尾田栄一郎

I received the following letter:
"Oda Sensei, you're such a weird, irresponsible person."
Just to be clear, I'm always writing silly things in my
comments these days, but in my youth there was a boy
who was always being praised by all the adults in the
neighborhood. He was a genius when it came to schoolwork
and was great at every sport.
...That would be my friend Tanaka. Please enjoy volume 30.

-Eiichiro Oda, 2003

Eiichiro Oda began his manga career at the age of 17, when his one-shot cowboy manga **Wanted!** won second place in the coveted Tezuka manga awards. Oda went on to work as an assistant to some of the biggest manga artists in the industry, including Nobuhiro Watsuki, before winning the Hop Step Award for new artists. His pirate adventure **One Piece**, which debuted in **Weekly Shonen Jump** in 1997, quickly became one of the most popular manga in Japan.

ONE PIECE VOL. 30
SKYPIEA PART 7

SHONEN JUMP Manga Edition

STORY AND ART BY EIICHIRO ODA

English Adaptation/Megan Bates
Translation/Masumi Matsumoto, HC Language Solutions, Inc.
Touch-up Art & Lettering/HudsonYards
Design/Sean Lee
Editor/Yuki Murashige

Printed in the U.S.A.

Published by VIZ Media, LLC
P.O. Box 77010
San Francisco, CA 94107

10 9 8 7 6 5 4 3 2
First printing, February 2010
Second printing, April 2011

www.viz.com

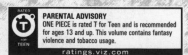

PARENTAL ADVISORY
ONE PIECE is rated T for Teen and is recommended
for ages 13 and up. This volume contains fantasy
violence and tobacco usage.
ratings.viz.com

THE WORLD'S
MOST POPULAR MANGA
SHONEN JUMP
www.shonenjump.com

SHONEN JUMP MANGA

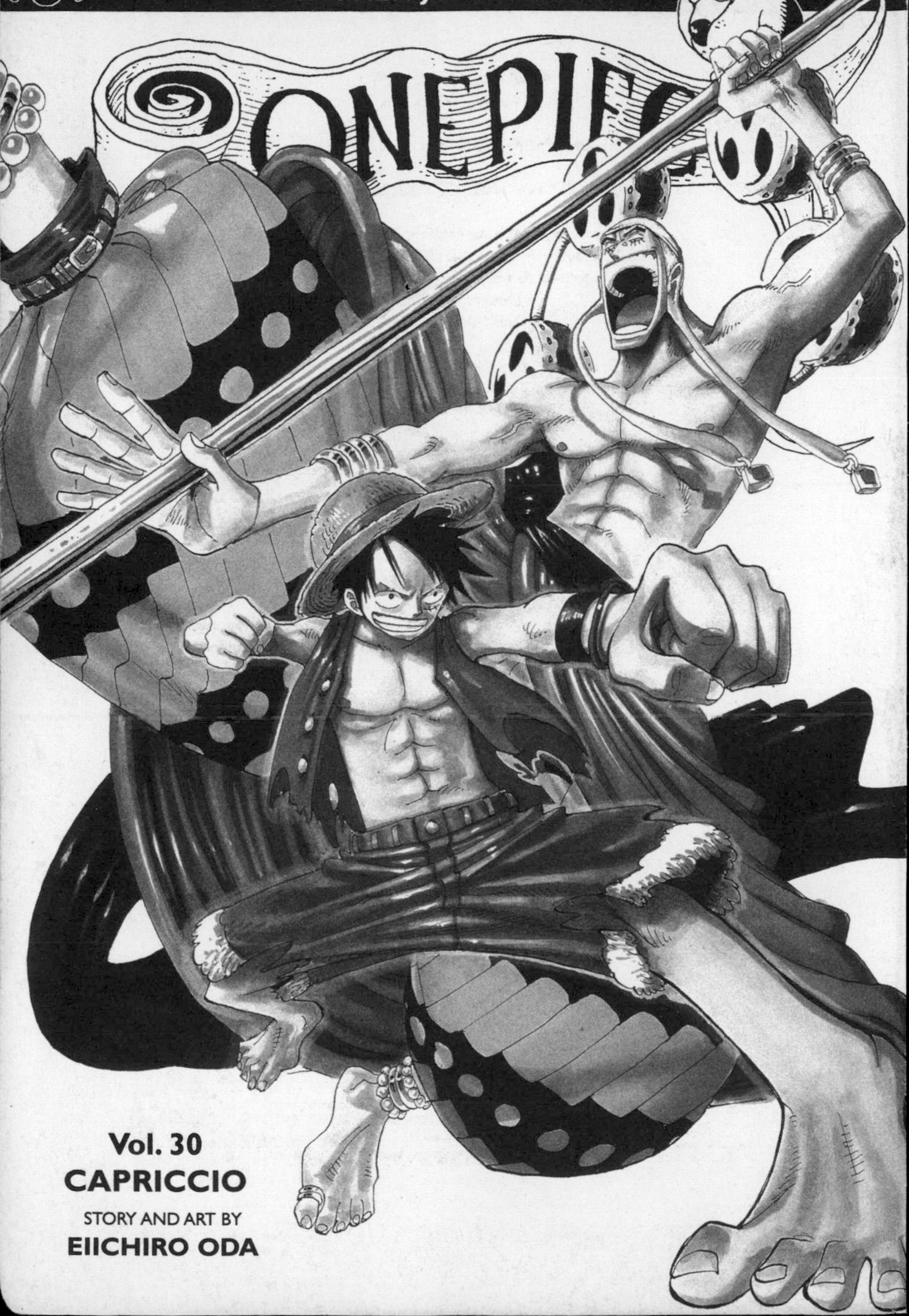

Vol. 30
CAPRICCIO

STORY AND ART BY
EIICHIRO ODA

The Shandians

The native inhabitants of Upper Yard. They're fighting to regain control of their homeland, which was seized by the Skypieans.

Wyper

Kamakiri

Braham

Genbo

Raki

Aisa

The Former Kami

"Sky Knight" Ganfor

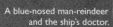

Conis

Pagaya

The Straw Hats

Boundlessly optimistic and able to stretch like rubber, he is determined to become King of the Pirates.

Monkey D. Luffy

A former bounty hunter and master of the "three-sword" style. He aspires to be the world's greatest swordsman.

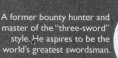

Roronoa Zolo

A thief who specializes in robbing pirates. Nami hates pirates, but Luffy convinced her to be his navigator.

Nami

A village boy with a talent for telling tall tales. His father, Yasopp, is a member of Shanks's crew.

Usopp

The big-hearted cook (and ladies' man) whose dream is to find the legendary sea, the "All Blue."

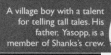

Sanji

A blue-nosed man-reindeer and the ship's doctor.

Tony Tony Chopper

A mysterious woman in search of the Ponegliff on which true history is recorded.

Nico Robin

Monkey D. Luffy started out as just a kid with a dream—to become the greatest pirate in history! Stirred by the tales of pirate "Red-Haired" Shanks, Luffy vowed to become a pirate himself. That was before the enchanted Devil Fruit gave Luffy the power to stretch like rubber, at the cost of being unable to swim—a serious handicap for an aspiring sea dog. Undeterred, Luffy set out to sea and recruited some crewmates—master swordsman Zolo; treasure-hunting thief Nami; lying sharp-shooter Usopp; the high-kicking chef Sanji; Chopper, the walkin' talkin' reindeer doctor; and the mysterious archaeologist Robin.

The Straw Hat pirates reach the land in the sky, Skypiea—a land ruled by the powerful Kami Eneru—but they're charged with trespassing. When the crew gets separated, Luffy, Sanji and Usopp face the tough challenges put up by the Kami's vassals, while the rest discover a shocking secret about their surroundings: mythical Upper Yard was originally part of Jaya Island! A treasure hunt for the island's legendary city of gold is in order, but before they can reach the riches the crew gets caught up in a battle between the Kami's army and the Shandians, a group of natives fighting to recapture their ancestral land. True to Kami Eneru's prophesy, "In three hours, only five people will remain alive," the Straw Hats are in a fight for survival. But against such an almighty enemy, will they be able to go home in one piece?!

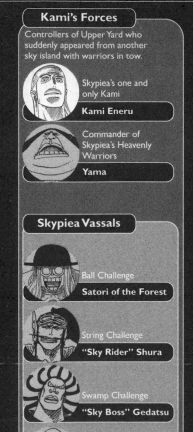

Kami's Forces

Controllers of Upper Yard who suddenly appeared from another sky island with warriors in tow.

Skypiea's one and only Kami

Kami Eneru

Commander of Skypiea's Heavenly Warriors

Yama

Skypiea Vassals

Ball Challenge

Satori of the Forest

String Challenge

"Sky Rider" Shura

Swamp Challenge

"Sky Boss" Gedatsu

Iron Challenge

"Sky Breeder" Ohm

A pirate that Luffy idolizes. Shanks gave Luffy his trademark straw hat.

"Red-Haired" Shanks

SKYPIEA

Vol. 30
Capriccio

CONTENTS

Chapter 276:
SHANDIAN RHYTHM

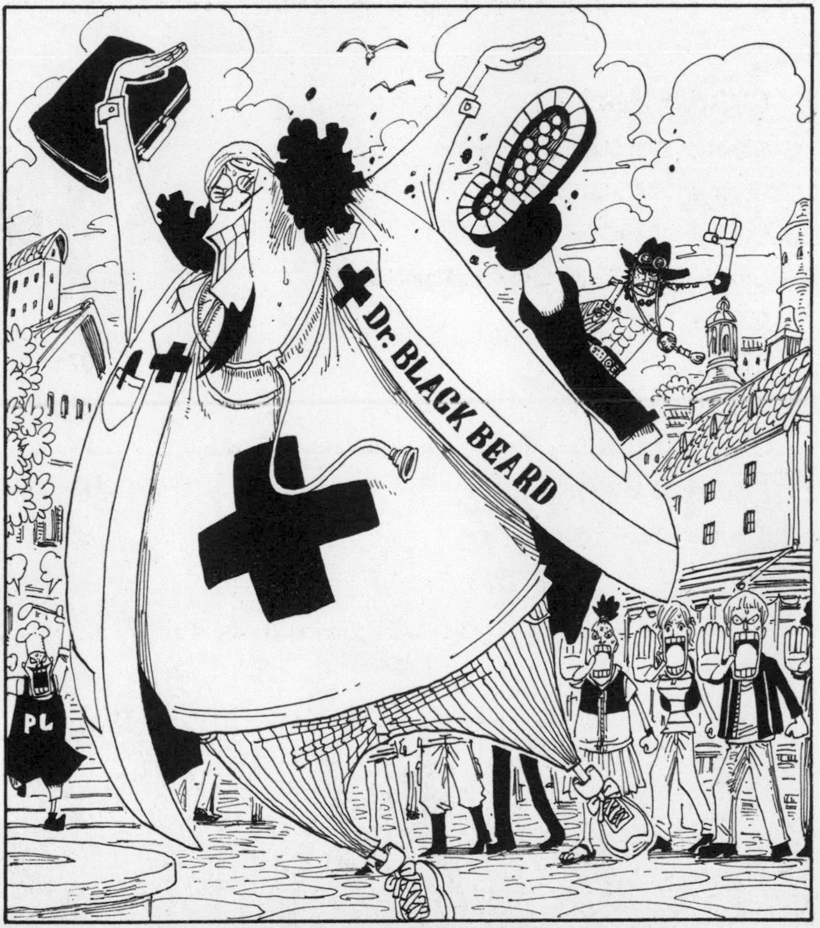
Dr. BLACK BEARD
PL

ACE'S GREAT SEARCH FOR BLACKBEARD, VOL. 4:
"THE WRONG PERSON"

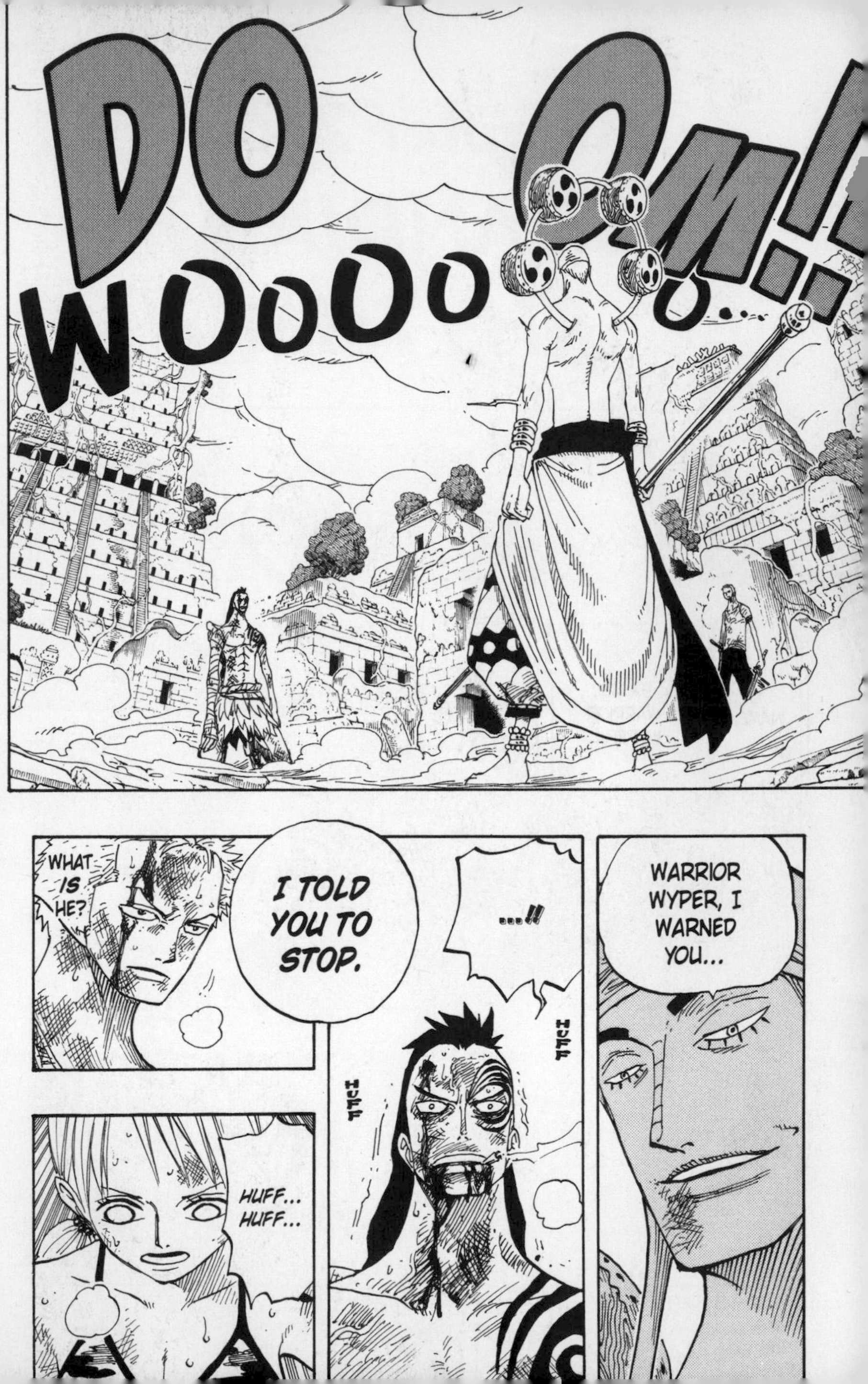
DOOM!!
WOOOOO...
WARRIOR WYPER, I WARNED YOU...
I TOLD YOU TO STOP.
...!!
HUFF
HUFF
WHAT IS HE?
HUFF... HUFF...

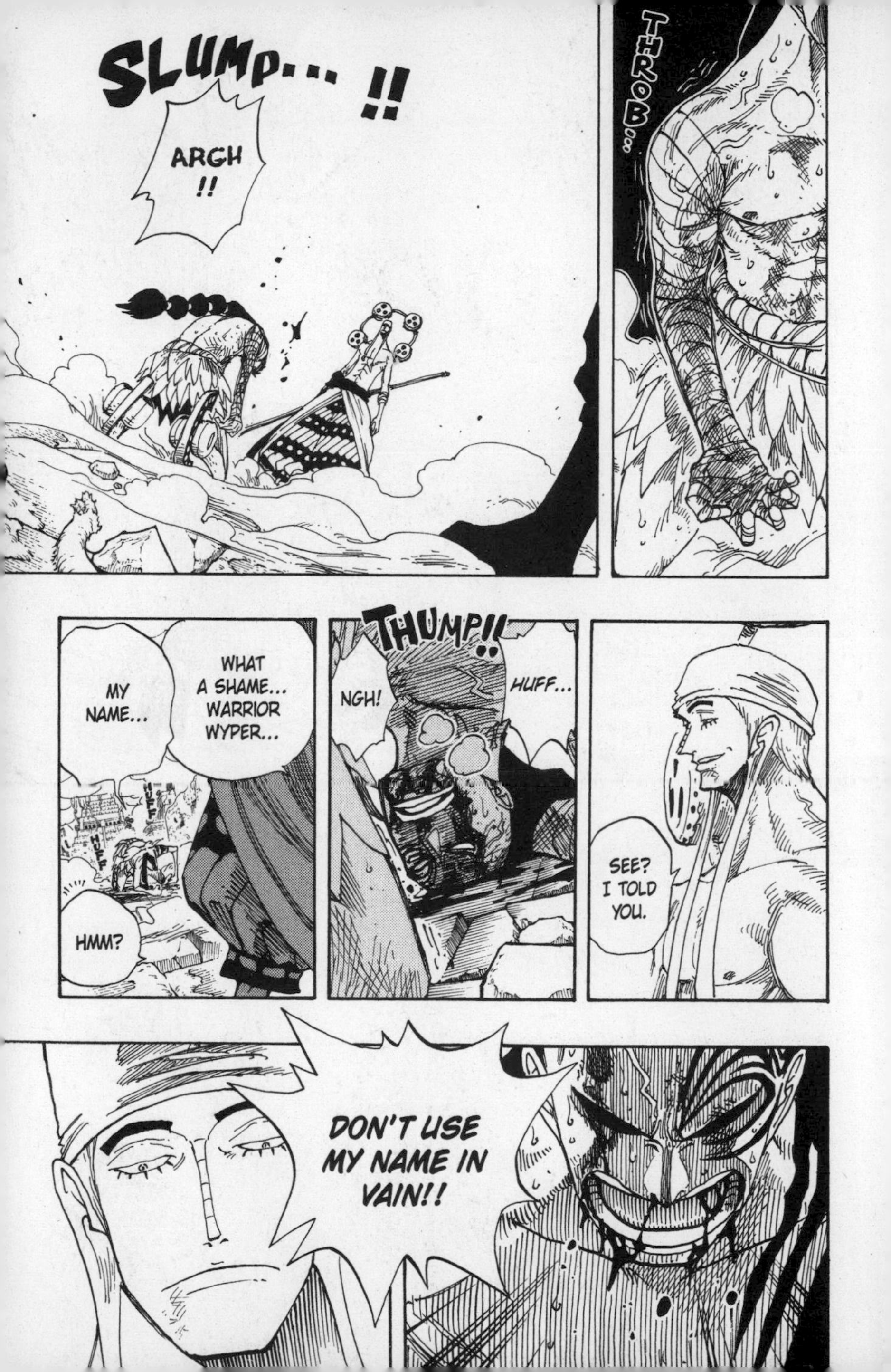
THROB...
SLUMP...!!
ARGH !!
SEE? I TOLD YOU.
THUMP!!
HUFF...
NGH!
WHAT A SHAME... WARRIOR WYPER...
MY NAME...
HUFF
HUFF
HMM?
DON'T USE MY NAME IN VAIN!!

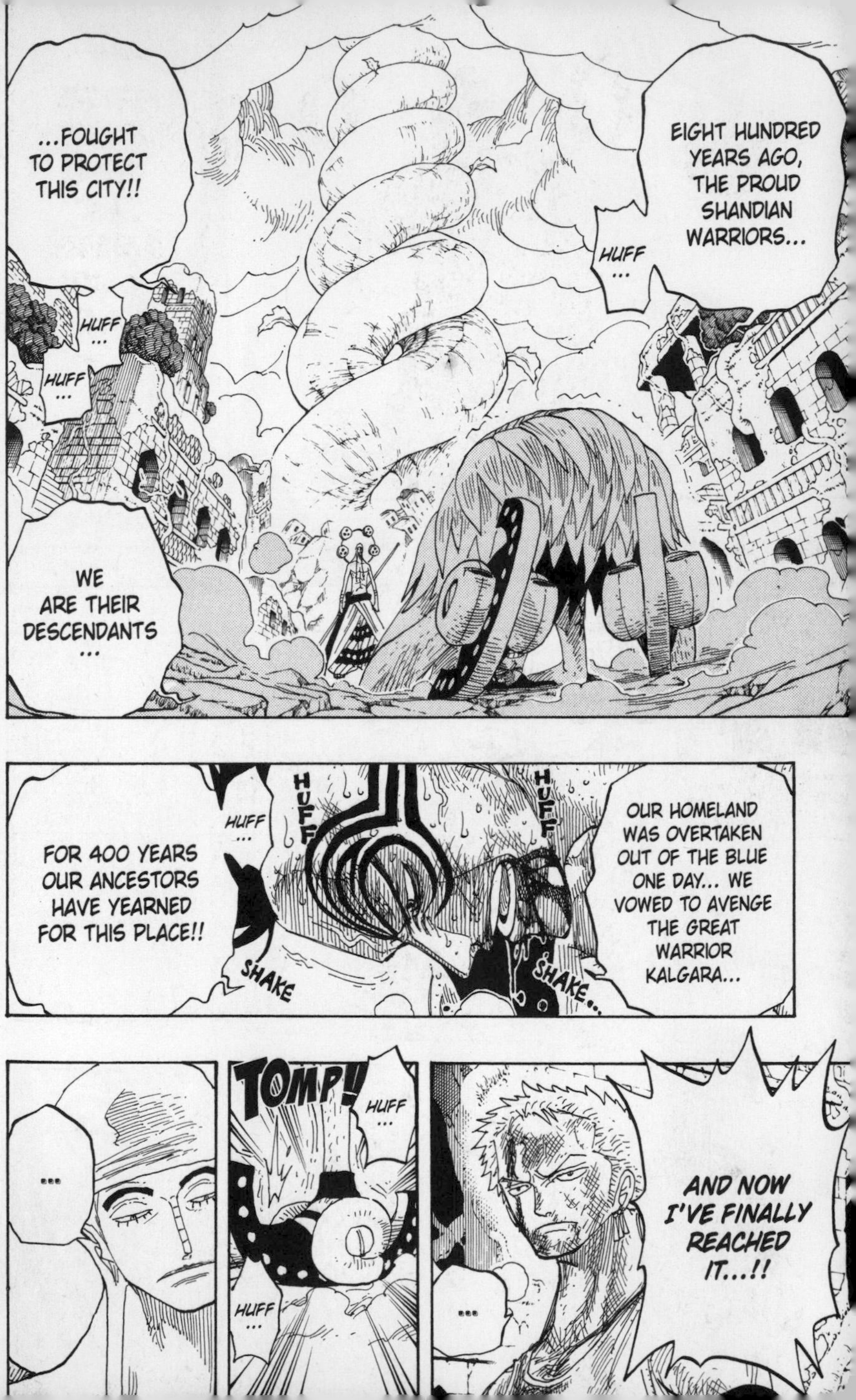
EIGHT HUNDRED YEARS AGO, THE PROUD SHANDIAN WARRIORS...
HUFF ...
...FOUGHT TO PROTECT THIS CITY!!
HUFF ...
HUFF ...
WE ARE THEIR DESCENDANTS ...
OUR HOMELAND WAS OVERTAKEN OUT OF THE BLUE ONE DAY... WE VOWED TO AVENGE THE GREAT WARRIOR KALGARA...
HUFF
HUFF
SHAKE...
HUFF ...
FOR 400 YEARS OUR ANCESTORS HAVE YEARNED FOR THIS PLACE!!
SHAKE
AND NOW I'VE FINALLY REACHED IT...!!
...
TOMP!!
HUFF ...
HUFF ...
...

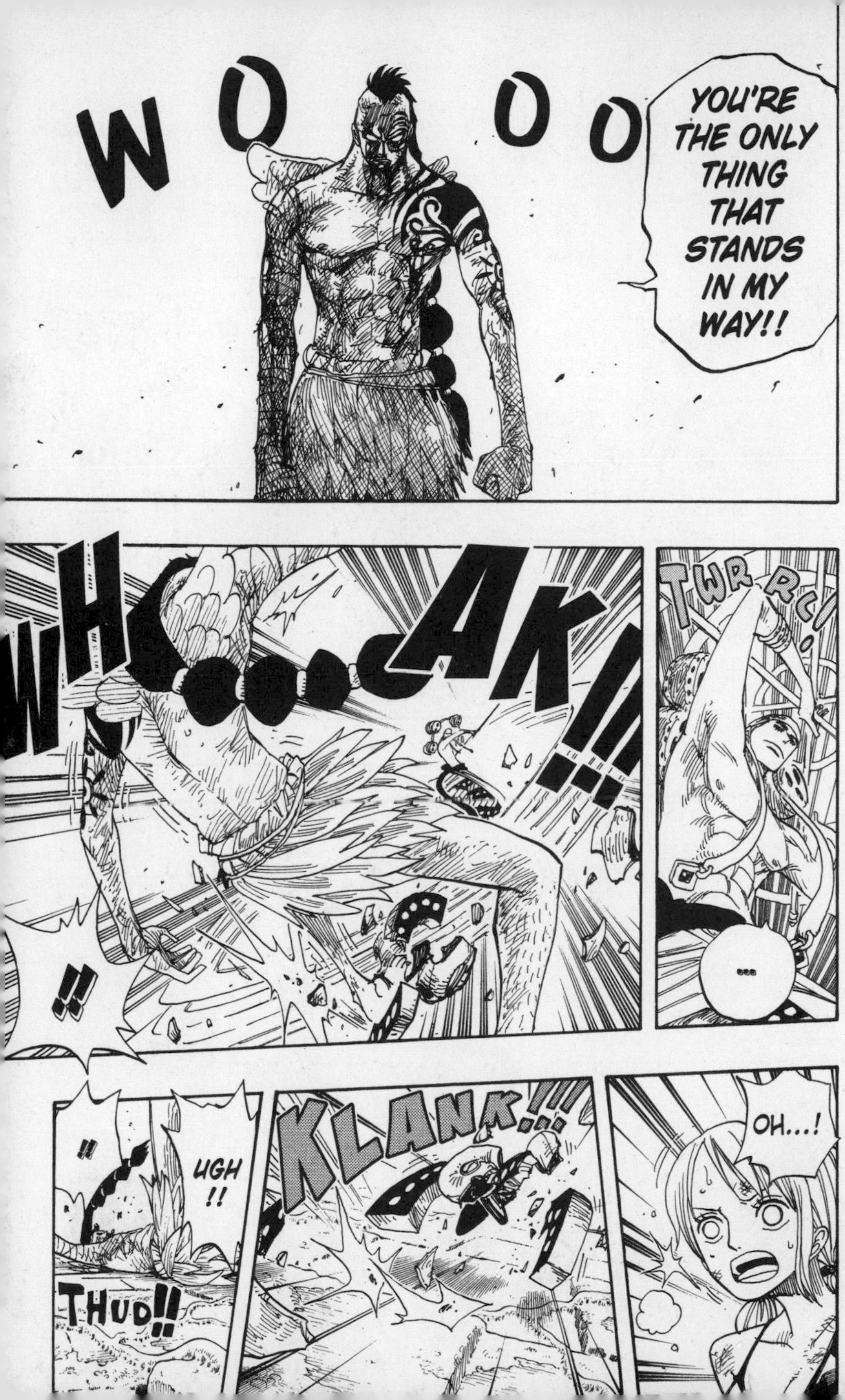

YOU'RE THE ONLY THING THAT STANDS IN MY WAY!!
WOOOO
TWRRL
...
WHAK!!!
!!
OH...!
KLANK!!!
!!
UGH !!
THUD!!

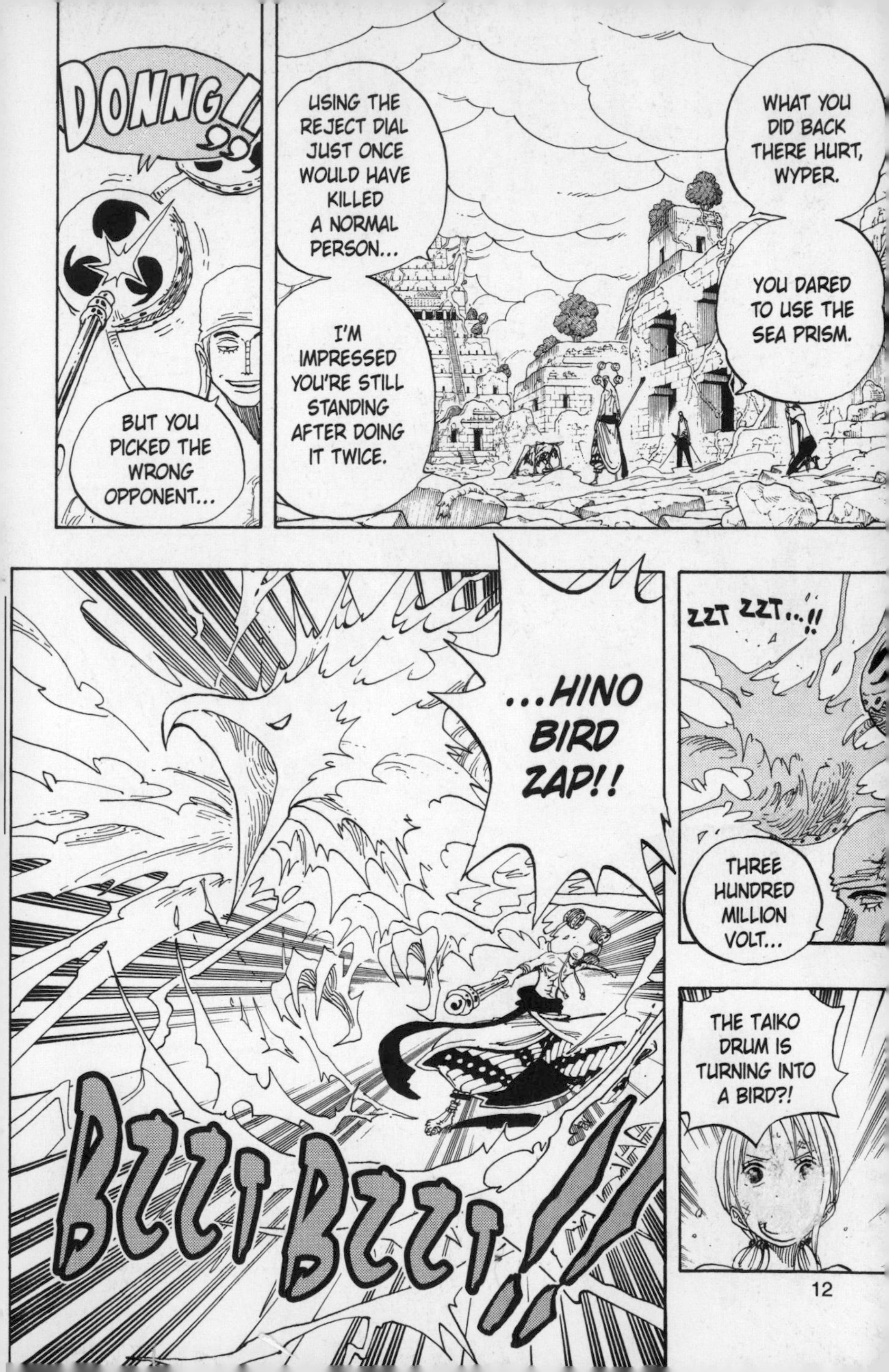
WHAT YOU DID BACK THERE HURT, WYPER.
YOU DARED TO USE THE SEA PRISM.
USING THE REJECT DIAL JUST ONCE WOULD HAVE KILLED A NORMAL PERSON...
I'M IMPRESSED YOU'RE STILL STANDING AFTER DOING IT TWICE.
DONNG!!
BUT YOU PICKED THE WRONG OPPONENT...
ZZT ZZT...!!
THREE HUNDRED MILLION VOLT...
THE TAIKO DRUM IS TURNING INTO A BIRD?!
...HINO BIRD ZAP!!
BZZT BZZT!!

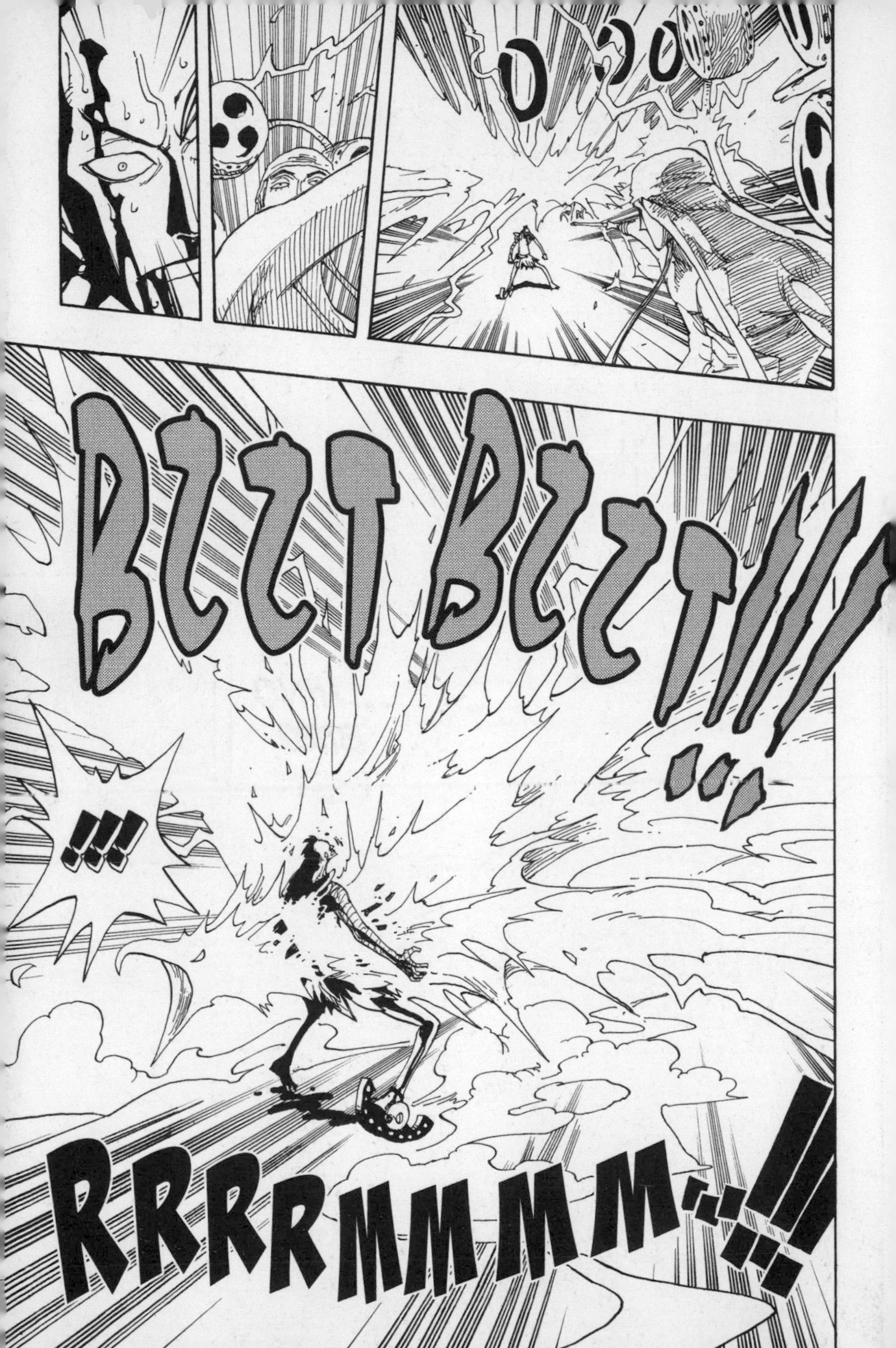
BZZT BZZT..!!
!!!
RRRRMMMMM..!!

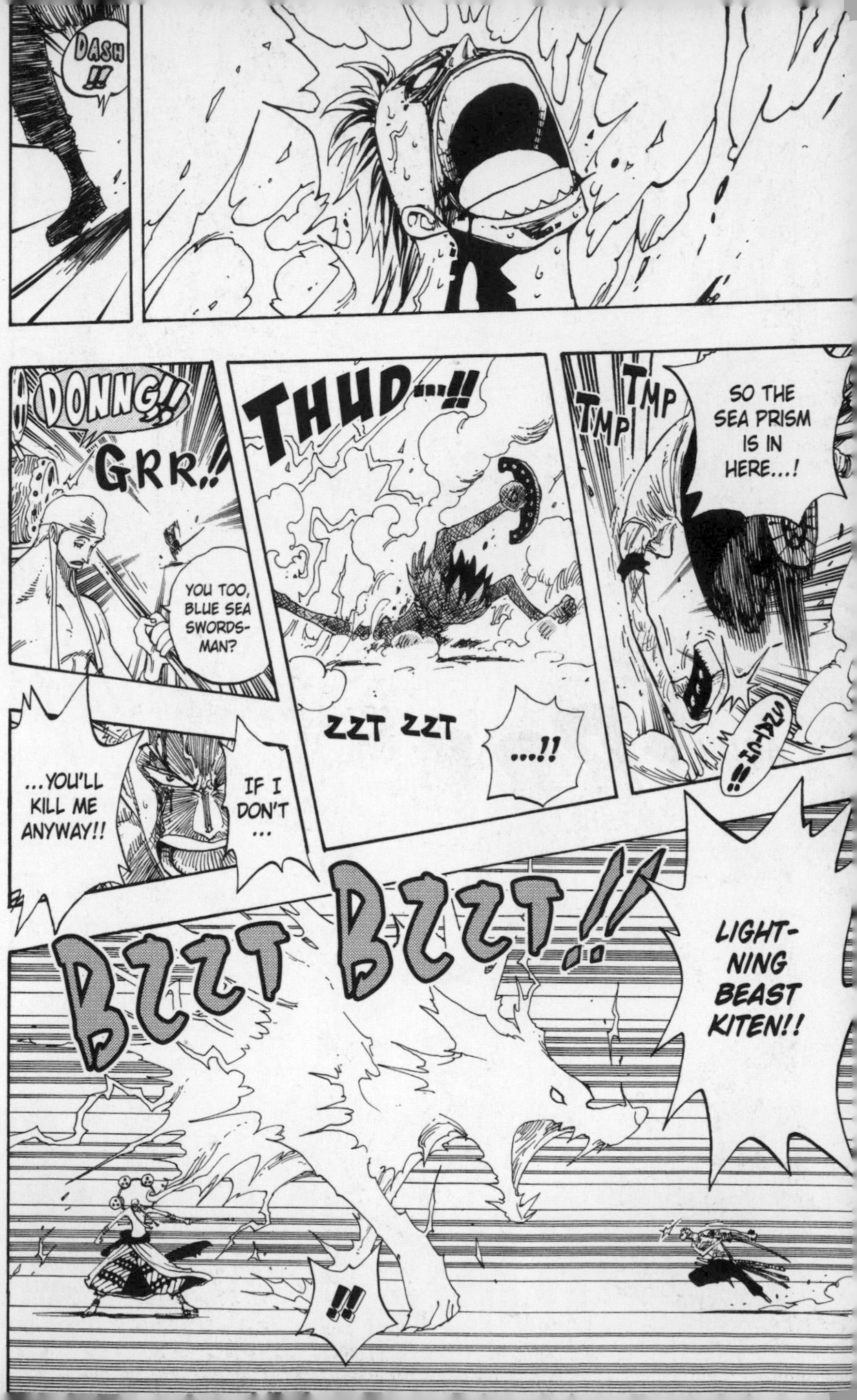
DASH!!
TMP TMP
SO THE SEA PRISM IS IN HERE...!
THUD...!!
ZZT ZZT
...!!
DONNG!!
GRR..!!
YOU TOO, BLUE SEA SWORDS-MAN?
IF I DON'T ...
...YOU'LL KILL ME ANYWAY!!
LIGHT-NING BEAST KITEN!!
BZZT BZZT!!
!!

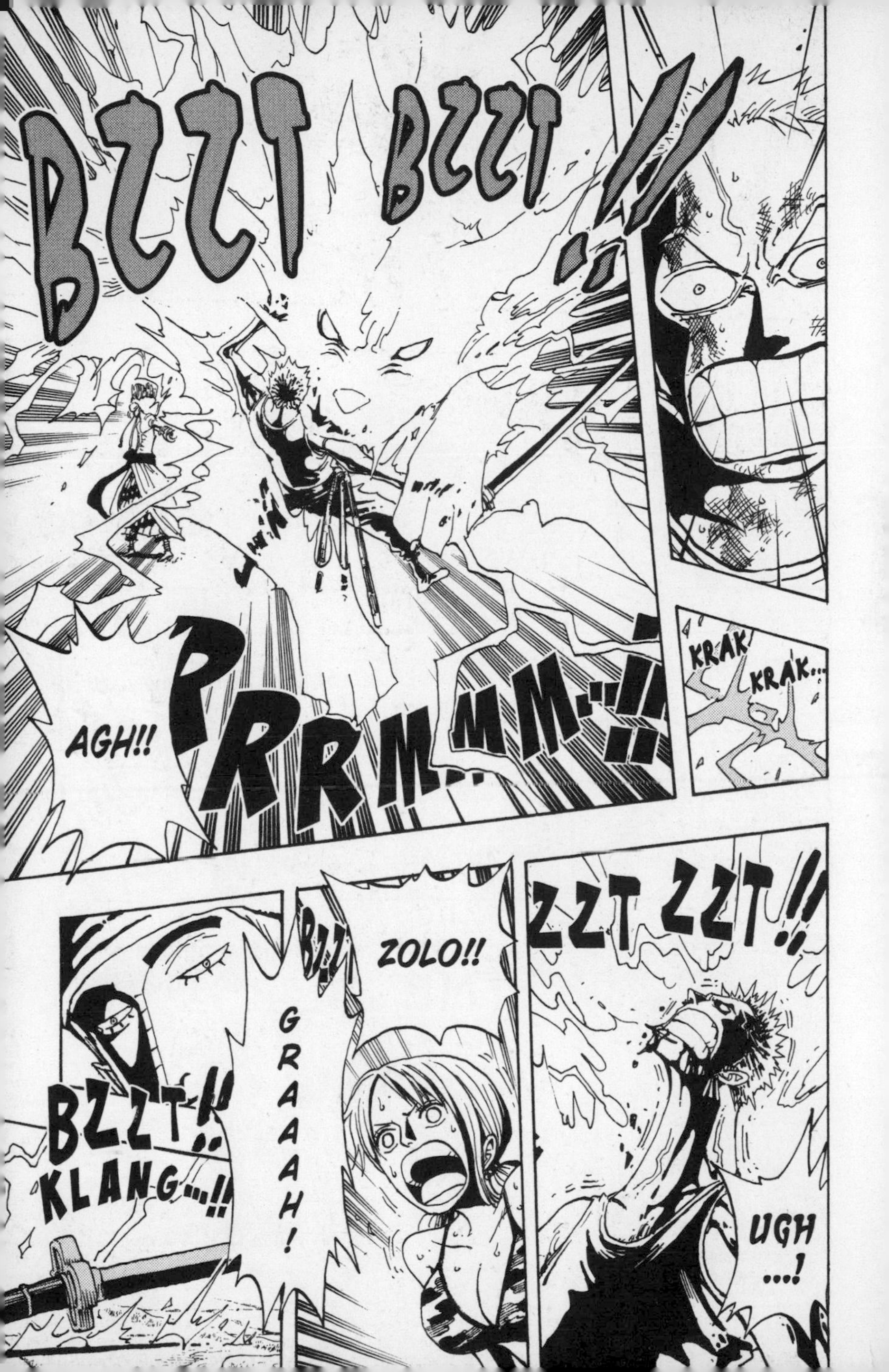
KRAK
KRAK...
BZZT BZZT!!
PRRMMM...!!
AGH!!
ZZT ZZT!!
UGH...!
BZZT
ZOLO!!
GRAAAAH!
BZZT!!
KLANG...!!

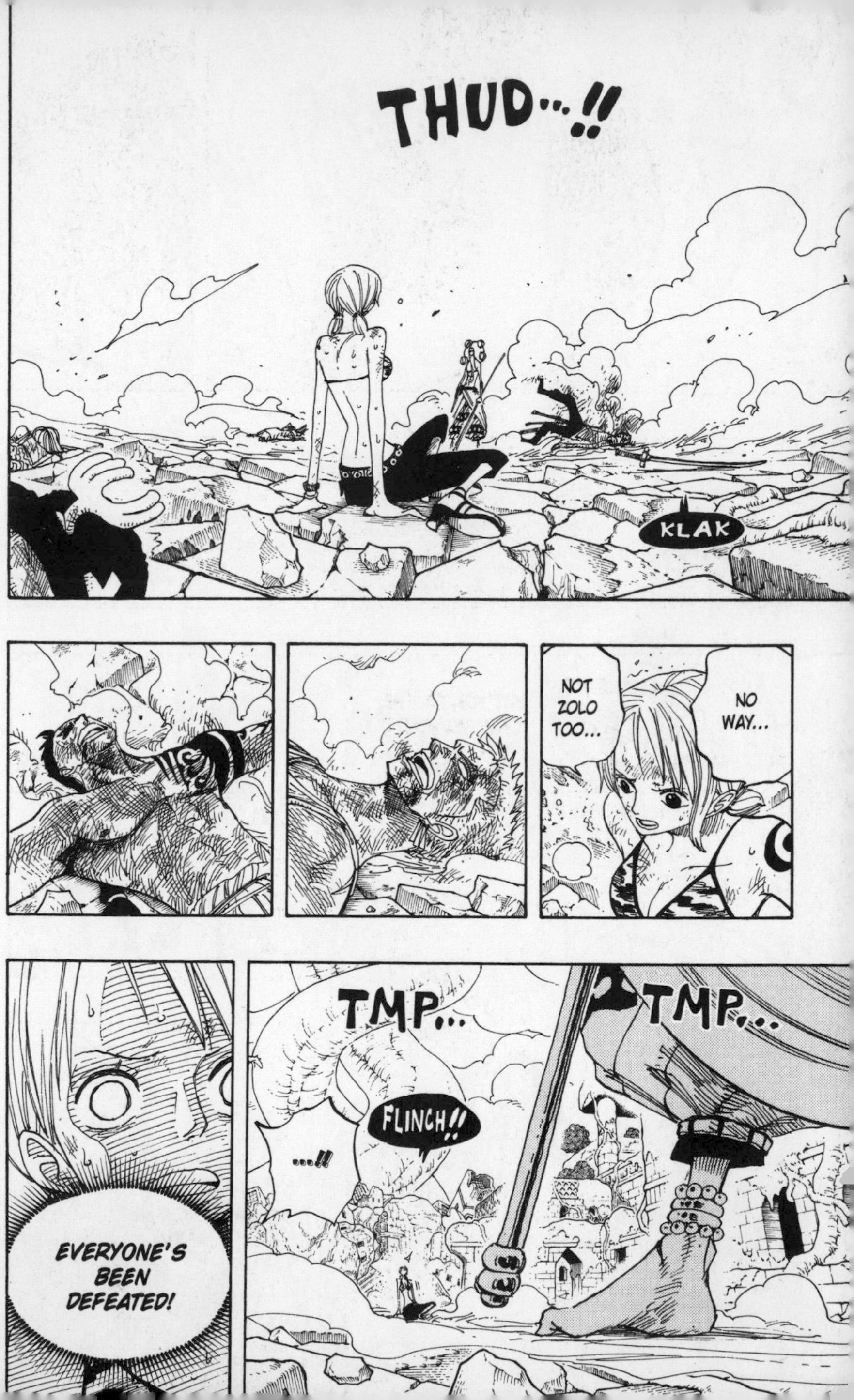
THUD...!!
KLAK
NO WAY...
NOT ZOLO TOO...
TMP...
TMP...
FLINCH!!
...!!
EVERYONE'S BEEN DEFEATED!

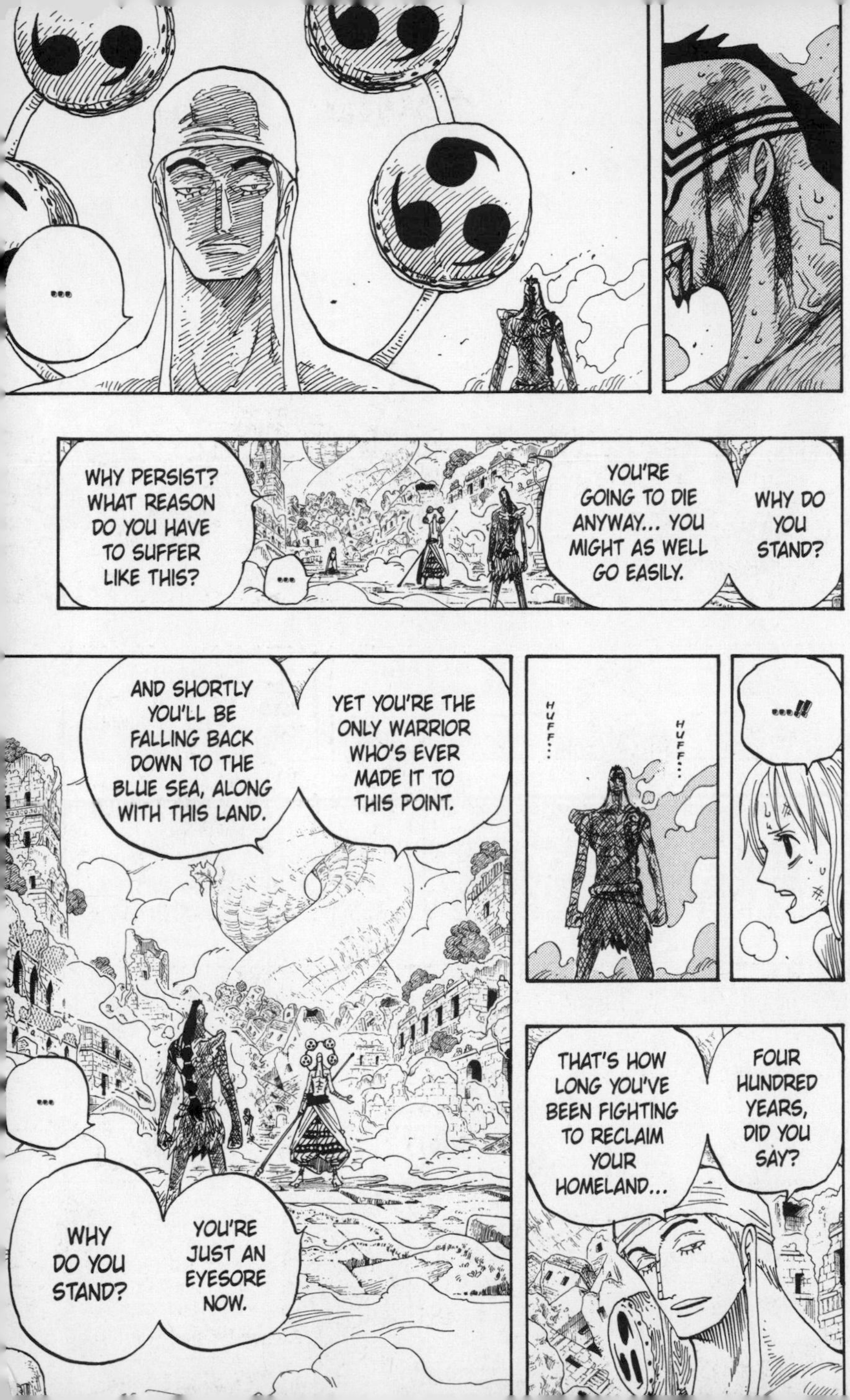

...
WHY DO YOU STAND?
YOU'RE GOING TO DIE ANYWAY... YOU MIGHT AS WELL GO EASILY.
WHY PERSIST? WHAT REASON DO YOU HAVE TO SUFFER LIKE THIS?
...
...!!
HUFF... HUFF...
FOUR HUNDRED YEARS, DID YOU SAY?
THAT'S HOW LONG YOU'VE BEEN FIGHTING TO RECLAIM YOUR HOMELAND...
YET YOU'RE THE ONLY WARRIOR WHO'S EVER MADE IT TO THIS POINT.
AND SHORTLY YOU'LL BE FALLING BACK DOWN TO THE BLUE SEA, ALONG WITH THIS LAND.
...
YOU'RE JUST AN EYESORE NOW.
WHY DO YOU STAND?

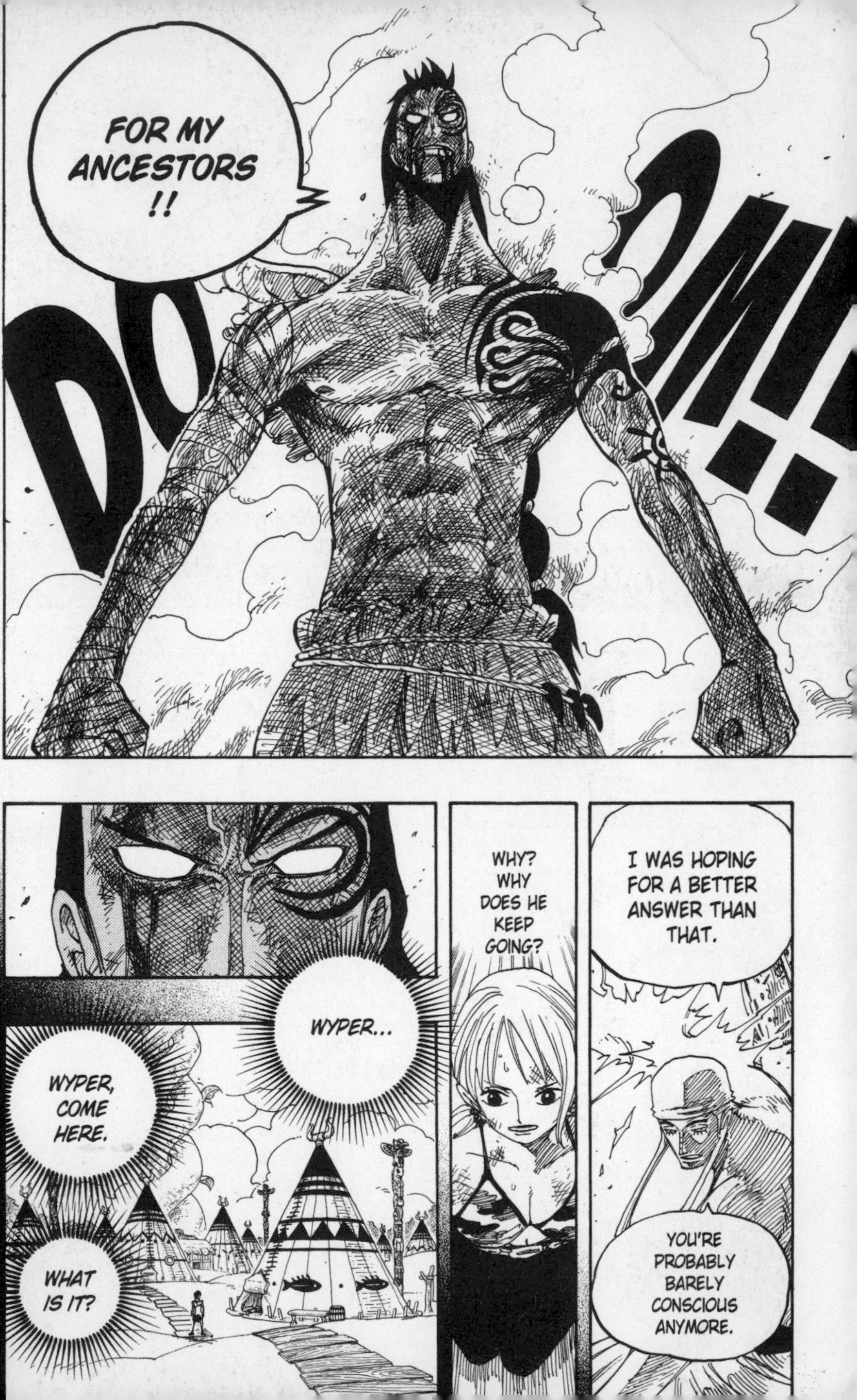
FOR MY ANCESTORS !!
DOOM!!
I WAS HOPING FOR A BETTER ANSWER THAN THAT.
YOU'RE PROBABLY BARELY CONSCIOUS ANYMORE.
WHY? WHY DOES HE KEEP GOING?
WYPER...
WYPER, COME HERE.
WHAT IS IT?

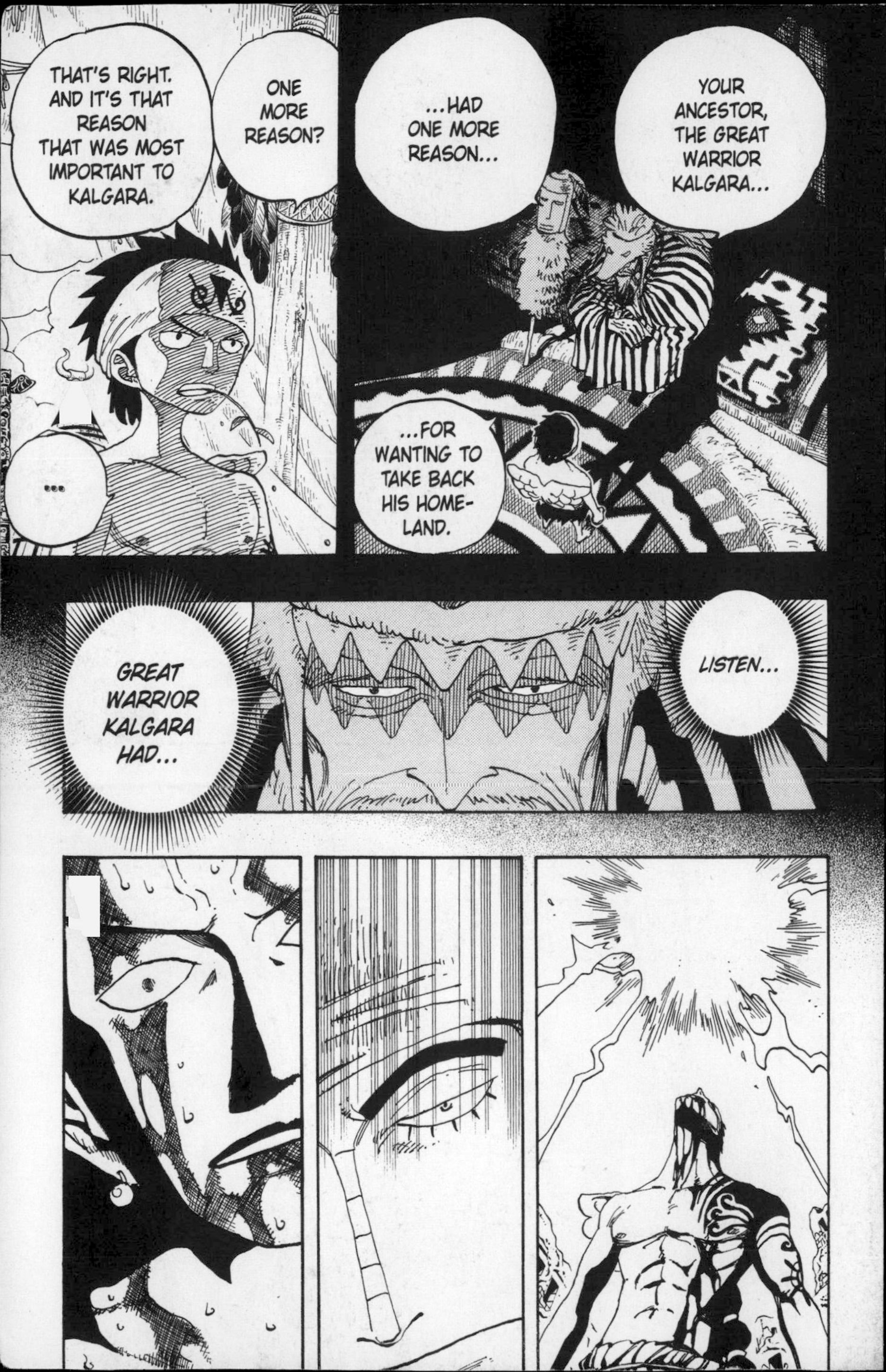
YOUR ANCESTOR, THE GREAT WARRIOR KALGARA...
...HAD ONE MORE REASON...
...FOR WANTING TO TAKE BACK HIS HOME-LAND.
ONE MORE REASON?
THAT'S RIGHT. AND IT'S THAT REASON THAT WAS MOST IMPORTANT TO KALGARA.
...
LISTEN...
GREAT WARRIOR KALGARA HAD...

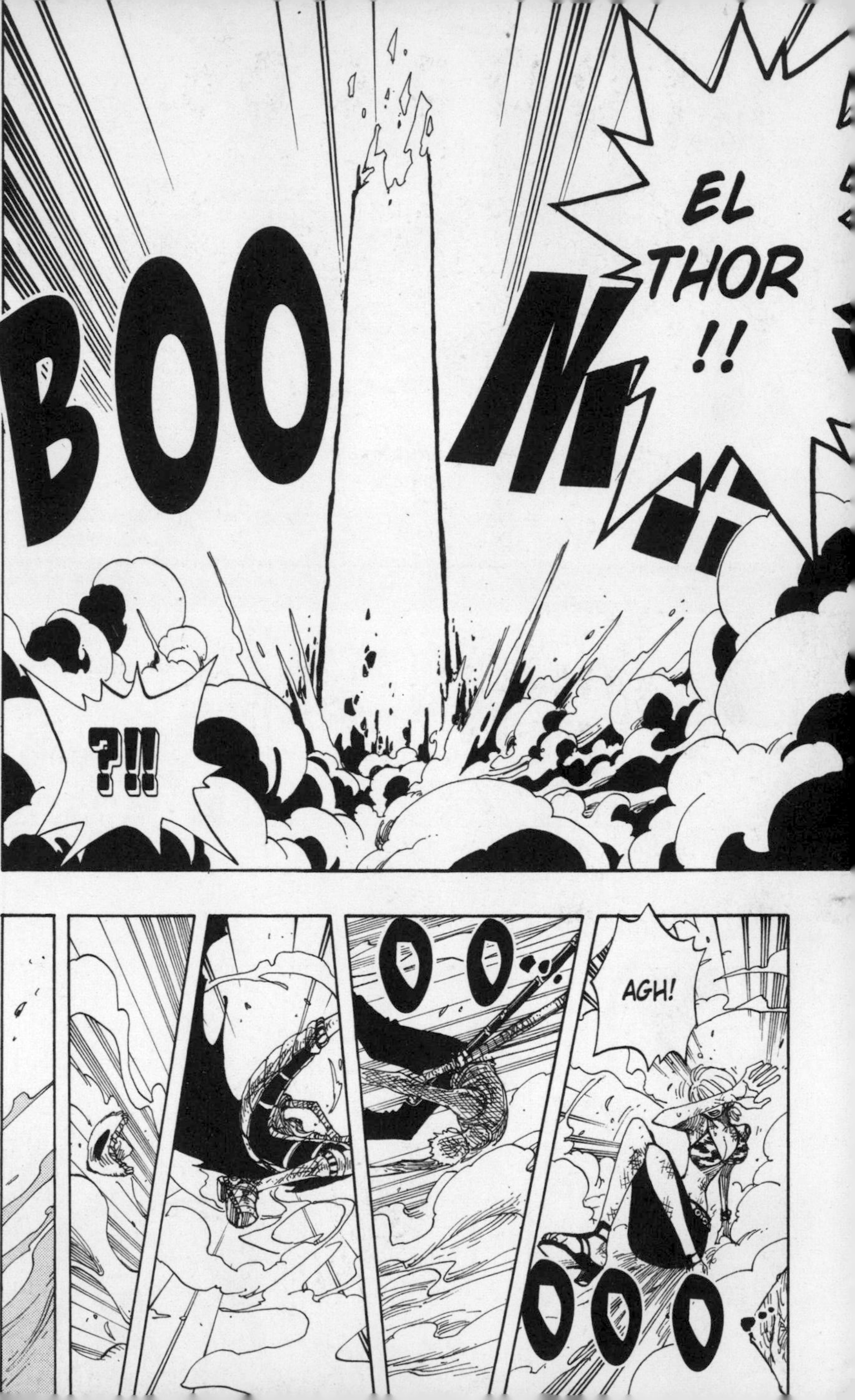
EL THOR!!
BOOM
?!!
AGH!

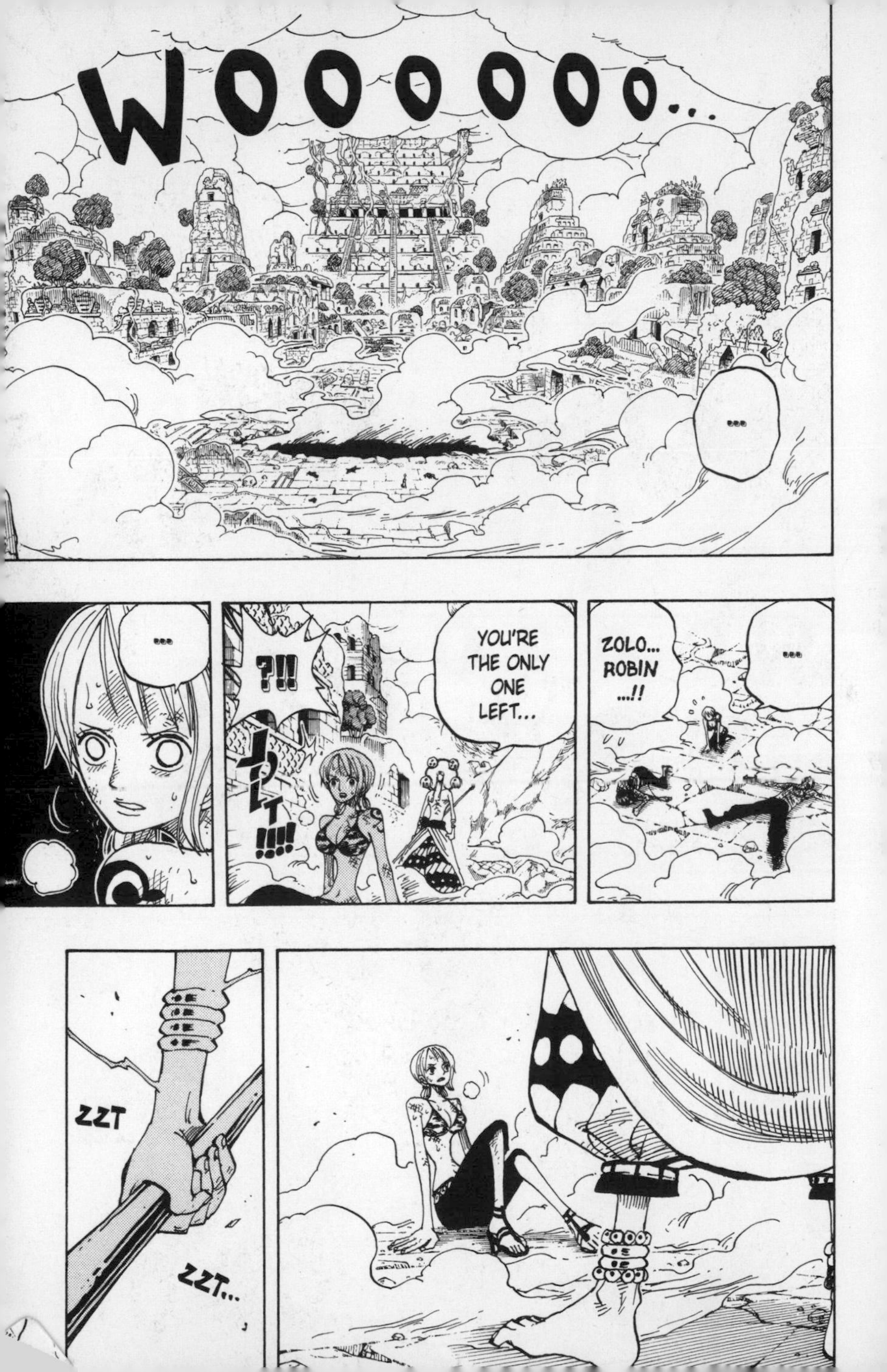
WOOOOOO...
...
...
ZOLO... ROBIN ...!!
YOU'RE THE ONLY ONE LEFT...
?!!
JOLT!!!!
...
ZZT
ZZT...

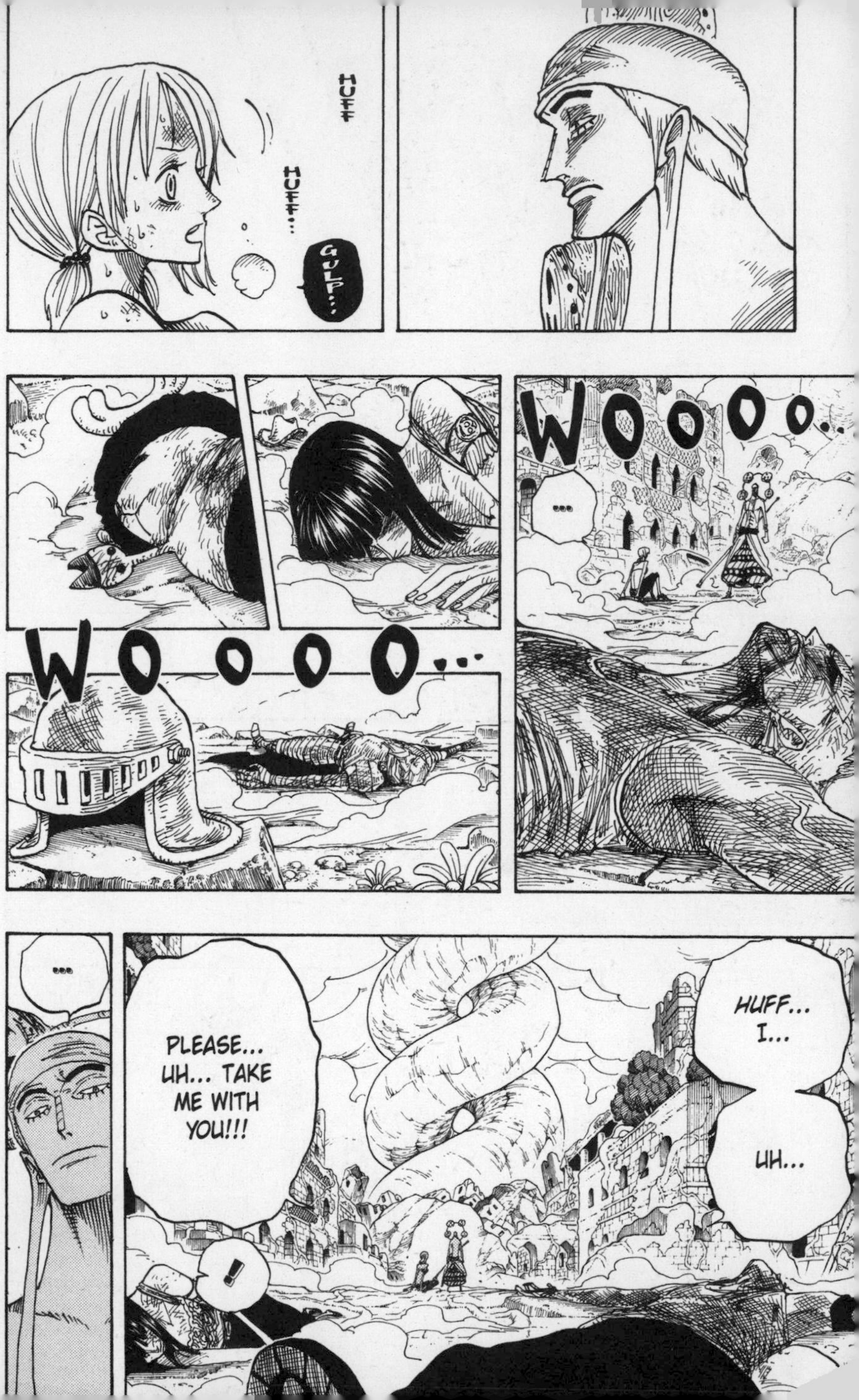
HUFF
HUFF...
GULP...
WOOOO...
...
WOOOO...
HUFF... I...
UH...
PLEASE... UH... TAKE ME WITH YOU!!!
!
...

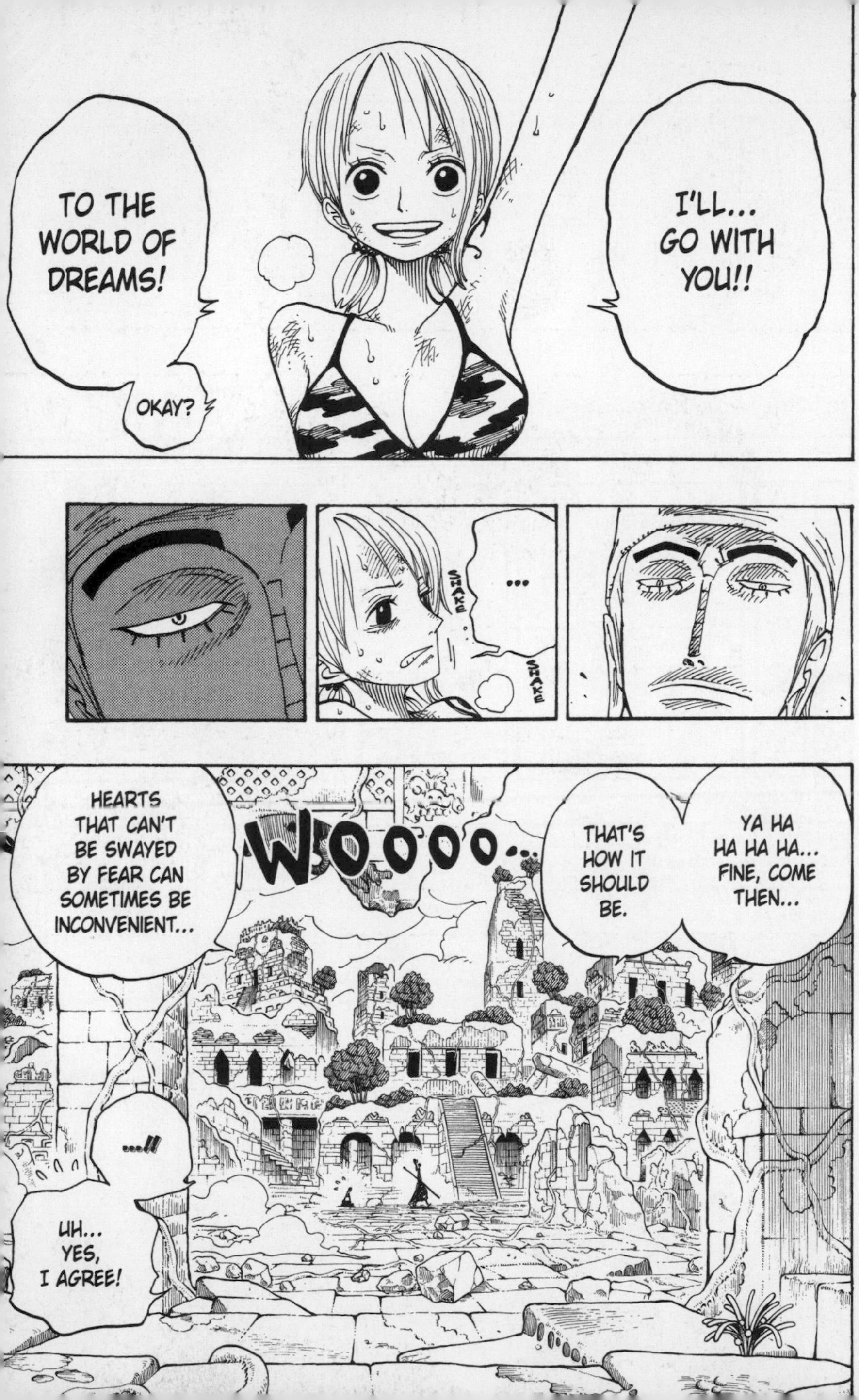
I'LL... GO WITH YOU!!
TO THE WORLD OF DREAMS!
OKAY?
SHAKE
...
SHAKE
YA HA HA HA HA... FINE, COME THEN...
THAT'S HOW IT SHOULD BE.
WOOOO...
HEARTS THAT CAN'T BE SWAYED BY FEAR CAN SOMETIMES BE INCONVENIENT...
...!!
UH... YES, I AGREE!

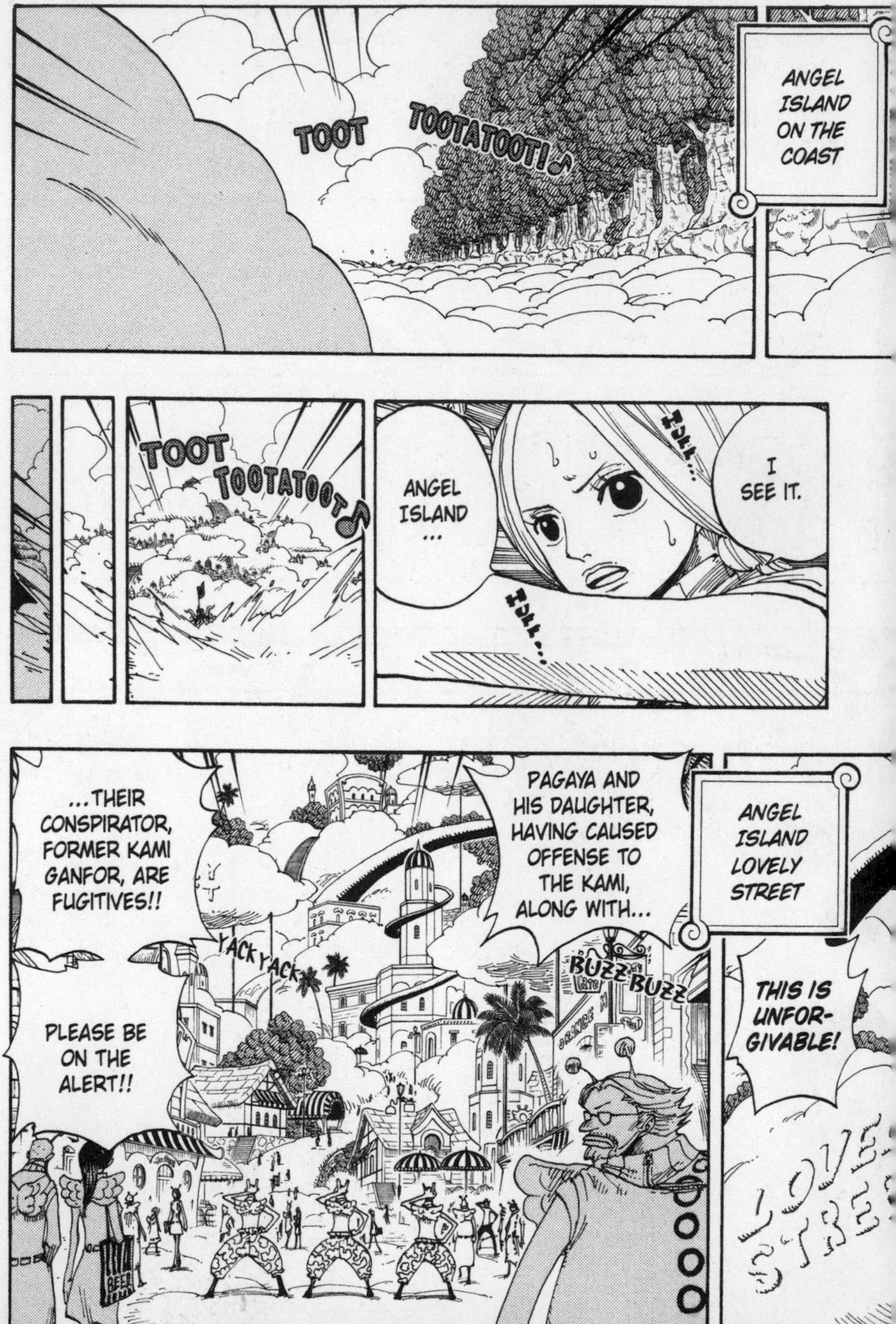
ANGEL ISLAND ON THE COAST
TOOT
TOOTATOOT!♪
HUFF...
I SEE IT.
ANGEL ISLAND...
HUFF...
TOOT
TOOTATOOT♪
THIS IS UNFORGIVABLE!
LOVE STRE
ANGEL ISLAND LOVELY STREET
PAGAYA AND HIS DAUGHTER, HAVING CAUSED OFFENSE TO THE KAMI, ALONG WITH...
...THEIR CONSPIRATOR, FORMER KAMI GANFOR, ARE FUGITIVES!!
BUZZ BUZZ
YACKYACK
PLEASE BE ON THE ALERT!!

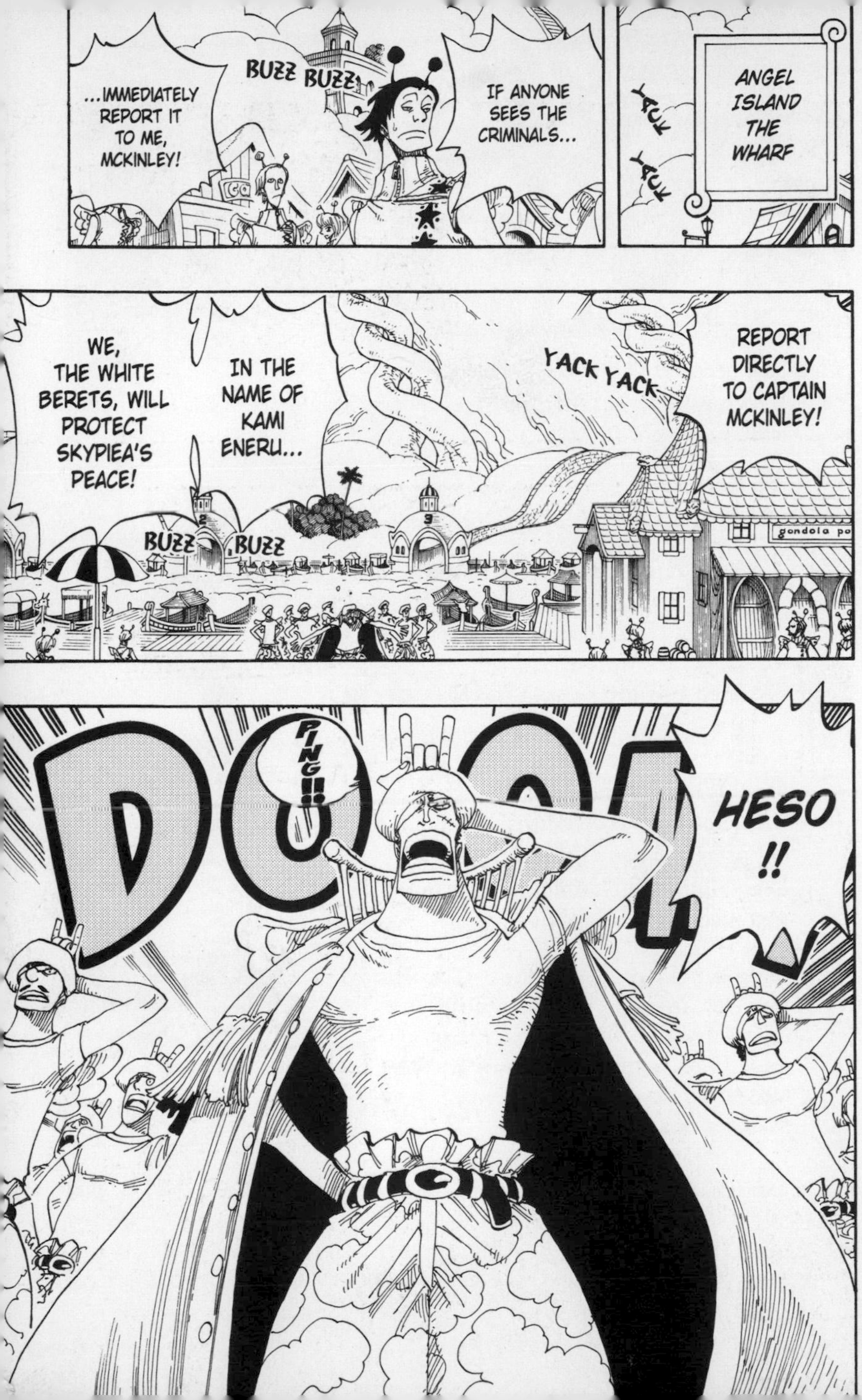
ANGEL ISLAND THE WHARF
YACK
YACK
IF ANYONE SEES THE CRIMINALS...
BUZZ BUZZ
...IMMEDIATELY REPORT IT TO ME, MCKINLEY!
REPORT DIRECTLY TO CAPTAIN MCKINLEY!
YACK YACK
IN THE NAME OF KAMI ENERU...
WE, THE WHITE BERETS, WILL PROTECT SKYPIEA'S PEACE!
BUZZ
BUZZ
HESO !!
PING!!

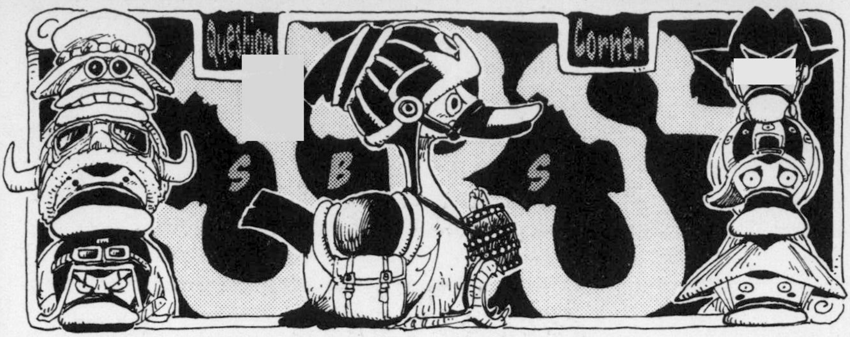
Question
Corner
S B S

Reader: Hee hee hee! ♡ Darling. ♡ Hee hee hee! ♡
Which would you rather do--take a bath, have dinner or go on a date with me?

What?

Oh…! You'd rather do the Question Corner… Oh, okay…

The Question Corner is now starting! ♡

Bye-bye,
--Mistress Missus #2

Oda: OK. Let's start now. (Totally normal.)

Q: Oda Sensei! In volume 22, page 144, panel 1, the Ponegliff has "Panda Man" written in Japanese! Is Panda Man an important person in the Alabasta Kingdom? (Is he even a ***person*** in the first place?) Please tell me!

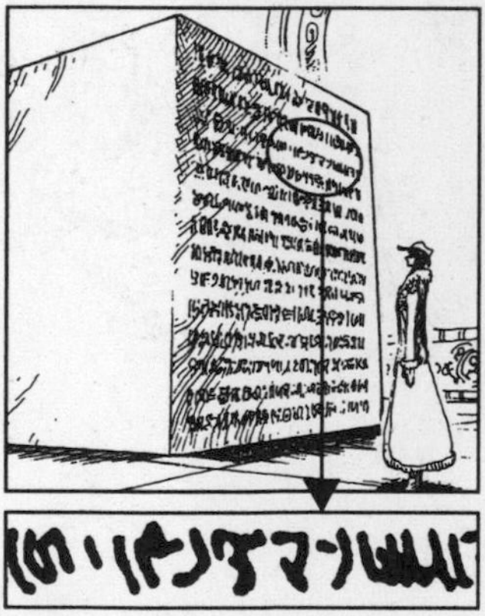

A: Give a round of applause! Clap clap clap clap. I'm glad you found it. Even I, myself, had forgotten that I had put that in there. The hidden panda isn't just in the art, so keep your eyes open.

Q: Odacchi! Can you draw the main seven characters with just your mouth?
--Shuichi

A: No way! I don't want to! Stop asking me to do stuff like that!

Chapter 277:
MAXIM

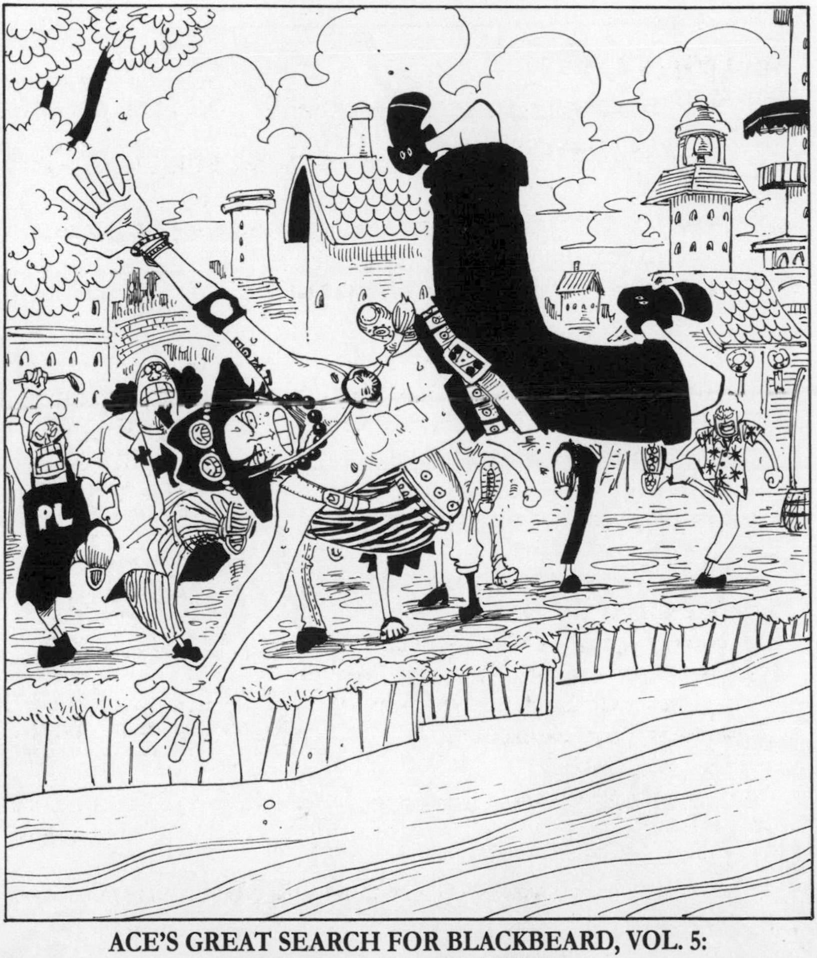

ACE'S GREAT SEARCH FOR BLACKBEARD, VOL. 5:
"THROWN IN THE RIVER"

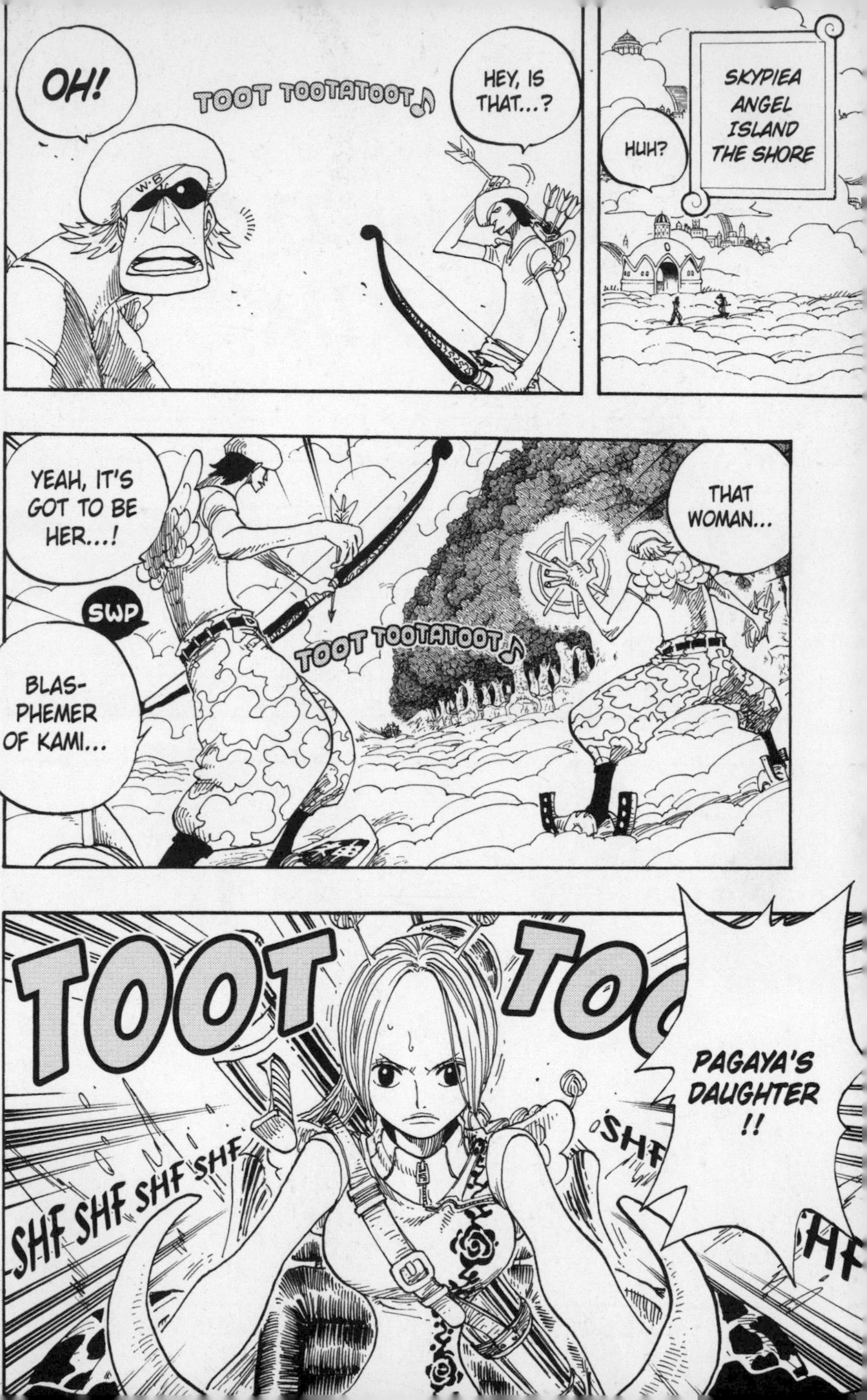
SKYPIEA ANGEL ISLAND THE SHORE
HUH?
HEY, IS THAT...?
TOOT TOOTATOOT♪
OH!
THAT WOMAN...
TOOT TOOTATOOT♪
YEAH, IT'S GOT TO BE HER...!
SWP
BLAS-PHEMER OF KAMI...
PAGAYA'S DAUGHTER !!
TOOT TOO
SHF
SHF
SHF SHF SHF SHF

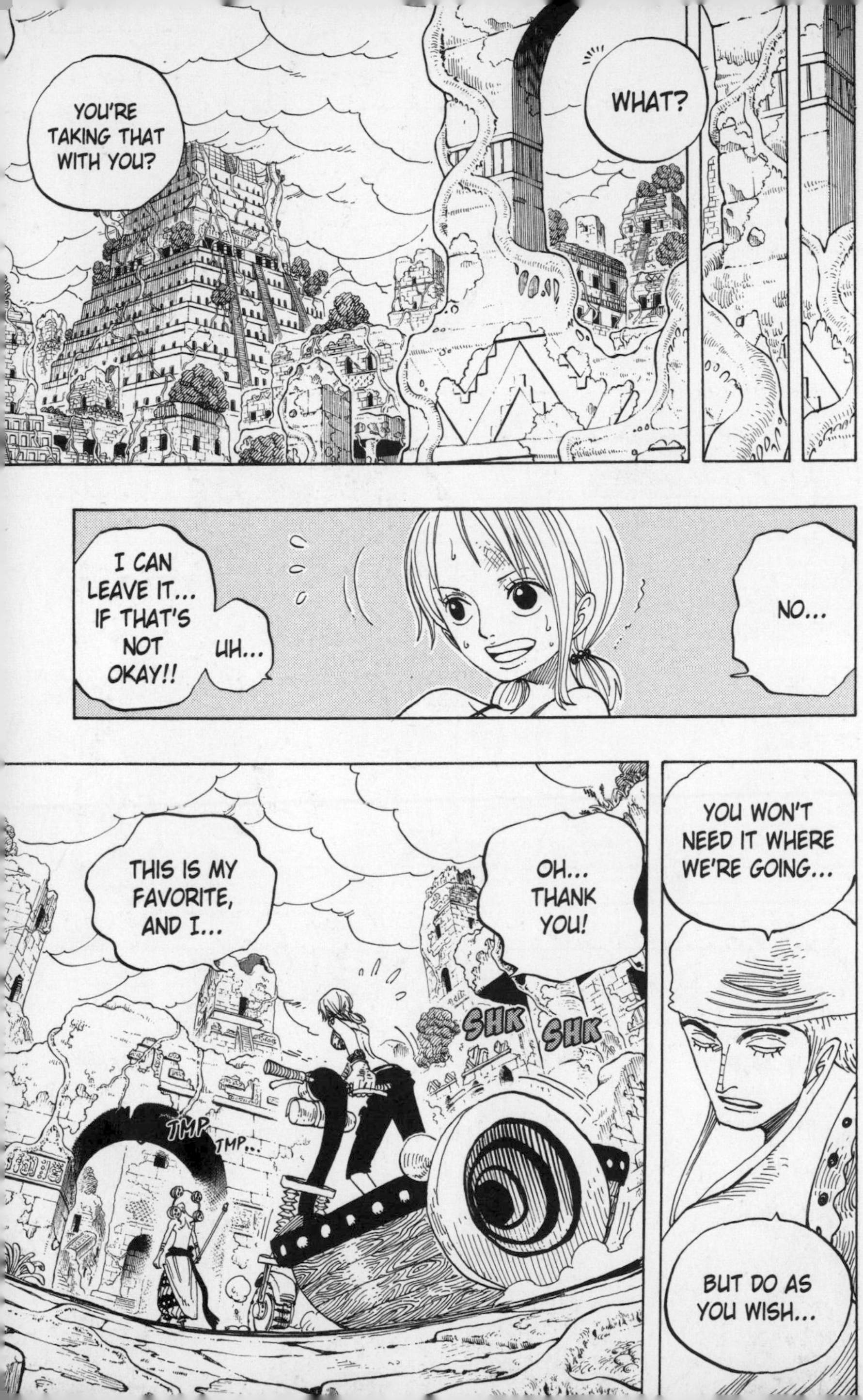
WHAT?
YOU'RE TAKING THAT WITH YOU?
NO...
UH...
I CAN LEAVE IT... IF THAT'S NOT OKAY!!
YOU WON'T NEED IT WHERE WE'RE GOING...
BUT DO AS YOU WISH...
OH... THANK YOU!
THIS IS MY FAVORITE, AND I...
SHK SHK
TMP TMP...

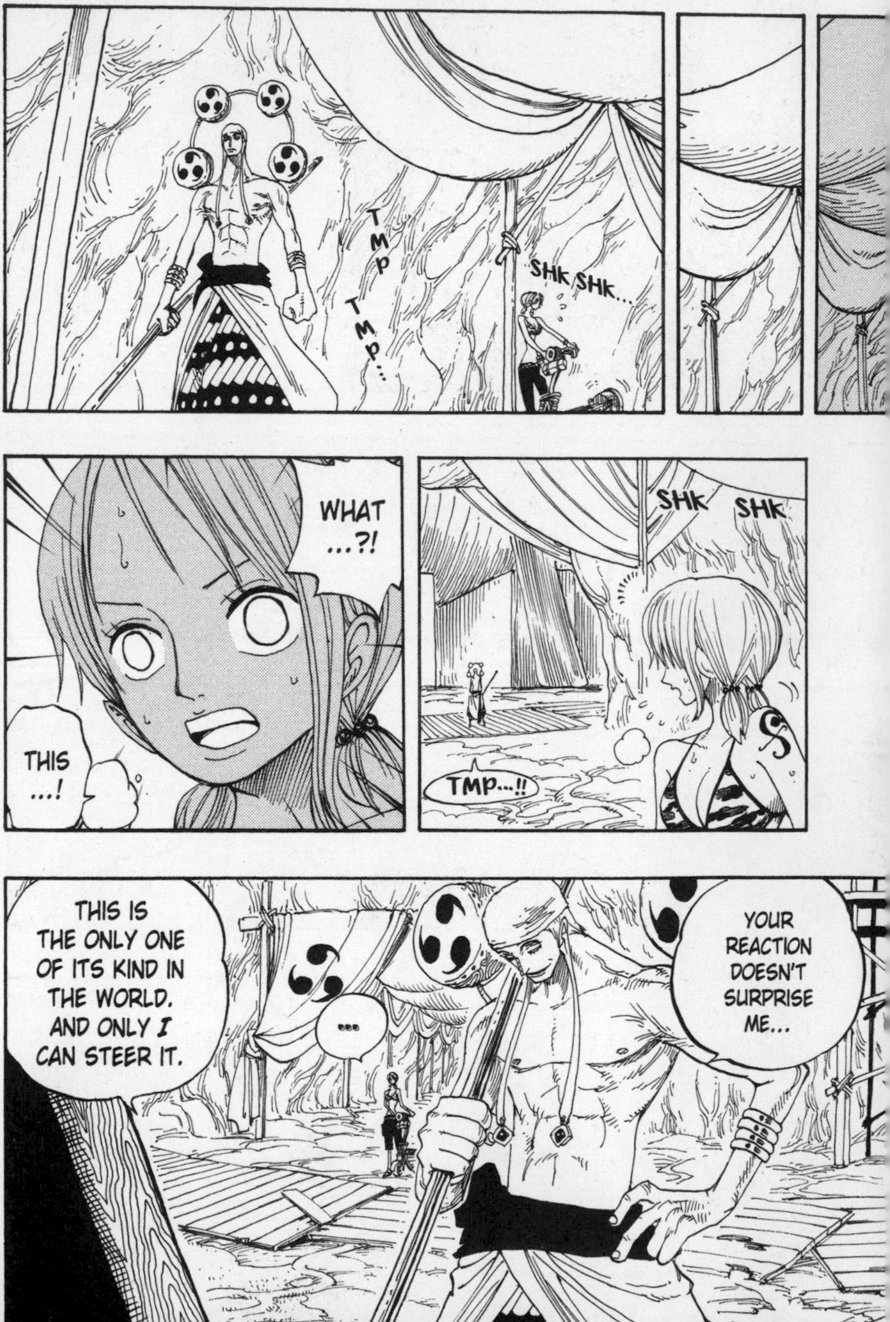
TMP
TMP...
SHK SHK...
SHK SHK
TMP...!!
WHAT ...?!
THIS ...!
YOUR REACTION DOESN'T SURPRISE ME...
...
THIS IS THE ONLY ONE OF ITS KIND IN THE WORLD. AND ONLY I CAN STEER IT.

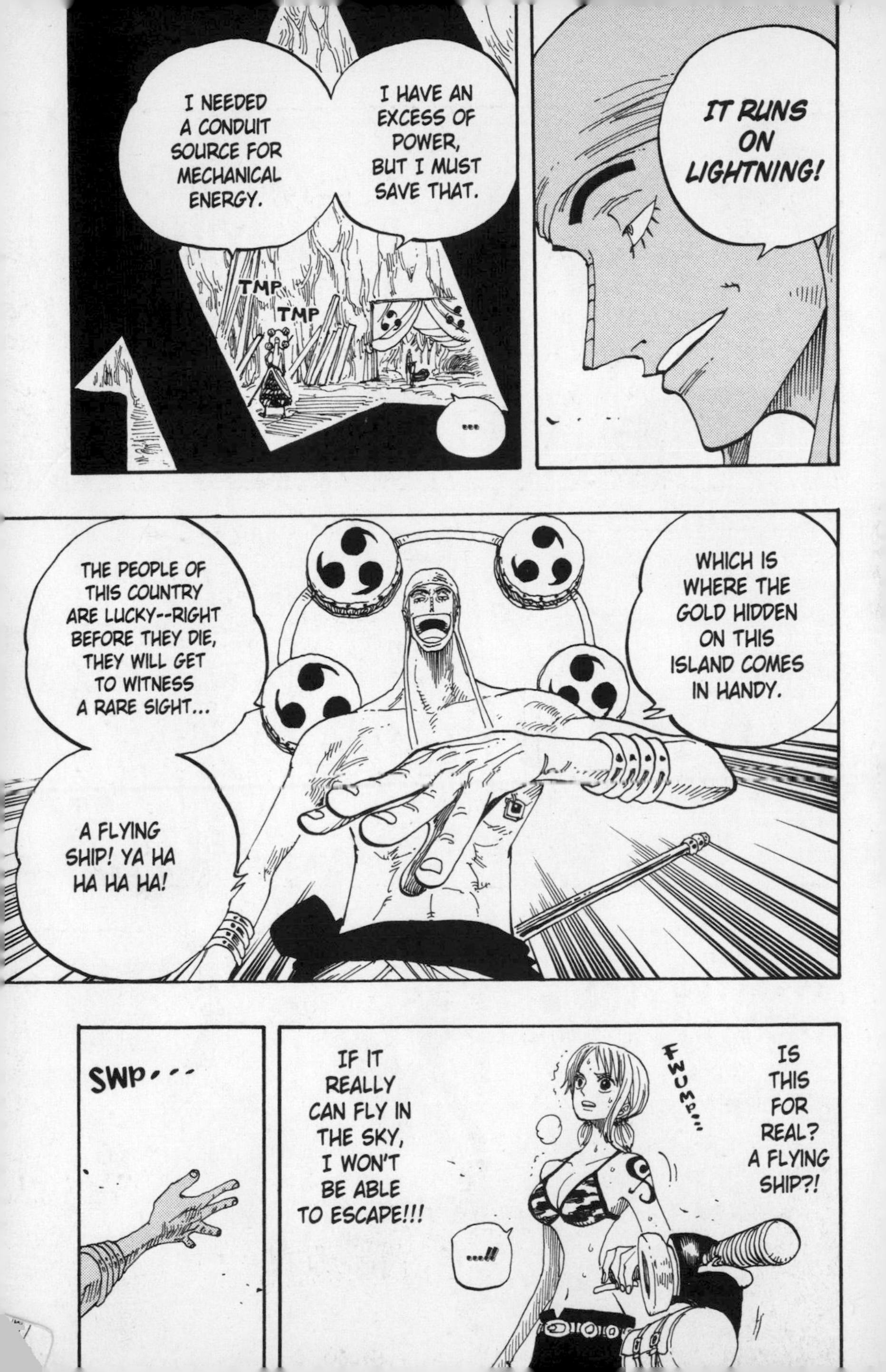
IT RUNS ON LIGHTNING!
I HAVE AN EXCESS OF POWER, BUT I MUST SAVE THAT.
I NEEDED A CONDUIT SOURCE FOR MECHANICAL ENERGY.
TMP
TMP
...
WHICH IS WHERE THE GOLD HIDDEN ON THIS ISLAND COMES IN HANDY.
THE PEOPLE OF THIS COUNTRY ARE LUCKY--RIGHT BEFORE THEY DIE, THEY WILL GET TO WITNESS A RARE SIGHT...
A FLYING SHIP! YA HA HA HA HA!
IS THIS FOR REAL? A FLYING SHIP?!
FWUMP...
IF IT REALLY CAN FLY IN THE SKY, I WON'T BE ABLE TO ESCAPE!!!
...!!
SWP...

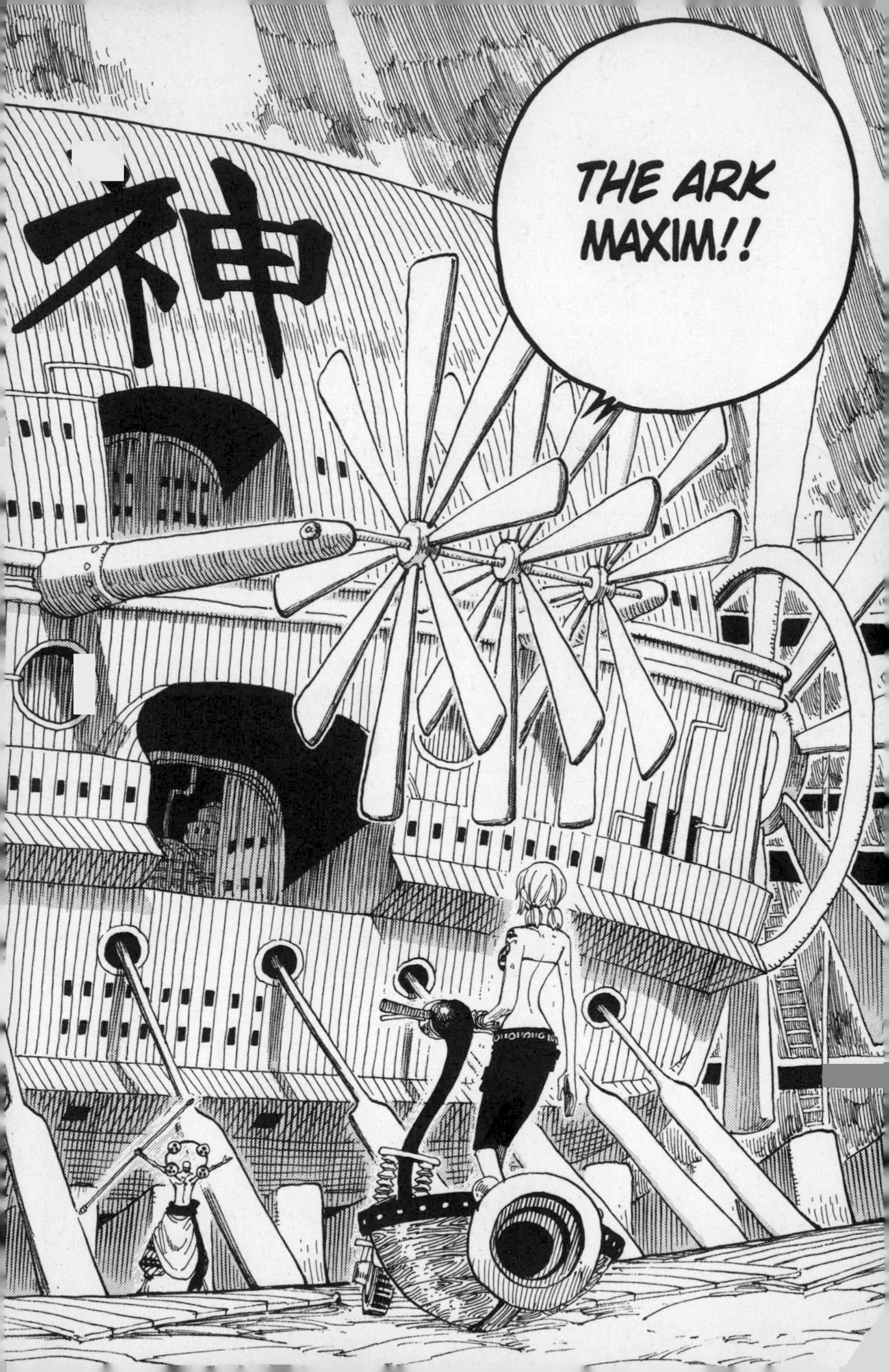
THE ARK MAXIM!!
神

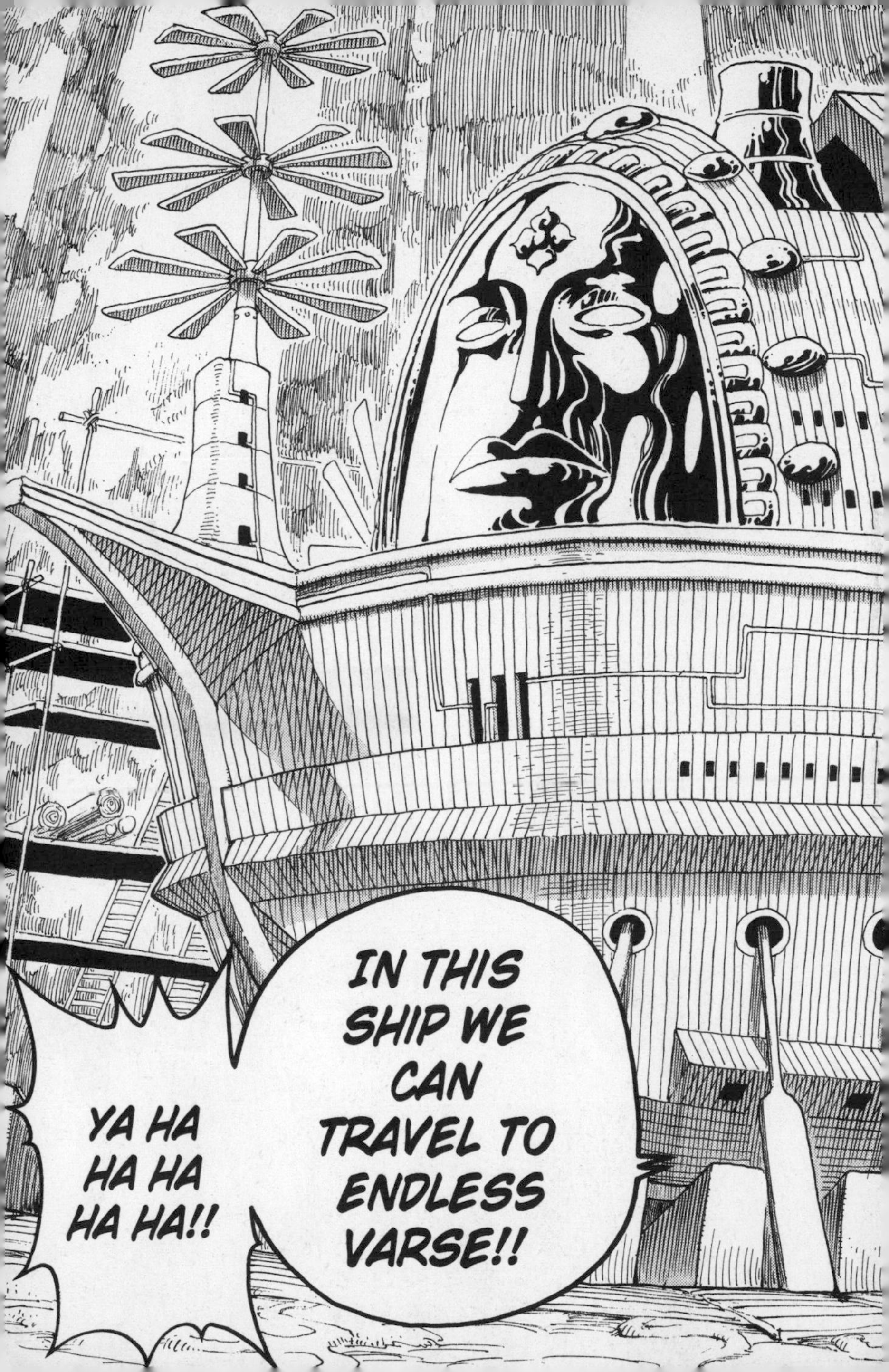
IN THIS SHIP WE CAN TRAVEL TO ENDLESS VARSE!!
YA HA HA HA HA HA!!

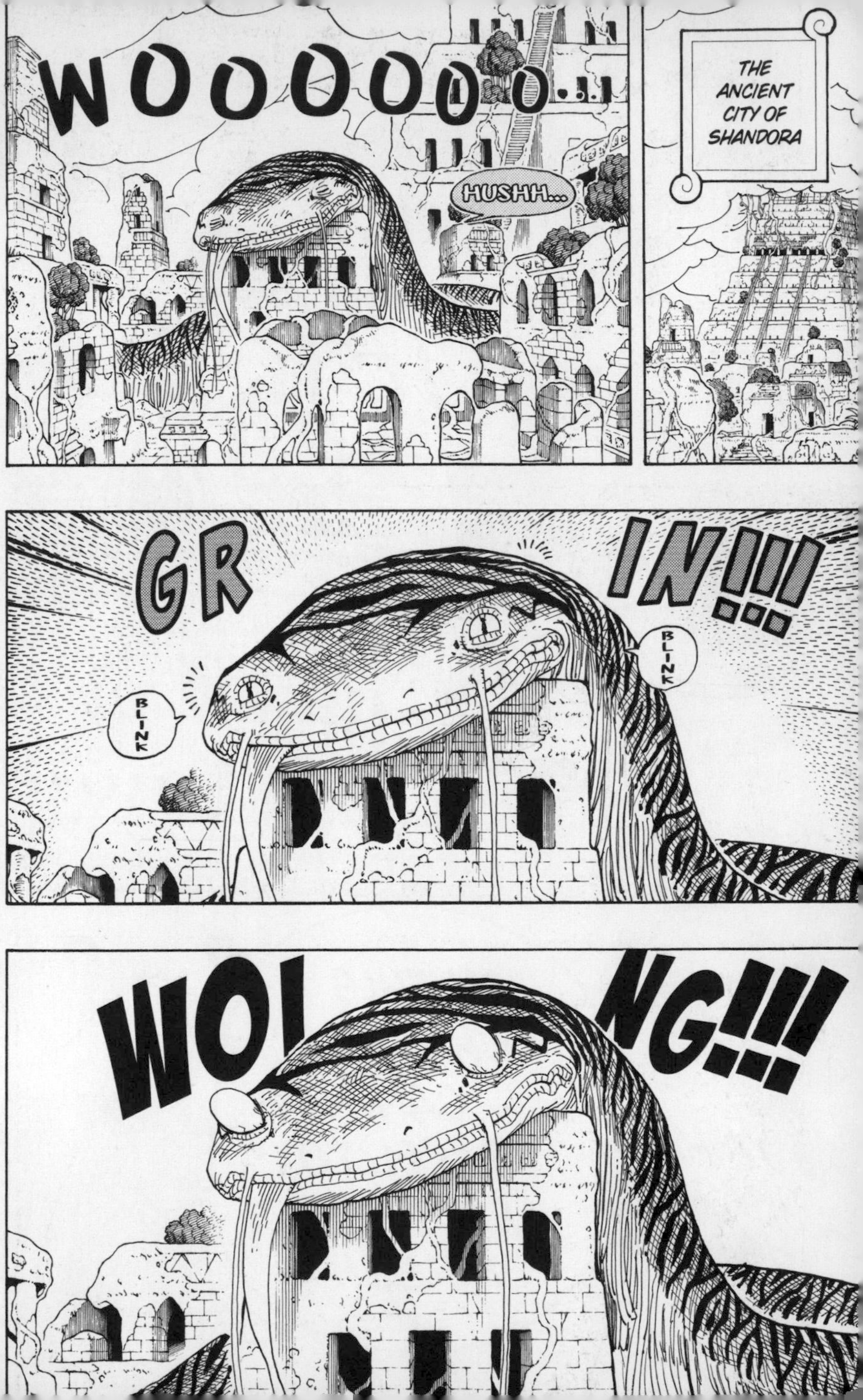
THE ANCIENT CITY OF SHANDORA
WOOOOOO...
HUSHH...
GR IN!!!
BLINK
BLINK
WO NG!!!

SILENCE...
BLINK
GR IN!!
YOINK
BLINK
TA-DAH

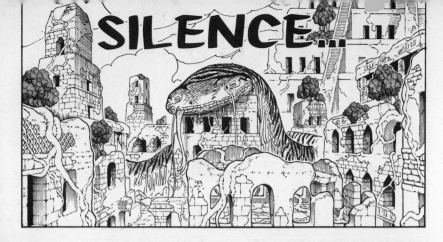

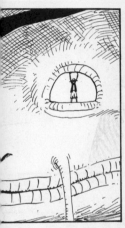

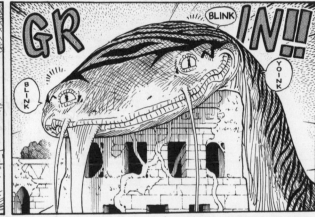

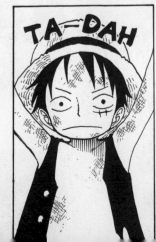

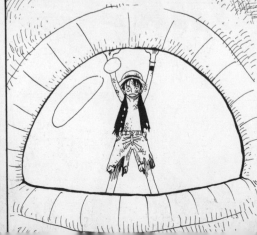

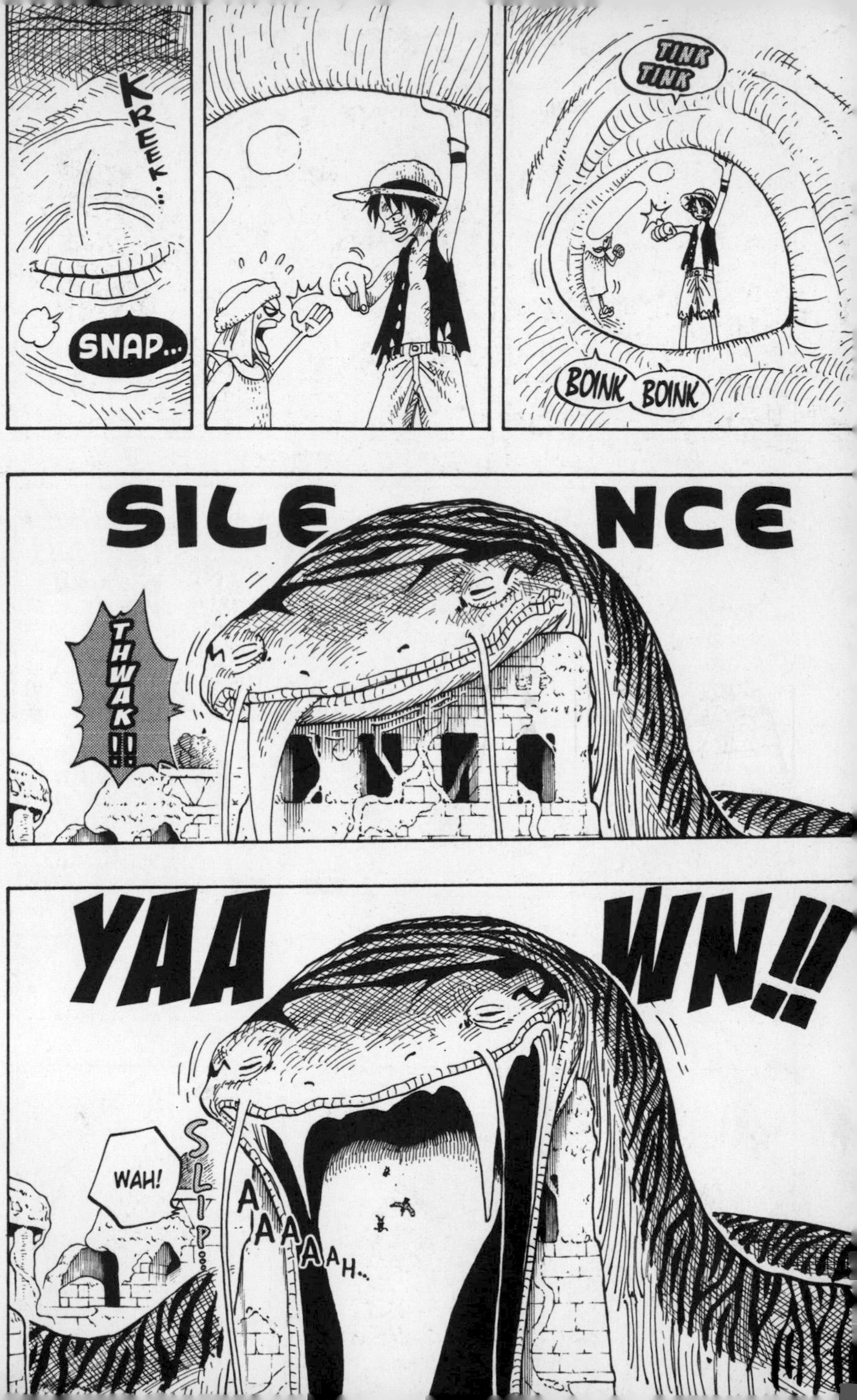
TINK TINK
BOINK BOINK
KREEK...
SNAP...
SILENCE
THWAK!!
YAAWN!!
SLIP...
WAH!
AAAAAAH..

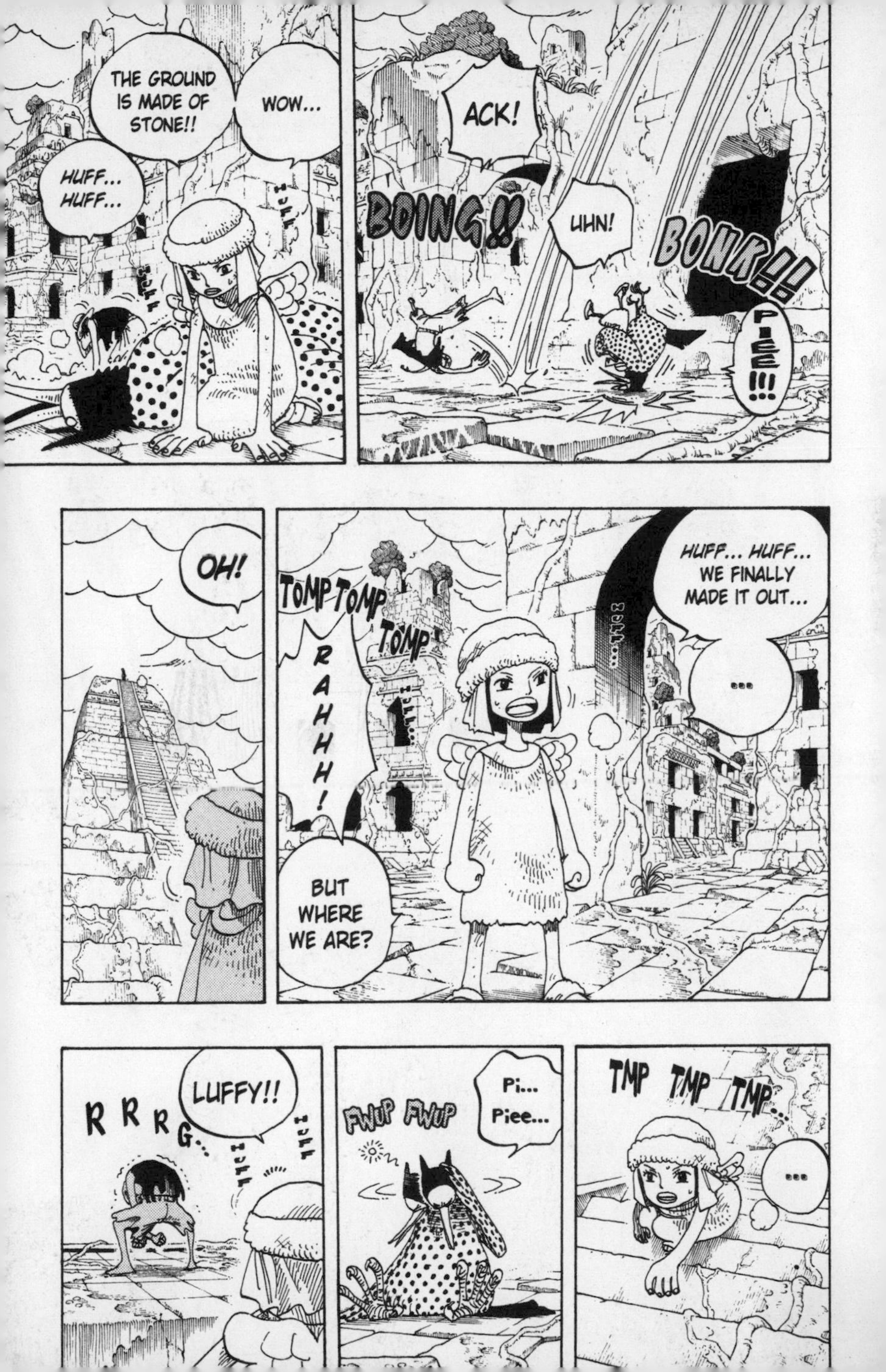
ACK!
BONK!!
PIEE!!!
UHN!
BOING!!
WOW...
THE GROUND IS MADE OF STONE!!
HUFF
HUFF... HUFF...
HUFF
HUFF... HUFF... WE FINALLY MADE IT OUT...
...
TOMP TOMP TOMP
RAHHH!
BUT WHERE WE ARE?
OH!
TMP TMP TMP...
...
Pi... Piee...
FWUP FWUP
LUFFY!!
HUFF
HUFF
RRRG...

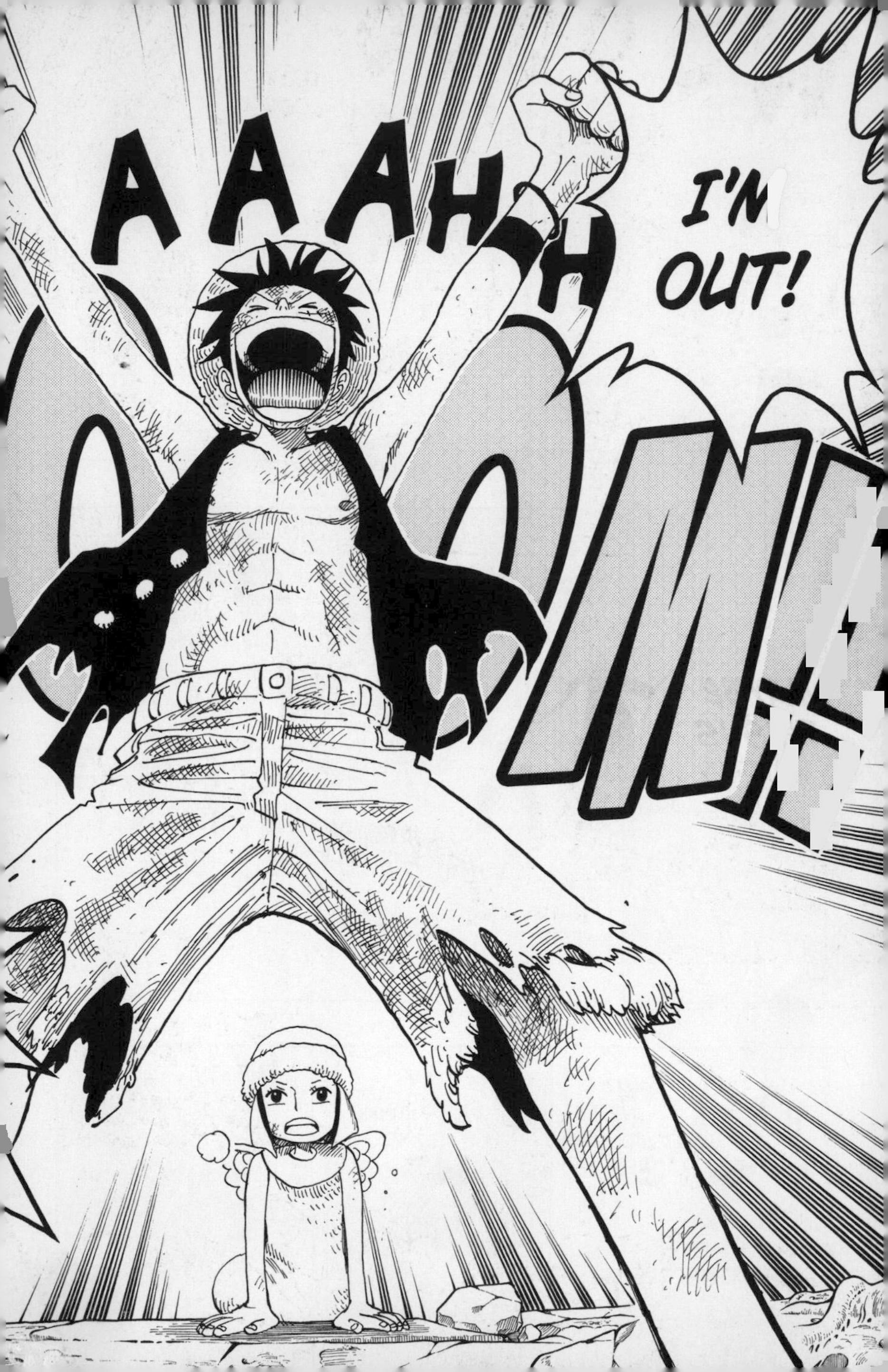
I'M OUT!
AAAAHH
OOM

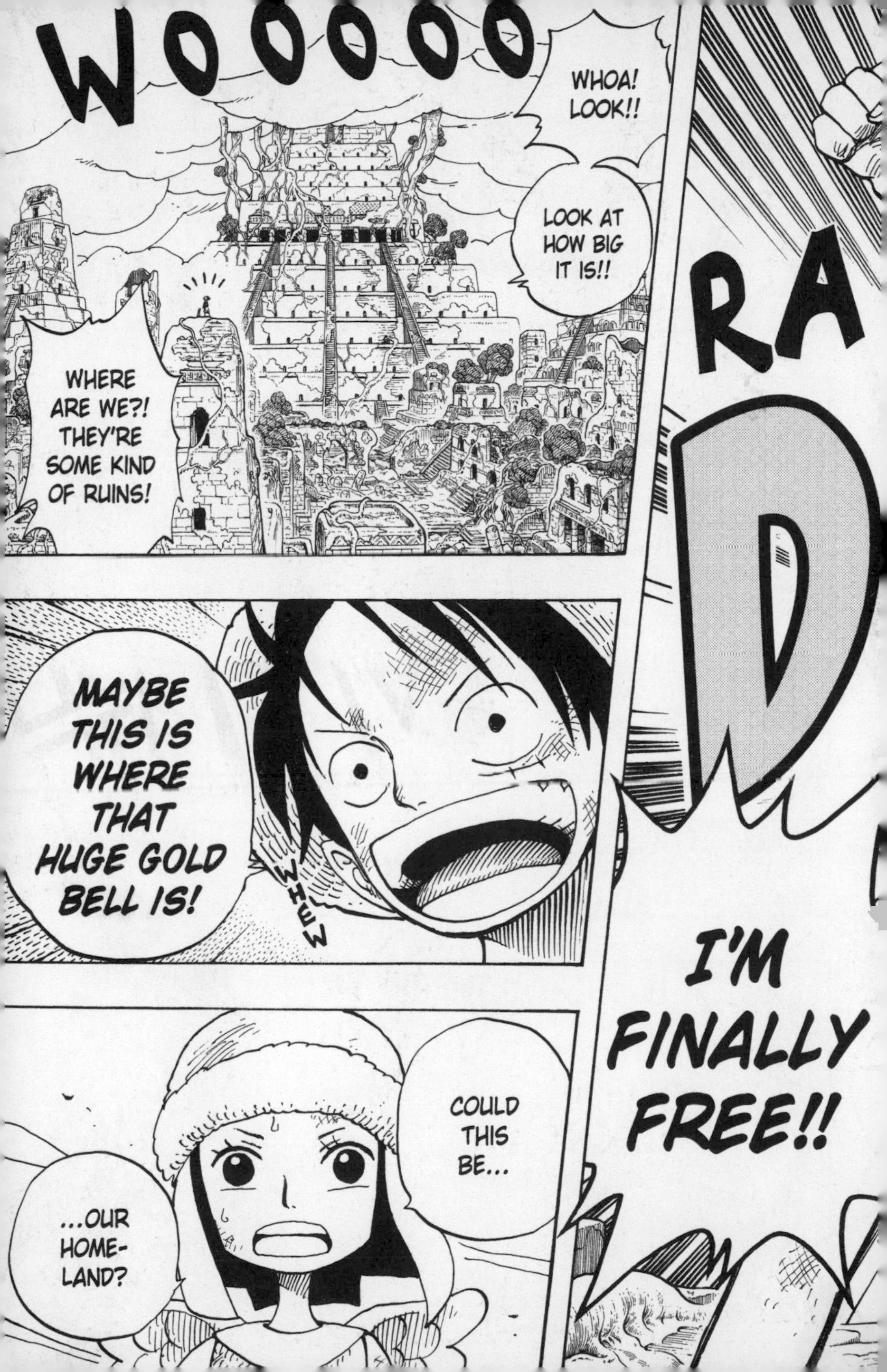
RA
D
I'M FINALLY FREE!!
WOOOOO
WHOA! LOOK!!
LOOK AT HOW BIG IT IS!!
WHERE ARE WE?! THEY'RE SOME KIND OF RUINS!
MAYBE THIS IS WHERE THAT HUGE GOLD BELL IS!
WHEW
COULD THIS BE...
...OUR HOMELAND?

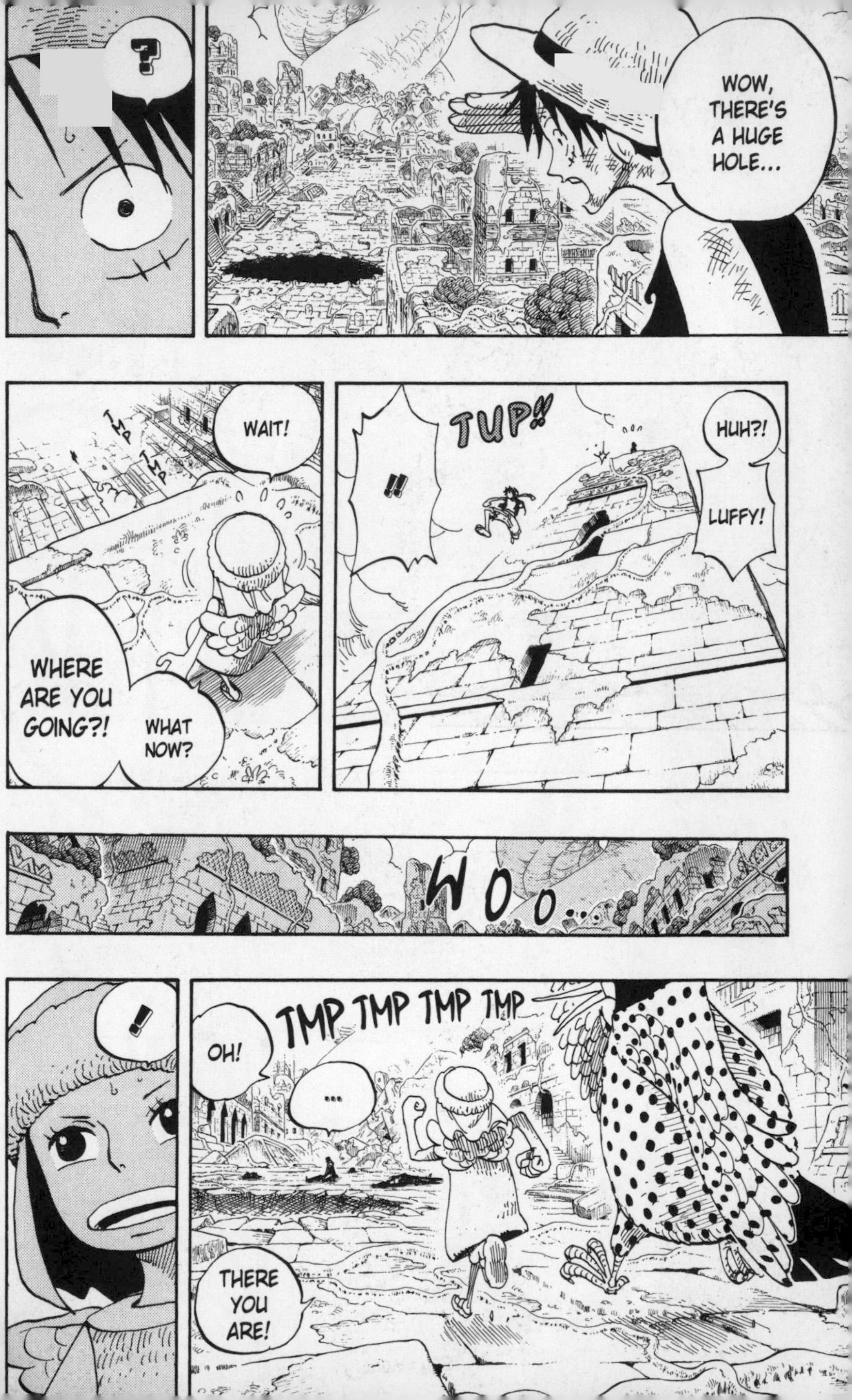
WOW, THERE'S A HUGE HOLE...
?
HUH?!
LUFFY!
TUP!!
!!
WAIT!
TMP TMP
WHAT NOW?
WHERE ARE YOU GOING?!
WOO...
TMP TMP TMP TMP
...
OH!
THERE YOU ARE!
!

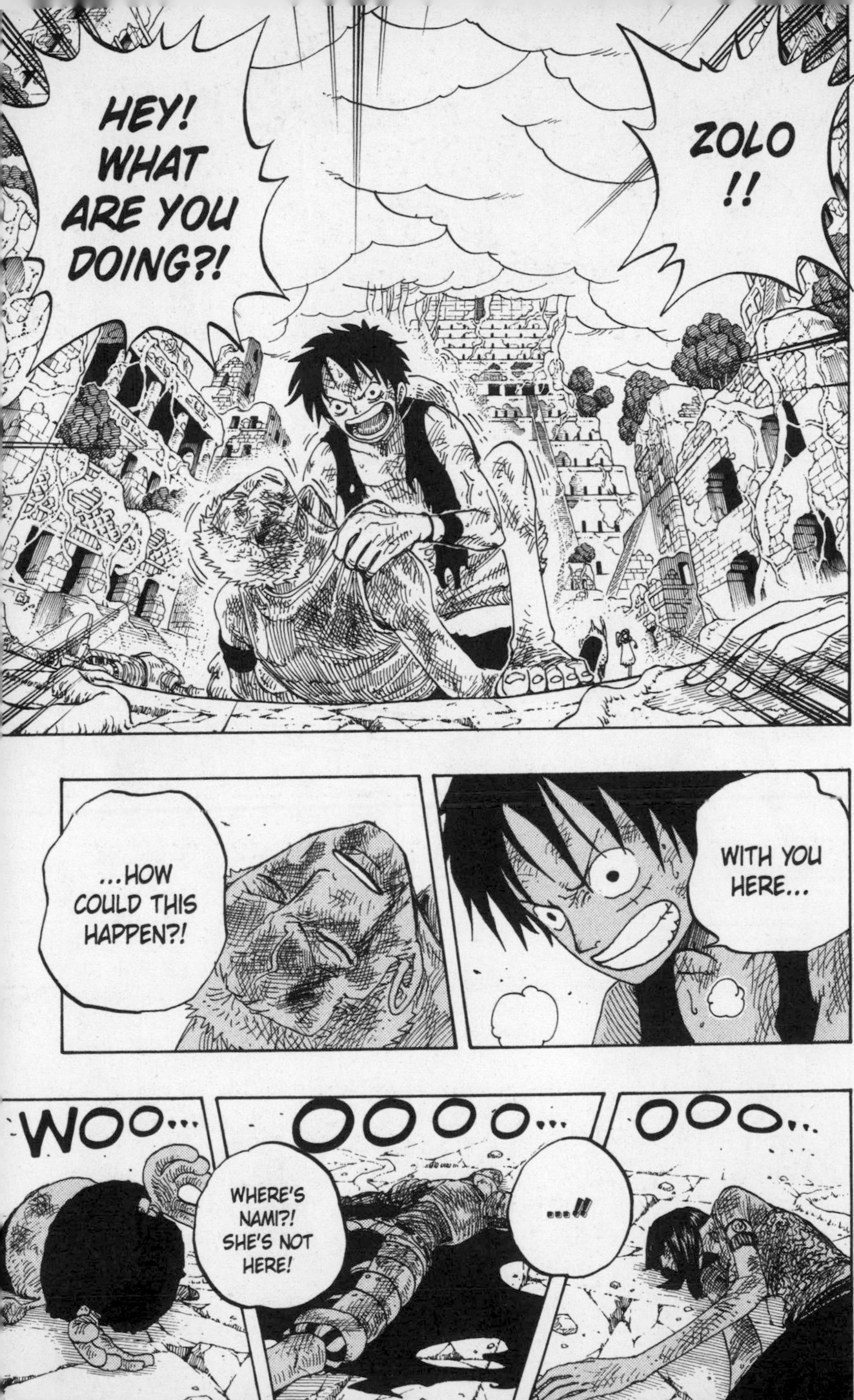
ZOLO !!
HEY! WHAT ARE YOU DOING?!
WITH YOU HERE...
...HOW COULD THIS HAPPEN?!
OOO...
OOOO...
WOO...
...!!
WHERE'S NAMI?! SHE'S NOT HERE!

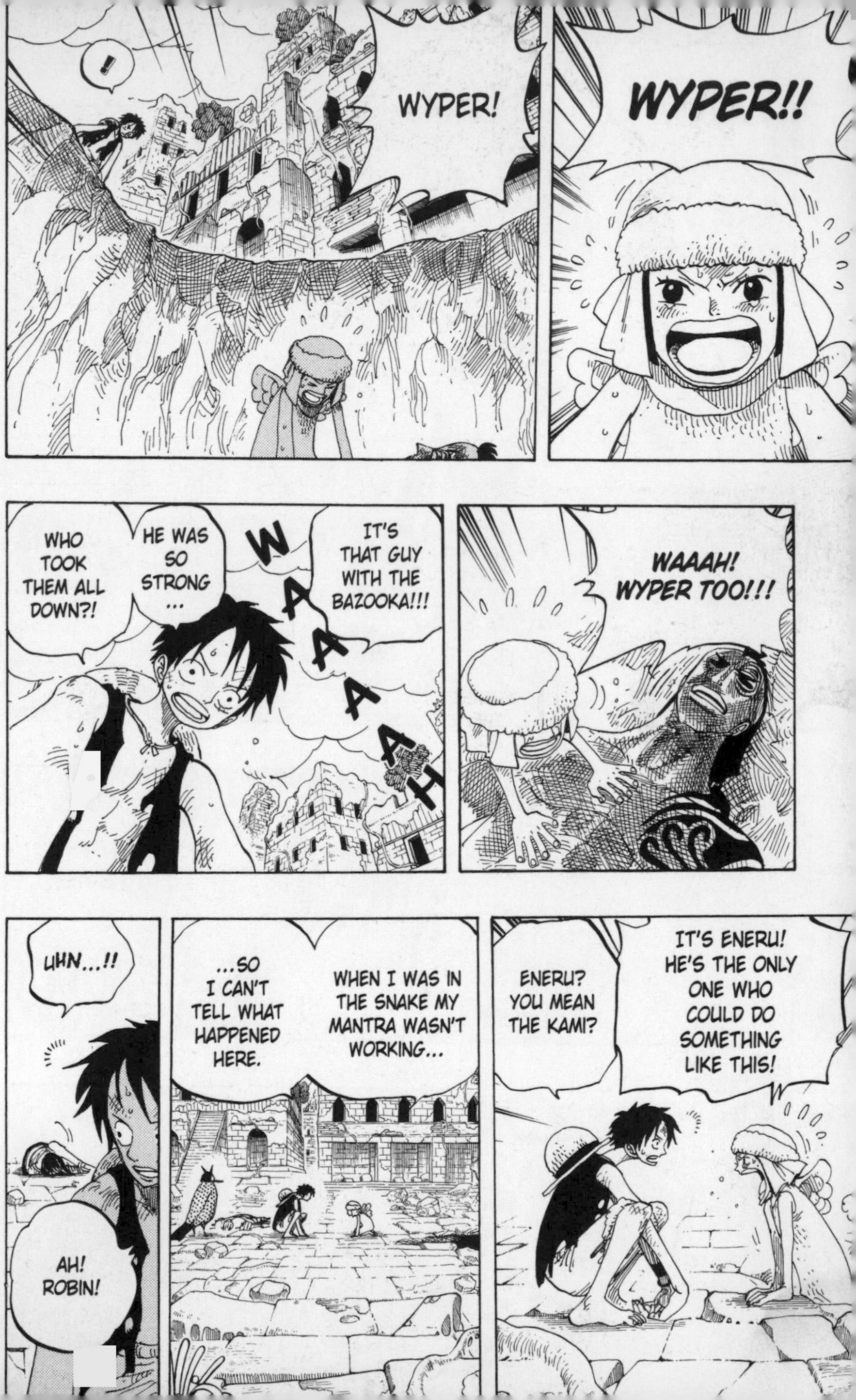
WYPER!!
WYPER!
!
WAAAH! WYPER TOO!!!
IT'S THAT GUY WITH THE BAZOOKA!!!
WAAAAH
HE WAS SO STRONG ...
WHO TOOK THEM ALL DOWN?!
IT'S ENERU! HE'S THE ONLY ONE WHO COULD DO SOMETHING LIKE THIS!
ENERU? YOU MEAN THE KAMI?
WHEN I WAS IN THE SNAKE MY MANTRA WASN'T WORKING...
...SO I CAN'T TELL WHAT HAPPENED HERE.
UHN...!!
AH! ROBIN!

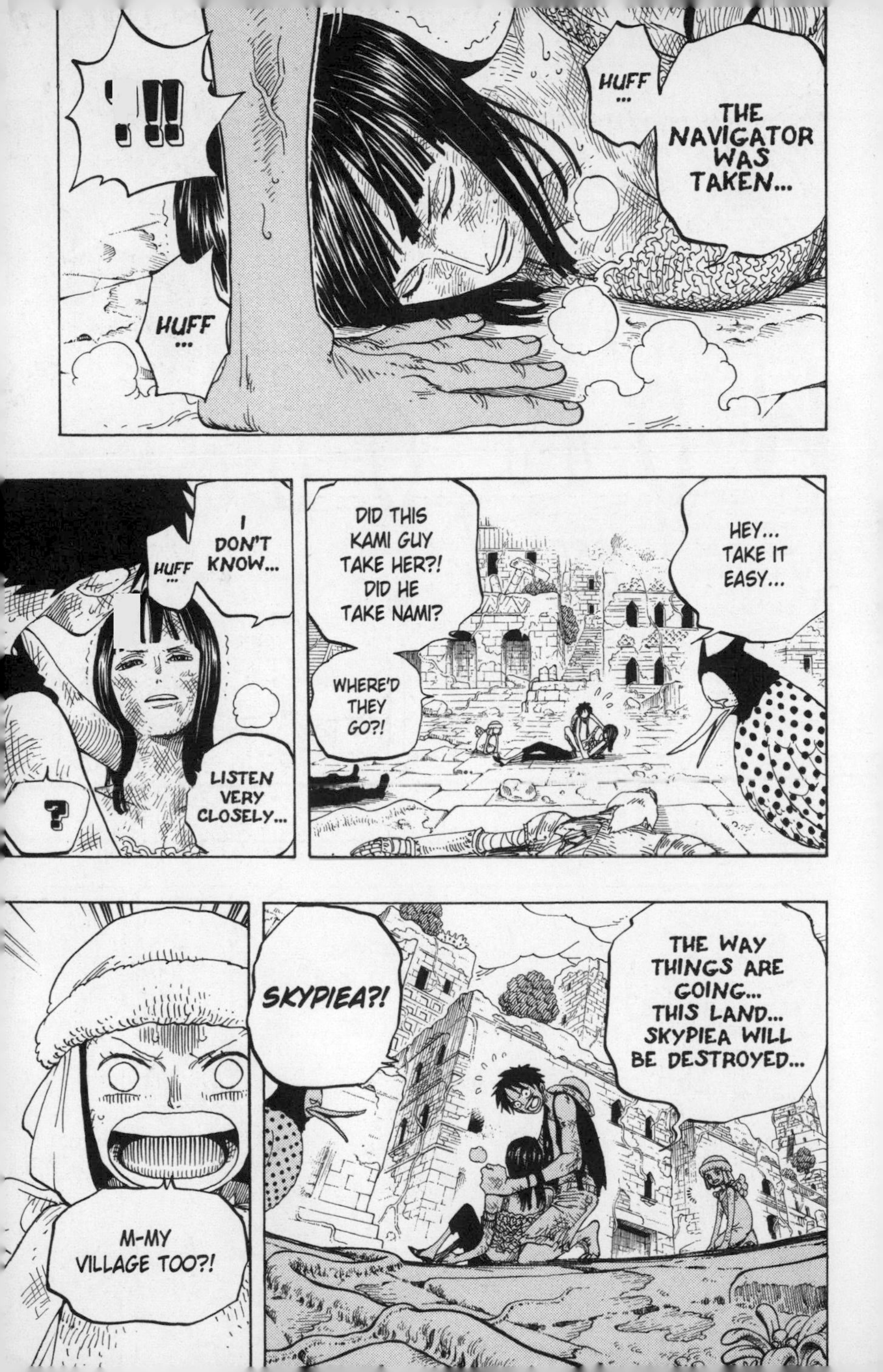
HUFF ...
THE NAVIGATOR WAS TAKEN...
!!
HUFF ...
HEY... TAKE IT EASY...
DID THIS KAMI GUY TAKE HER?! DID HE TAKE NAMI?
WHERE'D THEY GO?!
I DON'T KNOW...
HUFF ...
LISTEN VERY CLOSELY...
?
THE WAY THINGS ARE GOING... THIS LAND... SKYPIEA WILL BE DESTROYED...
SKYPIEA?!
M-MY VILLAGE TOO?!

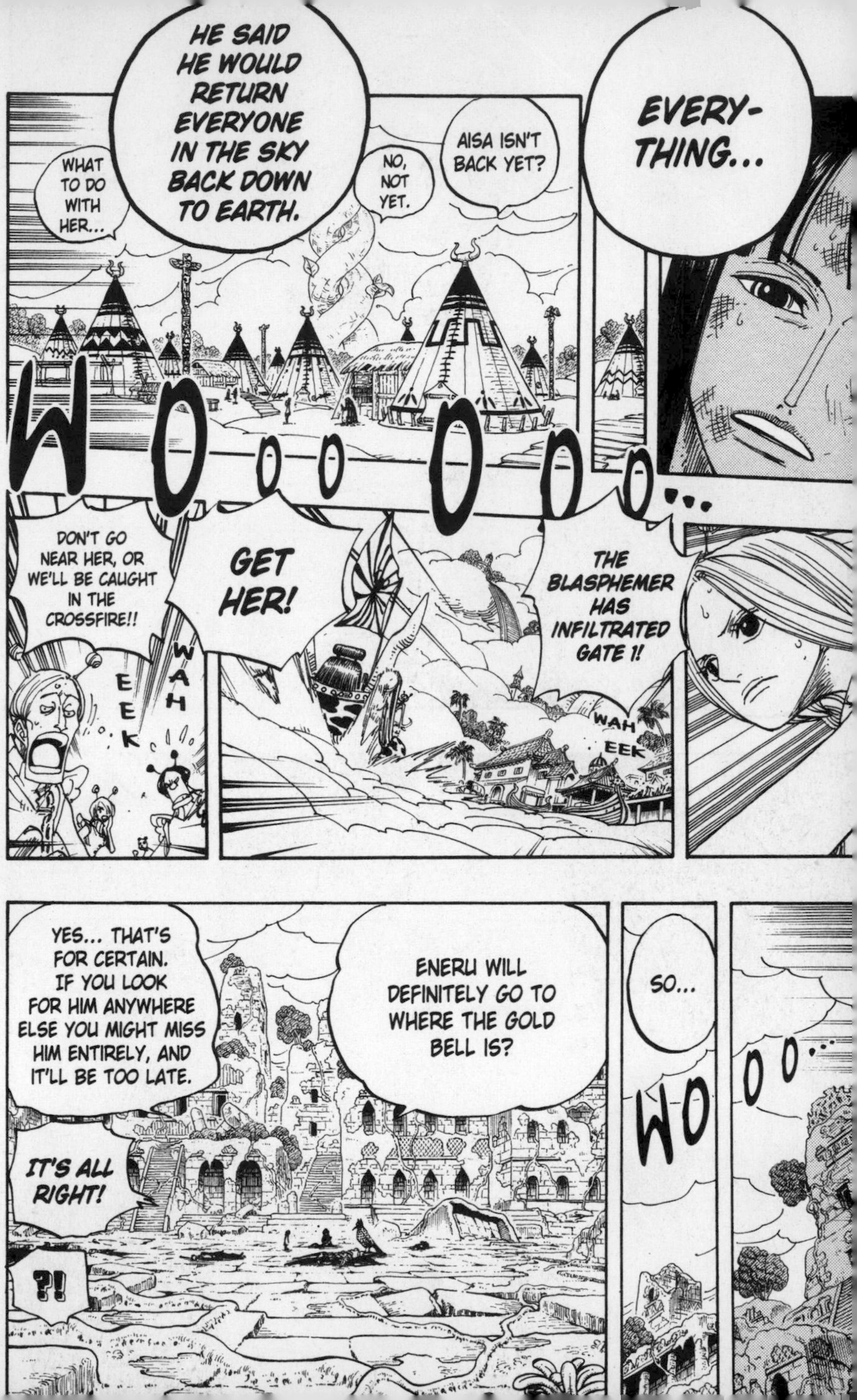
EVERY-THING...
HE SAID HE WOULD RETURN EVERYONE IN THE SKY BACK DOWN TO EARTH.
AISA ISN'T BACK YET?
NO, NOT YET.
WHAT TO DO WITH HER...
WOOOOOO...
THE BLASPHEMER HAS INFILTRATED GATE 1!
WAH
EEK
GET HER!
DON'T GO NEAR HER, OR WE'LL BE CAUGHT IN THE CROSSFIRE!!
WAH
EEK
WOO...
SO...
ENERU WILL DEFINITELY GO TO WHERE THE GOLD BELL IS?
YES... THAT'S FOR CERTAIN. IF YOU LOOK FOR HIM ANYWHERE ELSE YOU MIGHT MISS HIM ENTIRELY, AND IT'LL BE TOO LATE.
IT'S ALL RIGHT!
?!

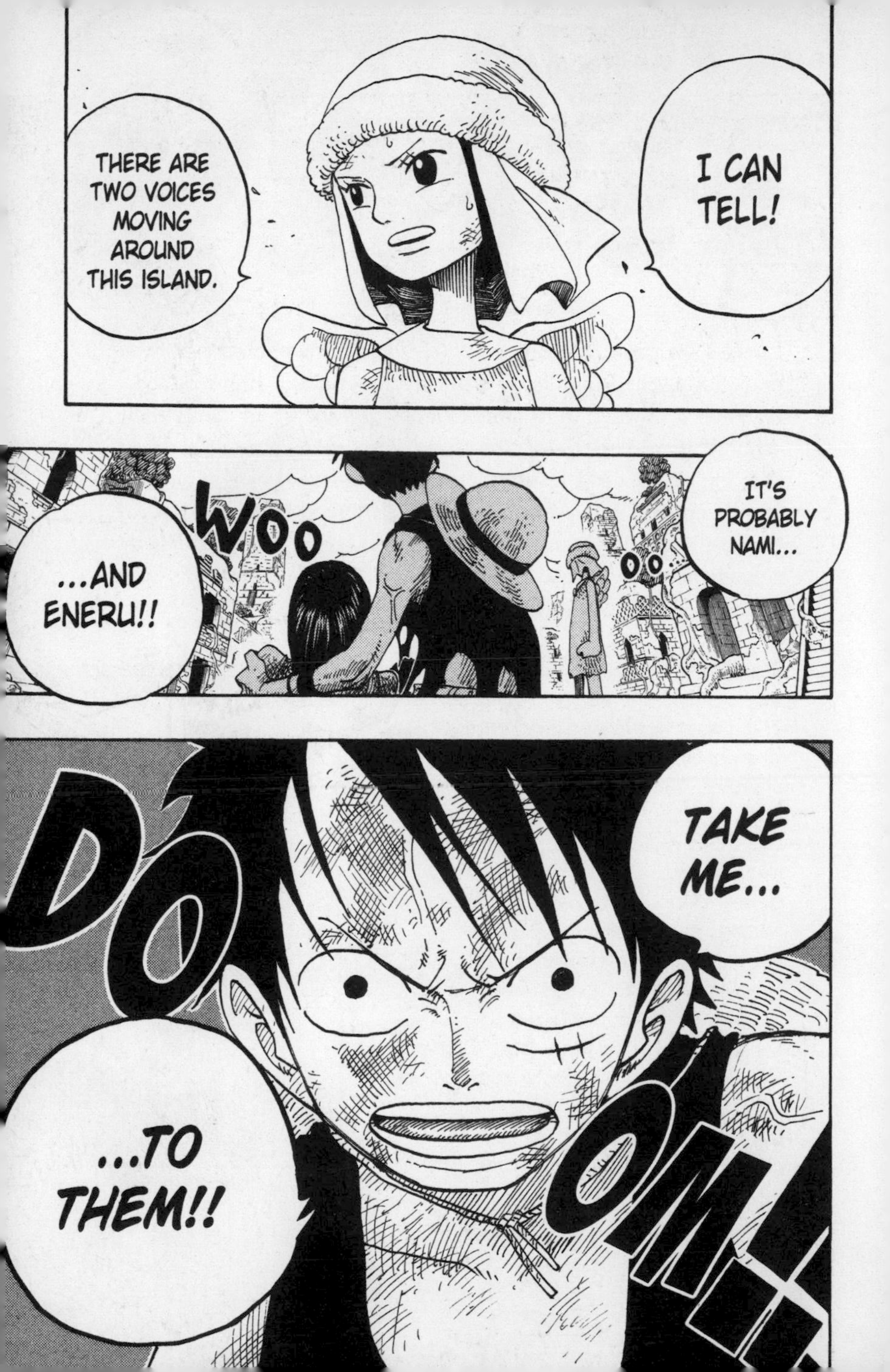
I CAN TELL!
THERE ARE TWO VOICES MOVING AROUND THIS ISLAND.
IT'S PROBABLY NAMI...
OO
WOO
...AND ENERU!!
TAKE ME...
...TO THEM!!
DOOM!!

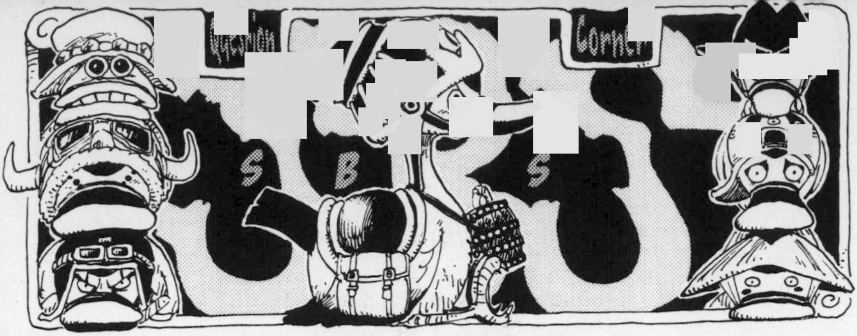
S B S

Q : I have a question. The other day I heard on the radio that it never rains during the Wimbledon tennis tournament in England. The reason is that when tournament organizers see a rain cloud, they send up a jet to blast away the cloud. That clears the sky above Wimbledon, but as a result, the neighboring towns are sometimes inundated with rain. After I heard this, I remembered the "Dance Powder" story in *One Piece*. I was surprised to find out that it's actually possible to change the weather, but did you use this fact as the basis for your storyline?

A : Rain or lack of it has always been a life-or-death situation for people's lives, and people have dreamt of controlling the weather since ancient times.
The artificial rainmaker that appears in the Alabasta arc was actually created by someone. But the experiment cost an inordinate amount of money. Even though it made rain, some people questioned whether it would rain anyway without the machine. No one has been able to prove it either way.
By the way, the idea for "Dance Powder" came from a substance called silver iodide. When it's burned and its smoke is put into clouds, the cloud gets bigger. It's a very interesting powder.

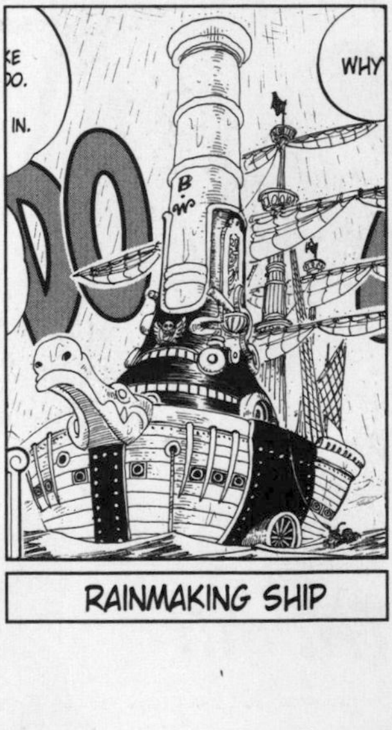
RAINMAKING SHIP

Chapter 278: CONIS

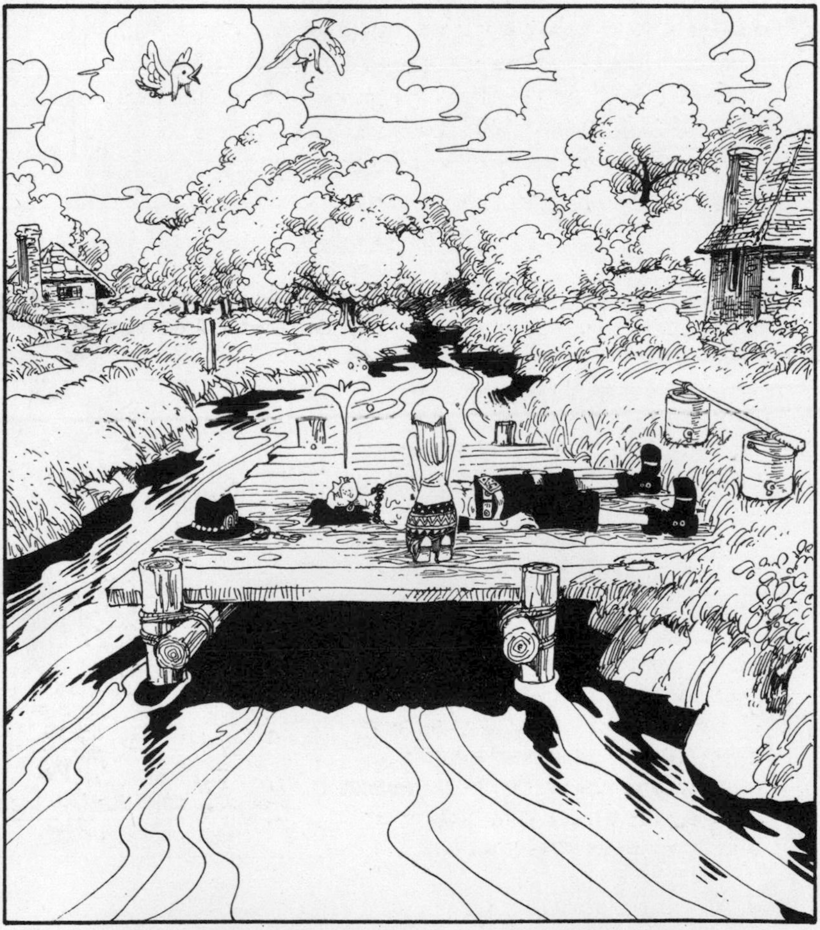

ACE'S GREAT SEARCH FOR BLACKBEARD, VOL. 6:
"SAVING A LIFE DOWNSTREAM FROM TOWN"

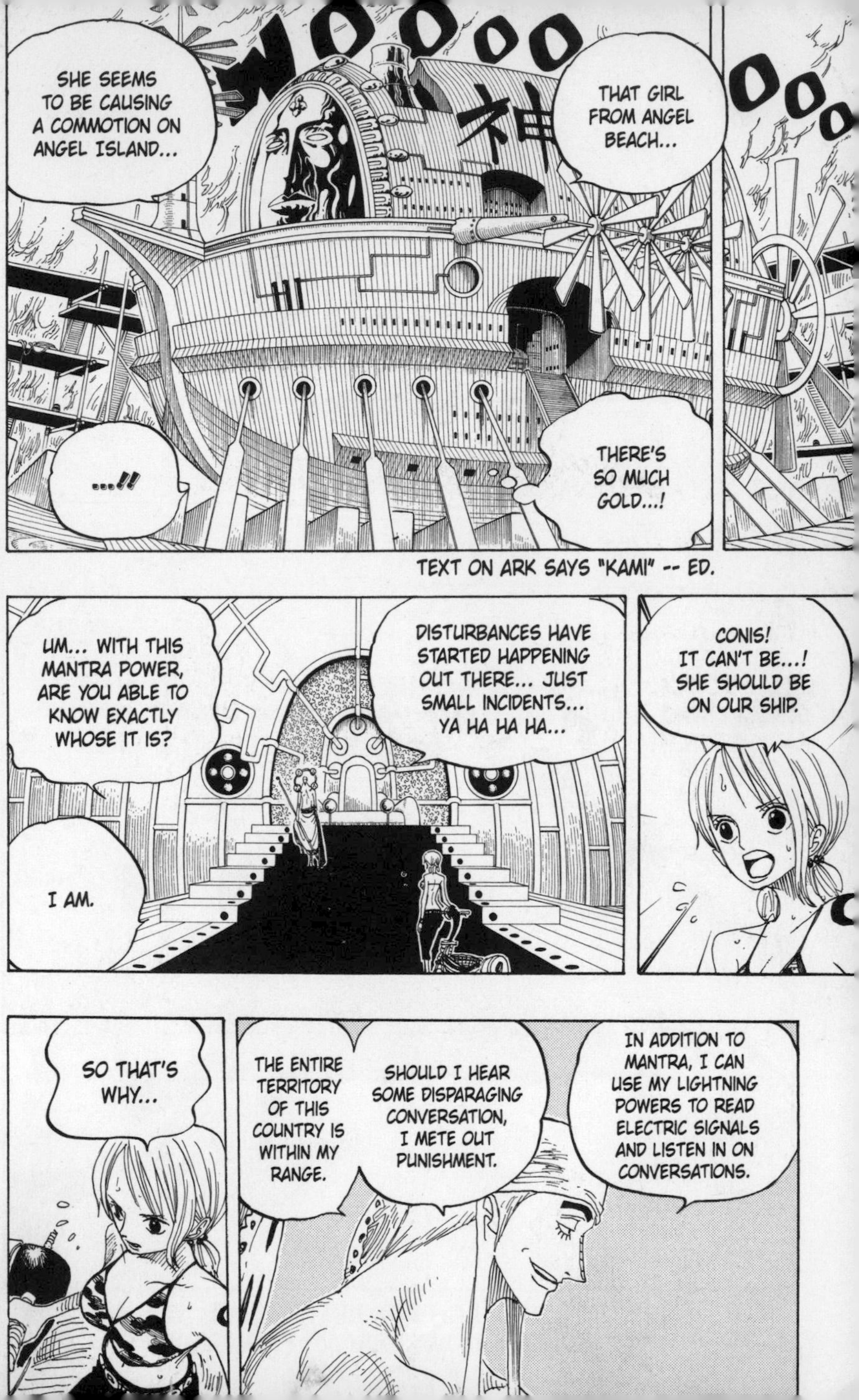
WOOOOOOO
神
THAT GIRL FROM ANGEL BEACH...
SHE SEEMS TO BE CAUSING A COMMOTION ON ANGEL ISLAND...
THERE'S SO MUCH GOLD...!
...!!
TEXT ON ARK SAYS "KAMI" -- ED.
CONIS! IT CAN'T BE...! SHE SHOULD BE ON OUR SHIP.
DISTURBANCES HAVE STARTED HAPPENING OUT THERE... JUST SMALL INCIDENTS... YA HA HA HA...
UM... WITH THIS MANTRA POWER, ARE YOU ABLE TO KNOW EXACTLY WHOSE IT IS?
I AM.
IN ADDITION TO MANTRA, I CAN USE MY LIGHTNING POWERS TO READ ELECTRIC SIGNALS AND LISTEN IN ON CONVERSATIONS.
SHOULD I HEAR SOME DISPARAGING CONVERSATION, I METE OUT PUNISHMENT.
THE ENTIRE TERRITORY OF THIS COUNTRY IS WITHIN MY RANGE.
SO THAT'S WHY...

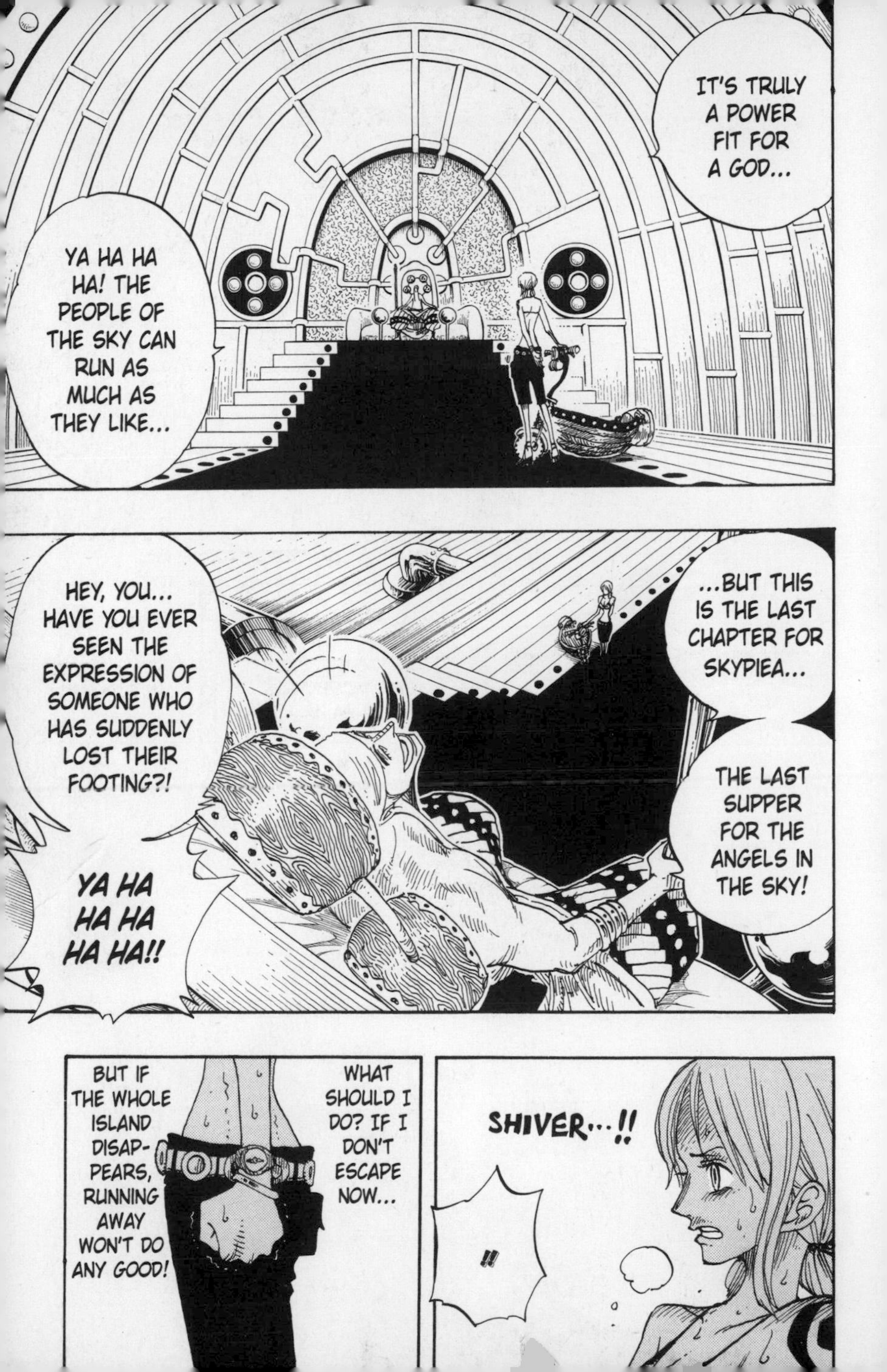
IT'S TRULY A POWER FIT FOR A GOD...
YA HA HA HA! THE PEOPLE OF THE SKY CAN RUN AS MUCH AS THEY LIKE...
...BUT THIS IS THE LAST CHAPTER FOR SKYPIEA...
THE LAST SUPPER FOR THE ANGELS IN THE SKY!
HEY, YOU... HAVE YOU EVER SEEN THE EXPRESSION OF SOMEONE WHO HAS SUDDENLY LOST THEIR FOOTING?!
YA HA HA HA HA HA!!
SHIVER...!!
!!
WHAT SHOULD I DO? IF I DON'T ESCAPE NOW...
BUT IF THE WHOLE ISLAND DISAP-PEARS, RUNNING AWAY WON'T DO ANY GOOD!

...

...

IS SOMETHING WRONG?

BA-BUMP

UM...

WHO IS THAT?

...

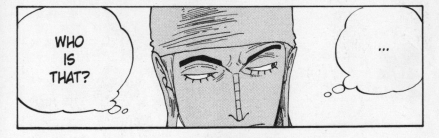

IT'S NOTHING...

TMP TMP

NO...

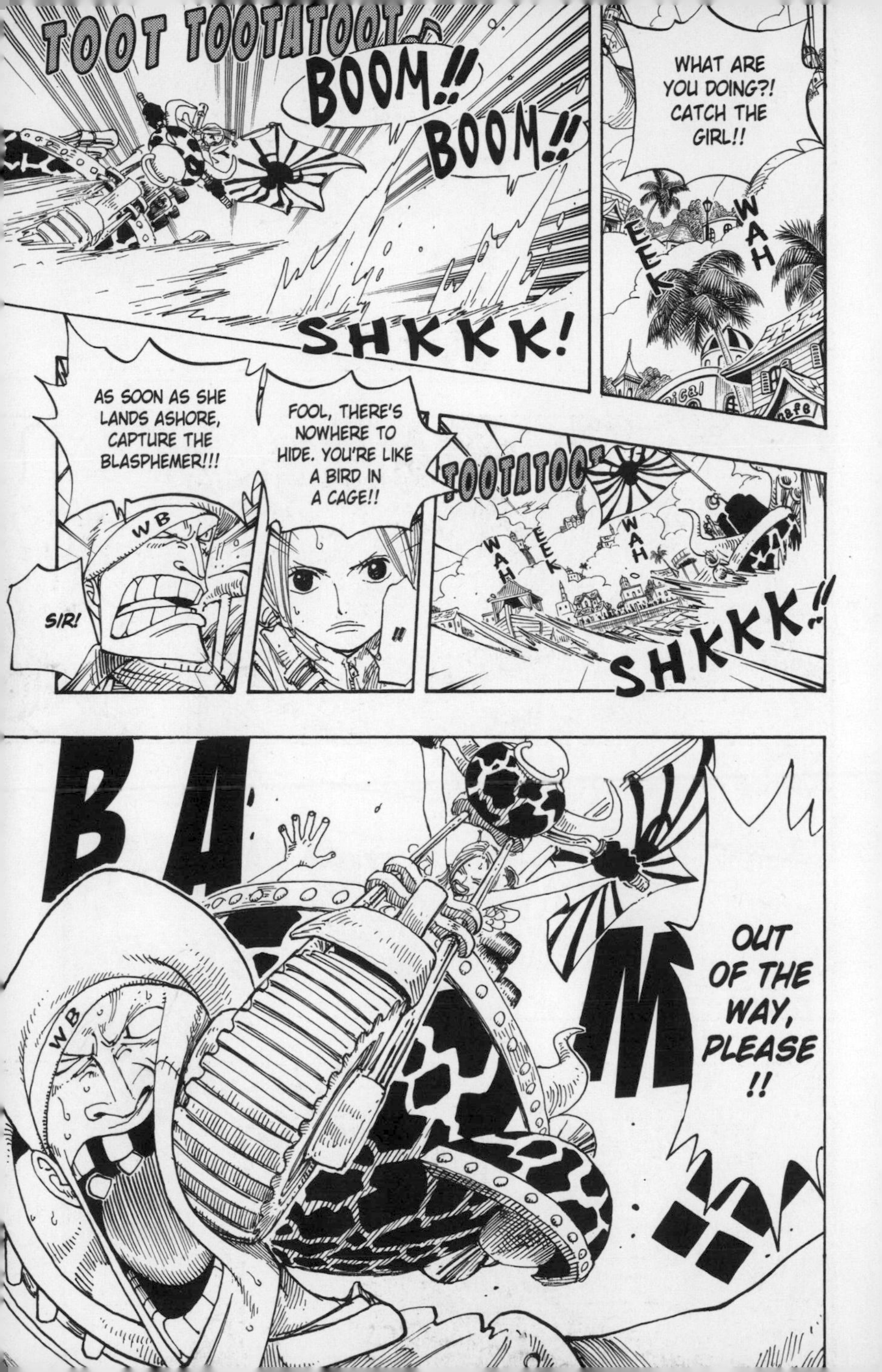
WHAT ARE YOU DOING?! CATCH THE GIRL!!
WAH
EEK
TOOT TOOTATOOT
BOOM!!
BOOM!!
SHKKK!
TOOTATOOT
WAH
EEK
WAH
SHKKK!!
FOOL, THERE'S NOWHERE TO HIDE. YOU'RE LIKE A BIRD IN A CAGE!!
!!
AS SOON AS SHE LANDS ASHORE, CAPTURE THE BLASPHEMER!!!
SIR!
BAM
OUT OF THE WAY, PLEASE!!

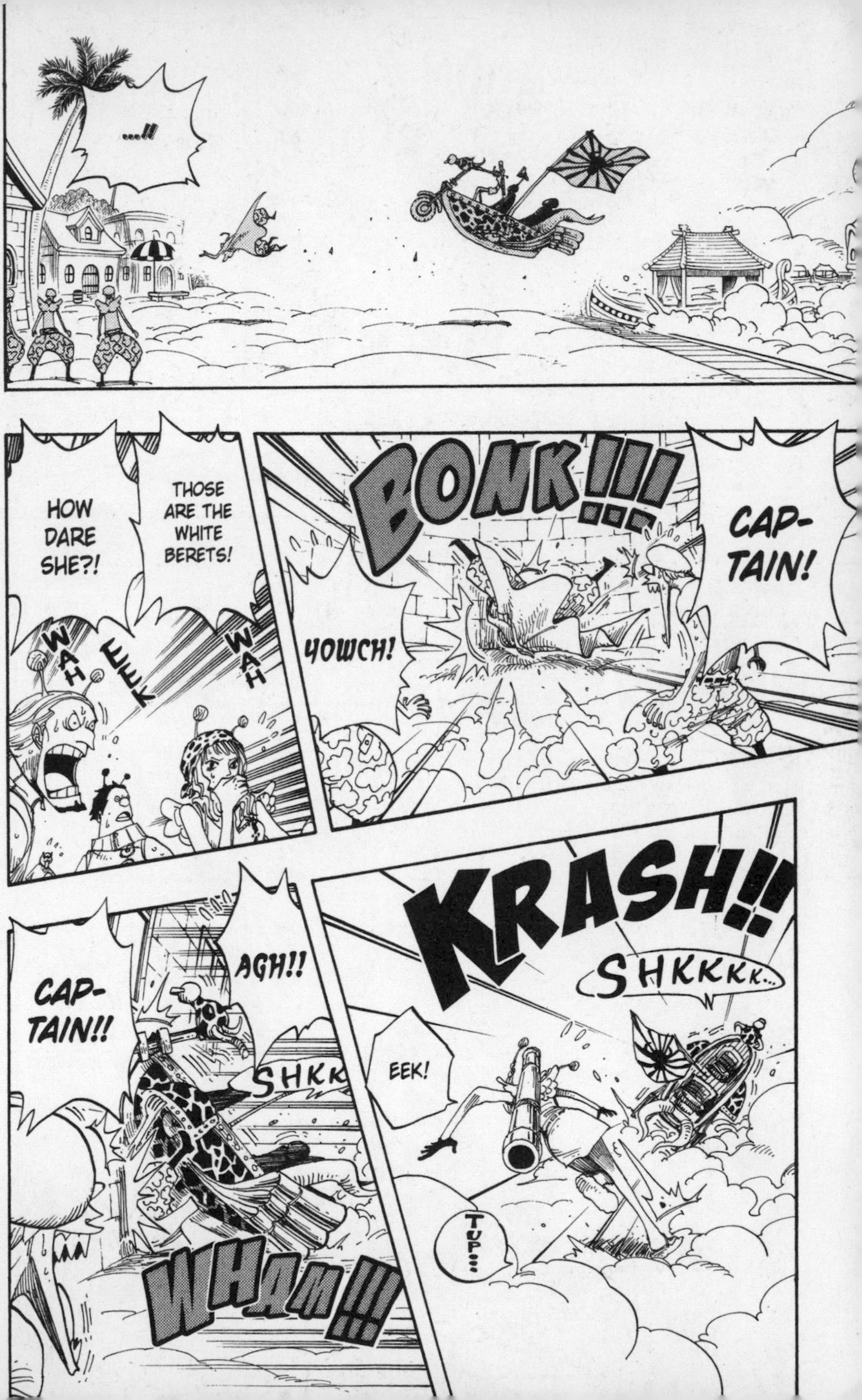
...!!
CAP-TAIN!
BONK!!!
YOWCH!
THOSE ARE THE WHITE BERETS!
HOW DARE SHE?!
WAH
WAH
EEK
KRASH!!
SHKKKK...
EEK!
TUP...
AGH!!
CAP-TAIN!!
SHKK
WHAM!!!

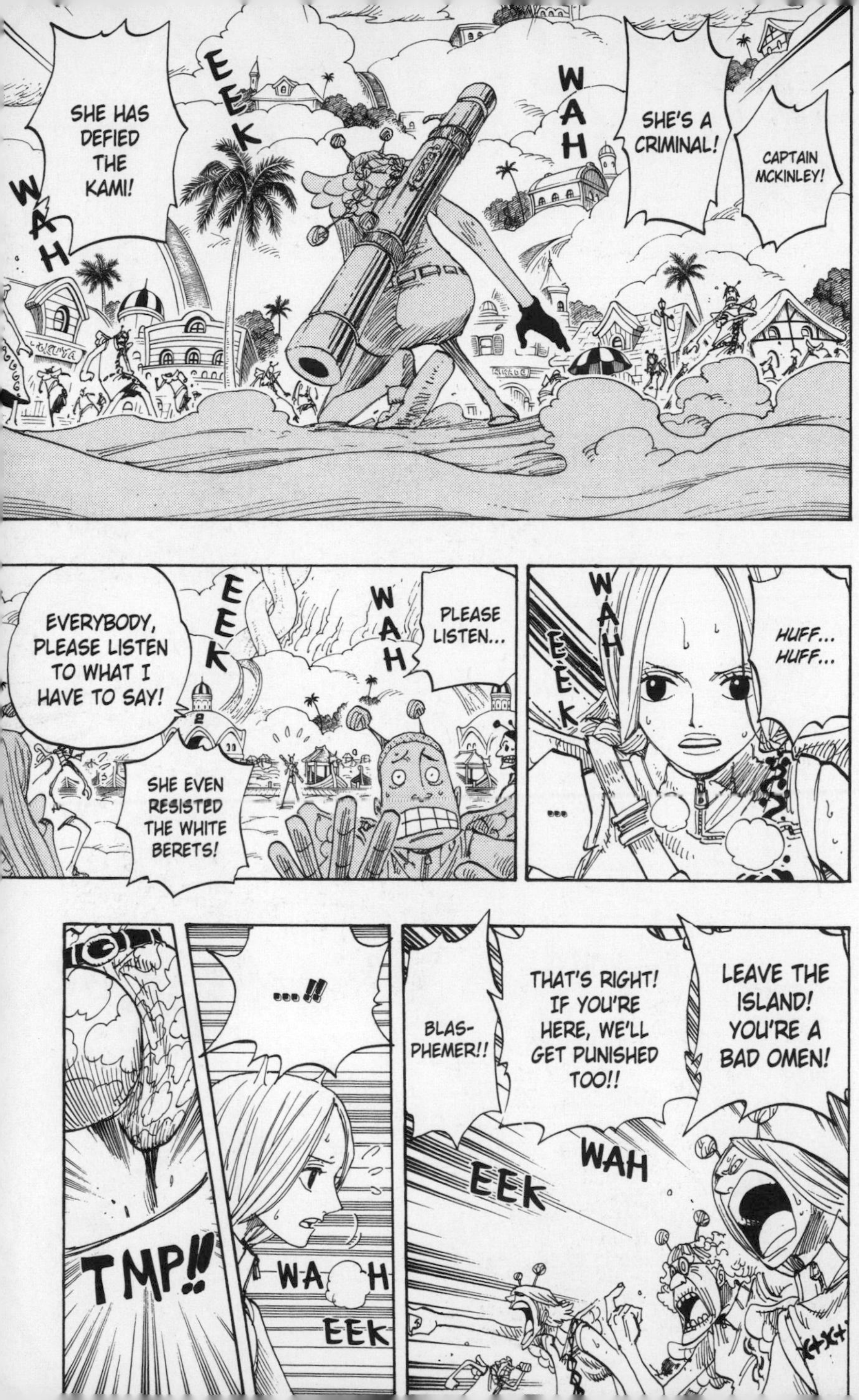
CAPTAIN MCKINLEY!
SHE'S A CRIMINAL!
WAH
EEK
SHE HAS DEFIED THE KAMI!
WAH
WAH
EEK
HUFF... HUFF...
...
PLEASE LISTEN...
WAH
EEK
EVERYBODY, PLEASE LISTEN TO WHAT I HAVE TO SAY!
SHE EVEN RESISTED THE WHITE BERETS!
LEAVE THE ISLAND! YOU'RE A BAD OMEN!
THAT'S RIGHT! IF YOU'RE HERE, WE'LL GET PUNISHED TOO!!
BLAS-PHEMER!!
WAH
EEK
...!!
WAH
EEK
TMP!!

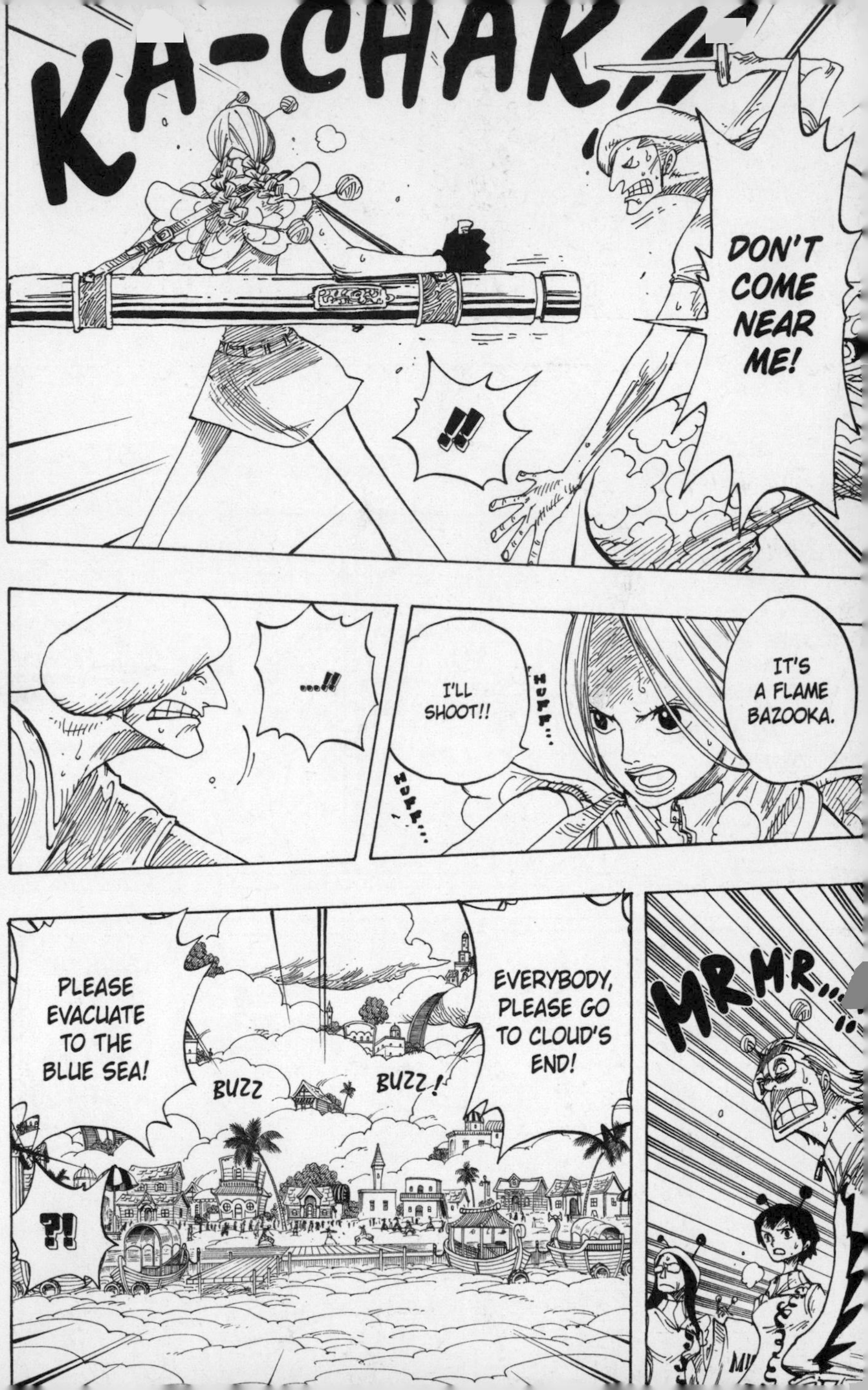
KA-CHAK!!
DON'T COME NEAR ME!
!!
IT'S A FLAME BAZOOKA.
HUFF...
HUFF...
I'LL SHOOT!!
...!!
MRMR...
EVERYBODY, PLEASE GO TO CLOUD'S END!
BUZZ!
BUZZ
PLEASE EVACUATE TO THE BLUE SEA!
?!

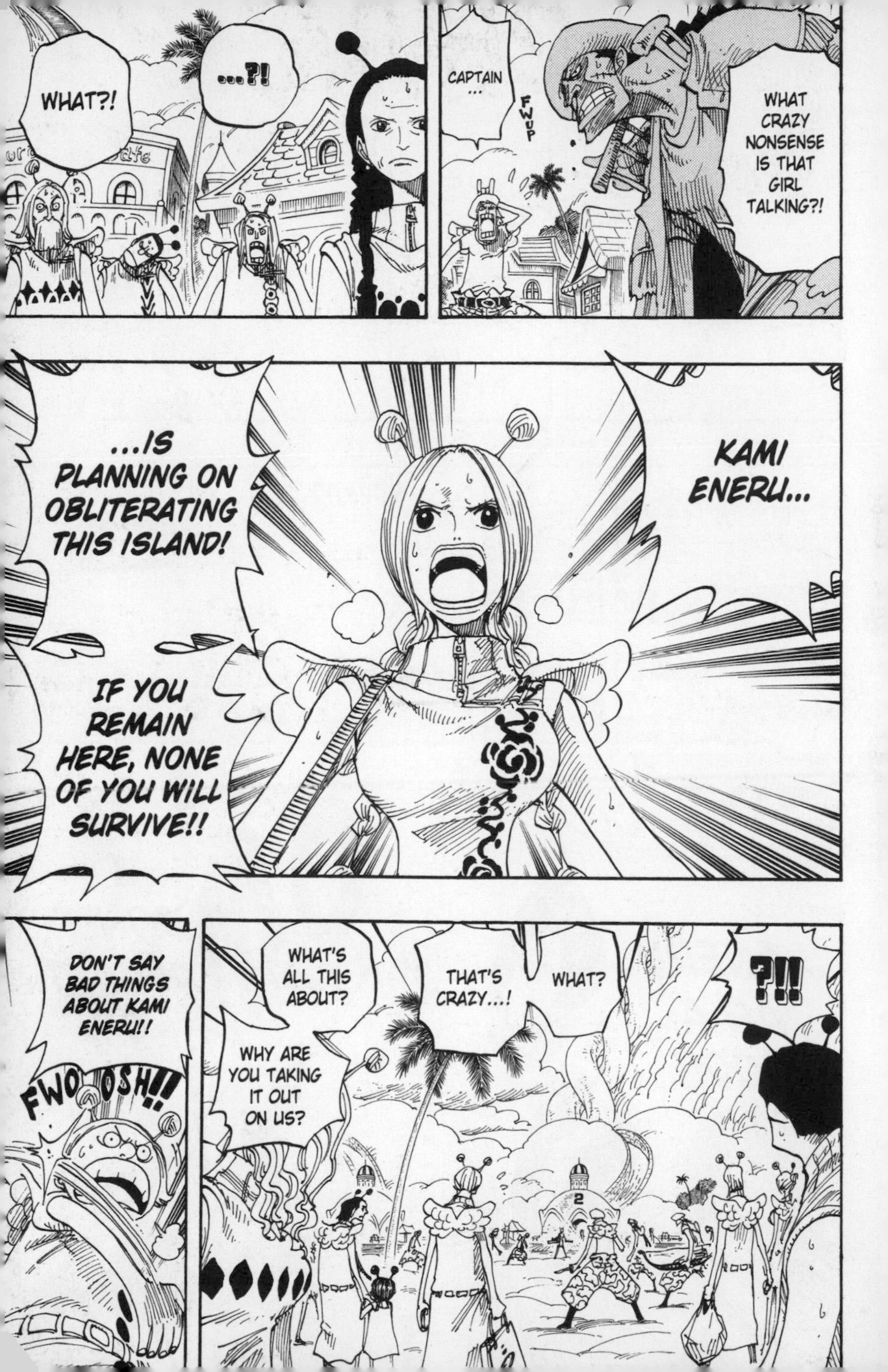
WHAT CRAZY NONSENSE IS THAT GIRL TALKING?!
CAPTAIN ...
FWUP
...?!
WHAT?!
KAMI ENERU...
...IS PLANNING ON OBLITERATING THIS ISLAND!
IF YOU REMAIN HERE, NONE OF YOU WILL SURVIVE!!
?!!
WHAT?
THAT'S CRAZY...!
WHAT'S ALL THIS ABOUT?
WHY ARE YOU TAKING IT OUT ON US?
DON'T SAY BAD THINGS ABOUT KAMI ENERU!!
FWOOSH!!

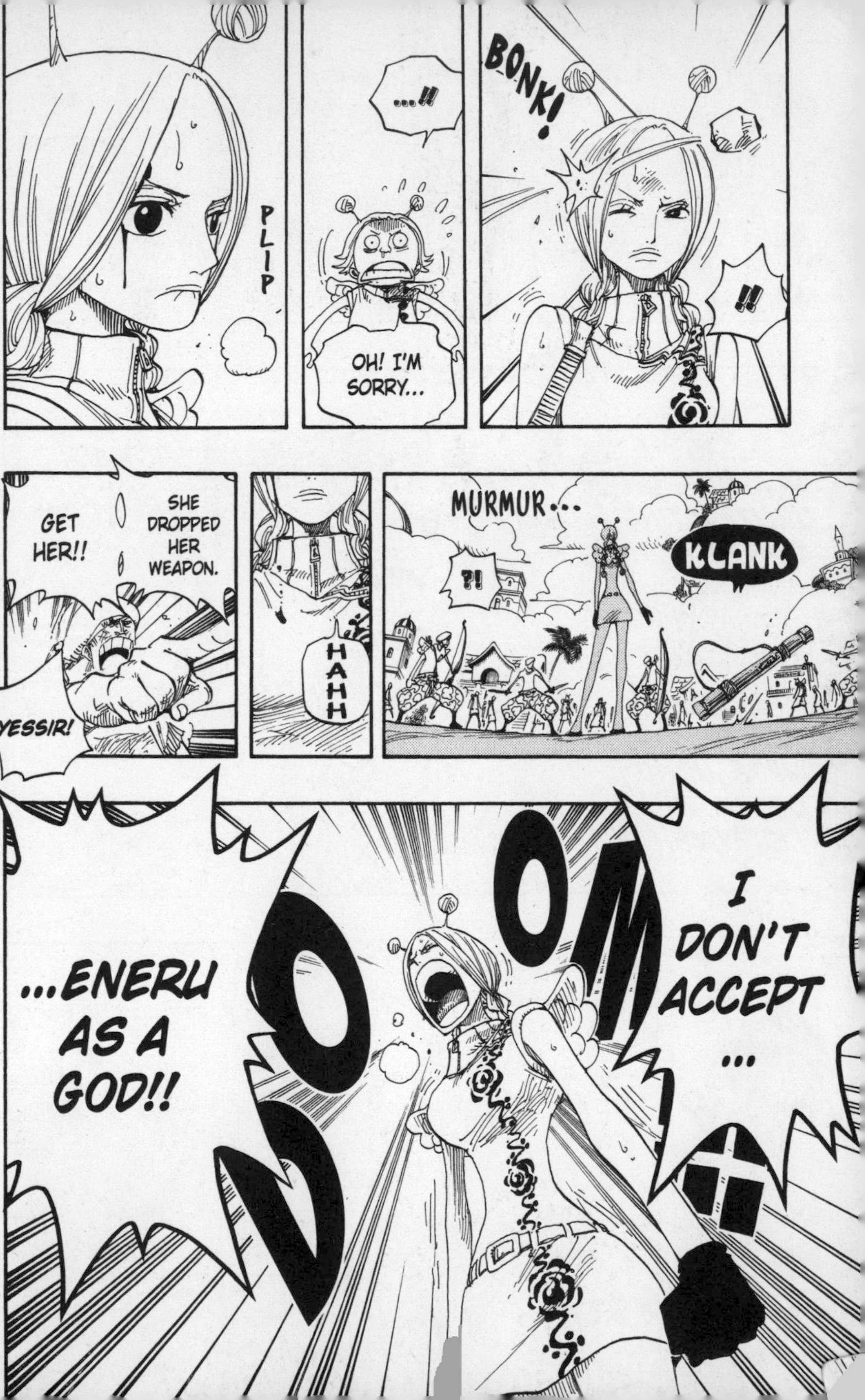
BONK!
!!
...!!
OH! I'M SORRY...
PLIP
MURMUR...
?!
KLANK
HAHH
SHE DROPPED HER WEAPON.
GET HER!!
YESSIR!
I DON'T ACCEPT...
DOOM
...ENERU AS A GOD!!

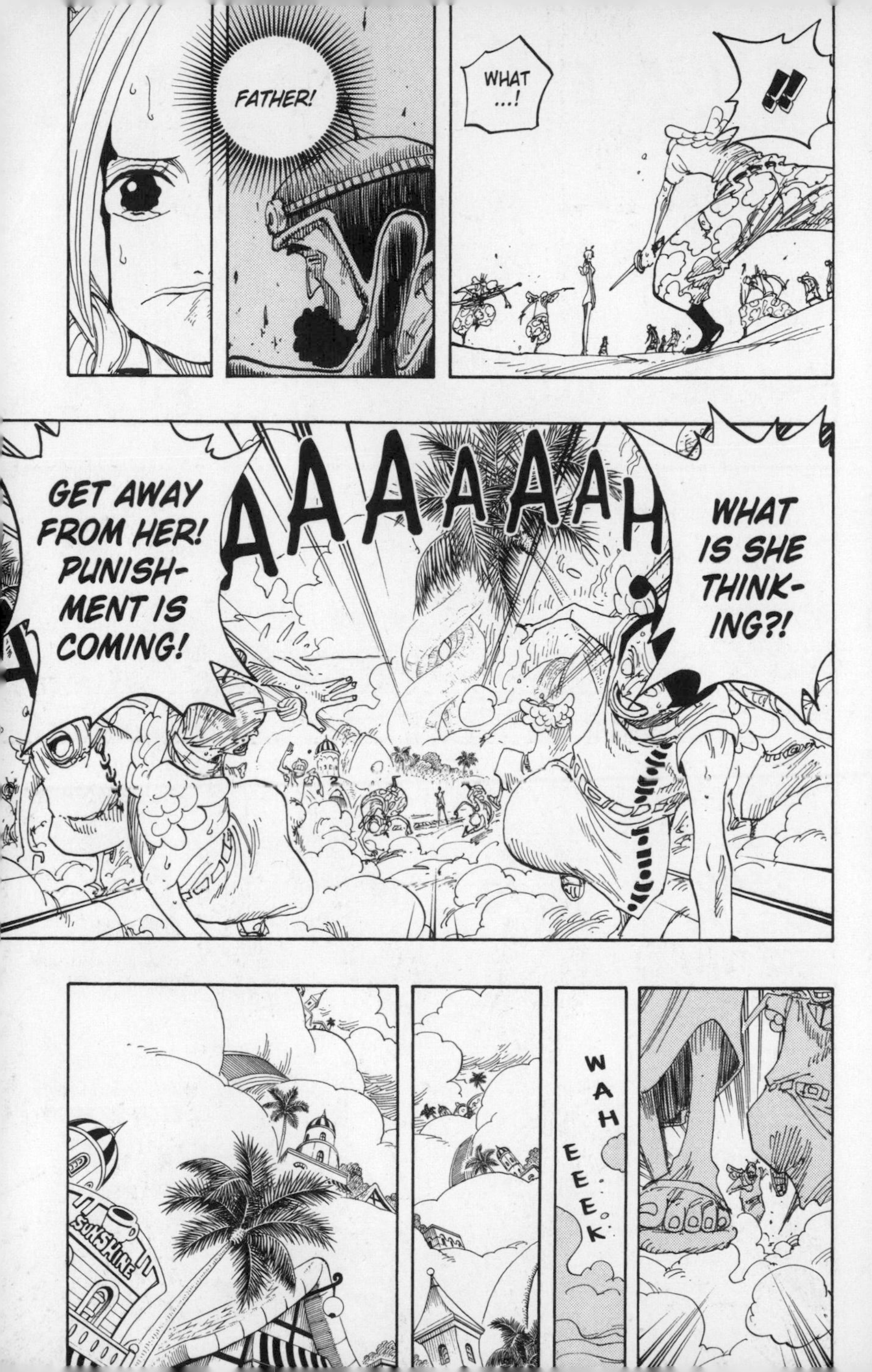
!!
WHAT ...!
FATHER!
WHAT IS SHE THINKING?!
AAAAAAH
GET AWAY FROM HER! PUNISHMENT IS COMING!
WAH EEEK
SUNSHINE

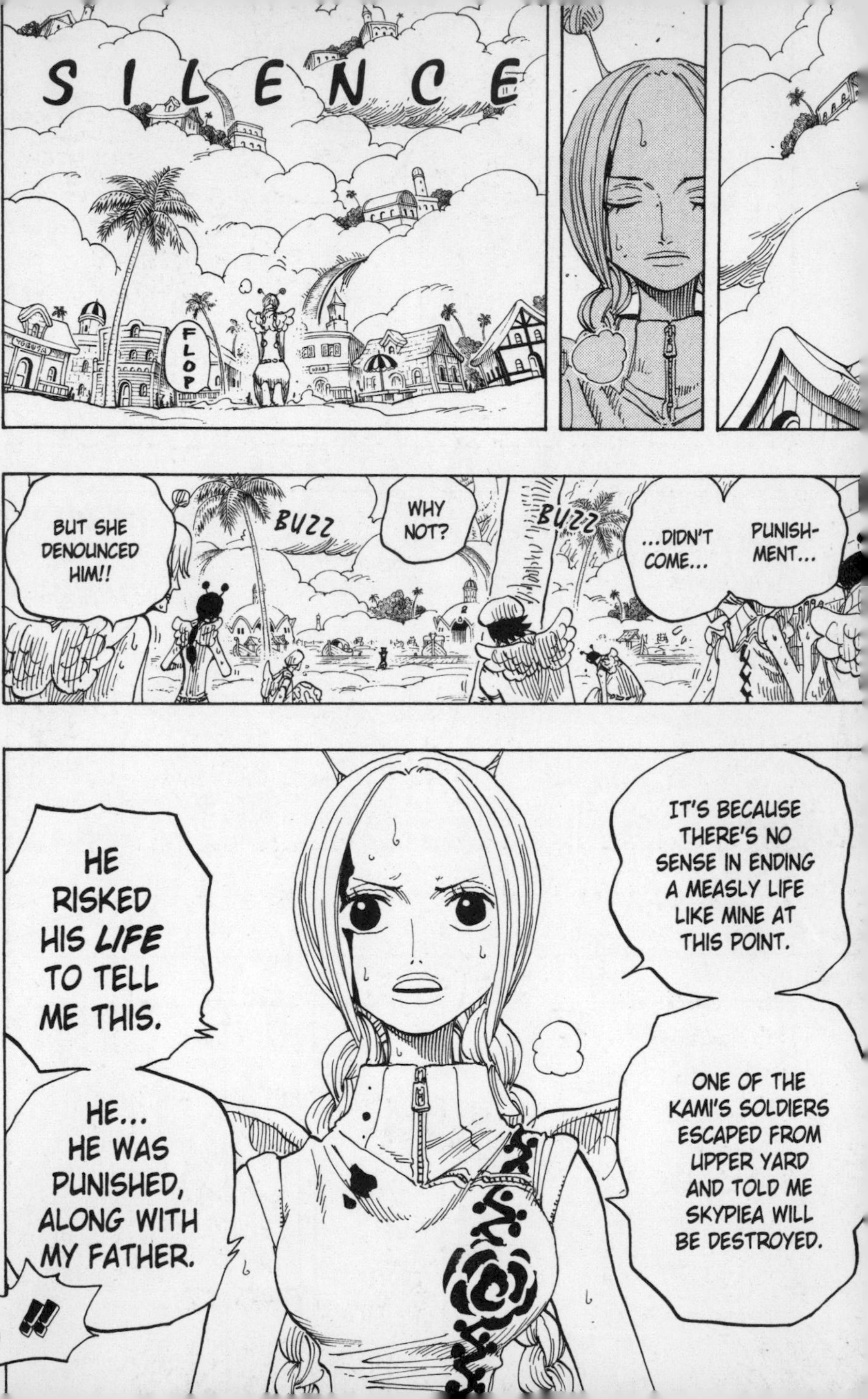

SILENCE
FLOP
PUNISHMENT...
...DIDN'T COME...
BUZZ
WHY NOT?
BUZZ
BUT SHE DENOUNCED HIM!!
IT'S BECAUSE THERE'S NO SENSE IN ENDING A MEASLY LIFE LIKE MINE AT THIS POINT.
ONE OF THE KAMI'S SOLDIERS ESCAPED FROM UPPER YARD AND TOLD ME SKYPIEA WILL BE DESTROYED.
HE RISKED HIS *LIFE* TO TELL ME THIS.
HE... HE WAS PUNISHED, ALONG WITH MY FATHER.
!!

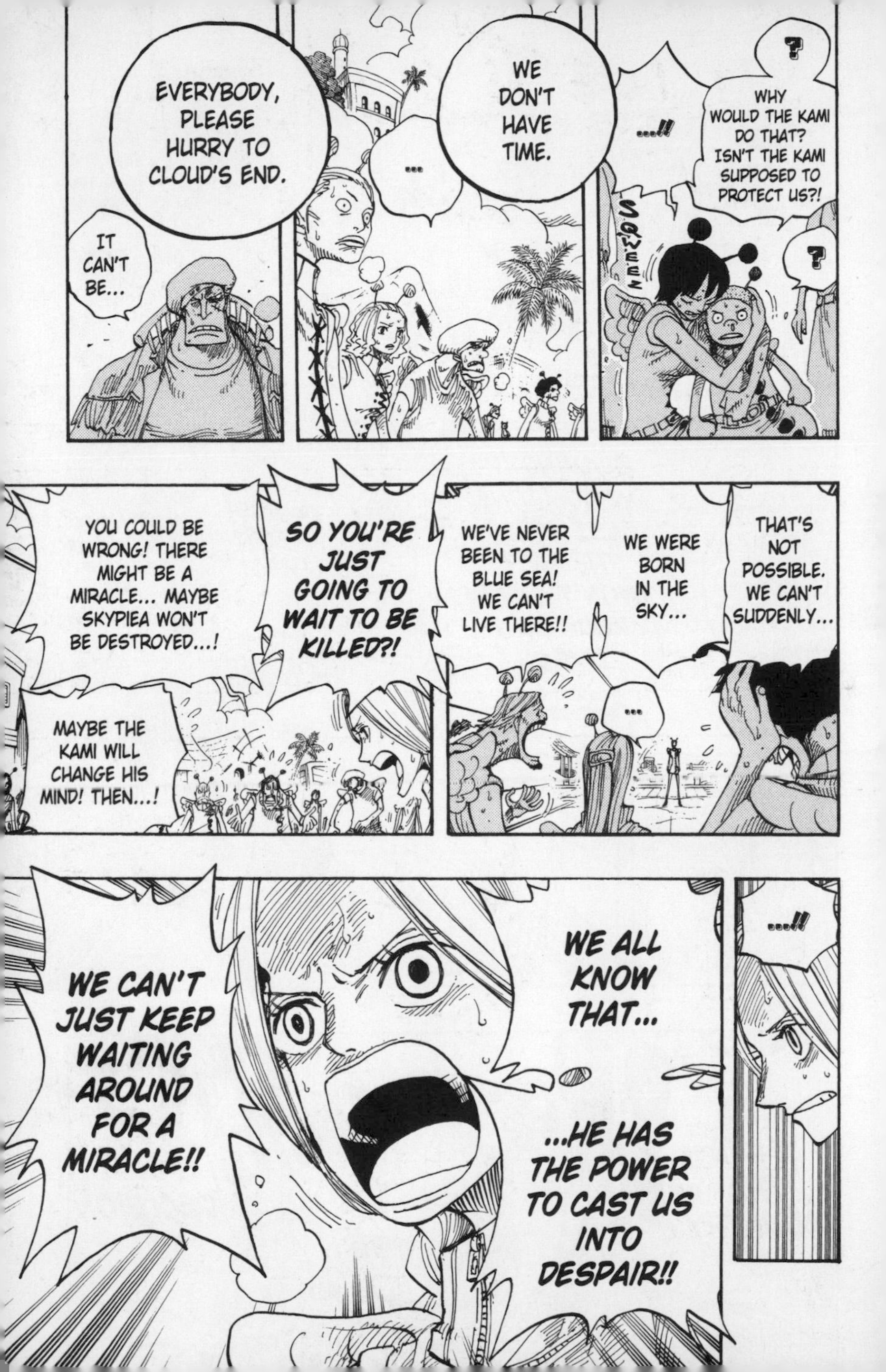
?
WHY WOULD THE KAMI DO THAT? ISN'T THE KAMI SUPPOSED TO PROTECT US?!
....!!
SQWEEZ
?
WE DON'T HAVE TIME.
...
EVERYBODY, PLEASE HURRY TO CLOUD'S END.
IT CAN'T BE...
THAT'S NOT POSSIBLE. WE CAN'T SUDDENLY...
WE WERE BORN IN THE SKY...
WE'VE NEVER BEEN TO THE BLUE SEA! WE CAN'T LIVE THERE!!
...
SO YOU'RE JUST GOING TO WAIT TO BE KILLED?!
YOU COULD BE WRONG! THERE MIGHT BE A MIRACLE... MAYBE SKYPIEA WON'T BE DESTROYED...!
MAYBE THE KAMI WILL CHANGE HIS MIND! THEN...!
....!!
WE ALL KNOW THAT...
...HE HAS THE POWER TO CAST US INTO DESPAIR!!
WE CAN'T JUST KEEP WAITING AROUND FOR A MIRACLE!!

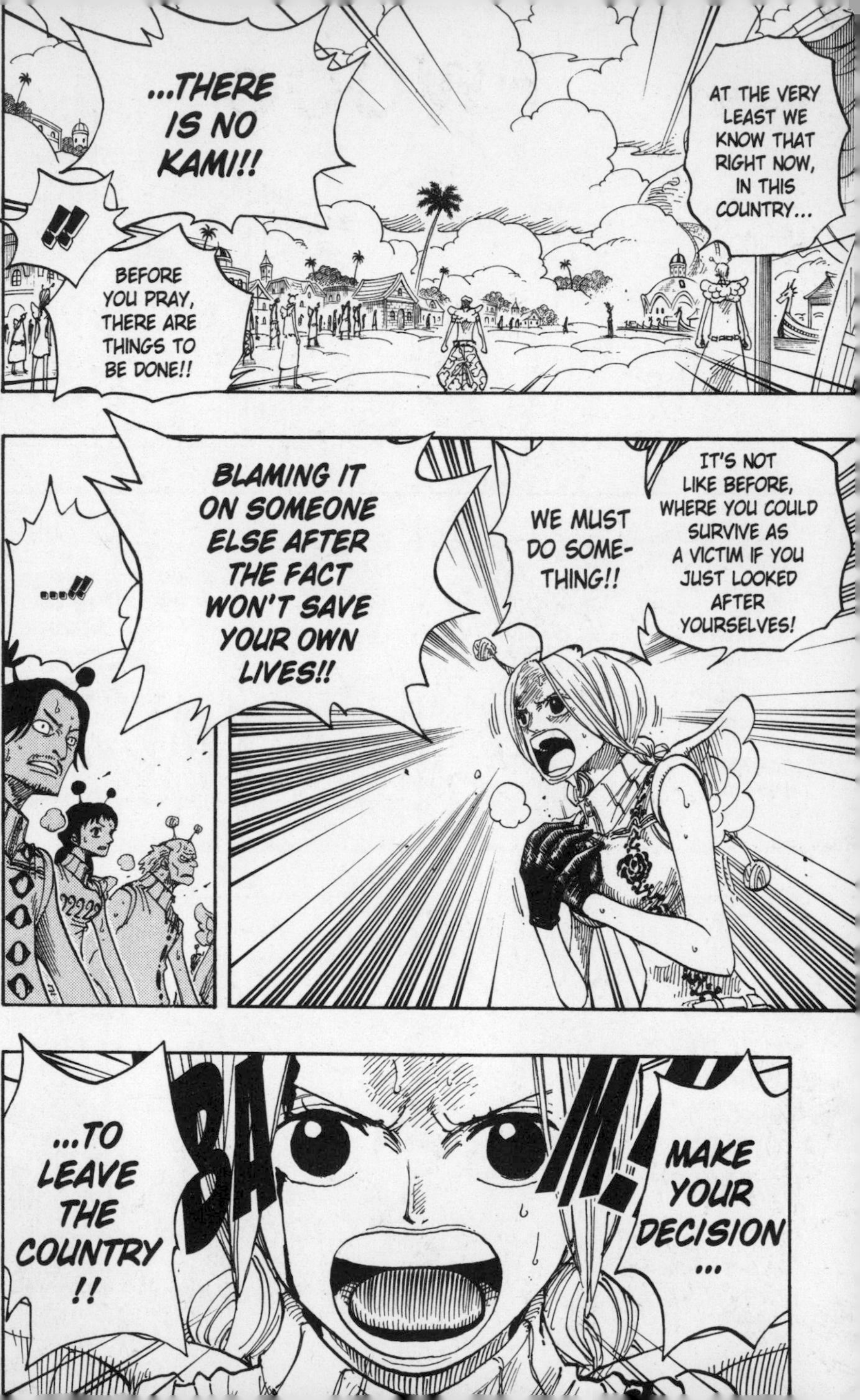
AT THE VERY LEAST WE KNOW THAT RIGHT NOW, IN THIS COUNTRY...
...THERE IS NO KAMI!!
!!
BEFORE YOU PRAY, THERE ARE THINGS TO BE DONE!!
IT'S NOT LIKE BEFORE, WHERE YOU COULD SURVIVE AS A VICTIM IF YOU JUST LOOKED AFTER YOURSELVES!
WE MUST DO SOME-THING!!
BLAMING IT ON SOMEONE ELSE AFTER THE FACT WON'T SAVE YOUR OWN LIVES!!
...!!
MAKE YOUR DECISION ...
BAM!
...TO LEAVE THE COUNTRY !!

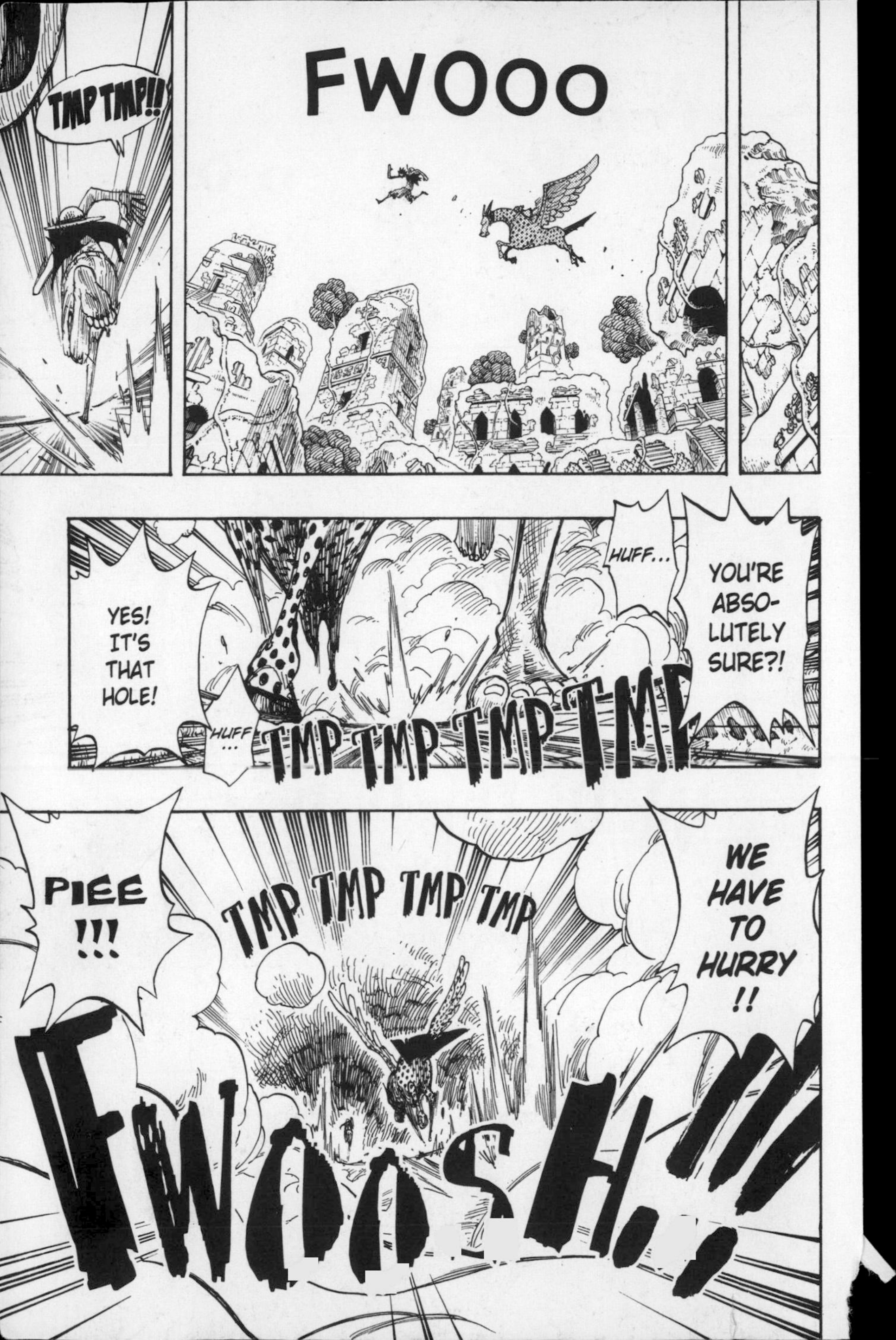
FWOOO
TMP TMP!!
HUFF...
YOU'RE ABSO-LUTELY SURE?!
YES! IT'S THAT HOLE!
HUFF...
TMP TMP TMP TMP
WE HAVE TO HURRY !!
TMP TMP TMP TMP
PIEE !!!
FWOOSH!!

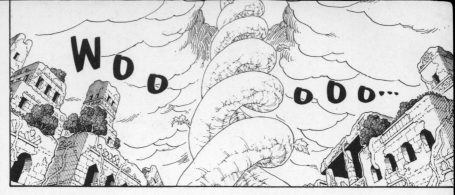

WOOOOOOO...
...
HUFF...
HUFF...
WE NEED TO GET OUT OF HERE...
AT LEAST GET UP TO THE TOP LEVEL...!!
I WON'T BE ABLE TO CARRY THEM ALL AT ONCE...
HUFF
HUFF
WOOOOO...

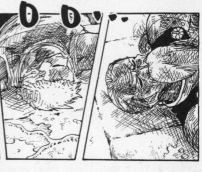

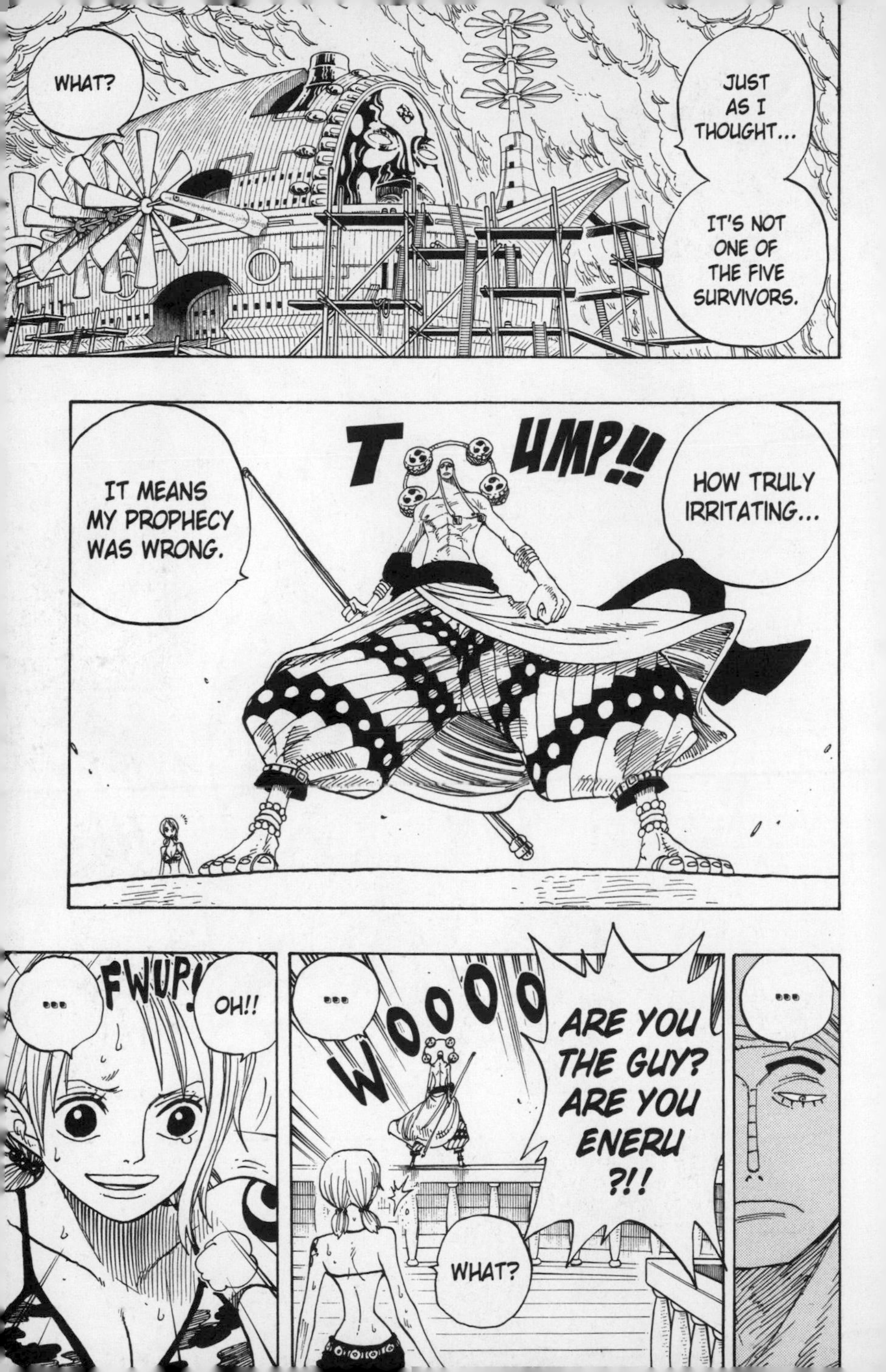
JUST AS I THOUGHT...
IT'S NOT ONE OF THE FIVE SURVIVORS.
WHAT?
HOW TRULY IRRITATING...
T UMP!!
IT MEANS MY PROPHECY WAS WRONG.
...
ARE YOU THE GUY? ARE YOU ENERU ?!!
WOOOO
...
WHAT?
OH!!
FWUP!
...

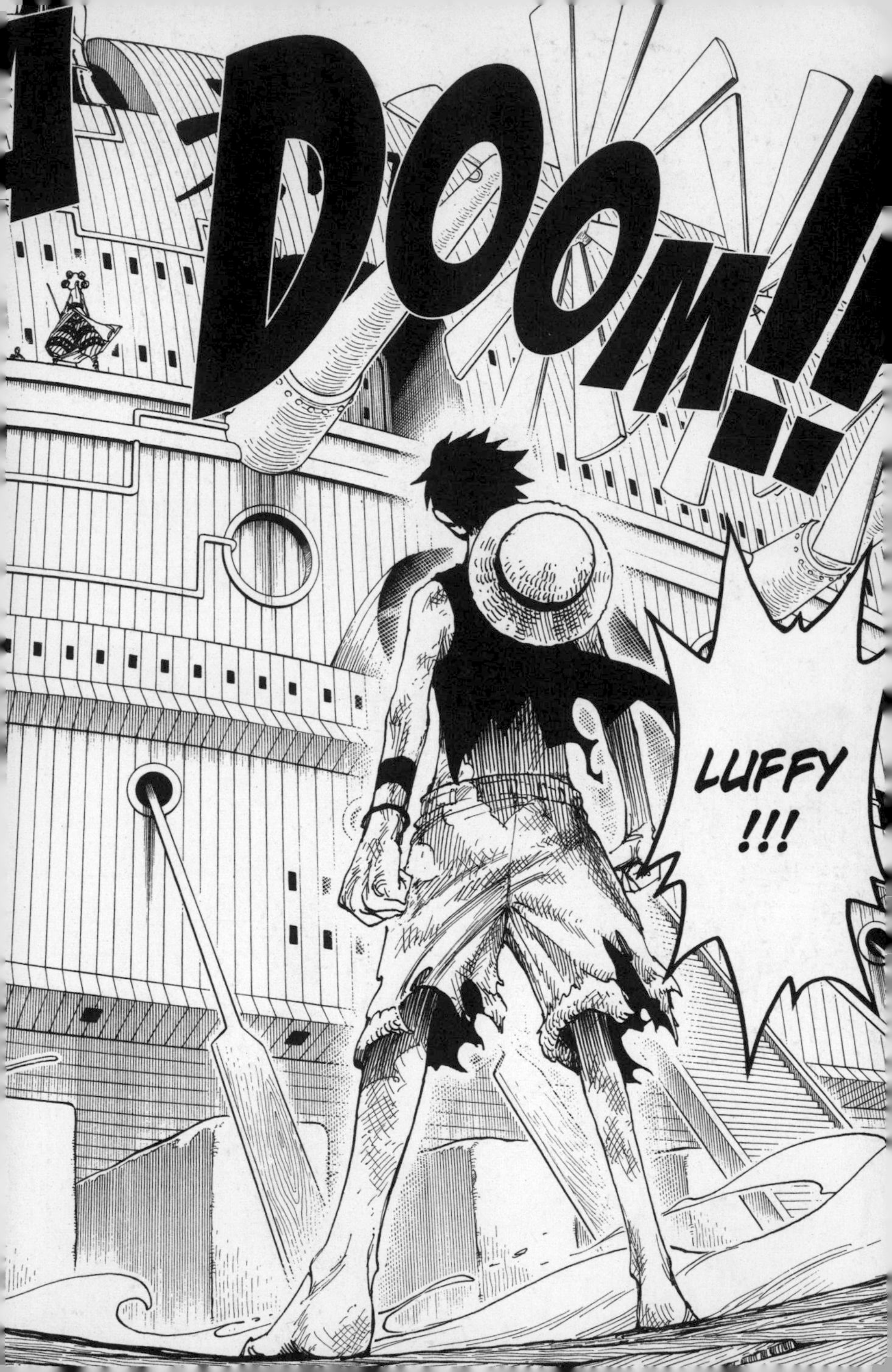
DOOM!!
LUFFY !!!

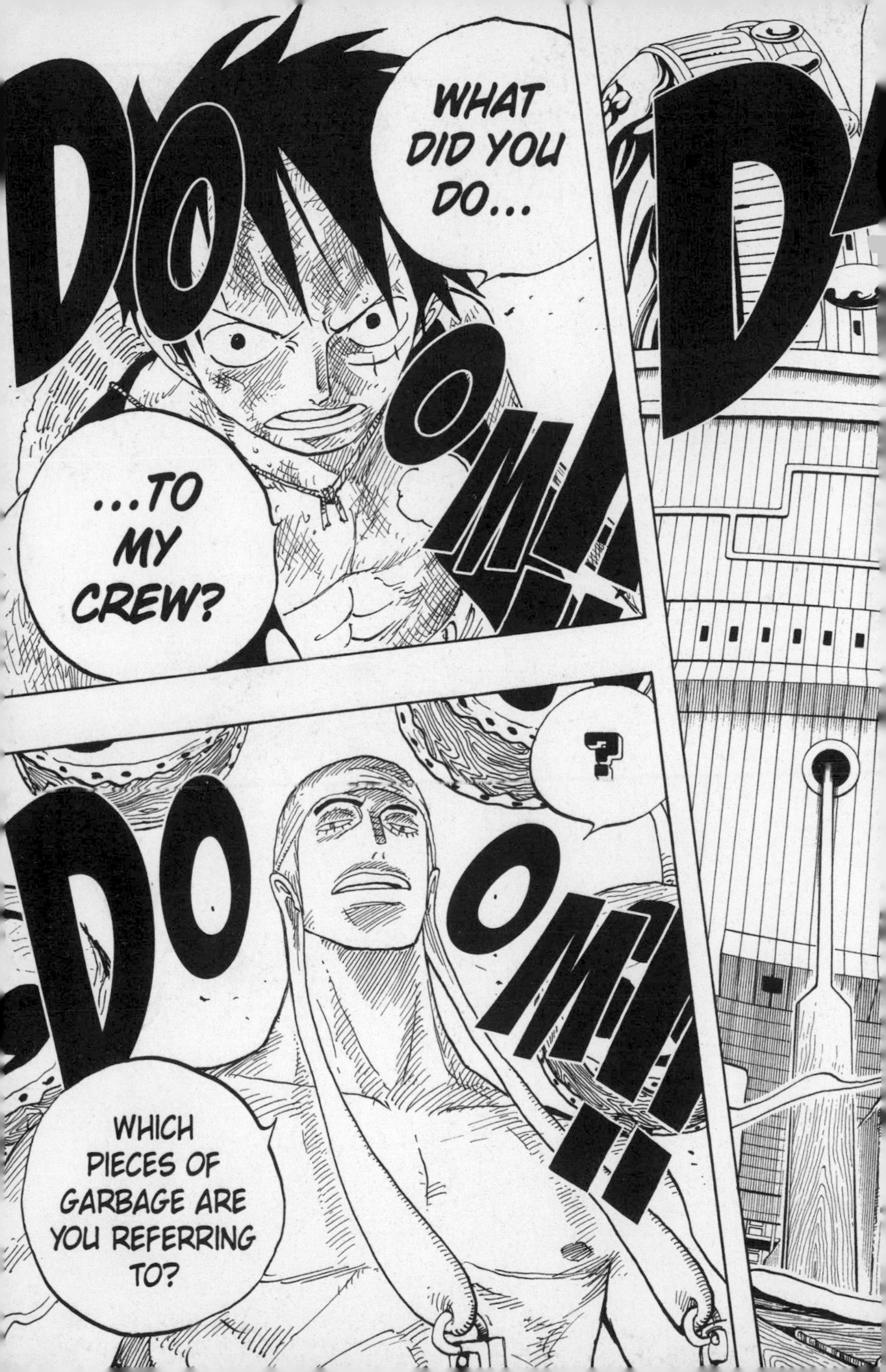

DA
WHAT DID YOU DO...
DOOM
...TO MY CREW?
?
DOOM
WHICH PIECES OF GARBAGE ARE YOU REFERRING TO?

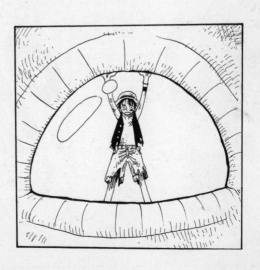

Chapter 279:
PIRATE LUFFY VS. KAMI ENERU

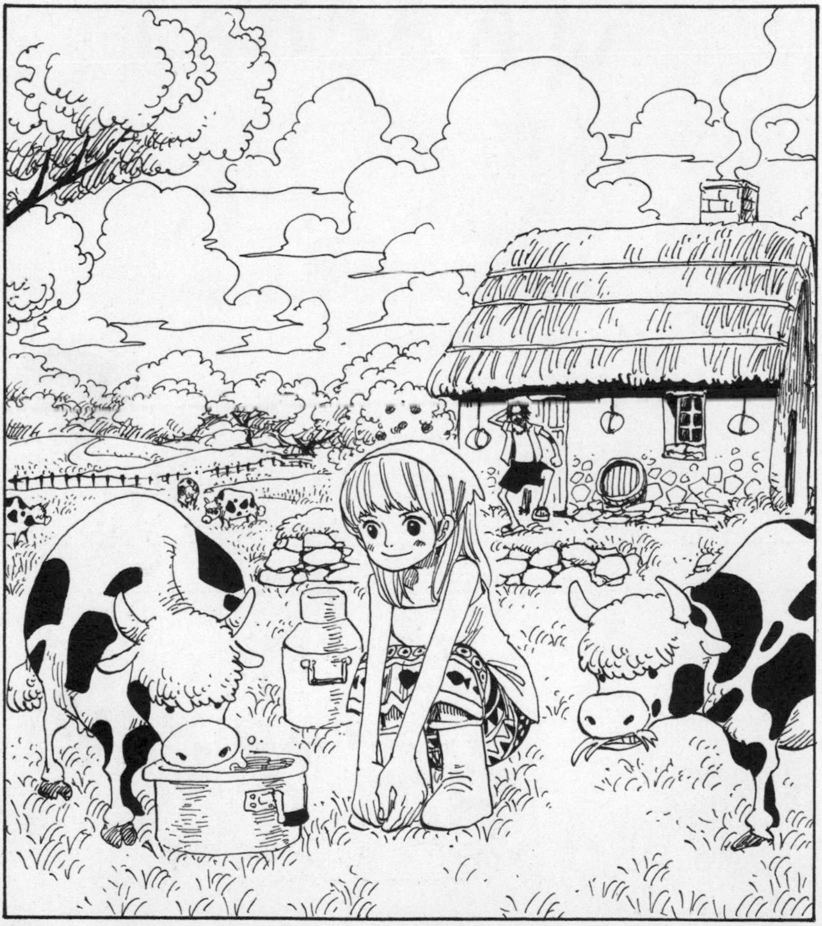

ACE'S GREAT SEARCH FOR BLACKBEARD, VOL. 7:
"ACE AWAKENS"

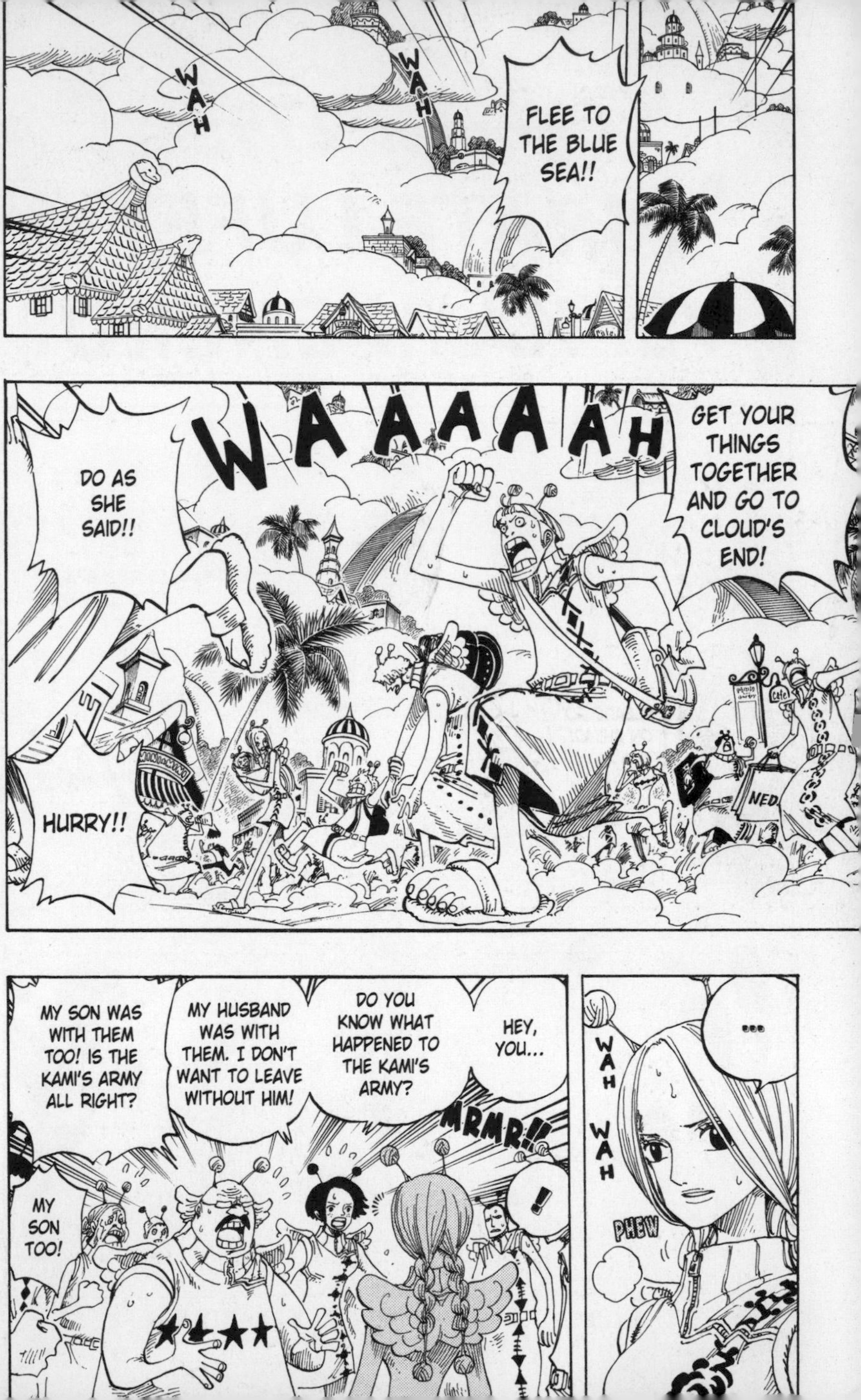
WAH
WAH
FLEE TO THE BLUE SEA!!
GET YOUR THINGS TOGETHER AND GO TO CLOUD'S END!
WAAAAAH
DO AS SHE SAID!!
HURRY!!
WAH WAH
...
PHEW
HEY, YOU...
DO YOU KNOW WHAT HAPPENED TO THE KAMI'S ARMY?
!
MRMR!!
MY HUSBAND WAS WITH THEM. I DON'T WANT TO LEAVE WITHOUT HIM!
MY SON WAS WITH THEM TOO! IS THE KAMI'S ARMY ALL RIGHT?
MY SON TOO!

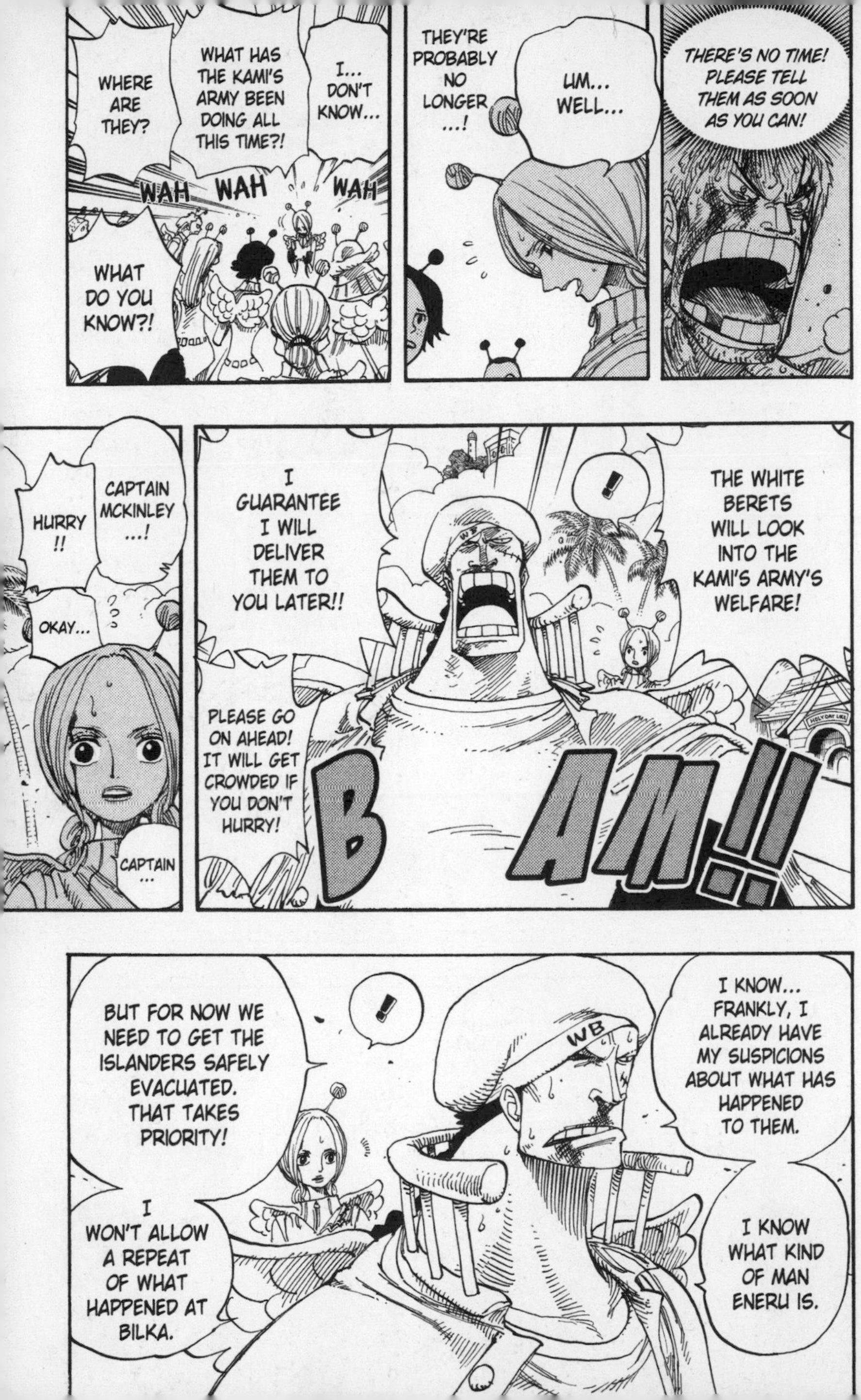
THERE'S NO TIME! PLEASE TELL THEM AS SOON AS YOU CAN!
UM... WELL...
THEY'RE PROBABLY NO LONGER ...!
I... DON'T KNOW...
WHAT HAS THE KAMI'S ARMY BEEN DOING ALL THIS TIME?!
WHERE ARE THEY?
WAH
WAH
WAH
WHAT DO YOU KNOW?!
!
THE WHITE BERETS WILL LOOK INTO THE KAMI'S ARMY'S WELFARE!
I GUARANTEE I WILL DELIVER THEM TO YOU LATER!!
PLEASE GO ON AHEAD! IT WILL GET CROWDED IF YOU DON'T HURRY!
BAM!!
CAPTAIN MCKINLEY ...!
HURRY !!
OKAY...
CAPTAIN ...
I KNOW... FRANKLY, I ALREADY HAVE MY SUSPICIONS ABOUT WHAT HAS HAPPENED TO THEM.
I KNOW WHAT KIND OF MAN ENERU IS.
!
BUT FOR NOW WE NEED TO GET THE ISLANDERS SAFELY EVACUATED. THAT TAKES PRIORITY!
I WON'T ALLOW A REPEAT OF WHAT HAPPENED AT BILKA.

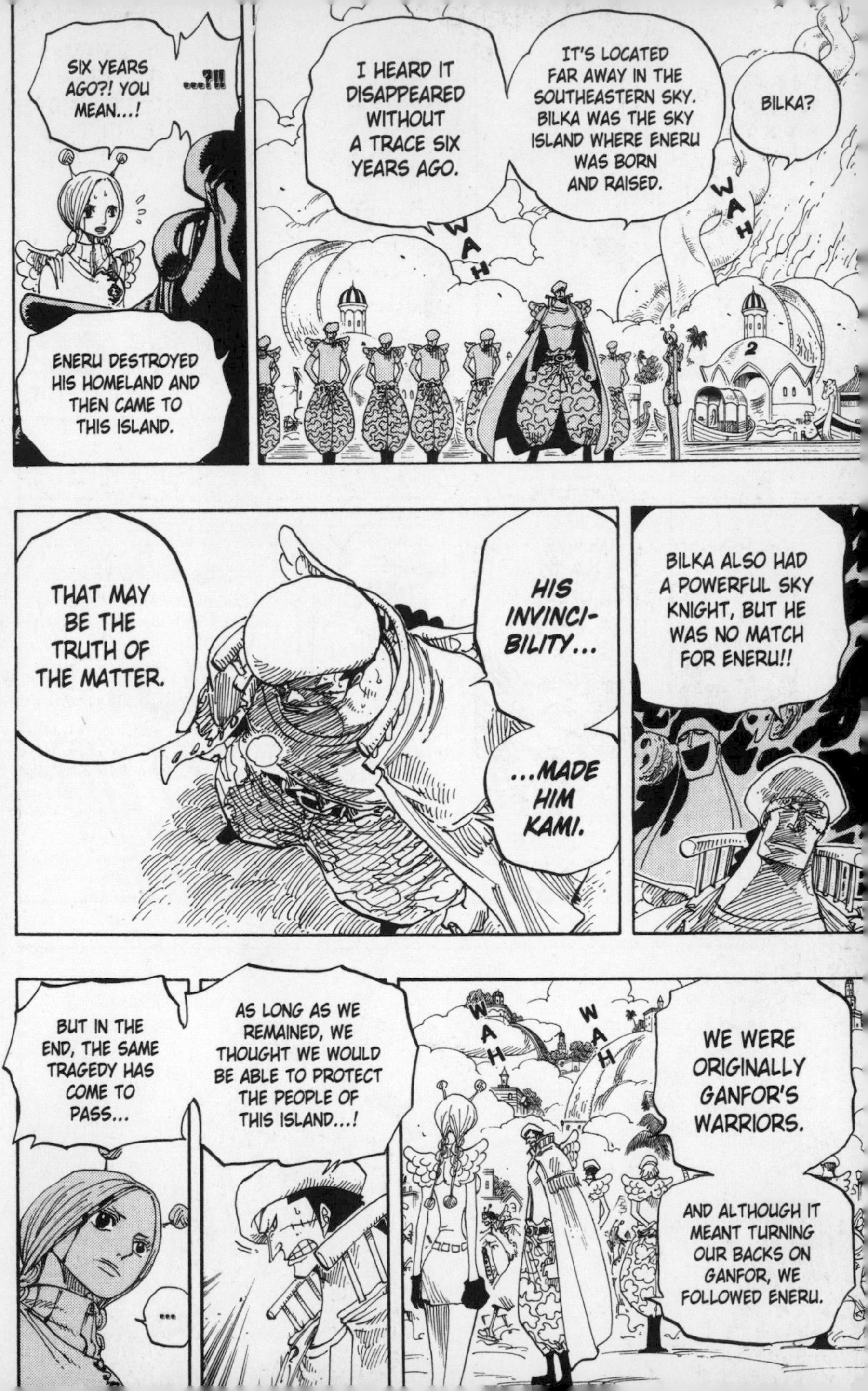
BILKA?
IT'S LOCATED FAR AWAY IN THE SOUTHEASTERN SKY. BILKA WAS THE SKY ISLAND WHERE ENERU WAS BORN AND RAISED.
I HEARD IT DISAPPEARED WITHOUT A TRACE SIX YEARS AGO.
WAH
WAH
...?!!
SIX YEARS AGO?! YOU MEAN...!
ENERU DESTROYED HIS HOMELAND AND THEN CAME TO THIS ISLAND.
BILKA ALSO HAD A POWERFUL SKY KNIGHT, BUT HE WAS NO MATCH FOR ENERU!!
HIS INVINCIBILITY...
...MADE HIM KAMI.
THAT MAY BE THE TRUTH OF THE MATTER.
WE WERE ORIGINALLY GANFOR'S WARRIORS.
AND ALTHOUGH IT MEANT TURNING OUR BACKS ON GANFOR, WE FOLLOWED ENERU.
WAH
WAH
AS LONG AS WE REMAINED, WE THOUGHT WE WOULD BE ABLE TO PROTECT THE PEOPLE OF THIS ISLAND...!
BUT IN THE END, THE SAME TRAGEDY HAS COME TO PASS...
...

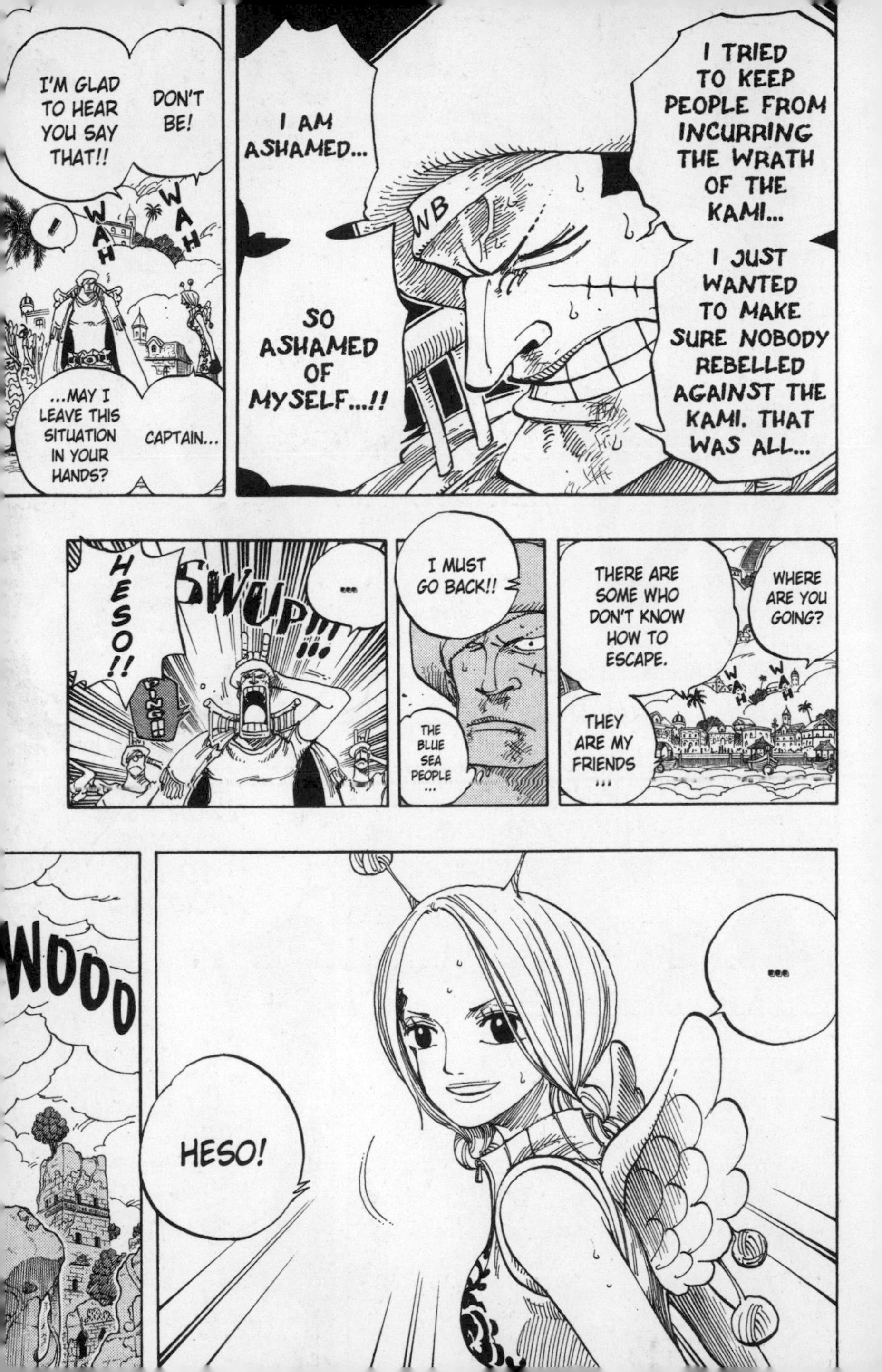
I TRIED TO KEEP PEOPLE FROM INCURRING THE WRATH OF THE KAMI...
I JUST WANTED TO MAKE SURE NOBODY REBELLED AGAINST THE KAMI. THAT WAS ALL...
I AM ASHAMED...
SO ASHAMED OF MYSELF...!!
DON'T BE!
I'M GLAD TO HEAR YOU SAY THAT!!
!
WAH
WAH
CAPTAIN...
...MAY I LEAVE THIS SITUATION IN YOUR HANDS?
WHERE ARE YOU GOING?
THERE ARE SOME WHO DON'T KNOW HOW TO ESCAPE.
WAH
WAH
THEY ARE MY FRIENDS...
I MUST GO BACK!!
THE BLUE SEA PEOPLE...
...
SWUP!!!
HESO!!
PING!!
...
HESO!
WOOD

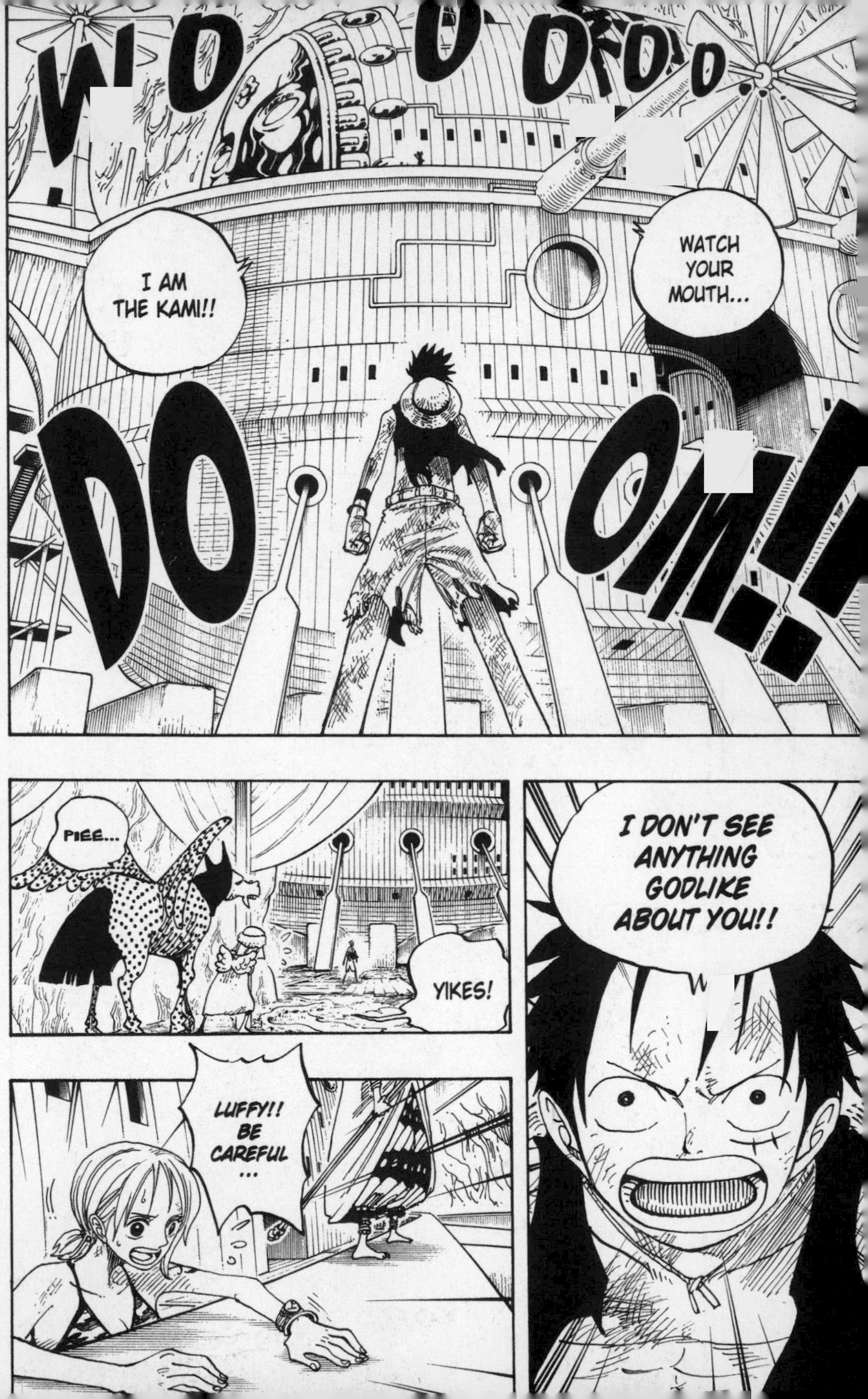
WATCH YOUR MOUTH...
I AM THE KAMI!!
I DON'T SEE ANYTHING GODLIKE ABOUT YOU!!
YIKES!
PIEE...
LUFFY!! BE CAREFUL ...

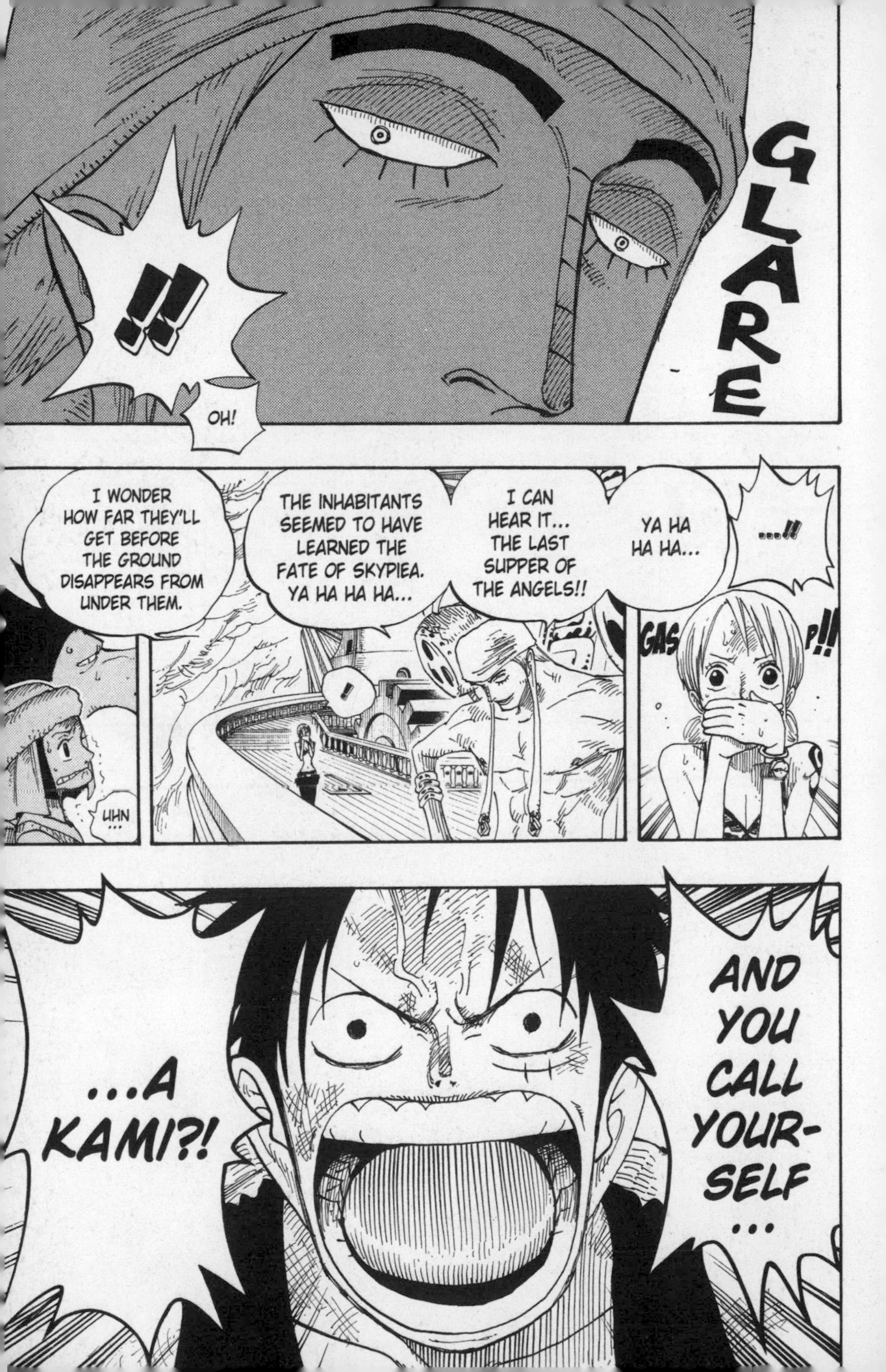

GLARE
!!
OH!
...!!
GASP!!
YA HA HA HA...
I CAN HEAR IT... THE LAST SUPPER OF THE ANGELS!!
THE INHABITANTS SEEMED TO HAVE LEARNED THE FATE OF SKYPIEA. YA HA HA HA...
!
I WONDER HOW FAR THEY'LL GET BEFORE THE GROUND DISAPPEARS FROM UNDER THEM.
UHN...
AND YOU CALL YOURSELF...
...A KAMI?!

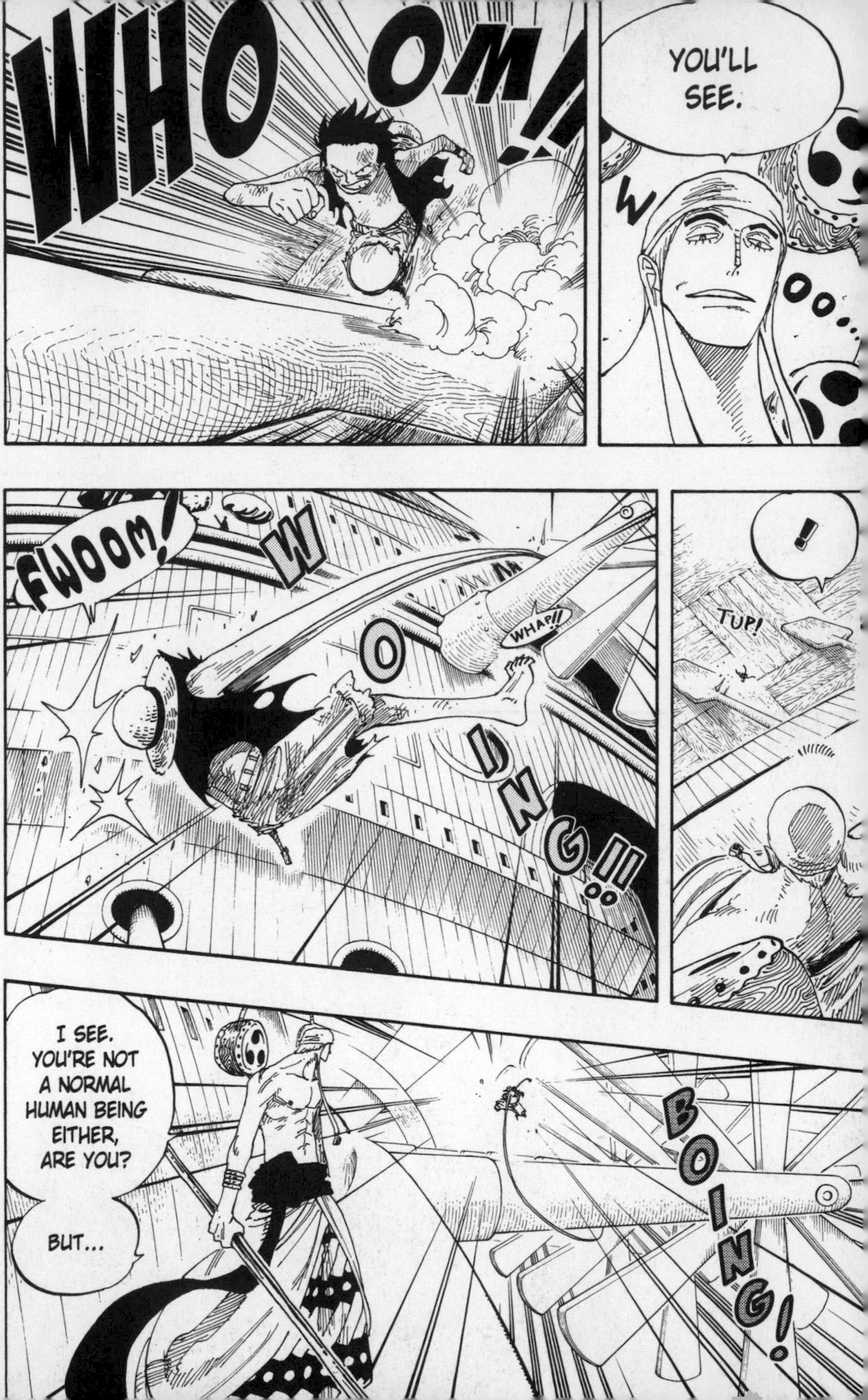

YOU'LL SEE.
WOO...
WHOOM!!
!
TUP!
FWOOM!
WOOING!!
WHAP!!
I SEE. YOU'RE NOT A NORMAL HUMAN BEING EITHER, ARE YOU?
BUT...
BOING!

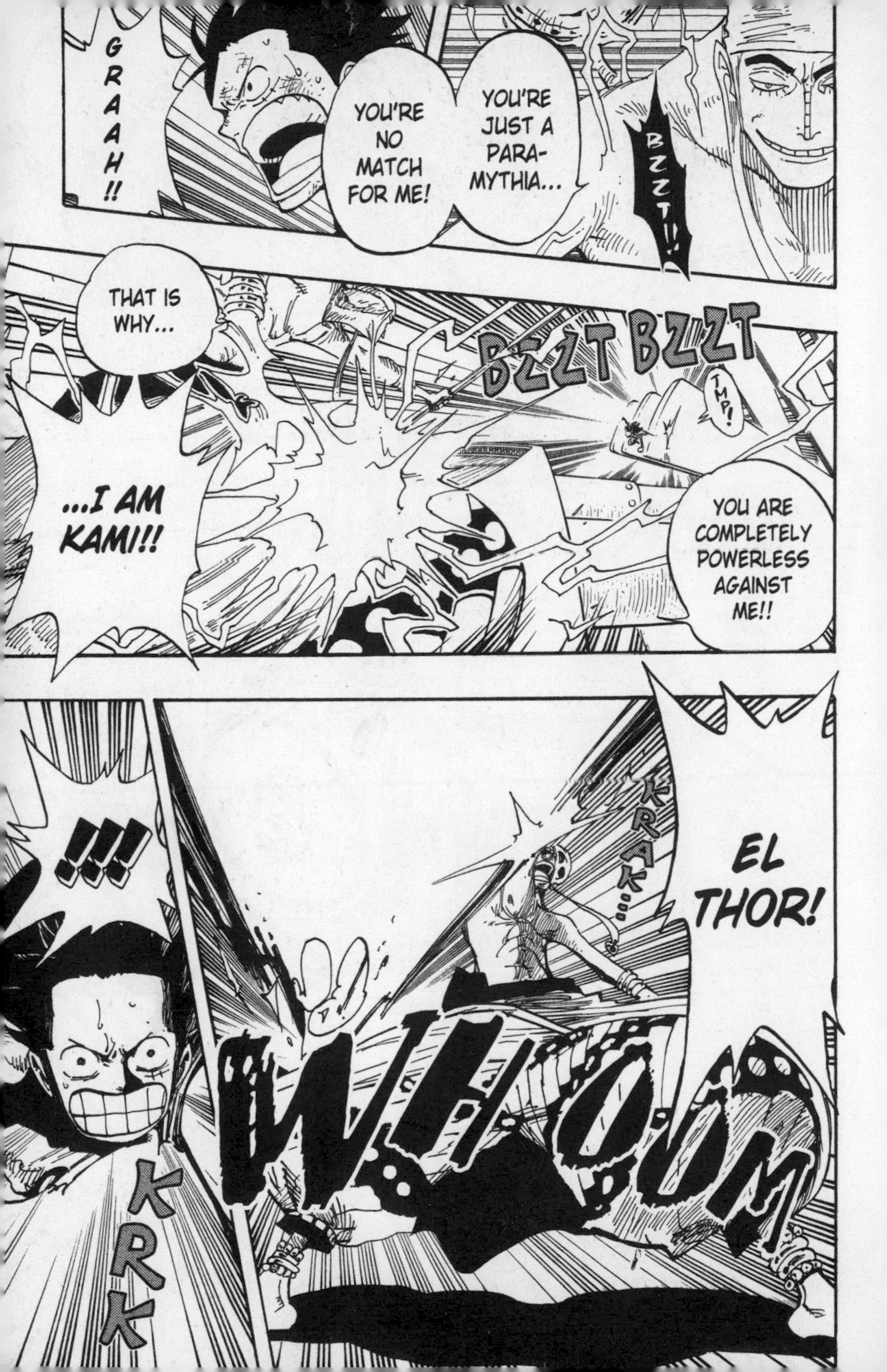
BZZT!!
YOU'RE JUST A PARA-MYTHIA...
YOU'RE NO MATCH FOR ME!
GRAAH!!
BZZT BZZT
TMP!
YOU ARE COMPLETELY POWERLESS AGAINST ME!!
THAT IS WHY...
...I AM KAMI!!
EL THOR!
KRAK...
WHOOM
!!!
KRK

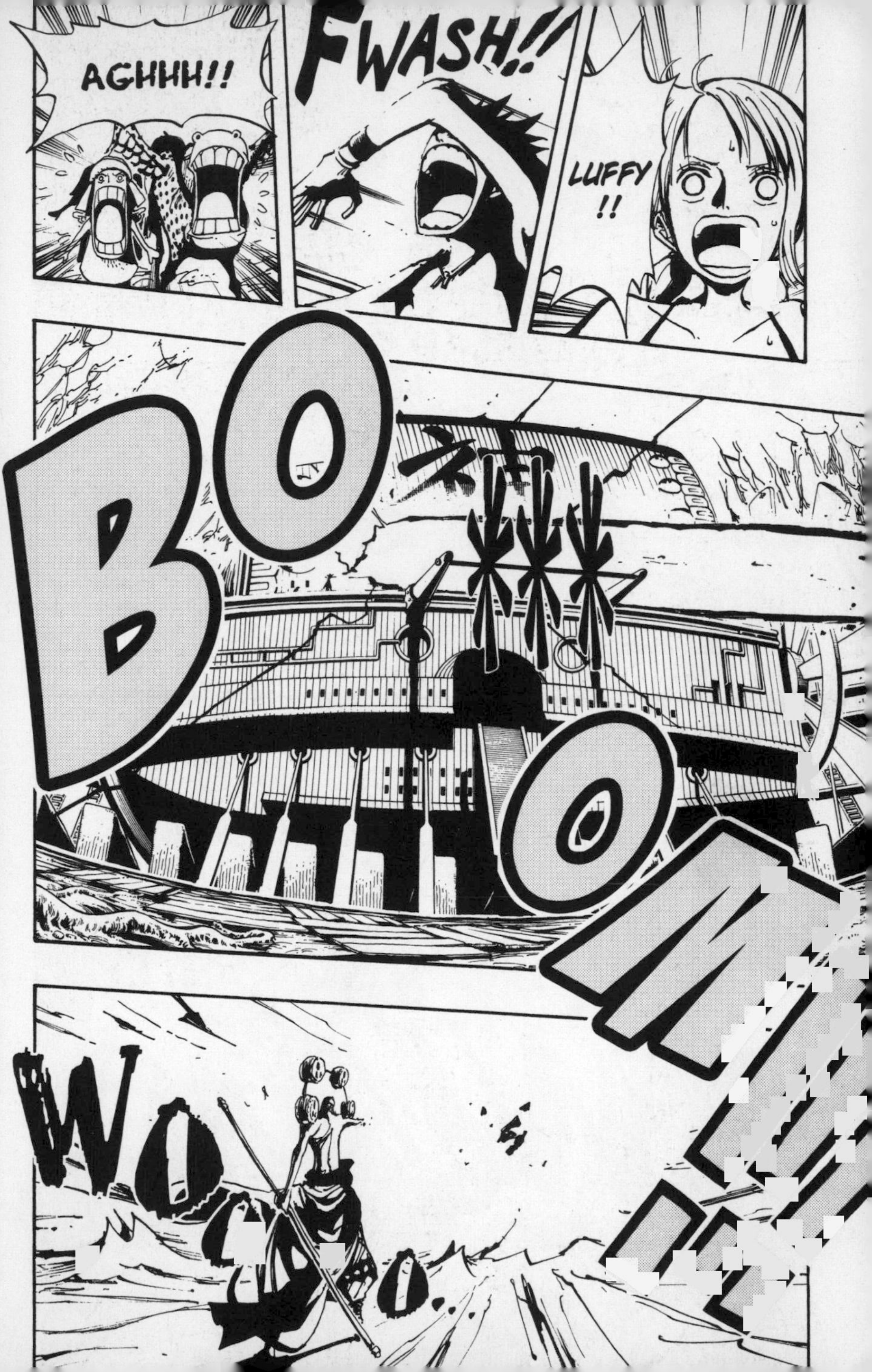
LUFFY !!
FWASH!!
AGHHH!!
BOOM
WOOO

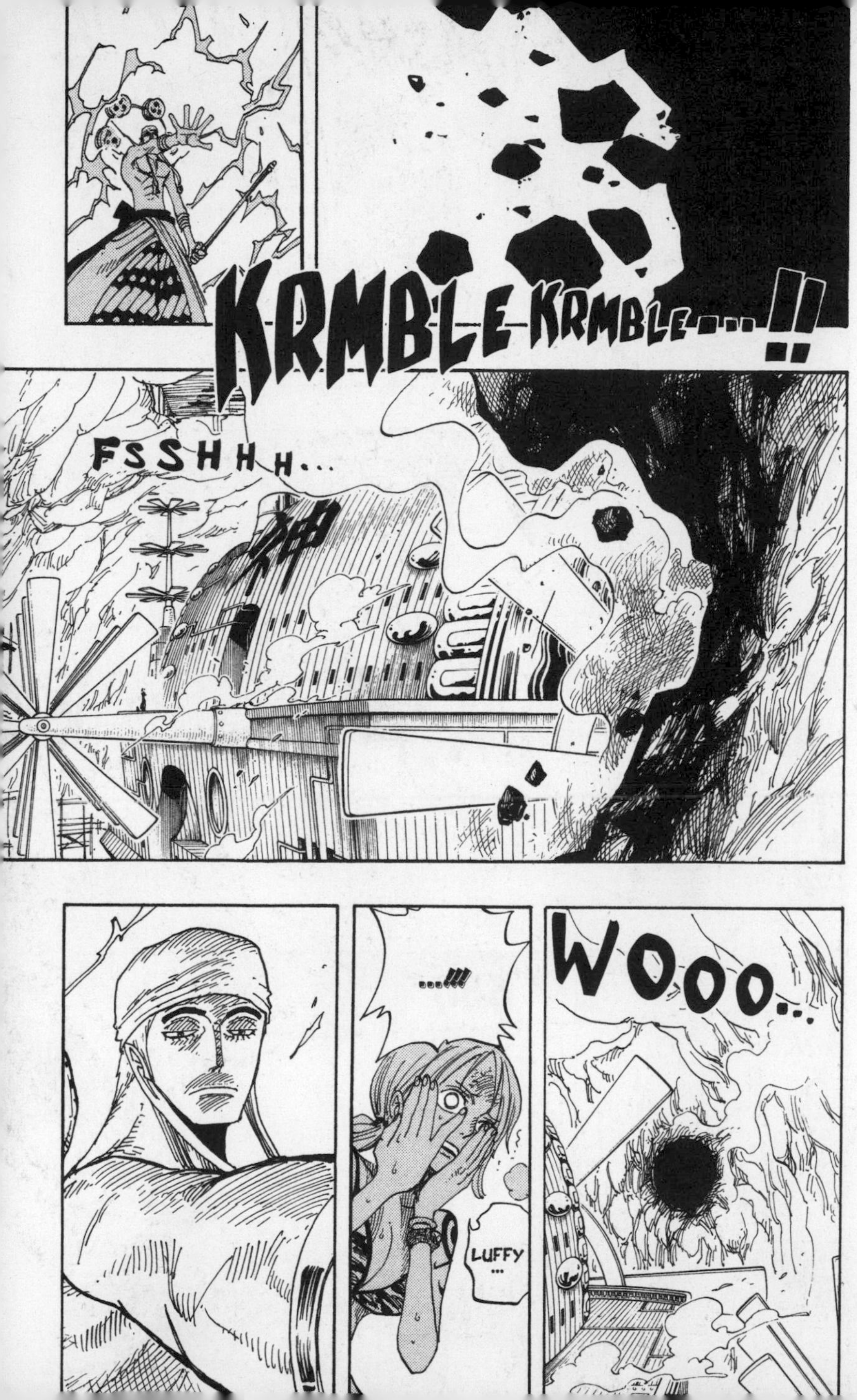
KRMBLE KRMBLE...!!
FSSHHH...
神
WOOO...
...!!!
LUFFY...

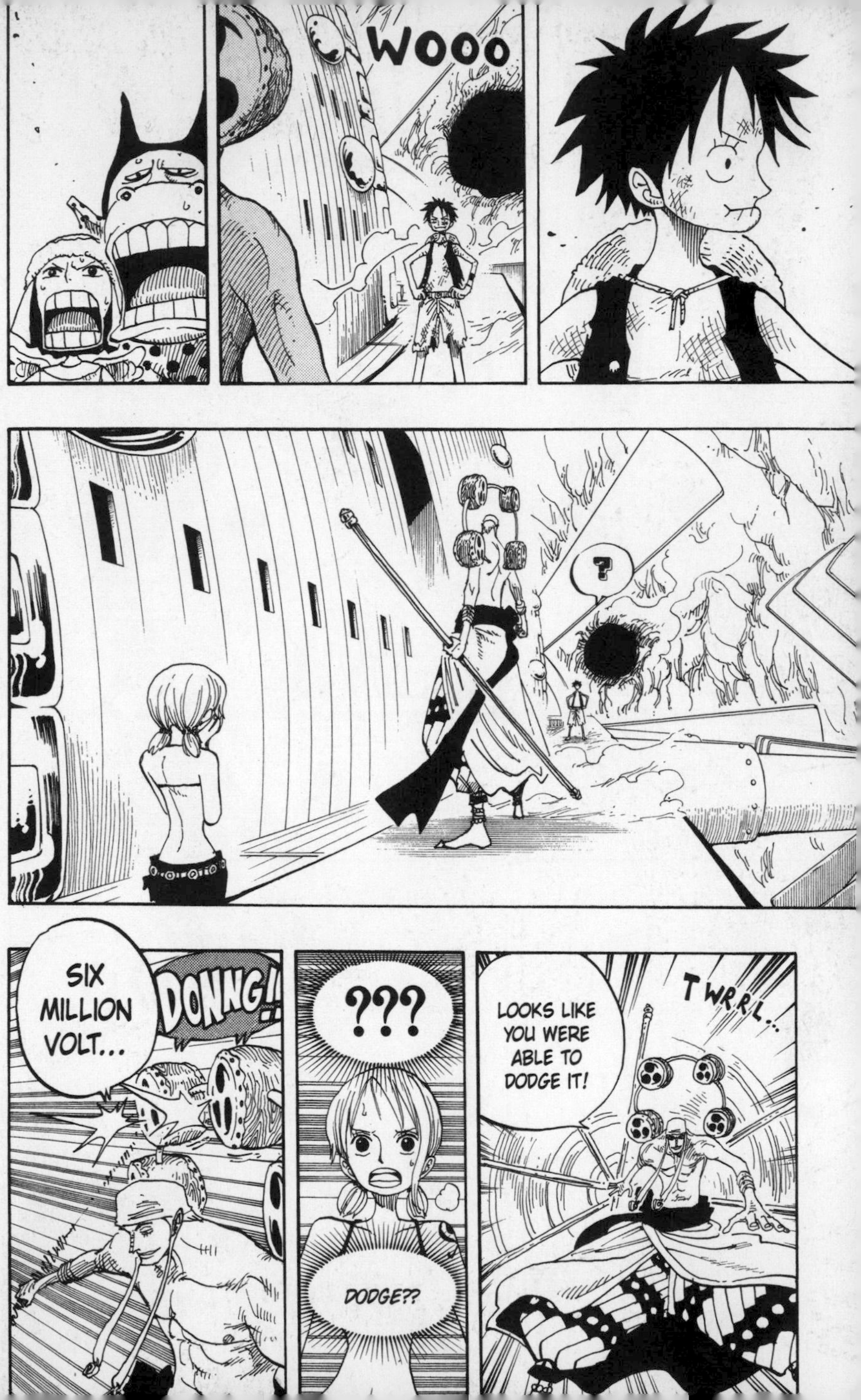
WOOO
?
TWRRL...
LOOKS LIKE YOU WERE ABLE TO DODGE IT!
???
DODGE??
SIX MILLION VOLT...
DONNG!!

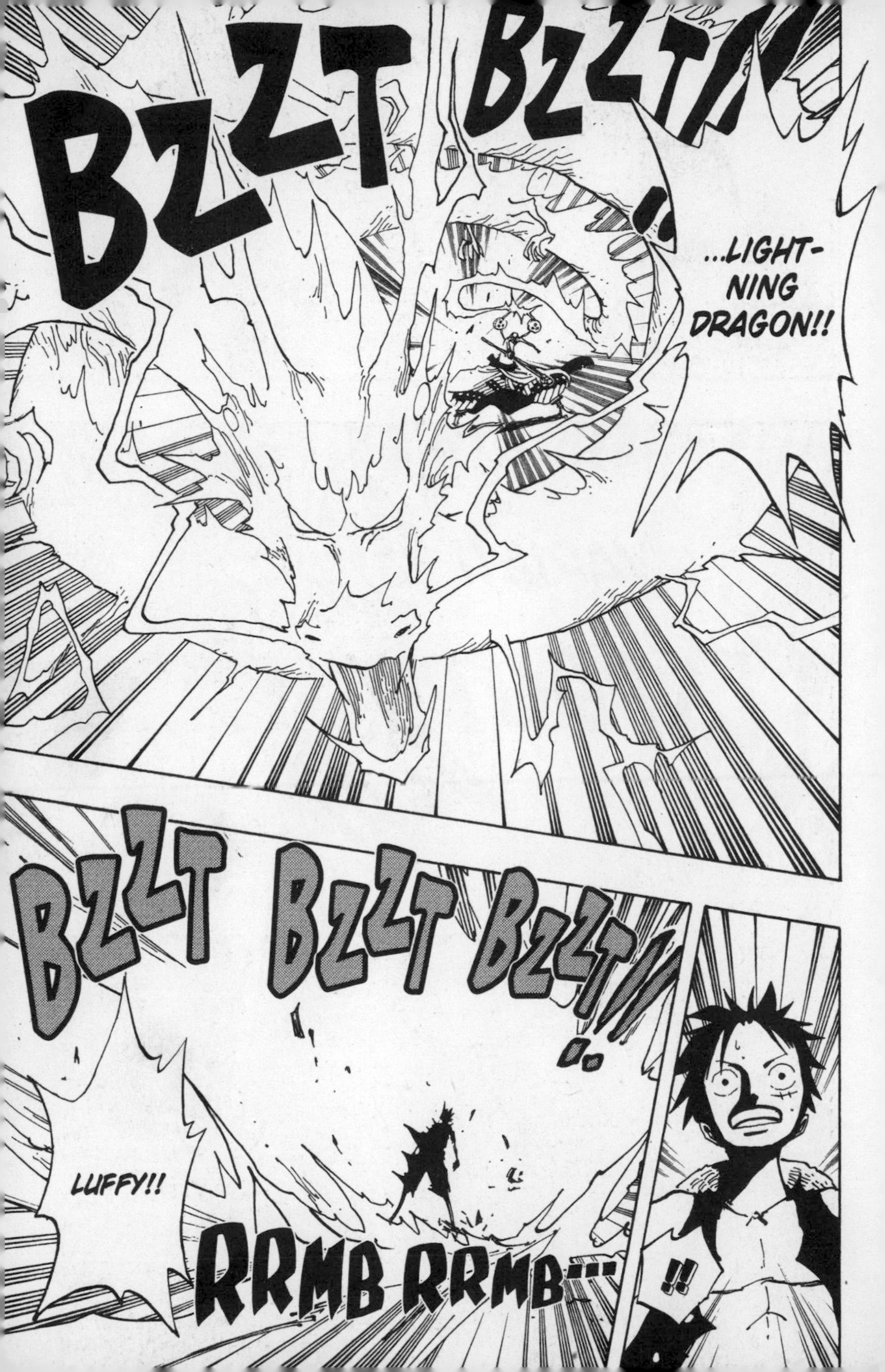
BZZT BZZT!!
...LIGHT-
NING
DRAGON!!
BZZT BZZT BZZT!!
!!
LUFFY!!
RRMB RRMB...
!!

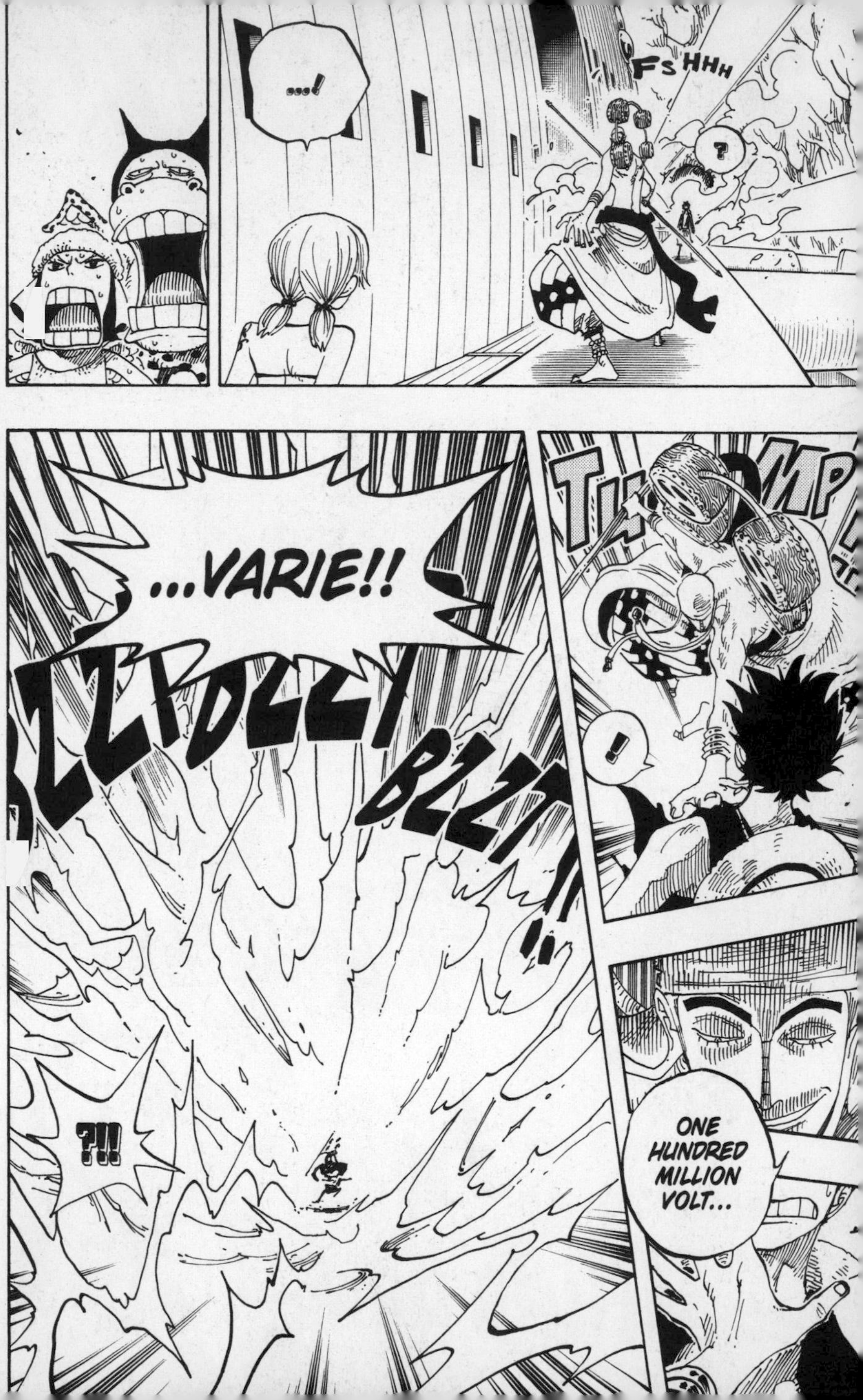
FSHHH
?
...!
!
ONE HUNDRED MILLION VOLT...
...VARIE!!
?!!

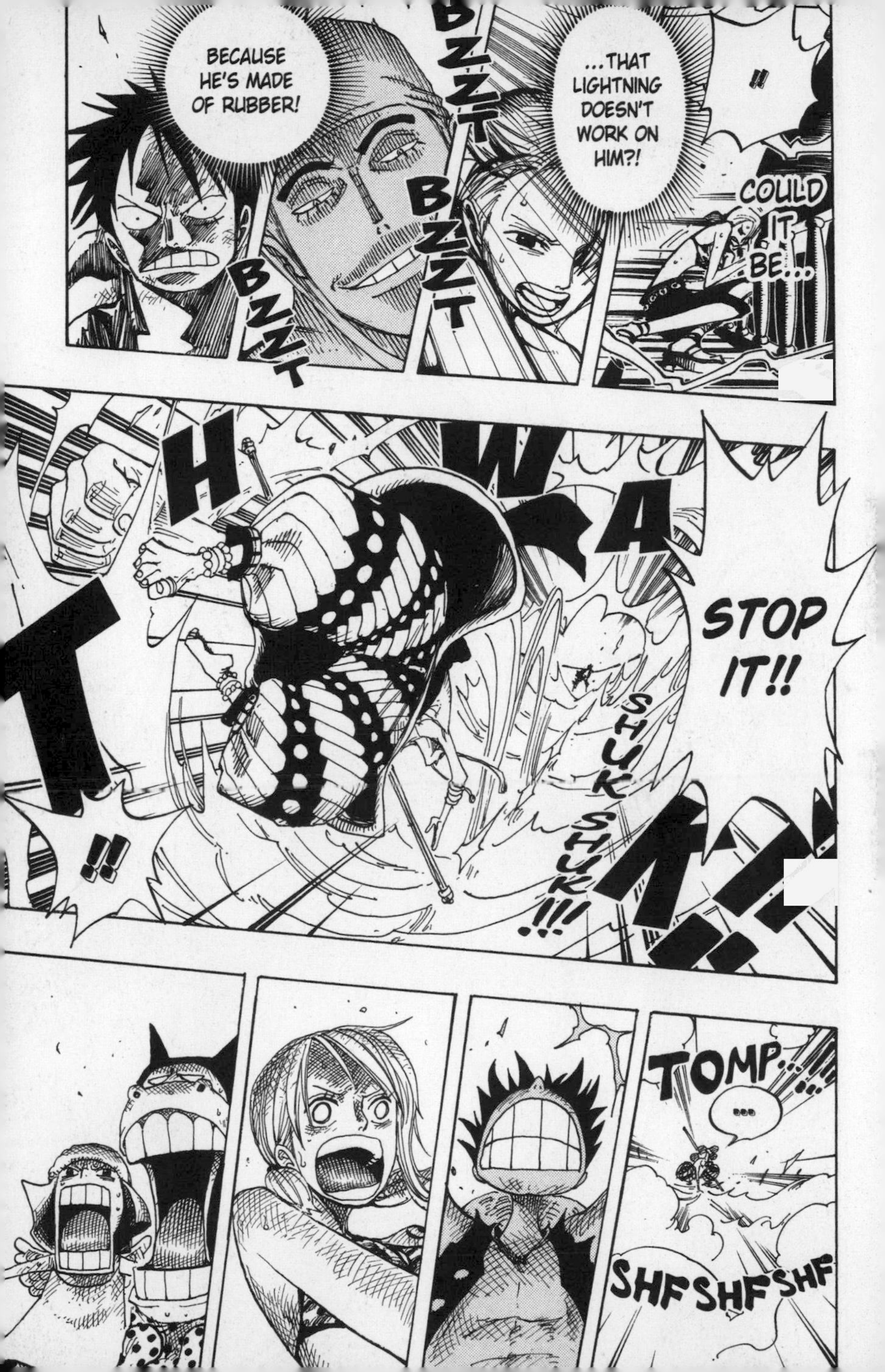
!!
COULD IT BE...
...THAT LIGHTNING DOESN'T WORK ON HIM?!
BZZZT
BZZZT
BECAUSE HE'S MADE OF RUBBER!
BZZZT
STOP IT!!
SHUK SHUK!!!
TOMP...
...
SHFSHFSHF

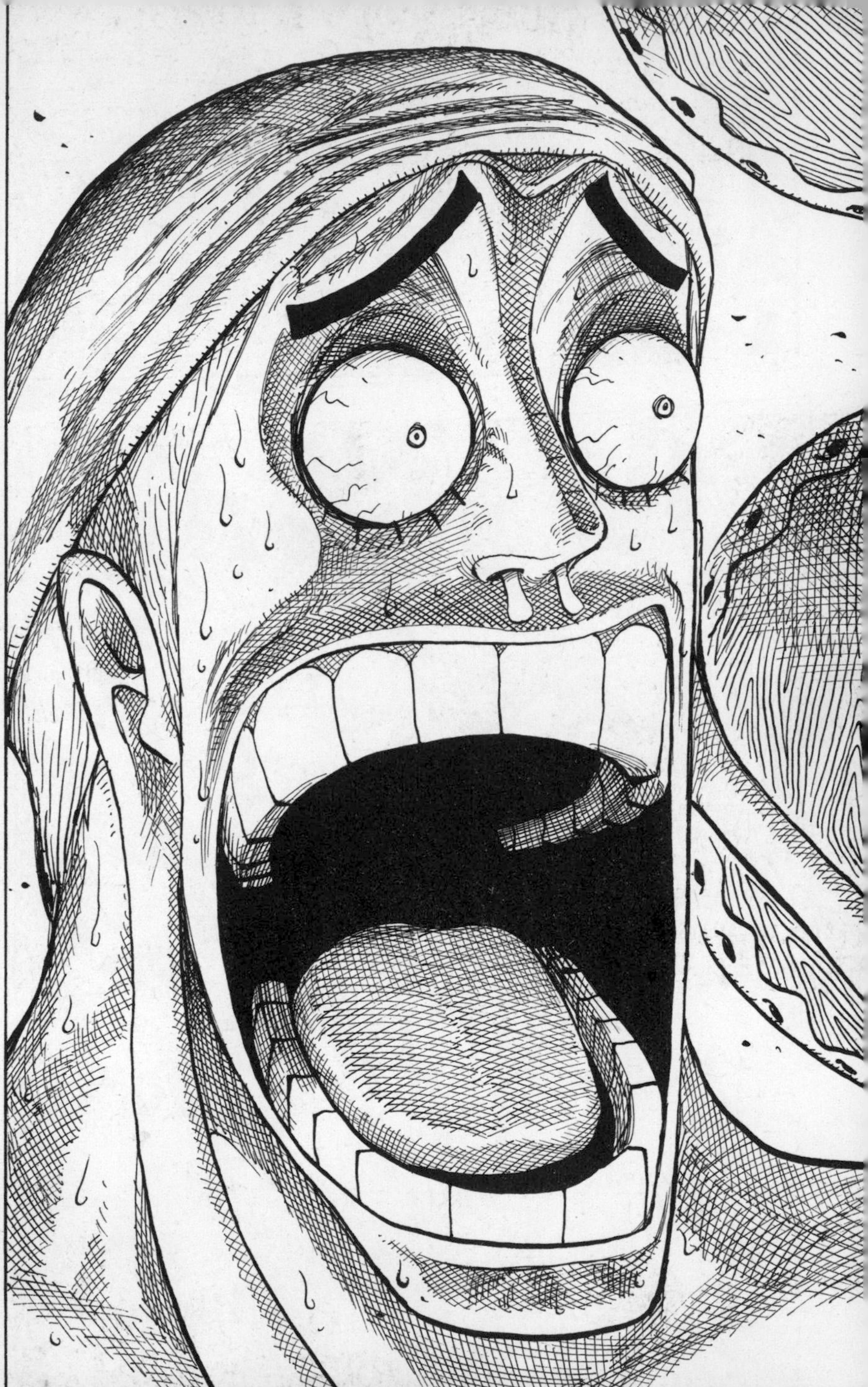

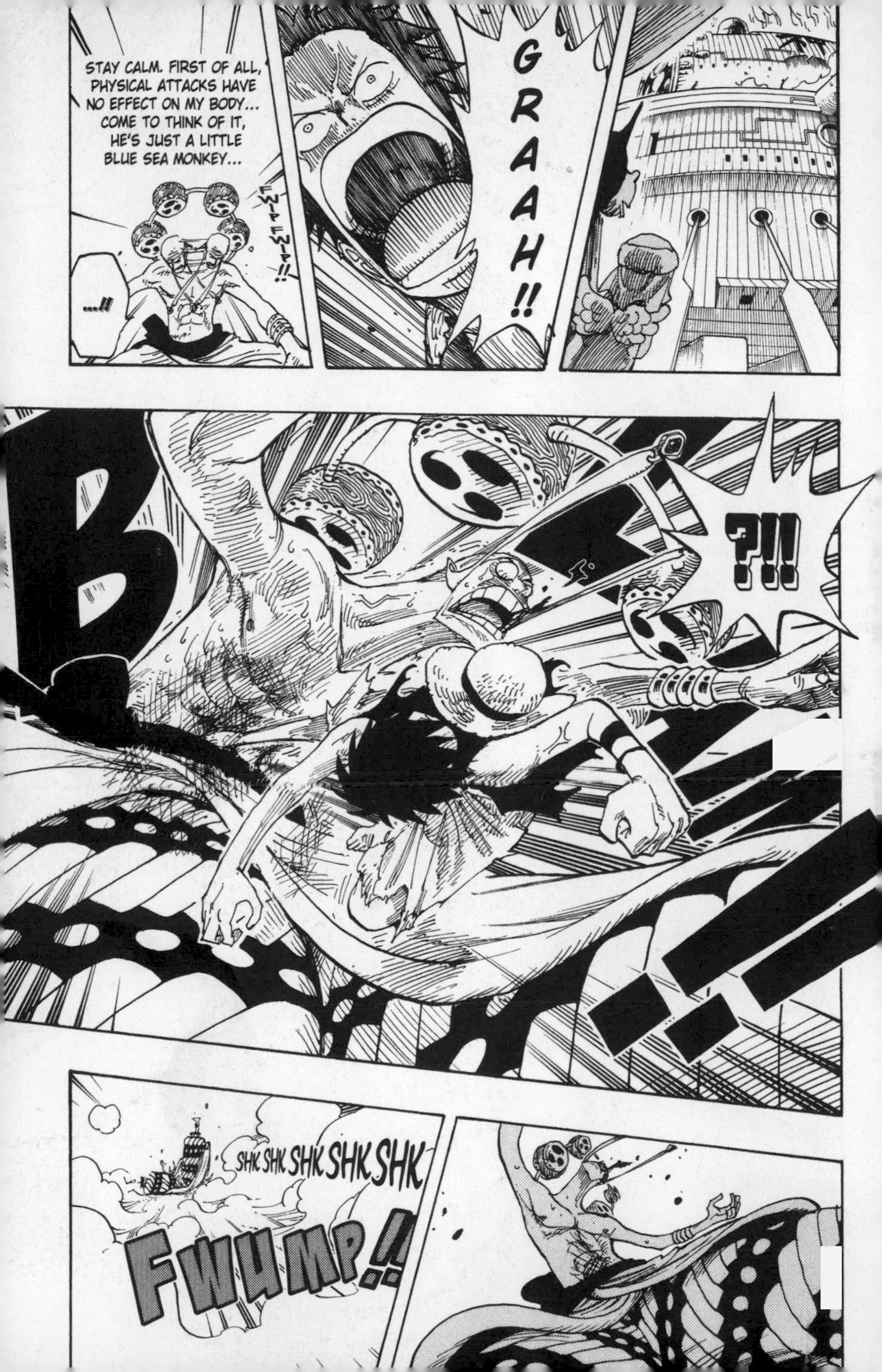
GRAAH!!
STAY CALM. FIRST OF ALL, PHYSICAL ATTACKS HAVE NO EFFECT ON MY BODY... COME TO THINK OF IT, HE'S JUST A LITTLE BLUE SEA MONKEY...
FWIP FWIP!!
...!!
B
?!!
SHK SHK SHK SHK SHK
FWUMP!!

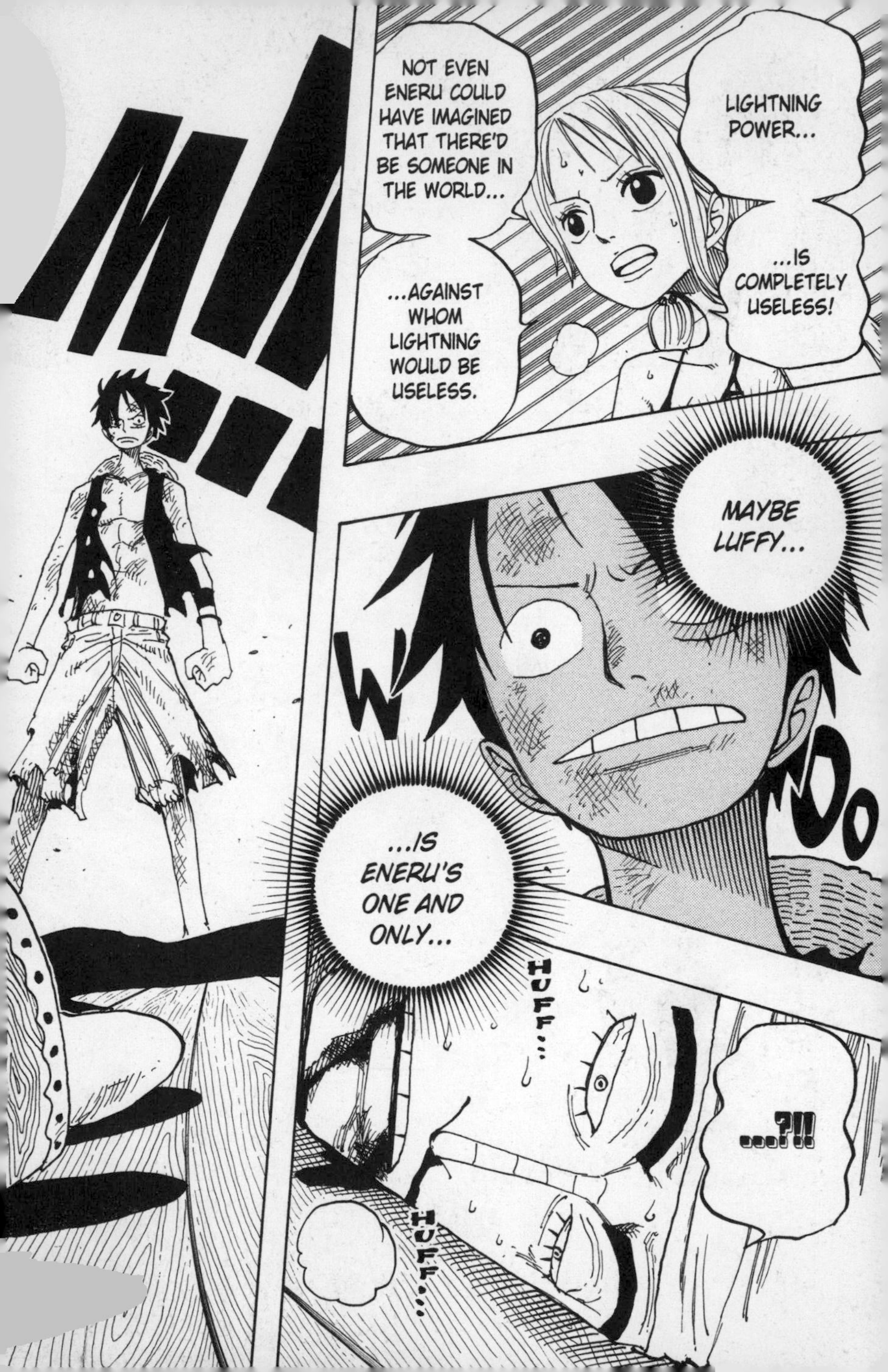
LIGHTNING POWER...
...IS COMPLETELY USELESS!
NOT EVEN ENERU COULD HAVE IMAGINED THAT THERE'D BE SOMEONE IN THE WORLD...
...AGAINST WHOM LIGHTNING WOULD BE USELESS.
MAYBE LUFFY...
DO
W
...IS ENERU'S ONE AND ONLY...
...?!!
HUFF...
HUFF...
M...

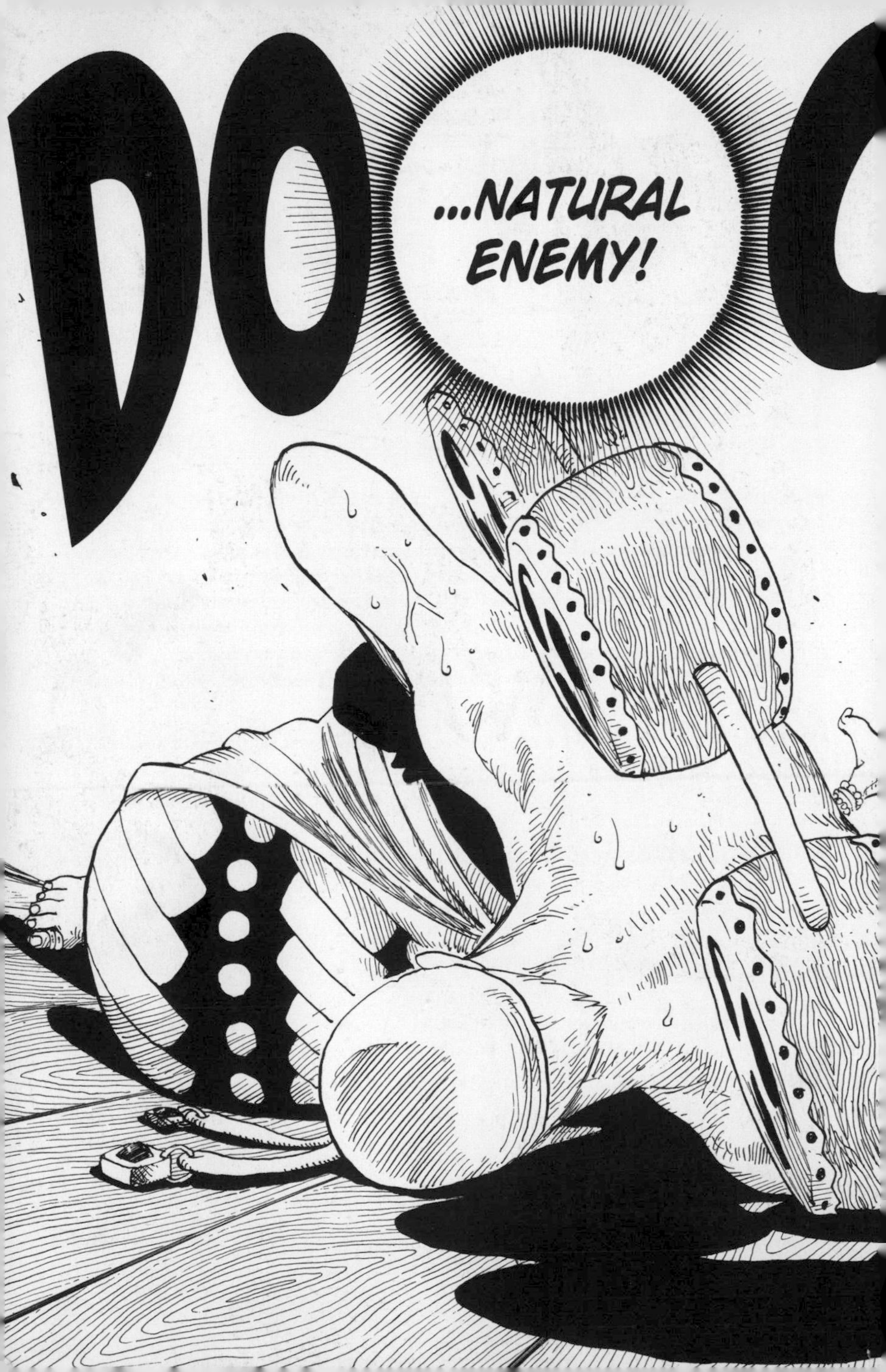
DOO
...NATURAL ENEMY!

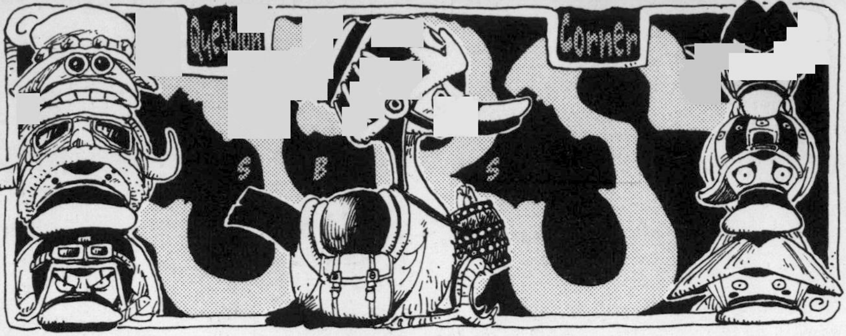
Question
Corner
S B S

Q: Dear Mr. Odacchi. I really really really x 1000 want a second timetable for *One Piece*… Would you please make one? Thank you.

--Shibu-san and Ishi-san

A: A timetable, huh… Yes, there was one a few volumes back that was very popular. Well, the crew has grown, and there have been a lot of requests for a new one. I want to make one, but the way school schedules are nowadays is different from when I was a student, so I don't know what kind of chart to make that would be the most useful. So if you have some free time, please make a copy of the one you're using now and send it to me.
I'll use that as an example and include a timetable next time. (^_^)

Q: Hello. There is a festival called "Shibugawa Heso Matsuri" in the region my friend is from. Conis would definitely participate, wouldn't she?

--Ponponchi

A: Oh, a heso festival? I wonder if it includes belly dancing?
Of course all the sky people would participate!
Even Eneru would go!!

HESO MEANS "BELLY BUTTON" IN JAPANESE. -EDITOR

Q: Why do all the beautiful women characters in *One Piece* have large breasts? Oda-chan, you're such an idiot!! There's more to women than just big breasts!! Sanji, you understand me, don't you? ♡

--Big Sanji Fan

Sanji: OF COURSE, YOUNG LADY!
WHAT MATTERS MOST IN A PERSON IS THEIR HEART!!
Oda: Hey, there's Nami wearing a swimsuit.
Sanji: OOOH, NAAAMI! ♡♡♡

Chapter 280:
FLOATING

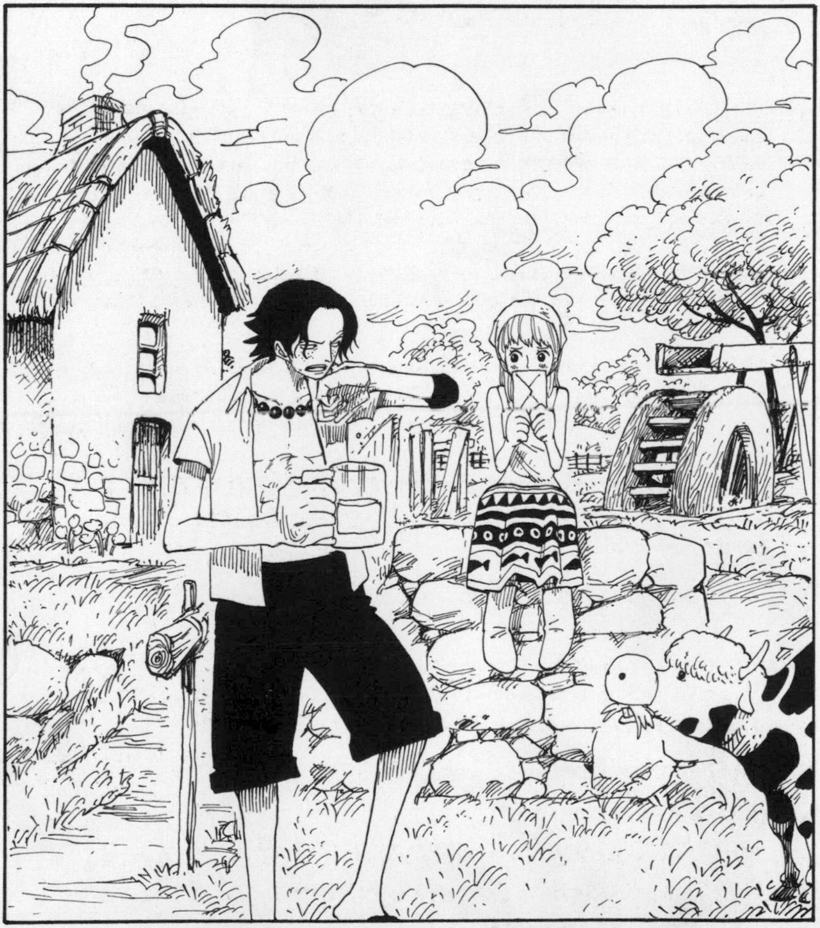

ACE'S GREAT SEARCH FOR BLACKBEARD, VOL. 8:
"THE DAIRY LASS MODA'S DILEMMA"

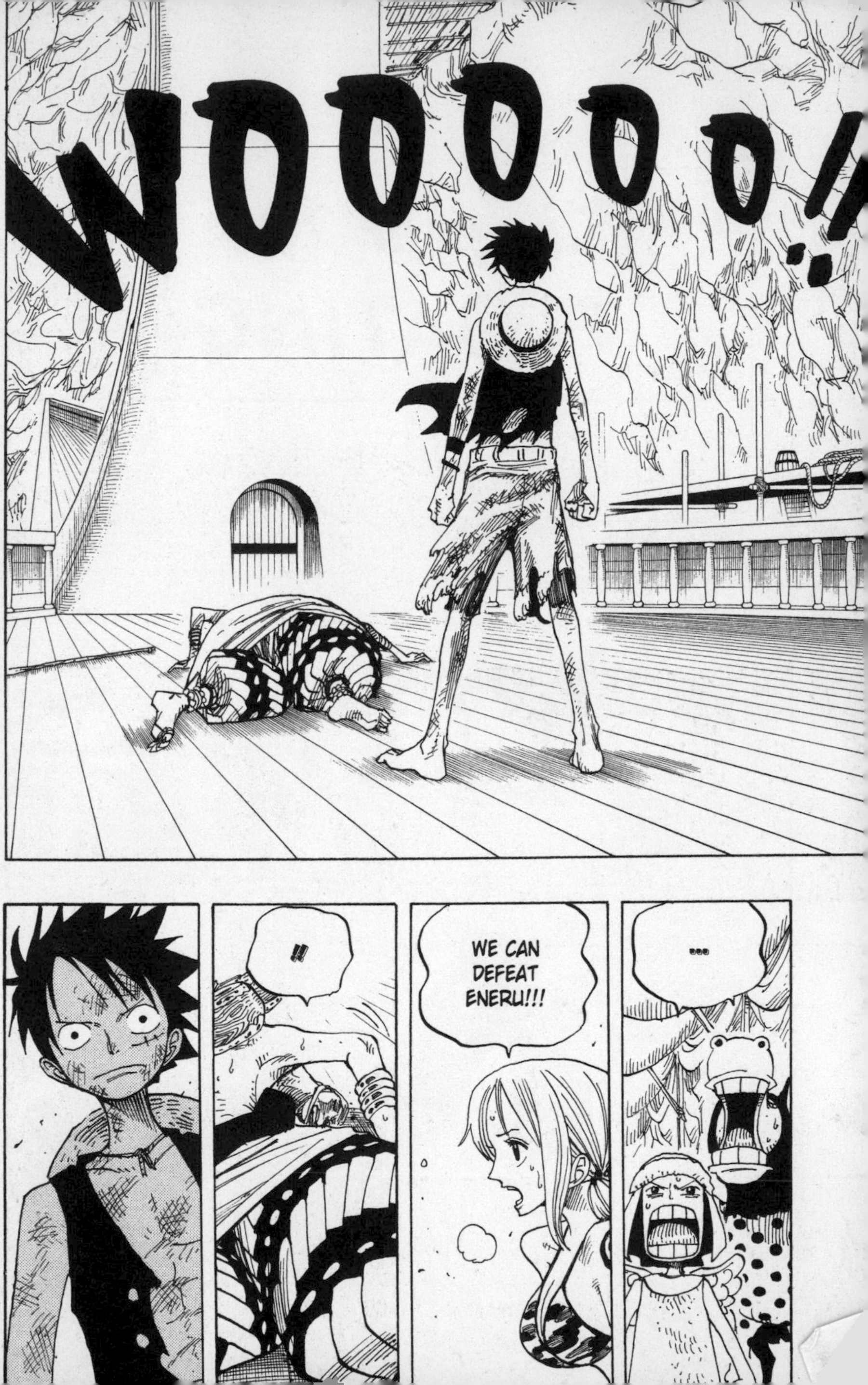
WOOOOO!!
...
WE CAN DEFEAT ENERU!!!
!!

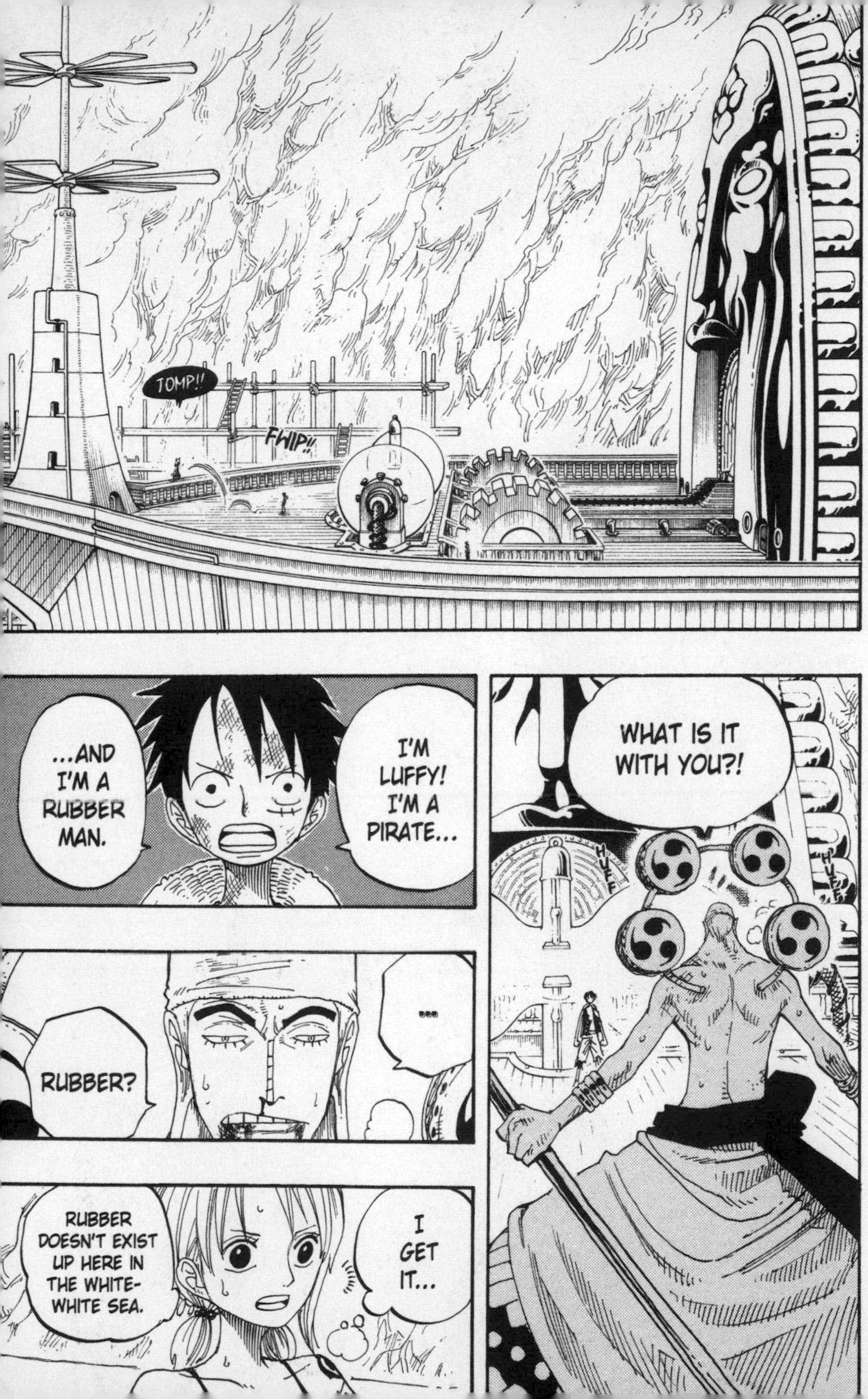
TOMP!!
FWIP!!
WHAT IS IT WITH YOU?!
HUFF
HUFF
I'M LUFFY! I'M A PIRATE...
...AND I'M A RUBBER MAN.
...
RUBBER?
I GET IT...
RUBBER DOESN'T EXIST UP HERE IN THE WHITE-WHITE SEA.

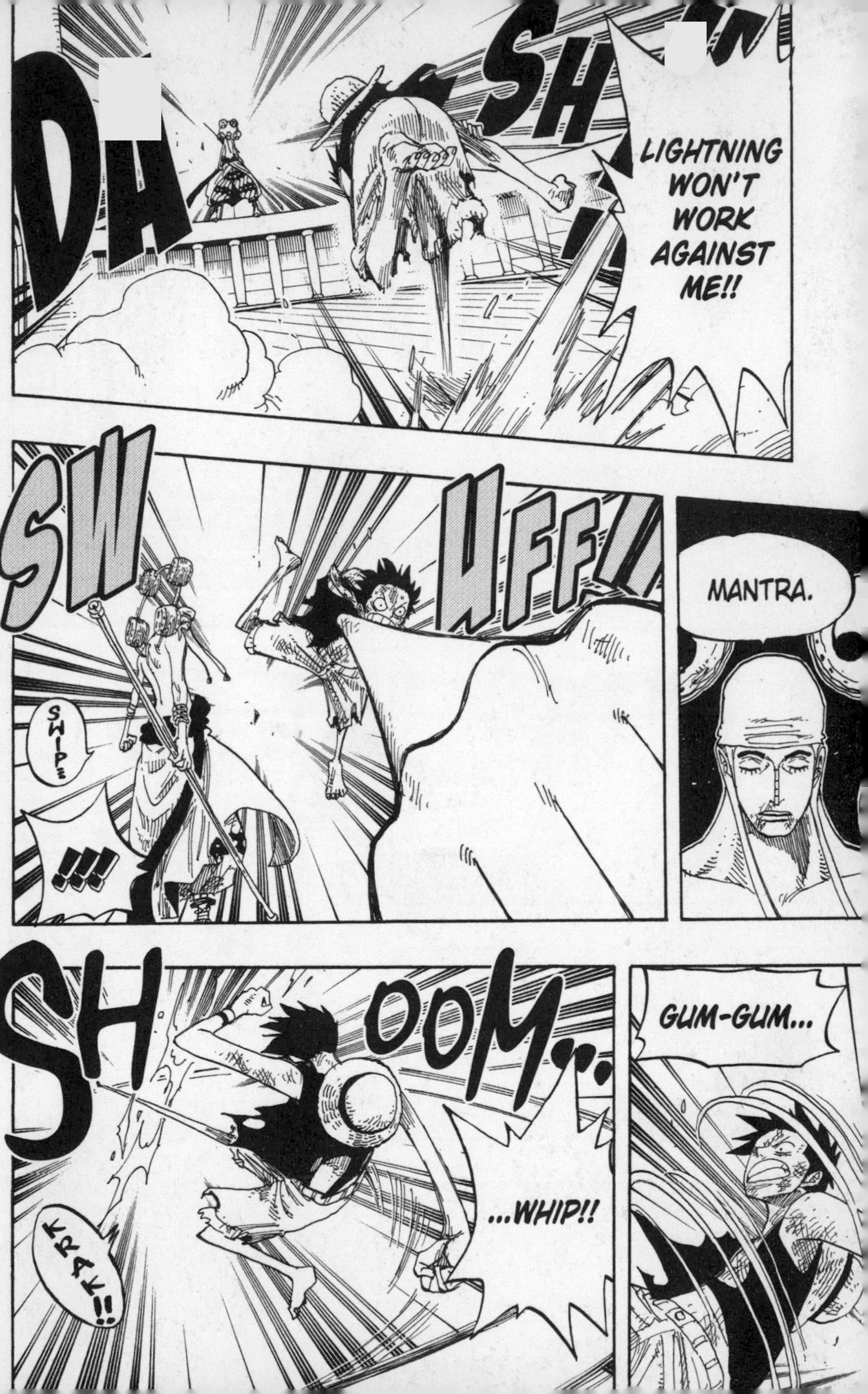
SH
LIGHTNING WON'T WORK AGAINST ME!!
DA
MANTRA.
HFF!!
SW
SWIPE
!!!
GUM-GUM...
OOM..
SH
...WHIP!!
KRAK!!

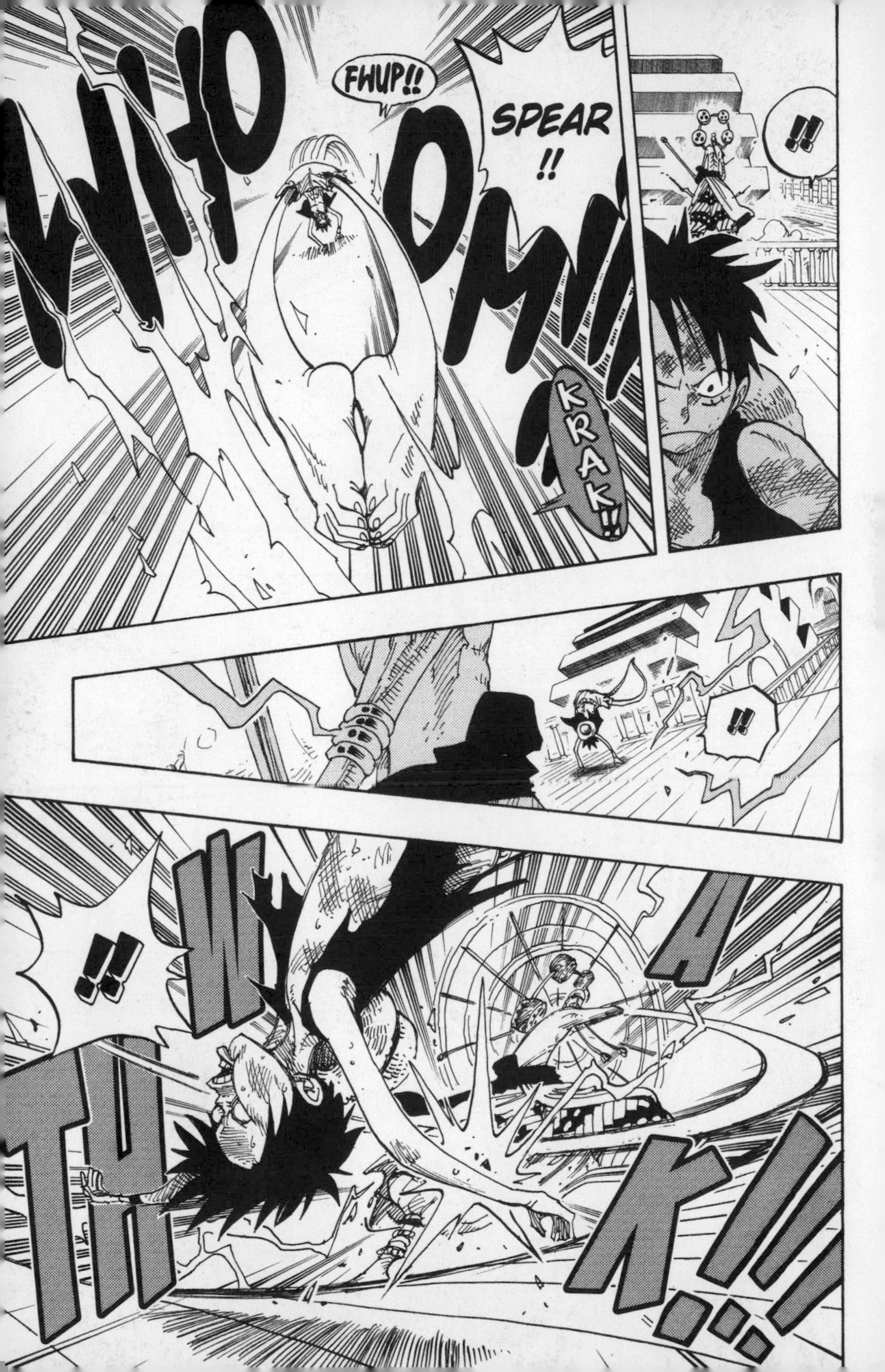
!!
SPEAR !!
FWUP!!
KRAK!!
!!
!!

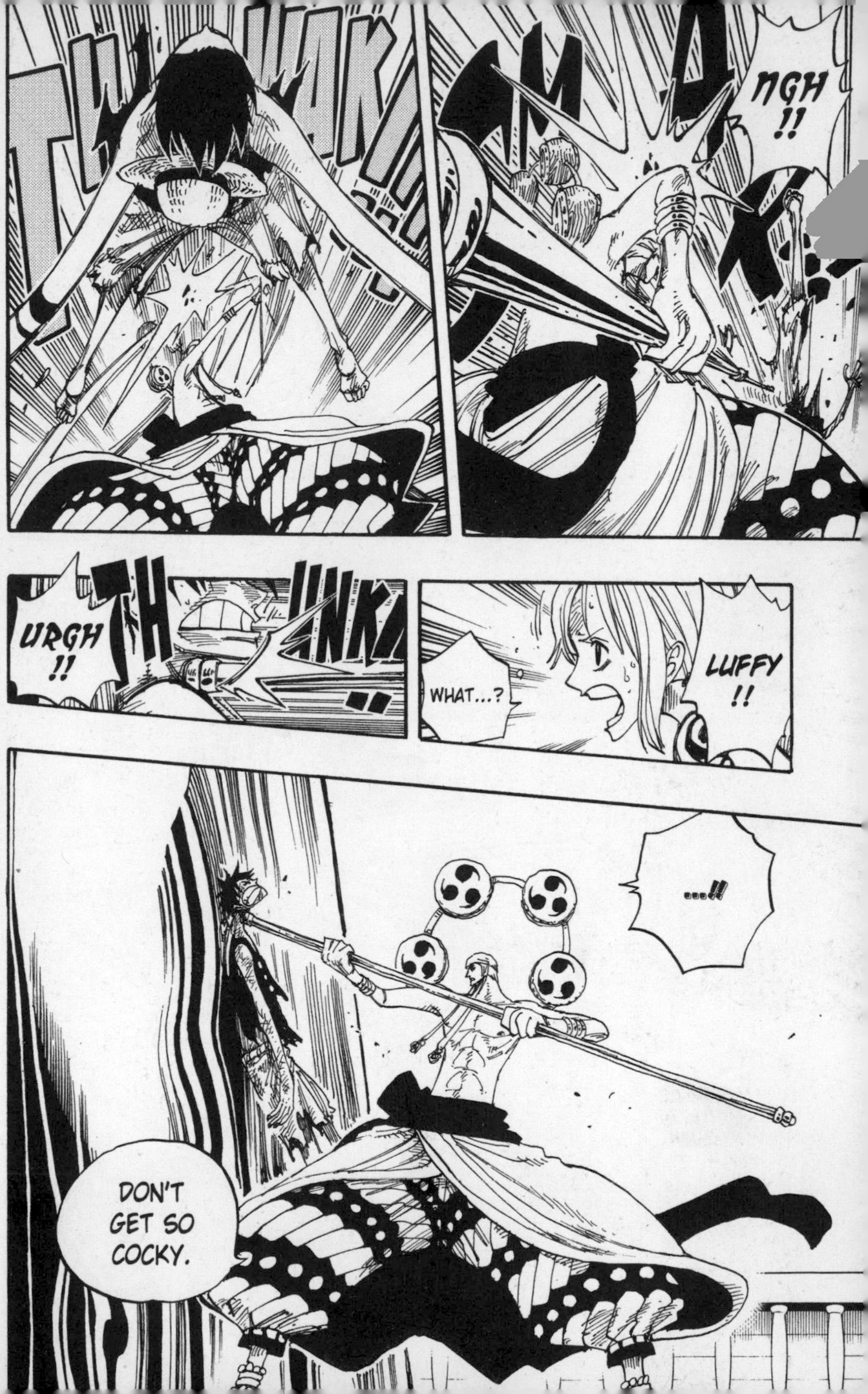
NGH !!
LUFFY !!
WHAT...?
URGH !!
...!!
DON'T GET SO COCKY.

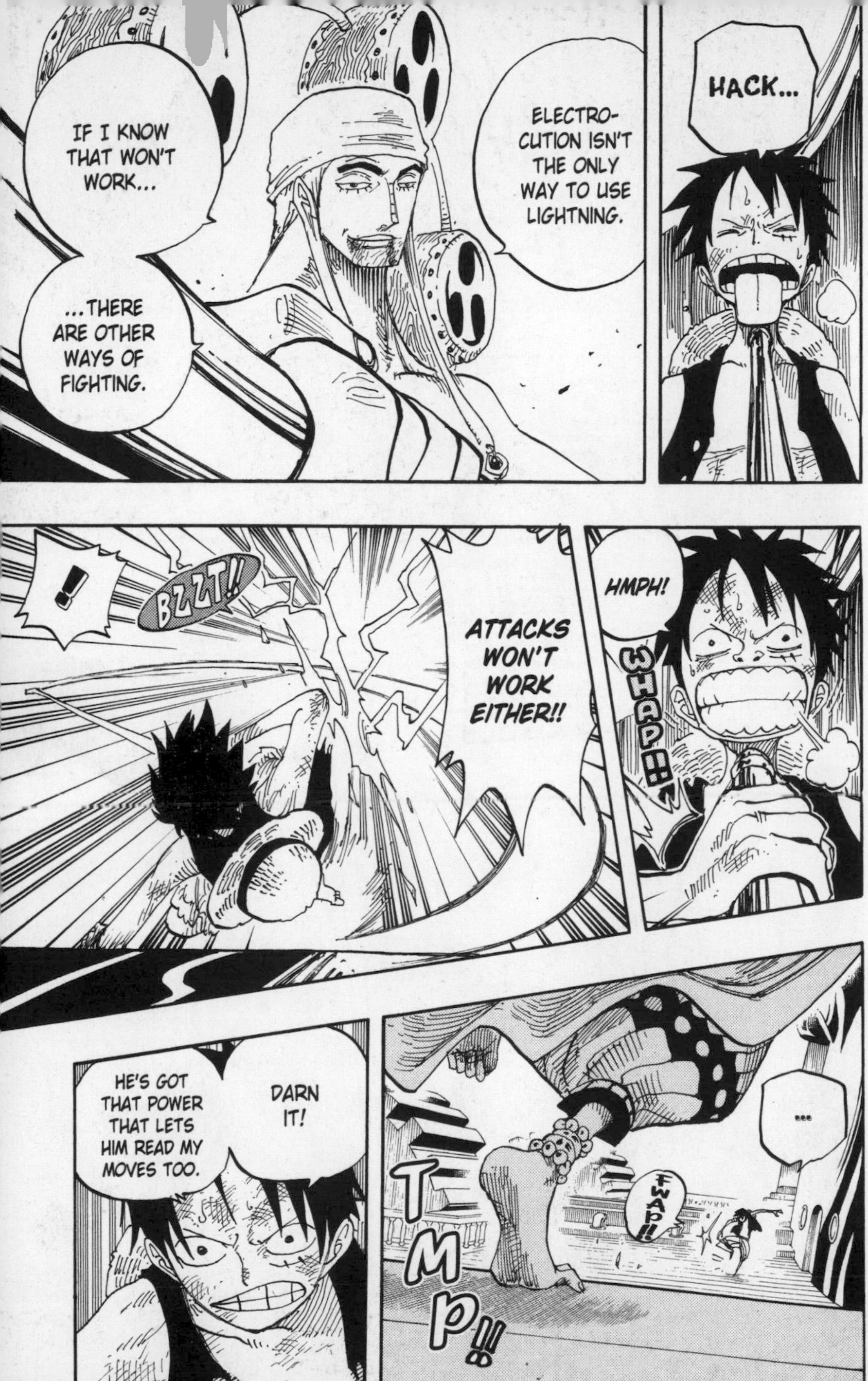
HACK...
ELECTRO-CUTION ISN'T THE ONLY WAY TO USE LIGHTNING.
IF I KNOW THAT WON'T WORK...
...THERE ARE OTHER WAYS OF FIGHTING.
HMPH!
WHAP!!
ATTACKS WON'T WORK EITHER!!
BZZT!!
!
...
FWAP!!
TMP!!
DARN IT!
HE'S GOT THAT POWER THAT LETS HIM READ MY MOVES TOO.

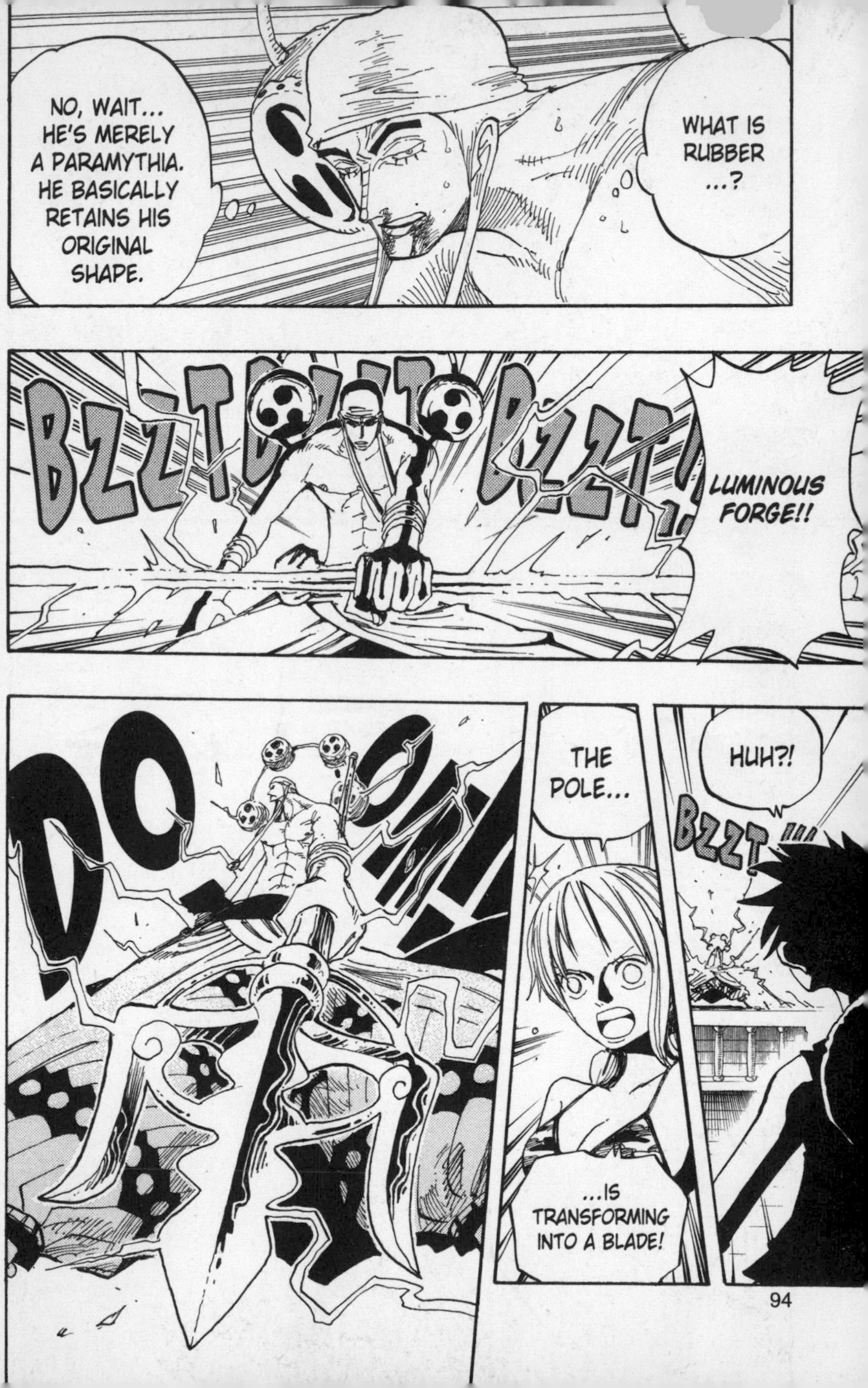
WHAT IS RUBBER ...?
NO, WAIT... HE'S MERELY A PARAMYTHIA. HE BASICALLY RETAINS HIS ORIGINAL SHAPE.
LUMINOUS FORGE!!
BZZT
BZZT
HUH?!
BZZT
THE POLE...
...IS TRANSFORMING INTO A BLADE!
DOOM

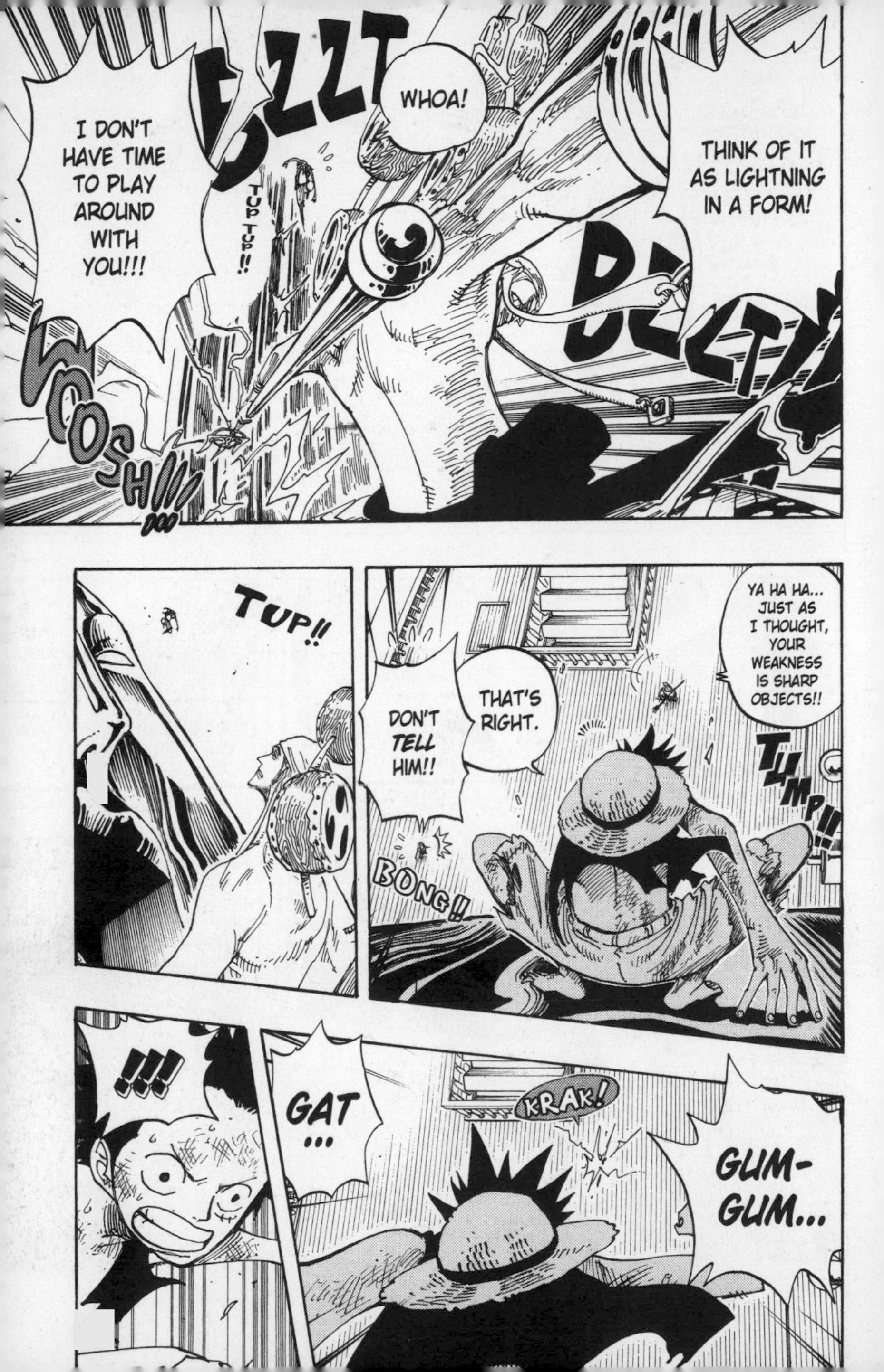
THINK OF IT AS LIGHTNING IN A FORM!
WHOA!
TUP TUP!!
I DON'T HAVE TIME TO PLAY AROUND WITH YOU!!!
WOOSH!!!
YA HA HA... JUST AS I THOUGHT, YOUR WEAKNESS IS SHARP OBJECTS!!
TUMP!!
THAT'S RIGHT.
DON'T *TELL* HIM!!
BONG!!
TUP!!
GUM-GUM...
KRAK!
GAT ...
!!!

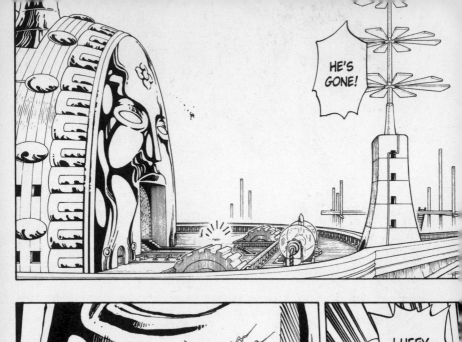

HE'S GONE!

LUFFY, BEHIND YOU!!

PIEE!

LUFFY, BEHIND YOU!!

HE TRAVELED THROUGH THE GOLD!

BZZT BZZT BZZT

BZZT...

BZZT BZZT

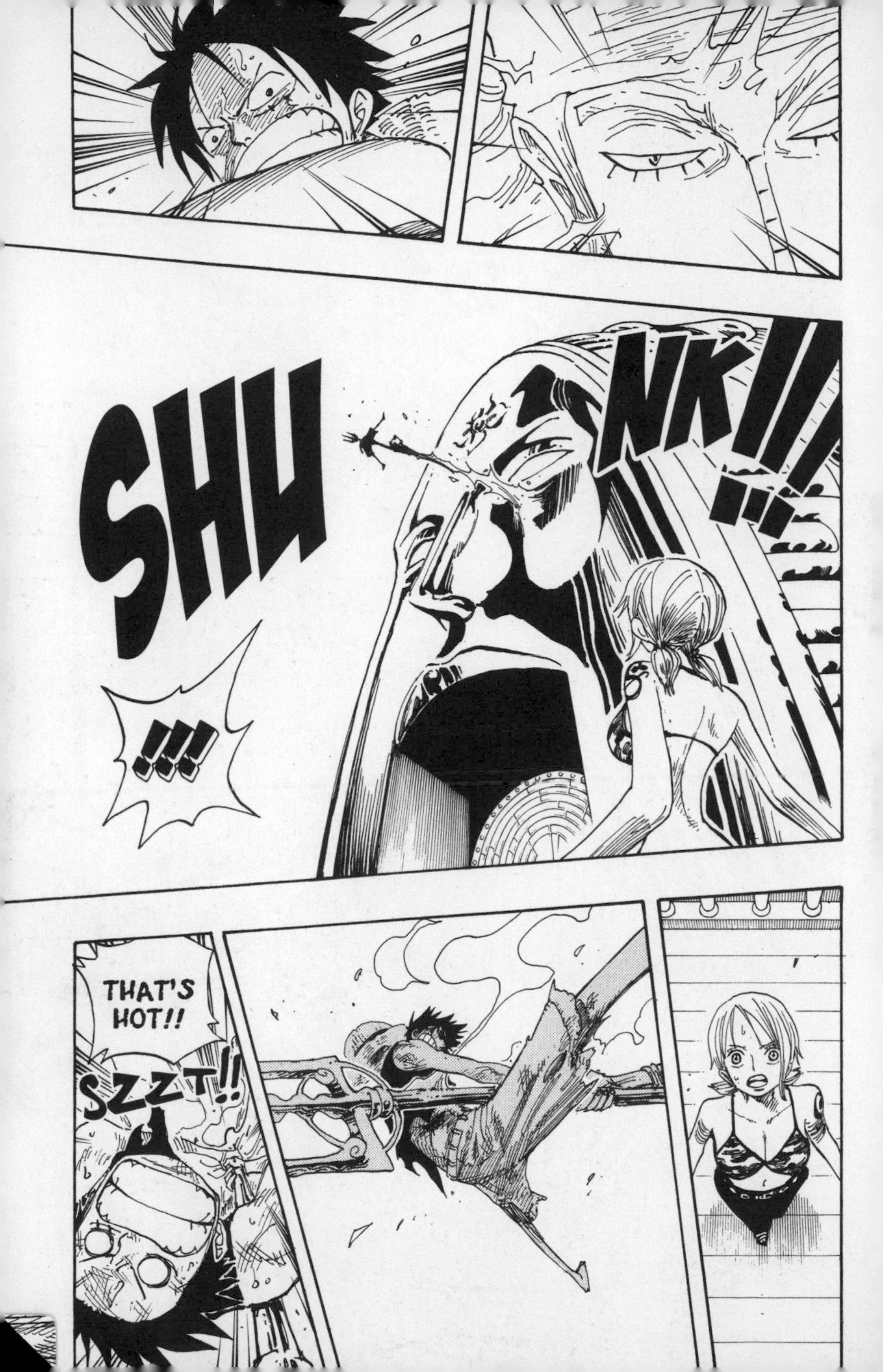
SHUNK!!
!!!
THAT'S HOT!!
SZZT!!

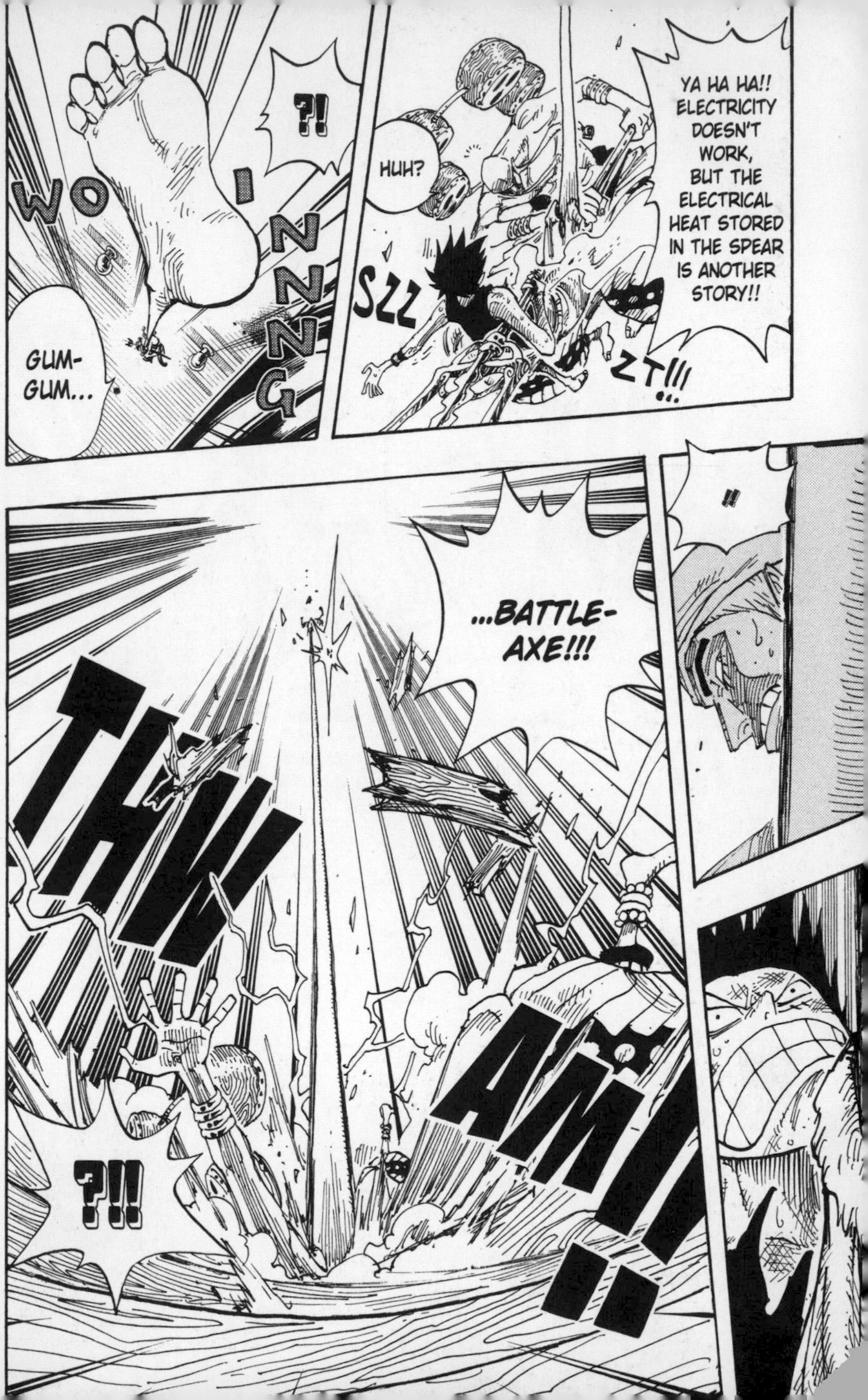
YA HA HA!! ELECTRICITY DOESN'T WORK, BUT THE ELECTRICAL HEAT STORED IN THE SPEAR IS ANOTHER STORY!!
HUH?
SZZ
ZT!!!
?!
WOINNNG
GUM-GUM...
!!
...BATTLE-AXE!!!
THWAM!!
?!!

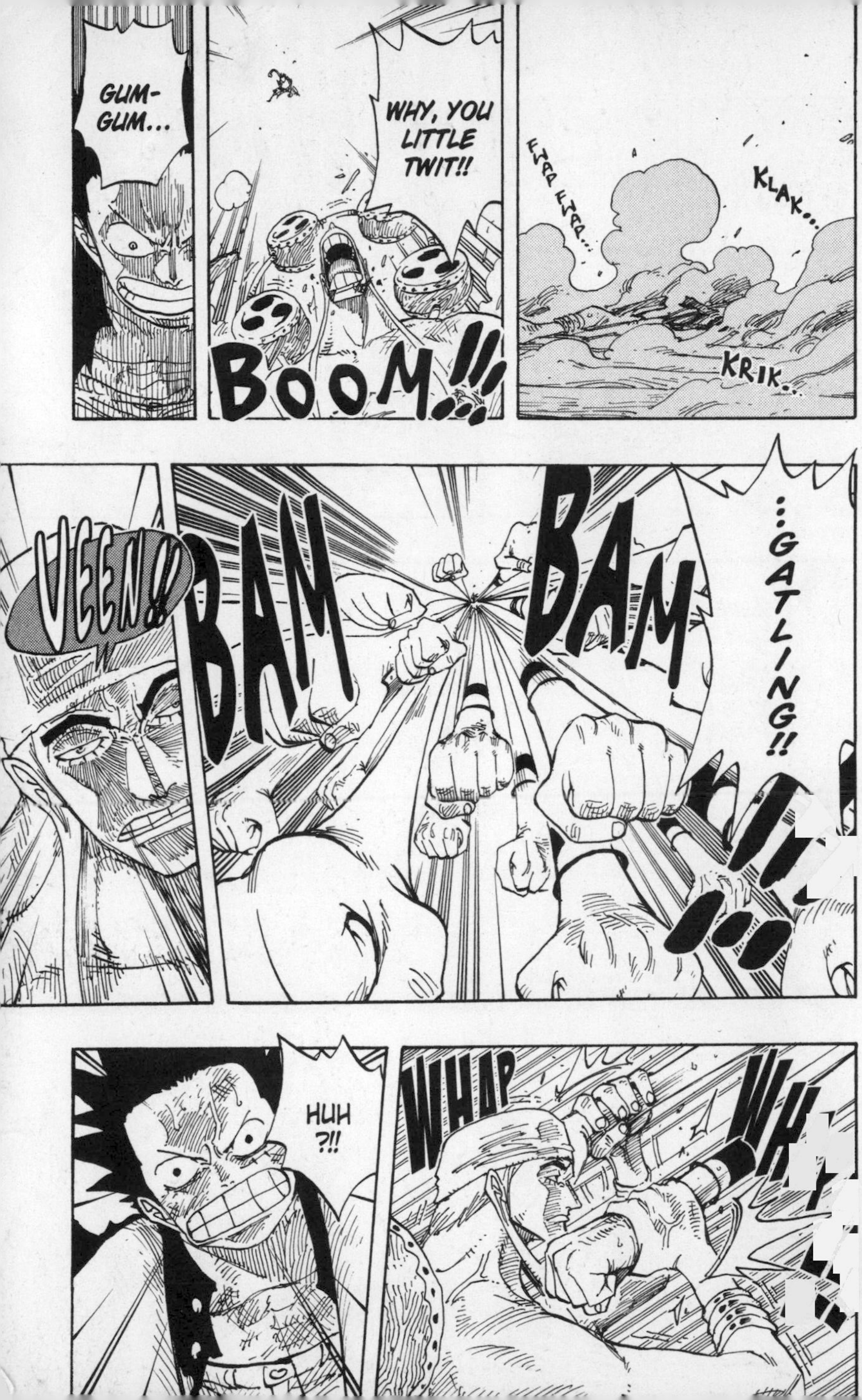
KLAK...
FWAP FWAP...
KRIK...
WHY, YOU LITTLE TWIT!!
BOOM!!!
GUM-GUM...
...GATLING!!
BAM
BAM
VEEN!!
WHOP
HUH?!!

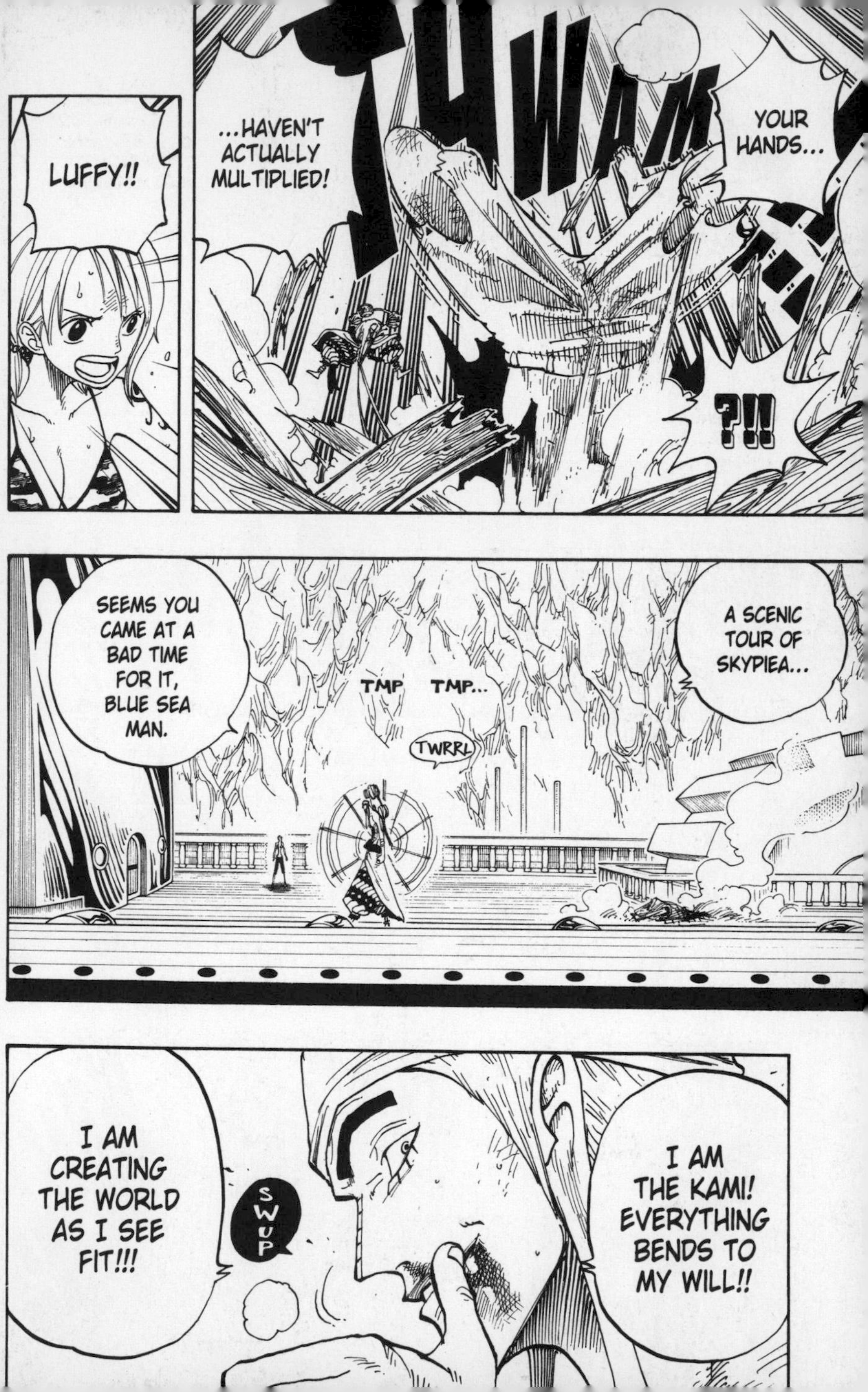
YOUR HANDS...
THWAM
?!!
...HAVEN'T ACTUALLY MULTIPLIED!
LUFFY!!
A SCENIC TOUR OF SKYPIEA...
TMP TMP...
TWRRL
SEEMS YOU CAME AT A BAD TIME FOR IT, BLUE SEA MAN.
I AM THE KAMI! EVERYTHING BENDS TO MY WILL!!
SWUP
I AM CREATING THE WORLD AS I SEE FIT!!!

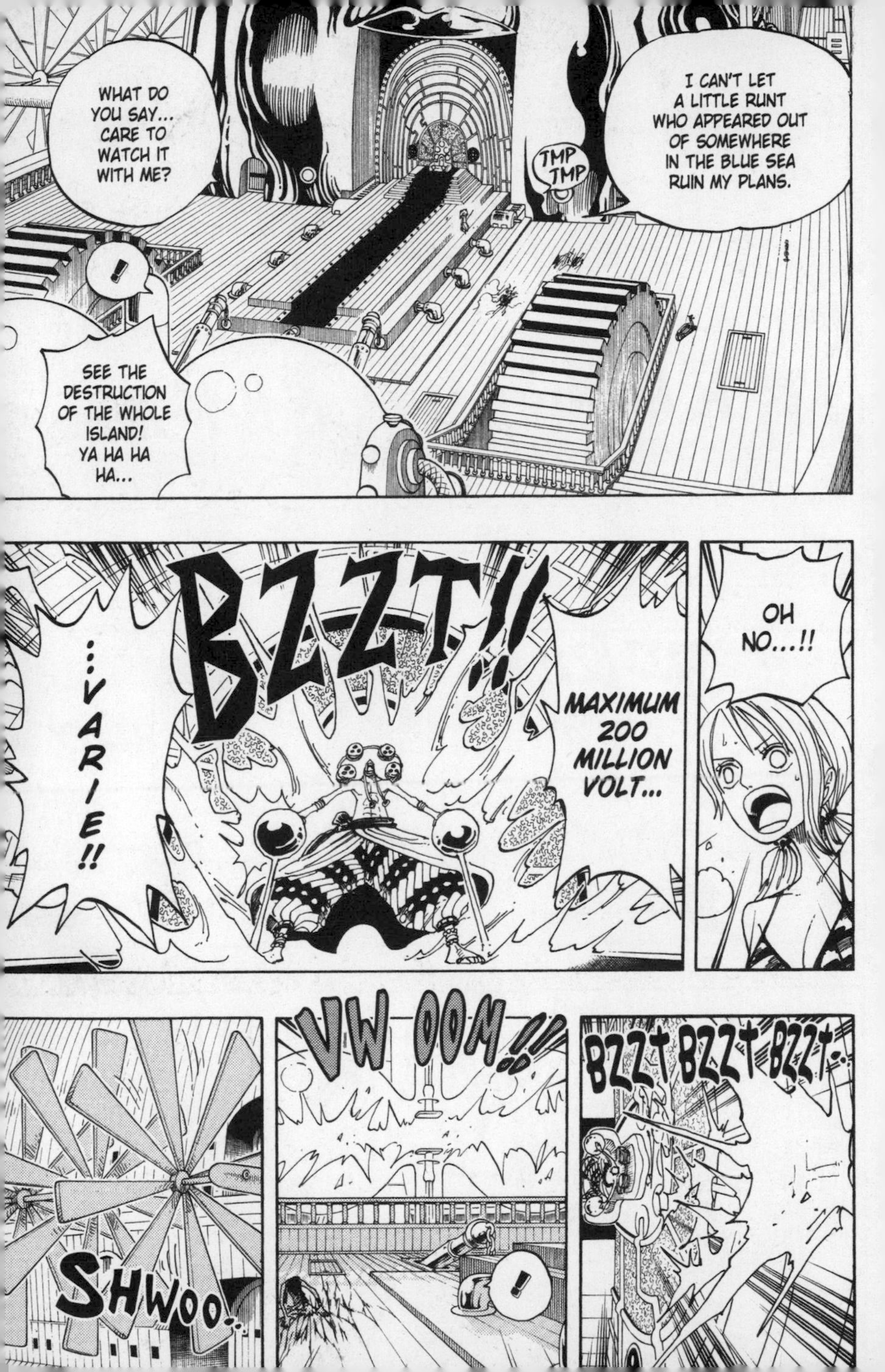
I CAN'T LET A LITTLE RUNT WHO APPEARED OUT OF SOMEWHERE IN THE BLUE SEA RUIN MY PLANS.
TMP TMP
WHAT DO YOU SAY... CARE TO WATCH IT WITH ME?
!
SEE THE DESTRUCTION OF THE WHOLE ISLAND! YA HA HA HA...
OH NO...!!
BZZT!!
MAXIMUM 200 MILLION VOLT...
...VARIE!!
BZZT BZZT BZZT...
VW OOM!!
!
SHWOO...

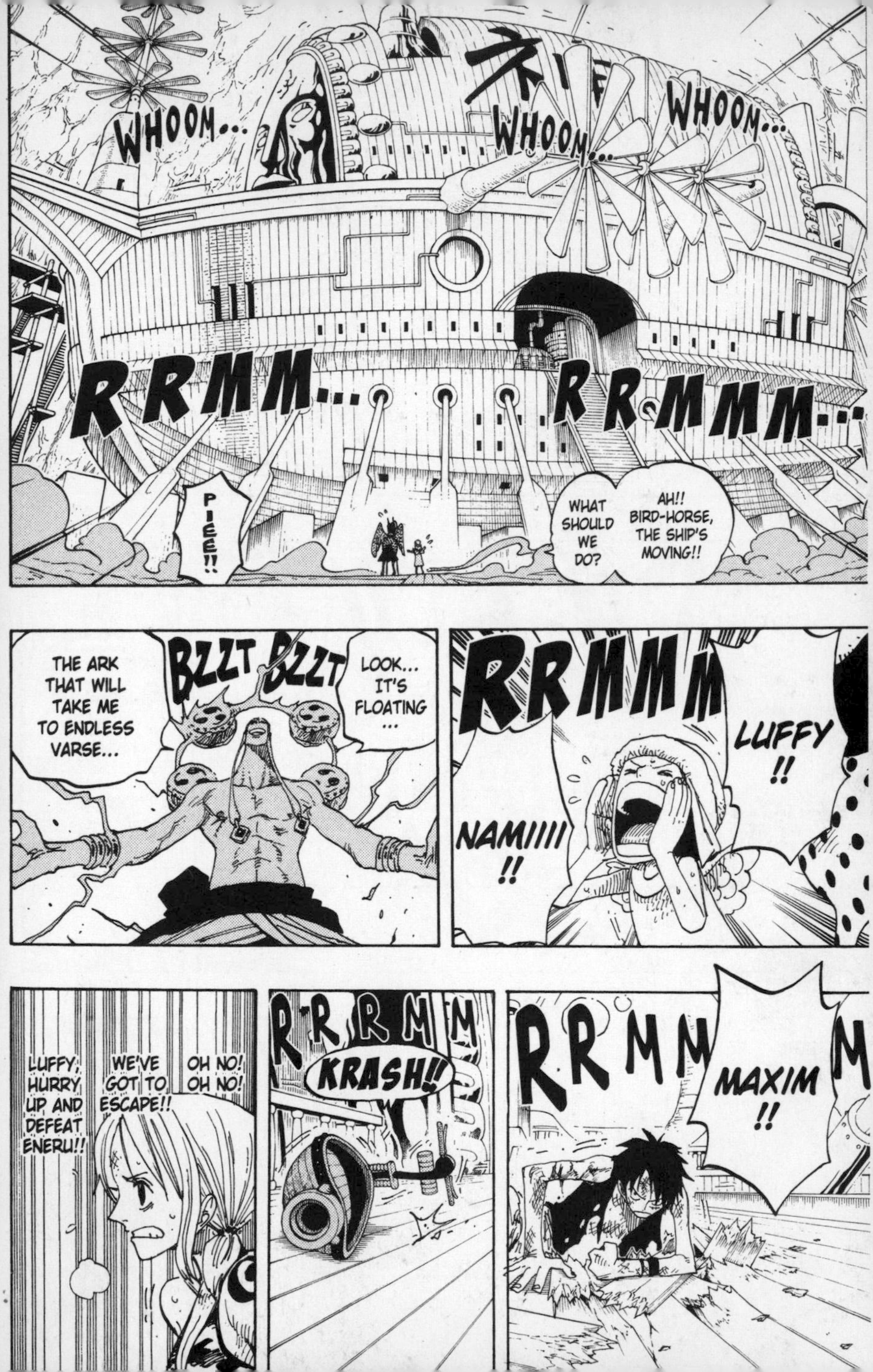
WHOOM...
WHOOM...
WHOOM...
RRMM...
RRMMMM...
AH!! BIRD-HORSE, THE SHIP'S MOVING!!
WHAT SHOULD WE DO?
PIEEE!!
LUFFY!!
NAMIIII!!
RRMMMM
LOOK... IT'S FLOATING...
BZZT BZZT
THE ARK THAT WILL TAKE ME TO ENDLESS VARSE...
MAXIM!!
RRMMMM
KRASH!!
RRRMM
OH NO! OH NO!
WE'VE GOT TO ESCAPE!!
LUFFY, HURRY UP AND DEFEAT ENERU!!

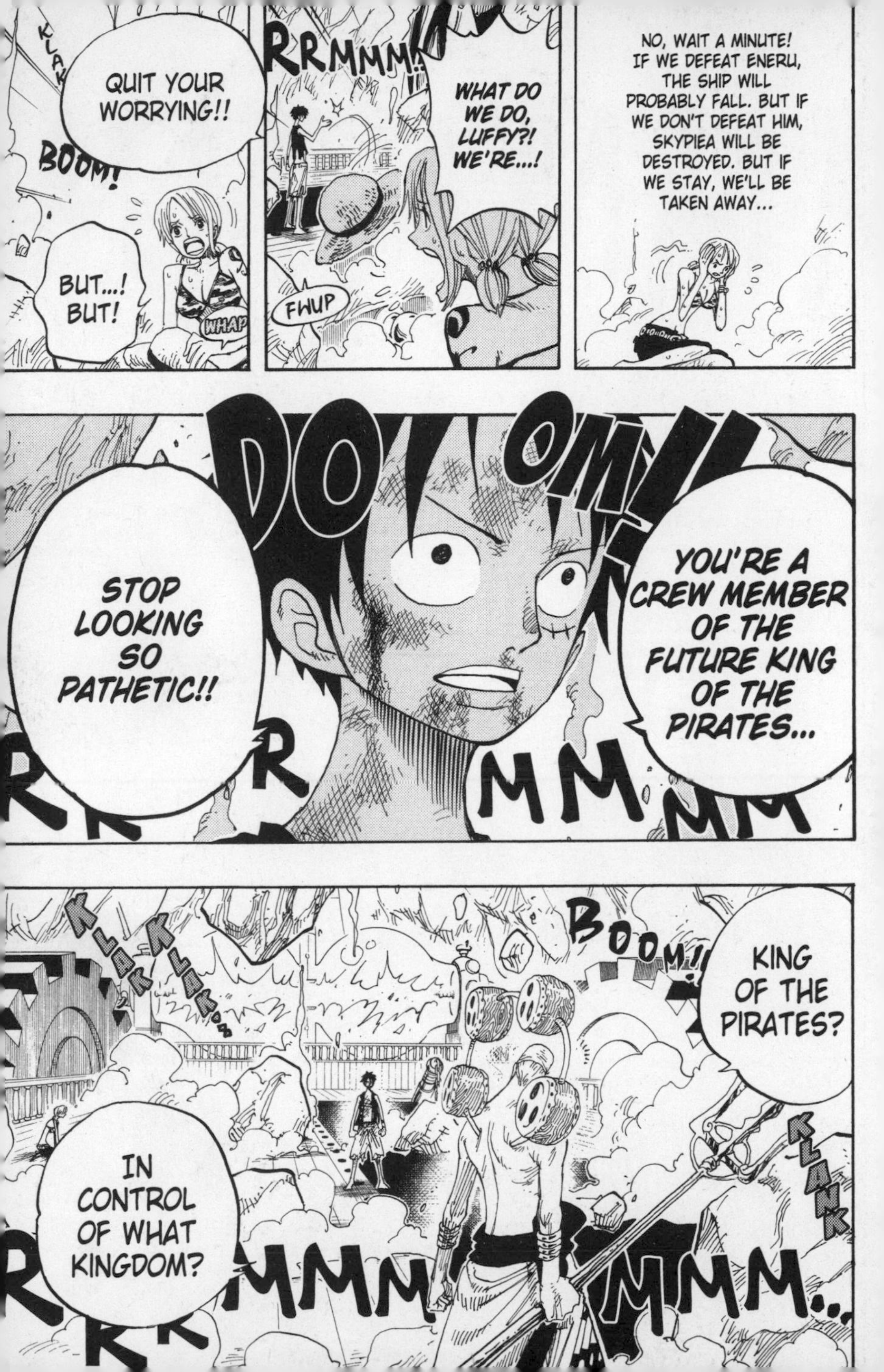
NO, WAIT A MINUTE! IF WE DEFEAT ENERU, THE SHIP WILL PROBABLY FALL. BUT IF WE DON'T DEFEAT HIM, SKYPIEA WILL BE DESTROYED. BUT IF WE STAY, WE'LL BE TAKEN AWAY...
RRMMM!
WHAT DO WE DO, LUFFY?! WE'RE...!
FWUP
KLAK
QUIT YOUR WORRYING!!
BOOM!
BUT...! BUT!
WHAP
DOOM!!
YOU'RE A CREW MEMBER OF THE FUTURE KING OF THE PIRATES...
STOP LOOKING SO PATHETIC!!
RRMMMM
KING OF THE PIRATES?
BOOM!
KLANK
KLAK KLAK
IN CONTROL OF WHAT KINGDOM?
RRRMMMM...

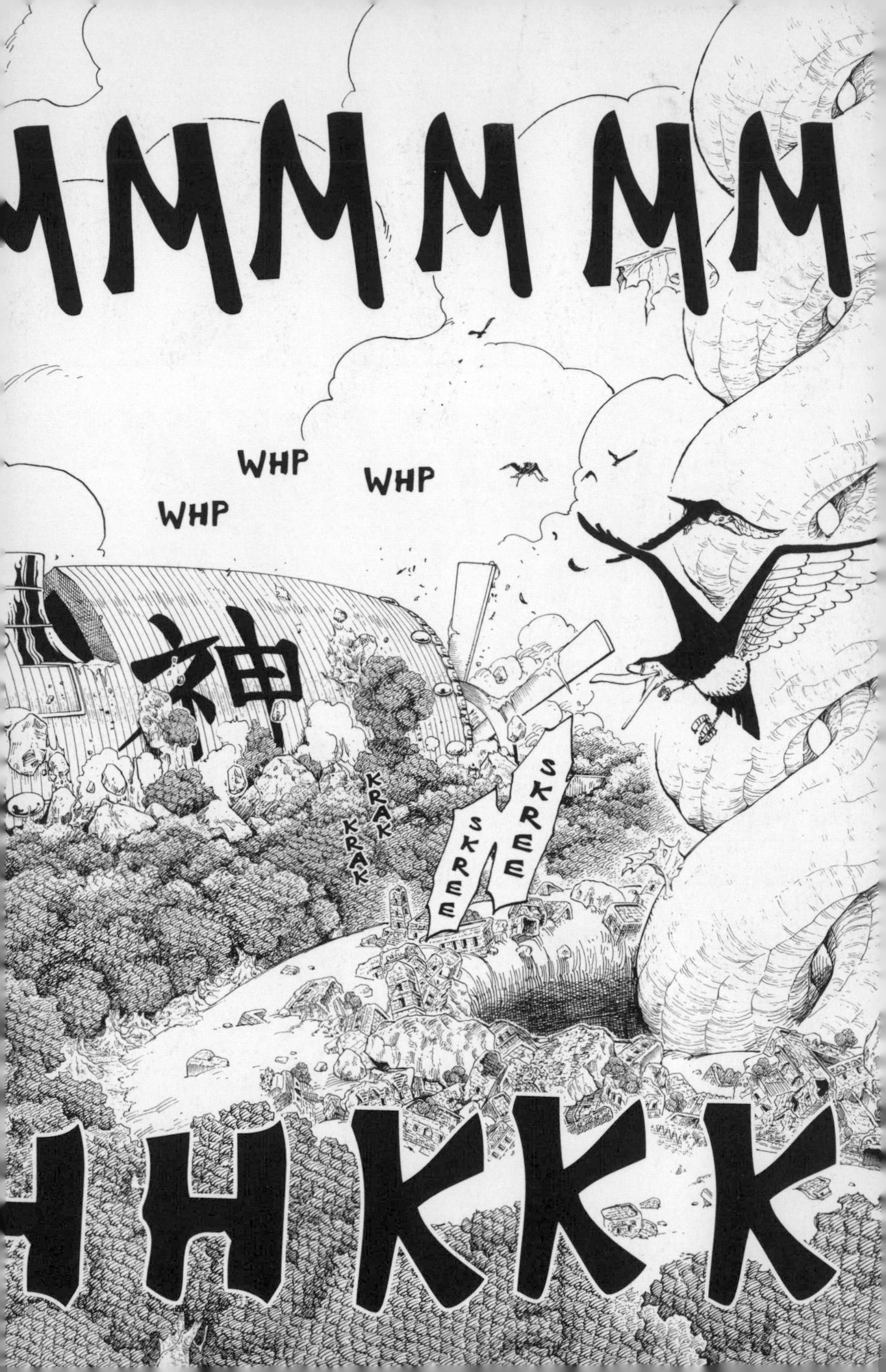
MMMMM
WHP
WHP
WHP
SKREE
SKREE
KRAK
KRAK
神
HKKK

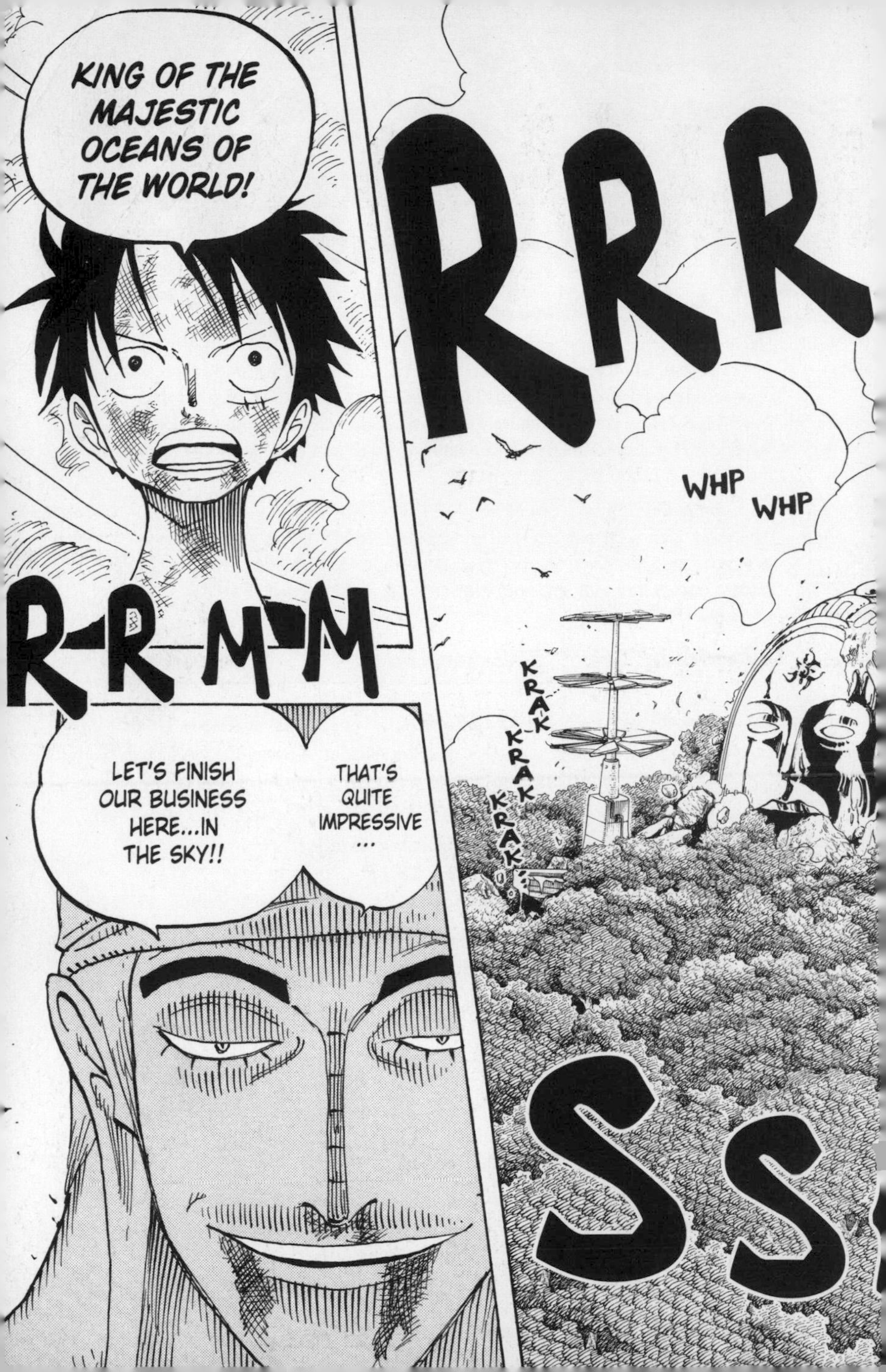
RRR
WHP
WHP
KRAK
KRAK
KRAK
KRAK
SS
KING OF THE MAJESTIC OCEANS OF THE WORLD!
RRMM
THAT'S QUITE IMPRESSIVE ...
LET'S FINISH OUR BUSINESS HERE...IN THE SKY!!

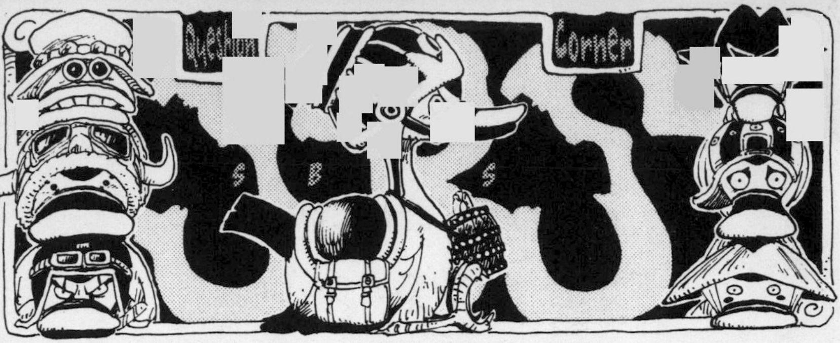
Question
Corner

Reader: Hello, Oda Sensei! I have a question about the Logia type of Devil's Fruit. In Chapter 280, Kami Eneru says that "Paramythias basically retain their original shape," but what about characters like Crocodile, who doesn't keep his shape with his Sand-Sand Fruit abilities, or Ace and Smoker? Are those not Logia abilities? If you don't answer, I won't allow you to go to the bathroom! You'll have to do it outdoors.

--LOL Jokes

Oda: I'm not going to do my business outdoors. You've got such a potty mouth. Going to the bathroom outside... I get this question a lot, so let me elaborate the answer more clearly in a chart.

Paramythia Type	Zoan Type	Logia Type
Gum-Gum Fruit	Ox-Ox Fruit	Plume-Plume Fruit
Chop-Chop Fruit	Bison Model	Flame-Flame Fruit
Slip-Slip Fruit	Human-Human Fruit	Sand-Sand Fruit
Bomb-Bomb Fruit	Tweet-Tweet Fruit	Rumble-Rumble Fruit
Kilo-Kilo Fruit	Falcon Model	
Wax-Wax Fruit	Diggy-Diggy Fruit	
Munch-Munch Fruit	Mutt-Mutt Fruit	
Clone-Clone Fruit	Dachshund Model	
Flower-Flower Fruit	Horse-Horse Fruit	
Dice-Dice Fruit		
Spike-Spike Fruit		
Bind-Bind Fruit		
Boing-Boing Fruit		

Does this give you a rough idea? The Logia type, which can change its shape into something found in nature, seems to rank higher than the other types.

Chapter 281:
DEATHPIEA

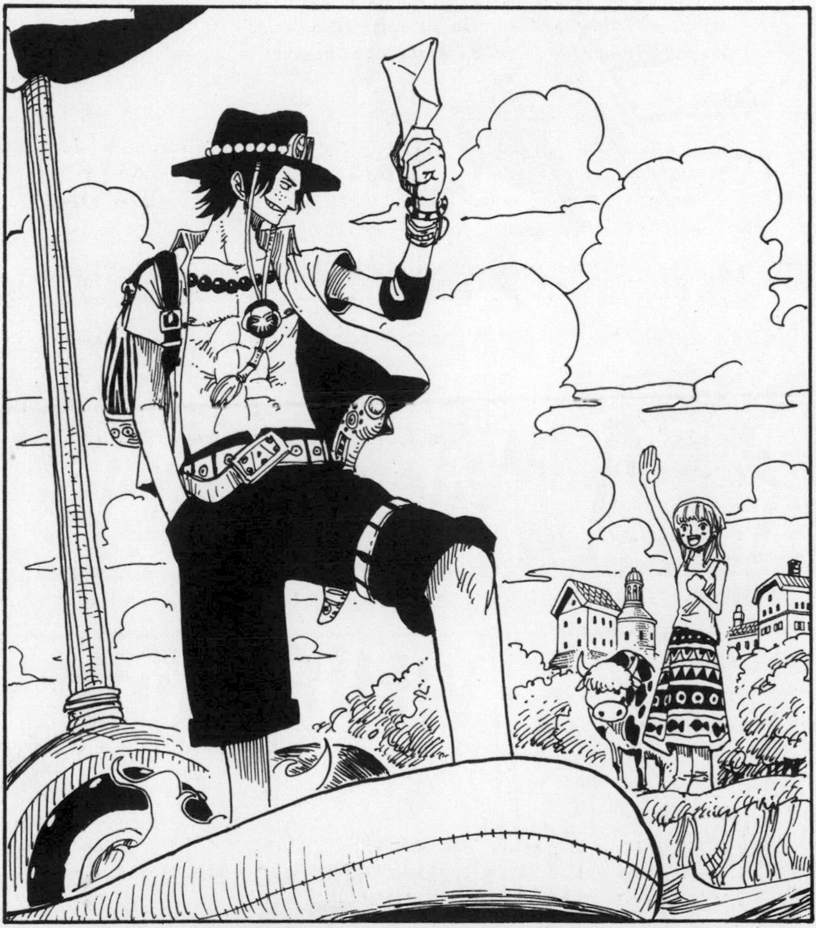

ACE'S GREAT SEARCH FOR BLACKBEARD, VOL. 9:
"A LITTLE FAVOR FOR SAVING MY LIFE"

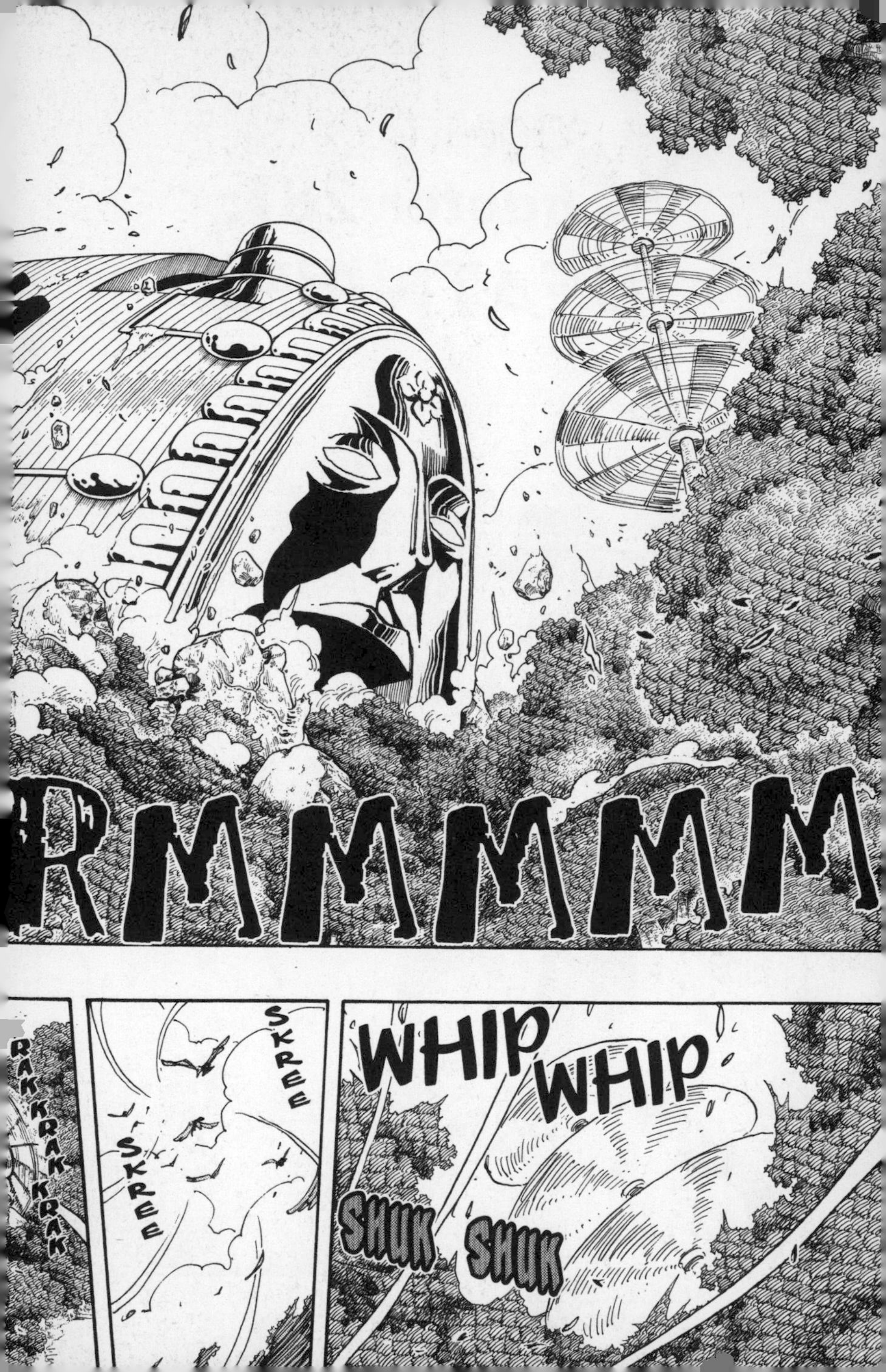
RMMMMM
WHIP WHIP
SHUK SHUK
SKREE SKREE
RAK KRAK KRAK

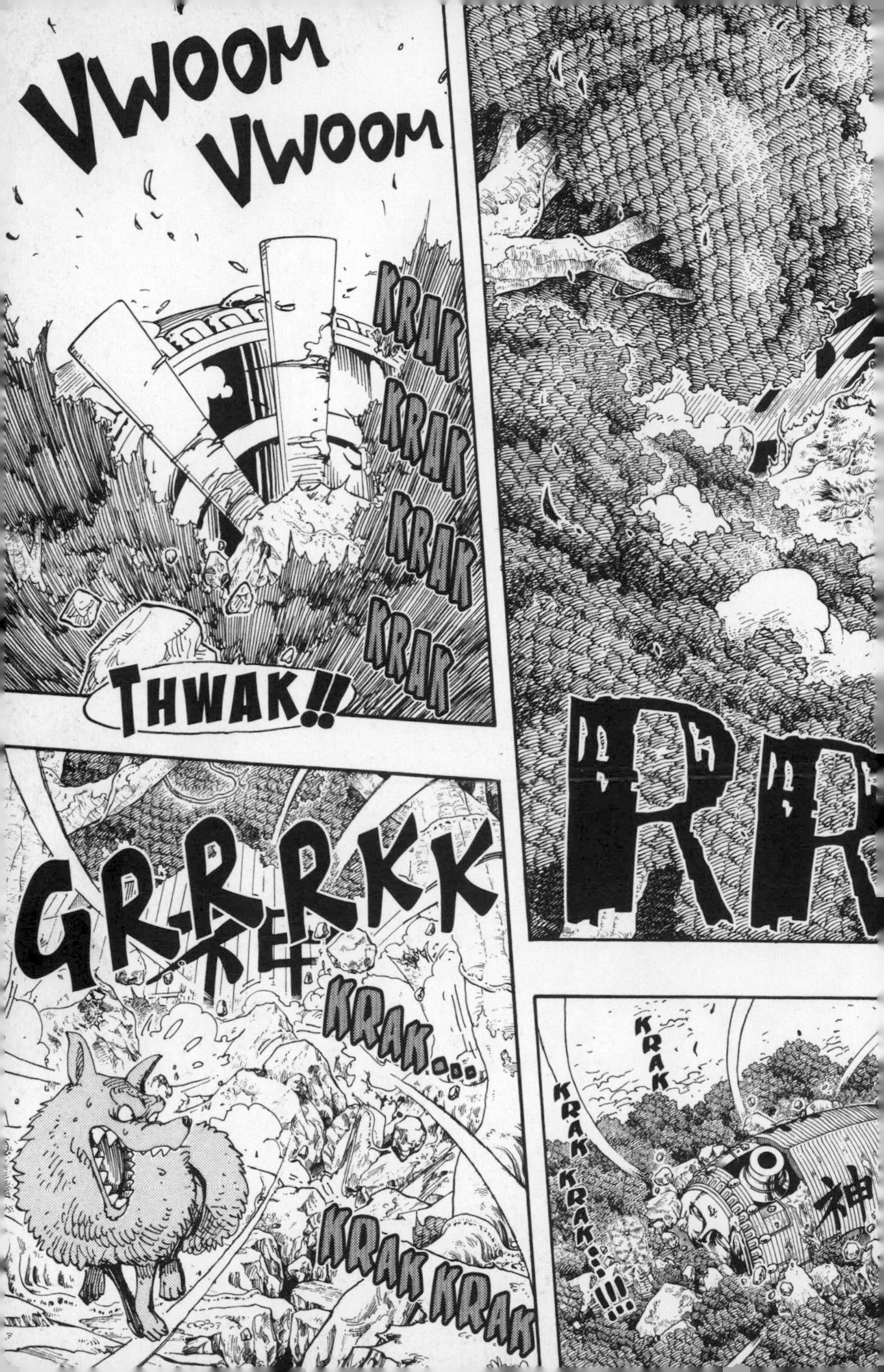
RR
VWOOM
VWOOM
KRAK KRAK KRAK KRAK
THWAK!!
GR-R-RKK
KRAK...
KRAK KRAK
KRAK
KRAK KRAK KRAK...!!!
神

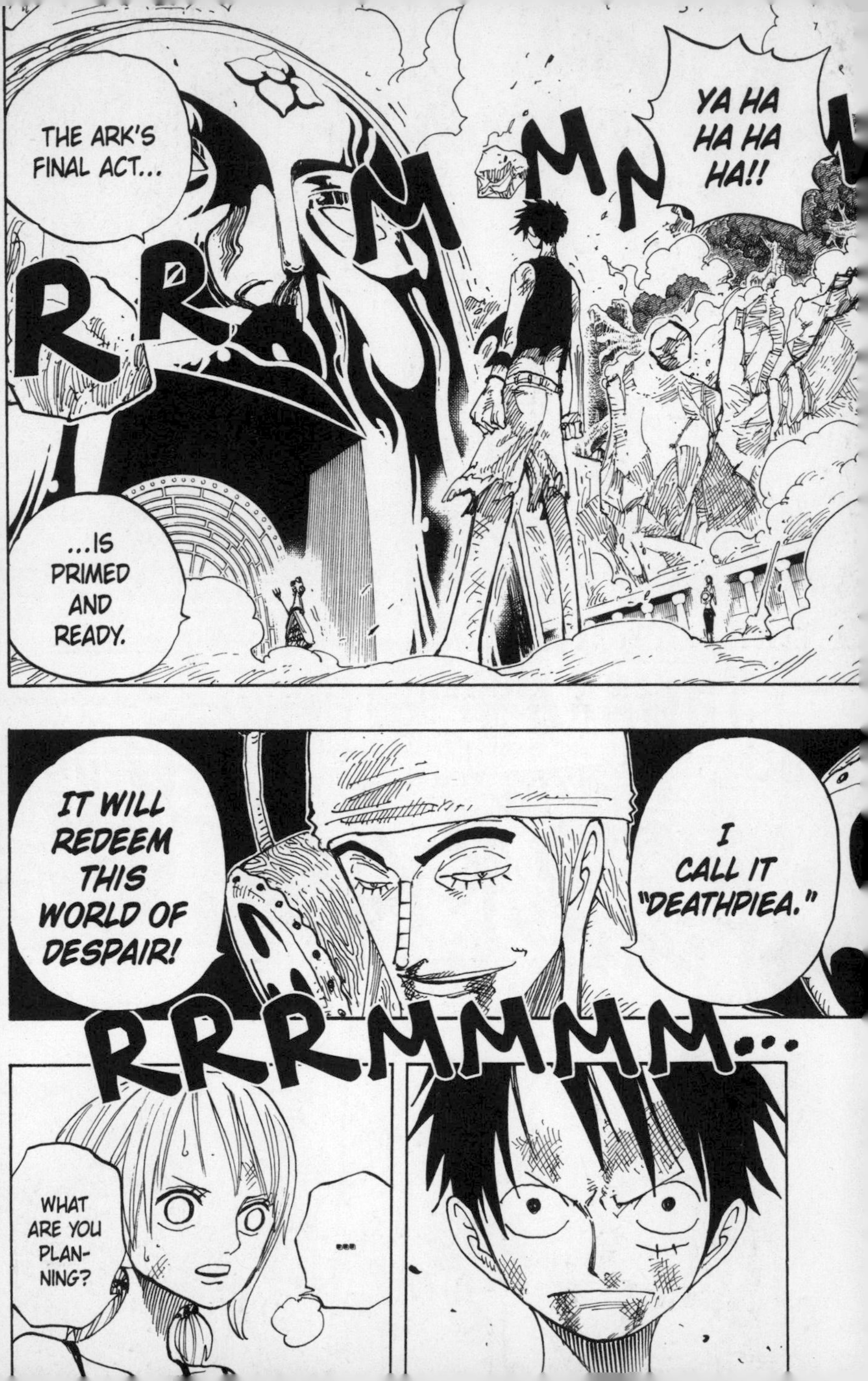
YA HA HA HA HA!!
RRMMM
THE ARK'S FINAL ACT...
...IS PRIMED AND READY.
I CALL IT "DEATHPIEA."
IT WILL REDEEM THIS WORLD OF DESPAIR!
RRRMMMM...
...
WHAT ARE YOU PLAN-NING?

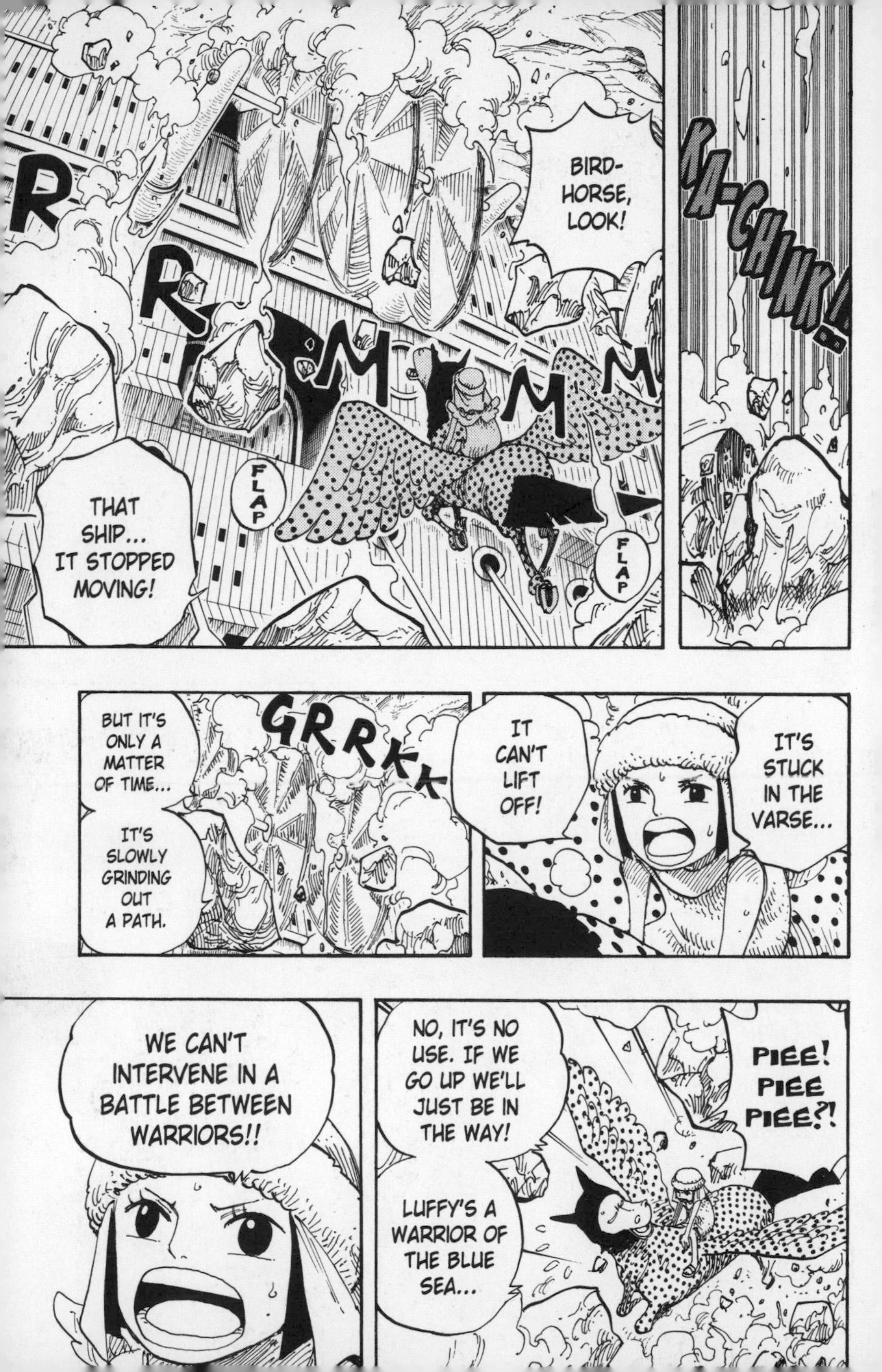
KA-CHINK!!
BIRD-HORSE, LOOK!
RRRMMMM
FLAP
FLAP
THAT SHIP... IT STOPPED MOVING!
IT'S STUCK IN THE VARSE...
IT CAN'T LIFT OFF!
GRRKK
BUT IT'S ONLY A MATTER OF TIME...
IT'S SLOWLY GRINDING OUT A PATH.
PIEE! PIEE PIEE?!
NO, IT'S NO USE. IF WE GO UP WE'LL JUST BE IN THE WAY!
LUFFY'S A WARRIOR OF THE BLUE SEA...
WE CAN'T INTERVENE IN A BATTLE BETWEEN WARRIORS!!

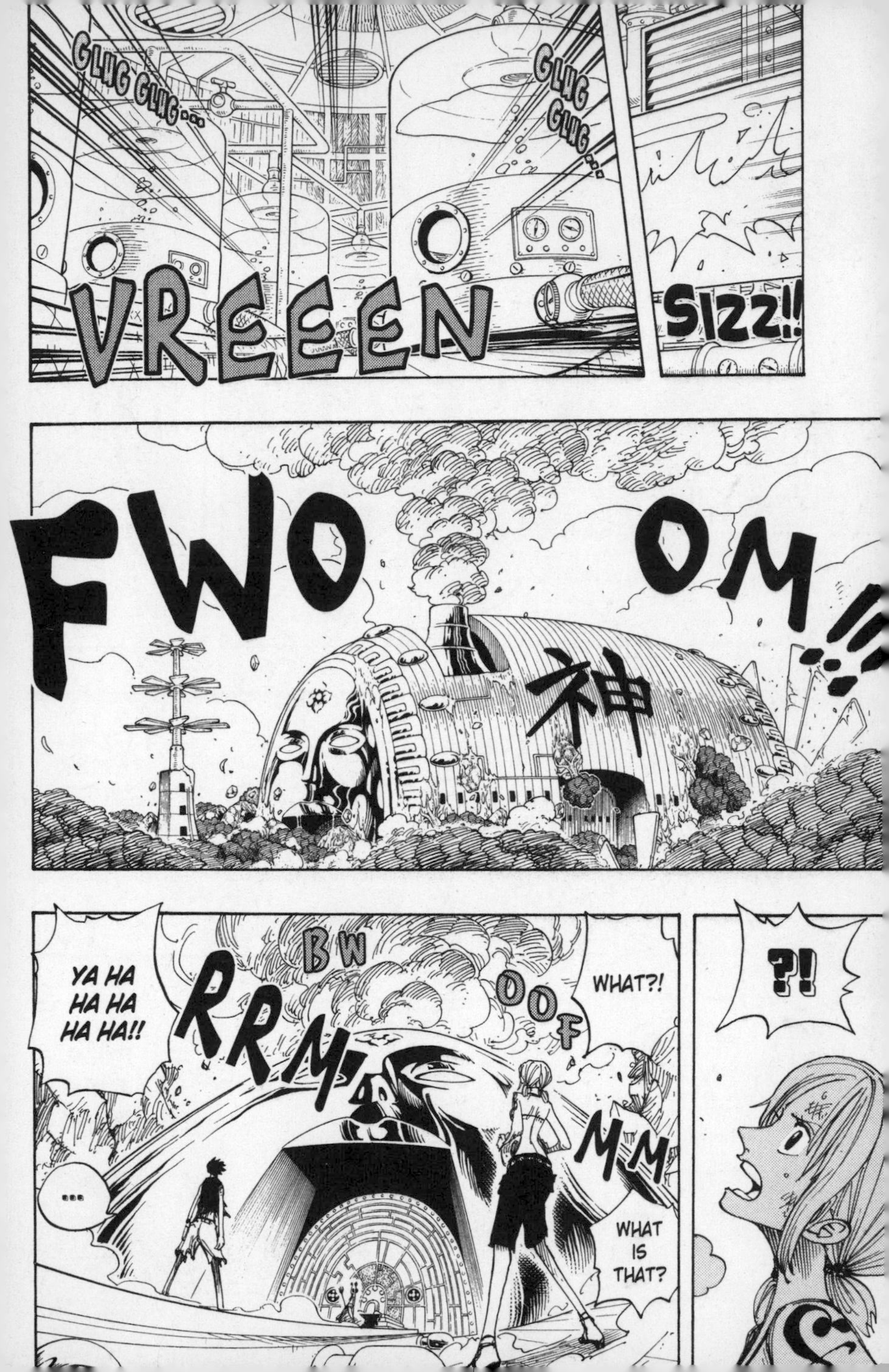
SIZZ!!
GLUG GLUG...
GLUG GLUG...
VREEEN
FWOOM!!
?!
WHAT?!
BWOOF
YA HA HA HA HA HA!!
RRMMM
WHAT IS THAT?
...

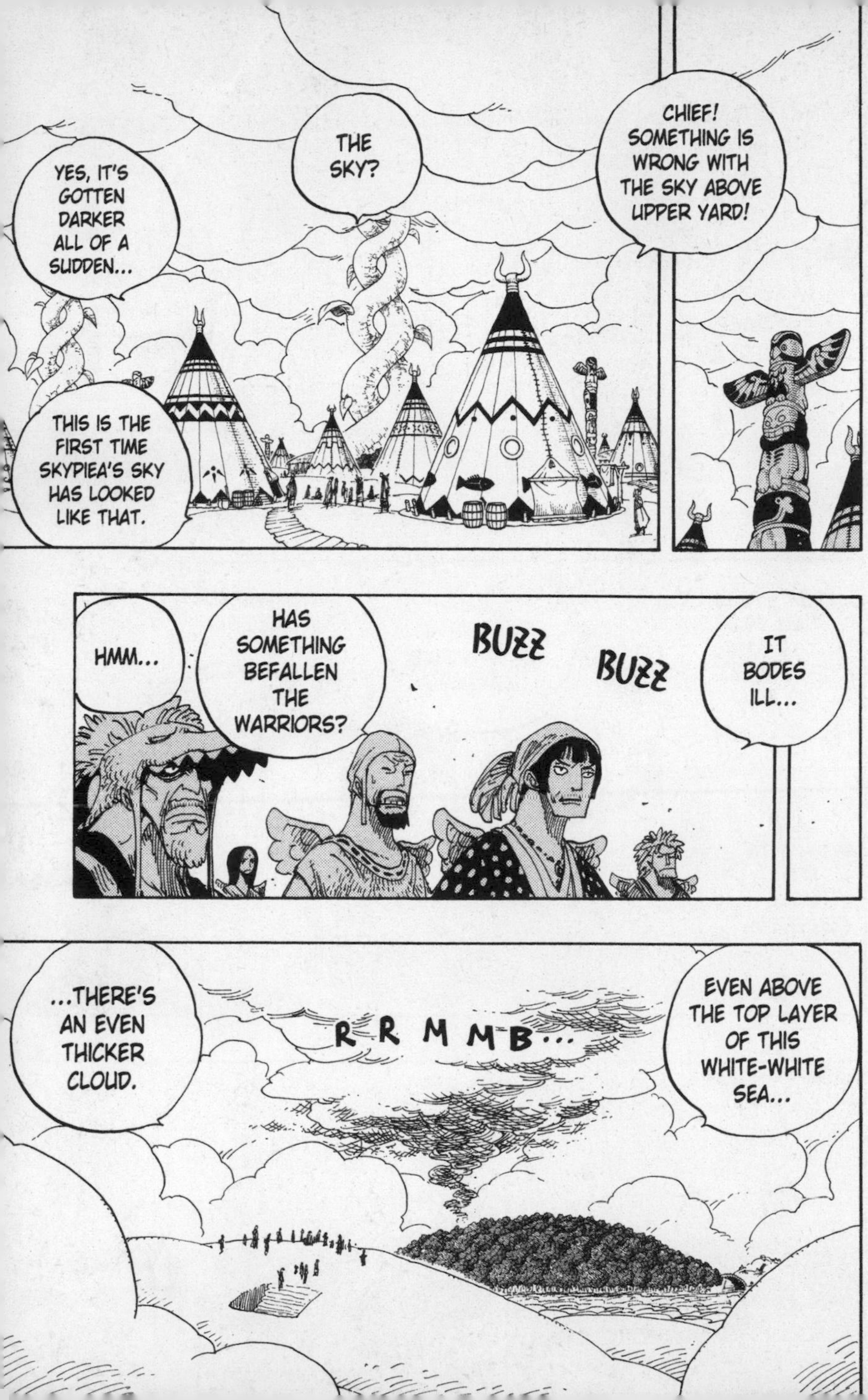
CHIEF! SOMETHING IS WRONG WITH THE SKY ABOVE UPPER YARD!
THE SKY?
YES, IT'S GOTTEN DARKER ALL OF A SUDDEN...
THIS IS THE FIRST TIME SKYPIEA'S SKY HAS LOOKED LIKE THAT.
IT BODES ILL...
BUZZ BUZZ
HAS SOMETHING BEFALLEN THE WARRIORS?
HMM...
EVEN ABOVE THE TOP LAYER OF THIS WHITE-WHITE SEA...
RRMMB...
...THERE'S AN EVEN THICKER CLOUD.

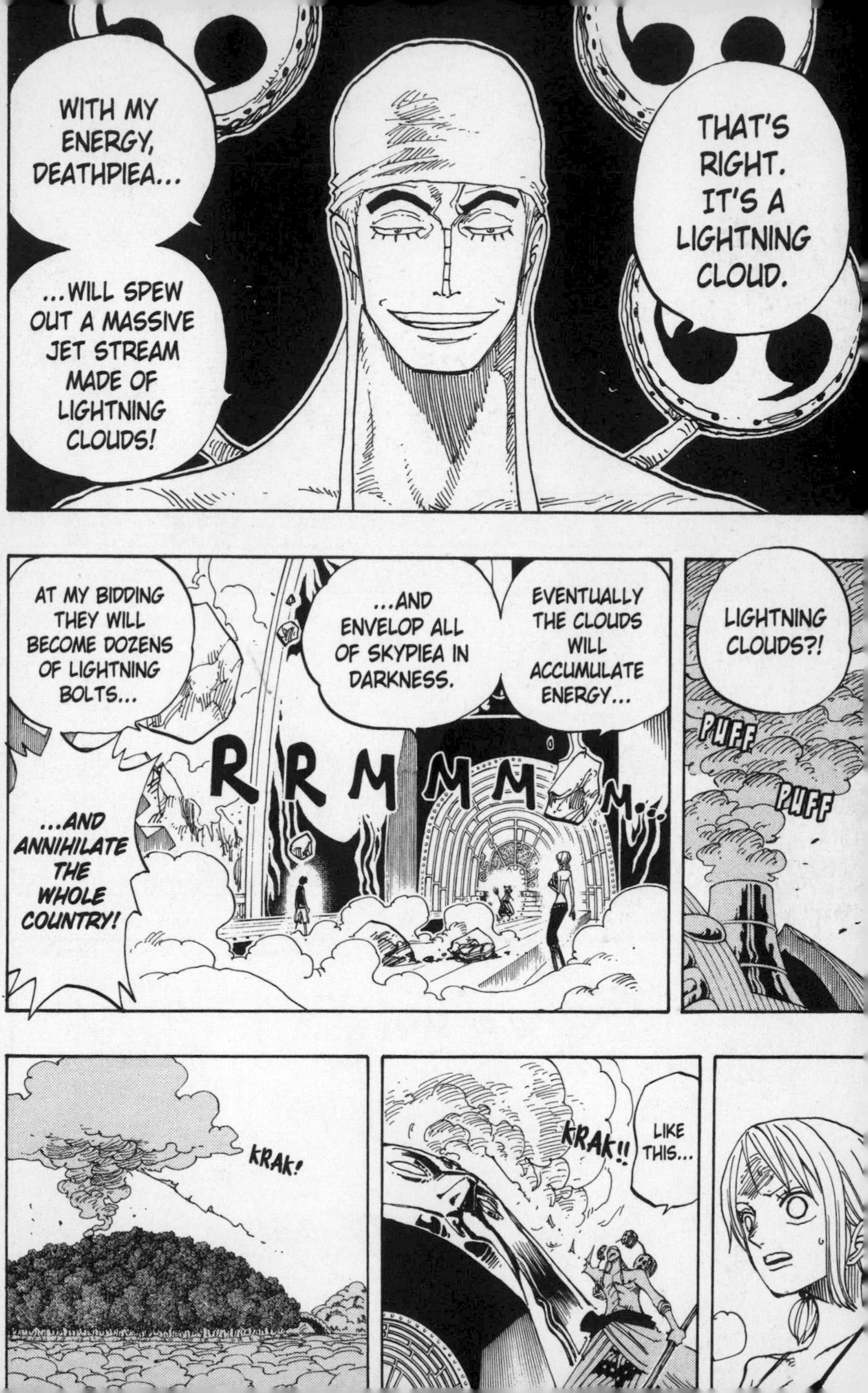
THAT'S RIGHT. IT'S A LIGHTNING CLOUD.
WITH MY ENERGY, DEATHPIEA...
...WILL SPEW OUT A MASSIVE JET STREAM MADE OF LIGHTNING CLOUDS!
LIGHTNING CLOUDS?!
PUFF
PUFF
EVENTUALLY THE CLOUDS WILL ACCUMULATE ENERGY...
...AND ENVELOP ALL OF SKYPIEA IN DARKNESS.
AT MY BIDDING THEY WILL BECOME DOZENS OF LIGHTNING BOLTS...
...AND ANNIHILATE THE WHOLE COUNTRY!
RRMMMMM...
LIKE THIS...
KRAK!!
KRAK!

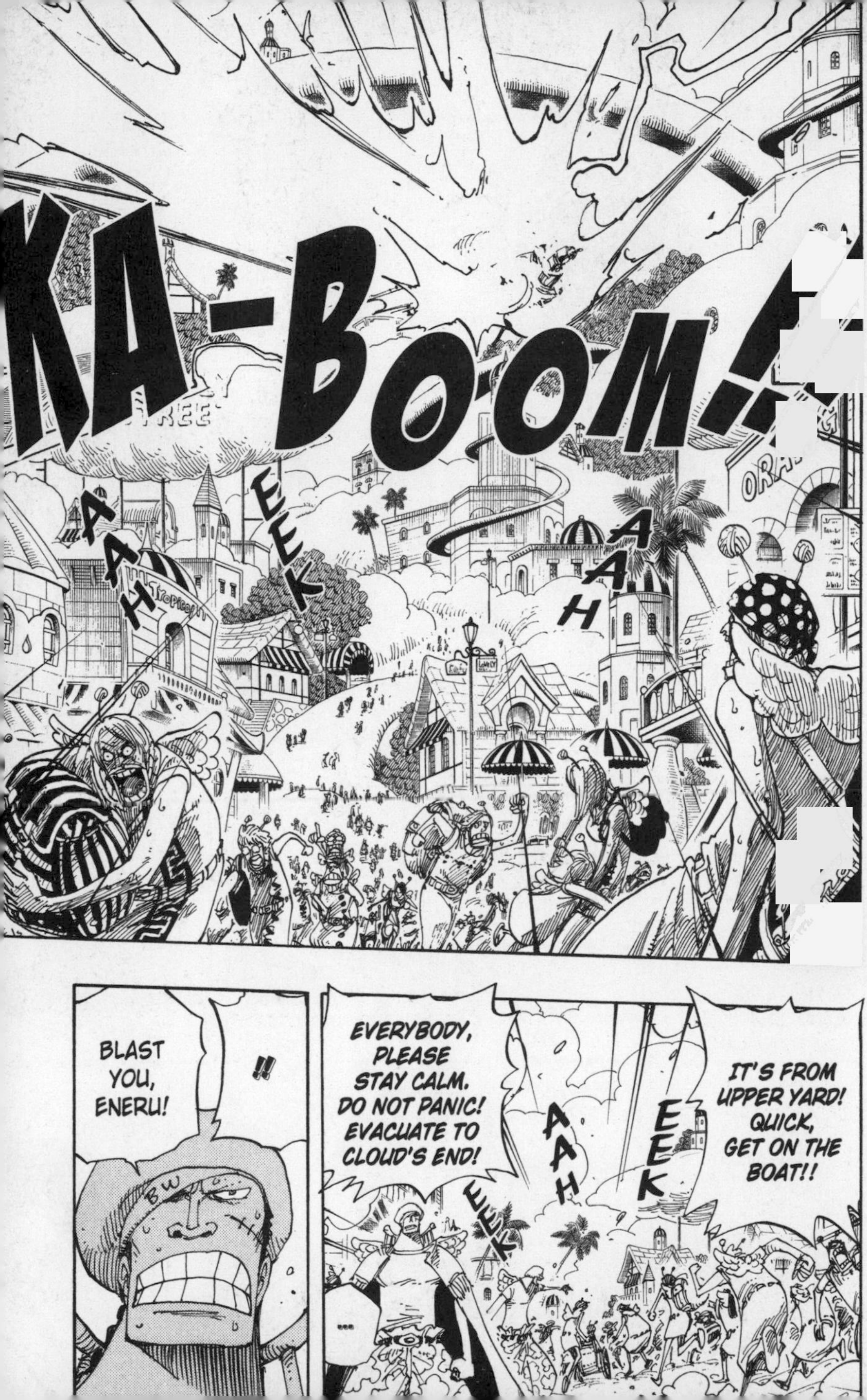
KA-BOOM!!
AAH
EEEK
AAH
IT'S FROM UPPER YARD! QUICK, GET ON THE BOAT!!
EEEK
AAH
EVERYBODY, PLEASE STAY CALM. DO NOT PANIC! EVACUATE TO CLOUD'S END!
EEEK
!!
BLAST YOU, ENERU!

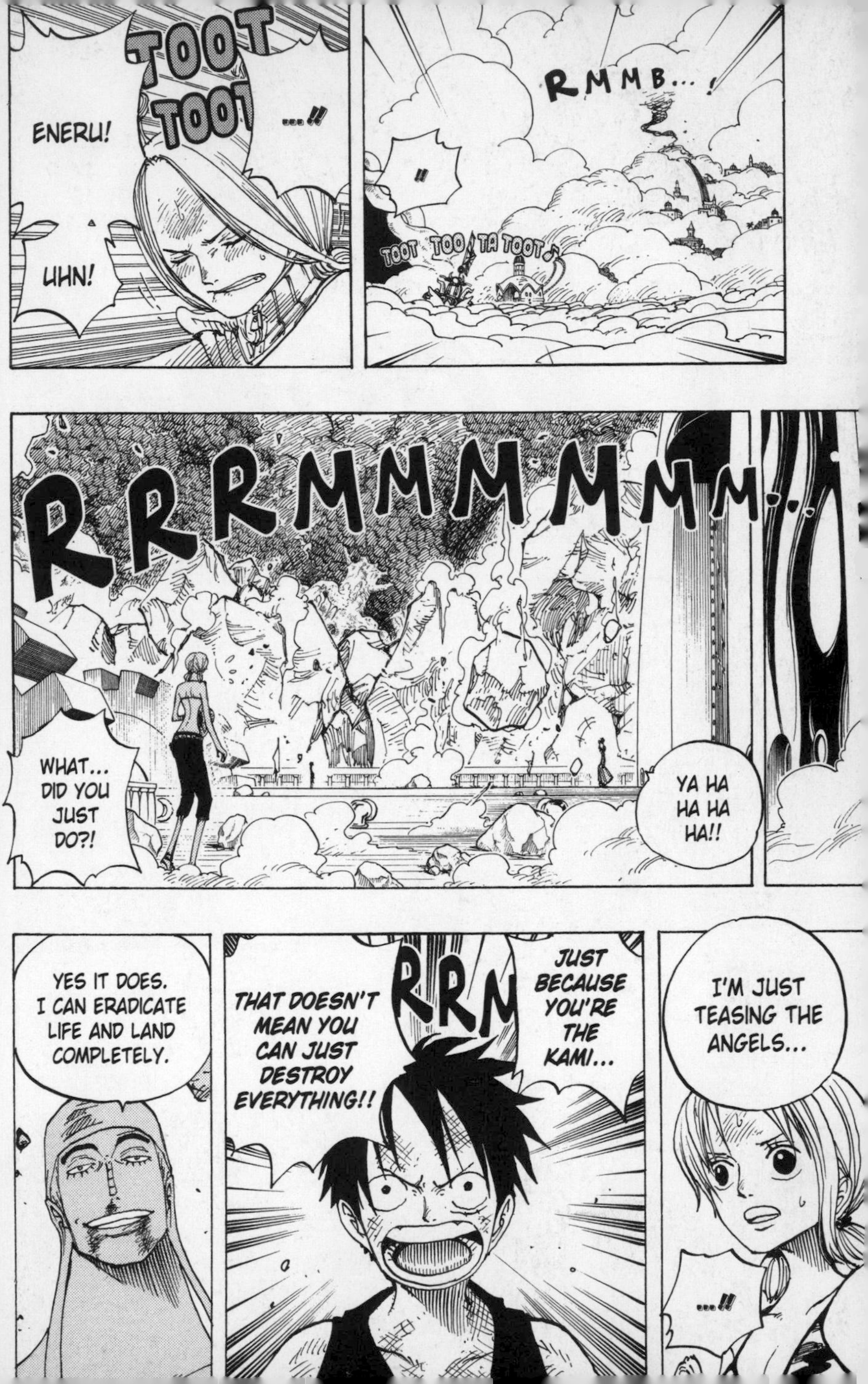
RMMB...!
!!
TOOT TOO TA TOOT♪
TOOT TOOT...!!
ENERU!
UHN!
RRRMMMMMMM...
YA HA HA HA HA!!
WHAT... DID YOU JUST DO?!
I'M JUST TEASING THE ANGELS...
...!!
JUST BECAUSE YOU'RE THE KAMI...
RRN
THAT DOESN'T MEAN YOU CAN JUST DESTROY EVERYTHING!!
YES IT DOES. I CAN ERADICATE LIFE AND LAND COMPLETELY.

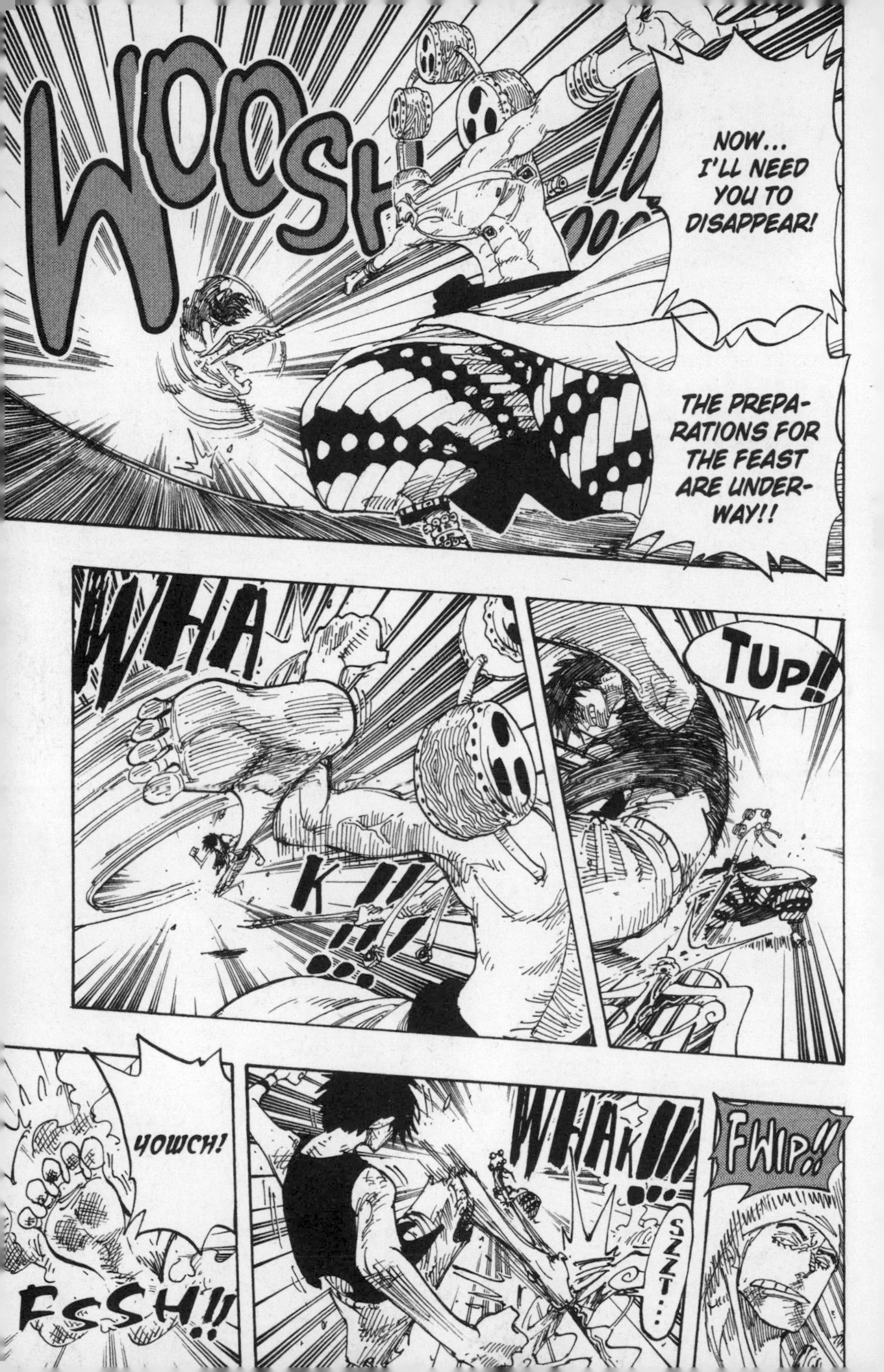
NOW... I'LL NEED YOU TO DISAPPEAR!
THE PREPARATIONS FOR THE FEAST ARE UNDERWAY!!
WOOSH
TUP!!
WHAK!!
FWIP!!
WHAK!!!
SZZT...
YOWCH!
FSSH!!

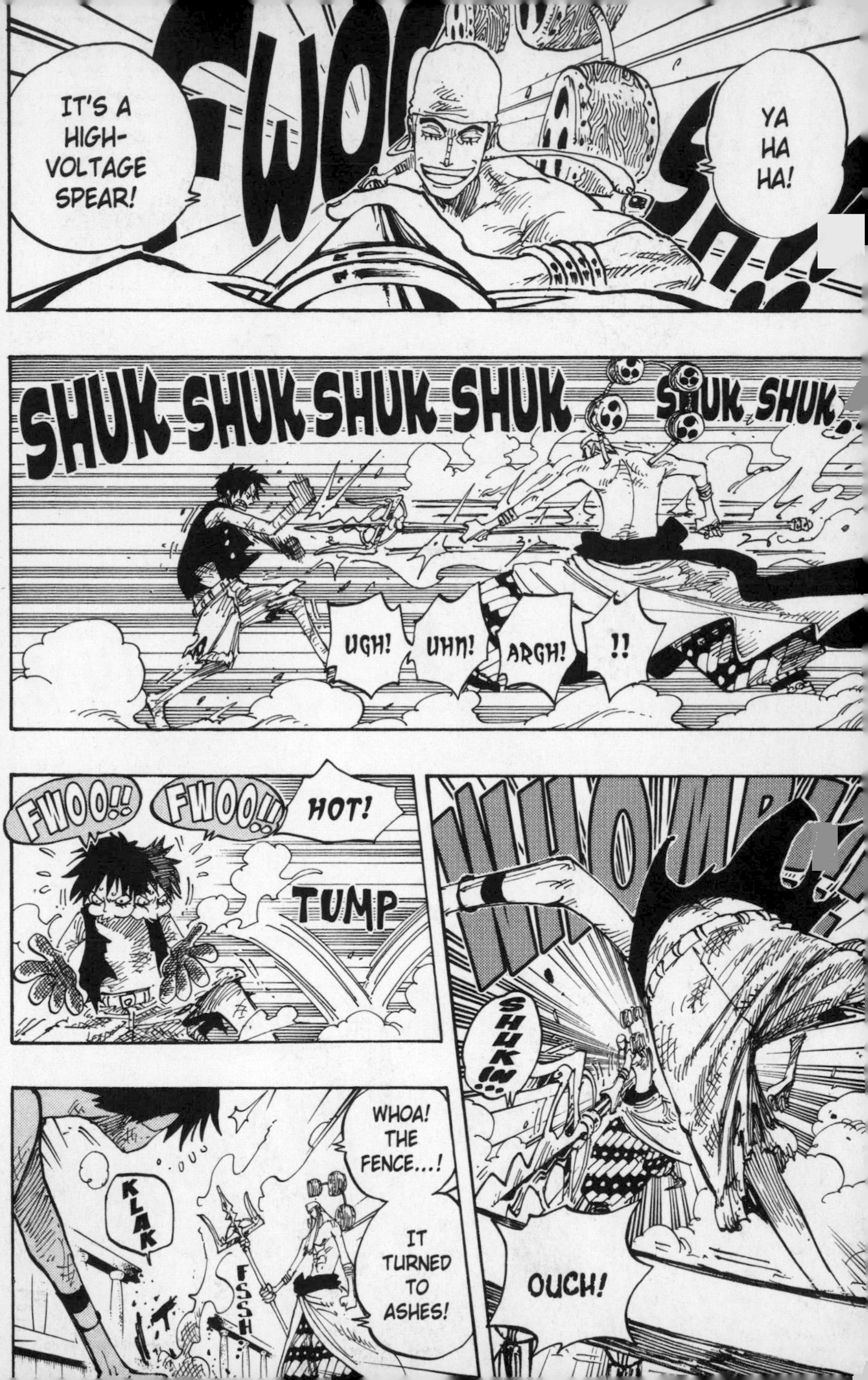

YA HA HA!
IT'S A HIGH-VOLTAGE SPEAR!
SHUK SHUK SHUK SHUK SHUK SHUK
!!
ARGH!
UHN!
UGH!
SHUKN!!
OUCH!
HOT!
FWOO!!
FWOO!!
TUMP
WHOA! THE FENCE...!
IT TURNED TO ASHES!
FSSSH...
KLAK

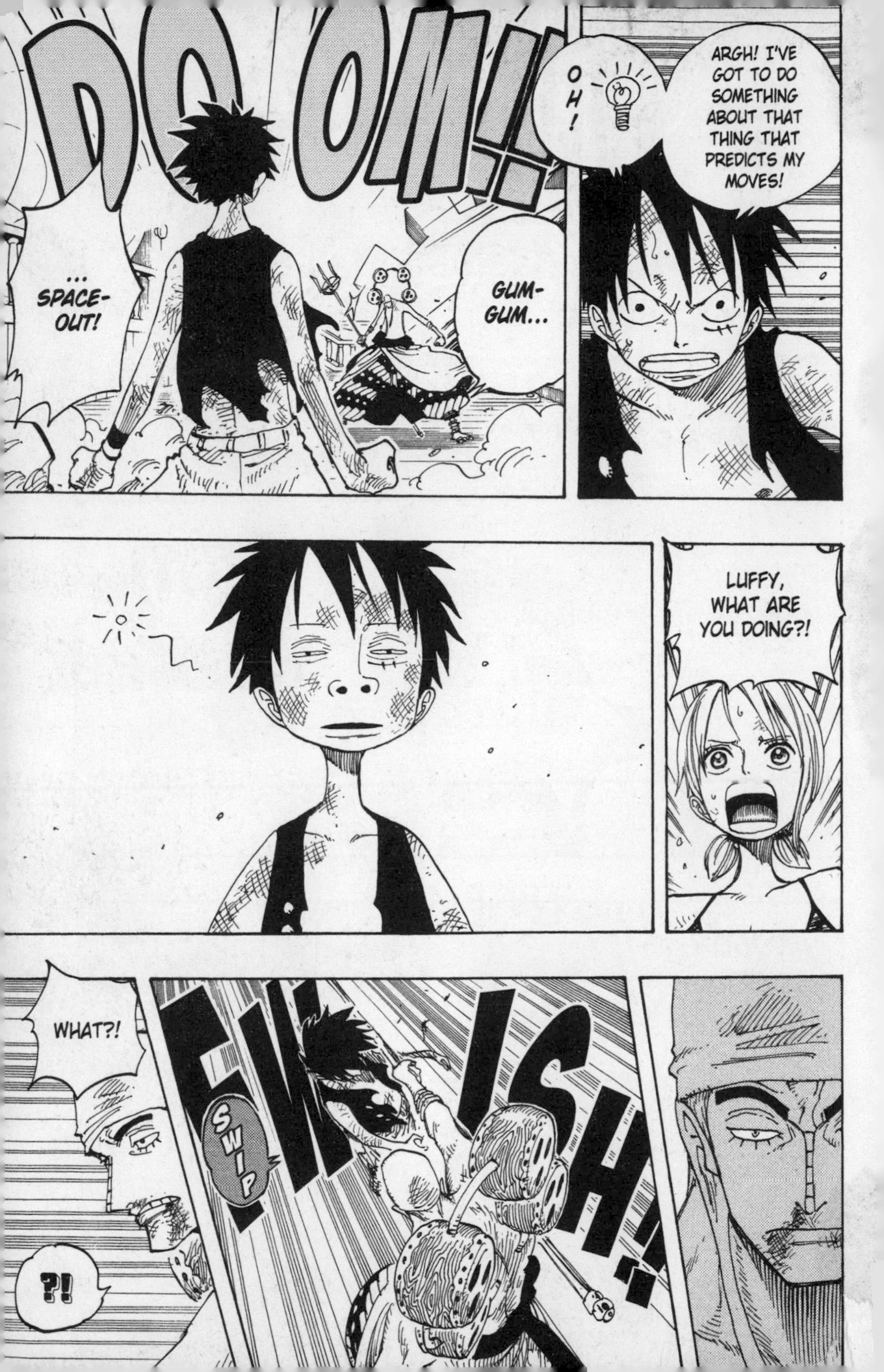
ARGH! I'VE GOT TO DO SOMETHING ABOUT THAT THING THAT PREDICTS MY MOVES!
OH!
DOOM!!
GUM-GUM...
... SPACE-OUT!
LUFFY, WHAT ARE YOU DOING?!
FWISH!!
SWIP
WHAT?!
?!

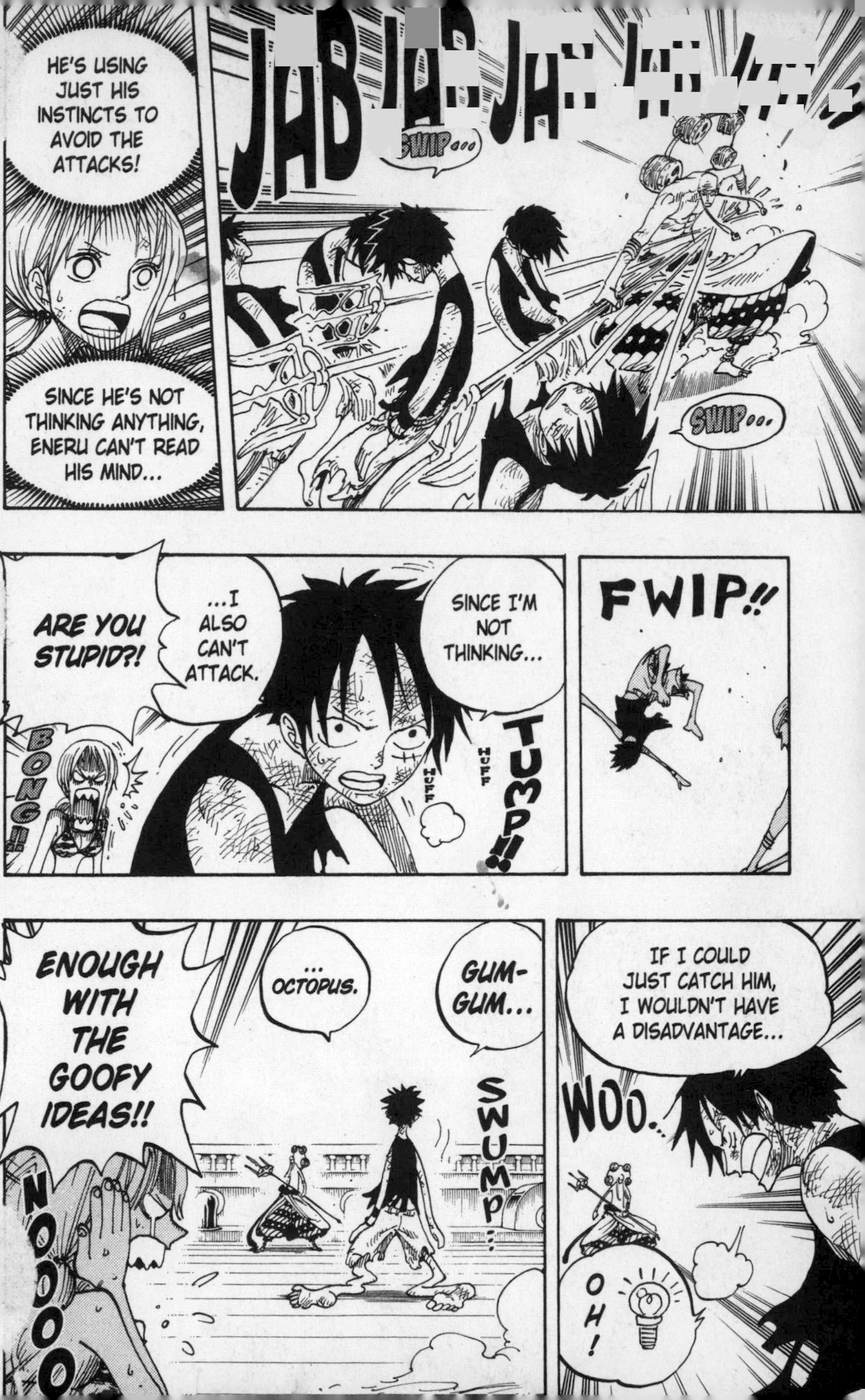
JAB JAB
SWIP...
SWIP...
HE'S USING JUST HIS INSTINCTS TO AVOID THE ATTACKS!
SINCE HE'S NOT THINKING ANYTHING, ENERU CAN'T READ HIS MIND...
FWIP!!
SINCE I'M NOT THINKING...
HUFF HUFF
TUMP!!
...I ALSO CAN'T ATTACK.
ARE YOU STUPID?!
BONG!!
IF I COULD JUST CATCH HIM, I WOULDN'T HAVE A DISADVANTAGE...
WOO...
OH!
GUM-GUM...
SWUMP!!
...OCTOPUS.
ENOUGH WITH THE GOOFY IDEAS!!
NOOOO

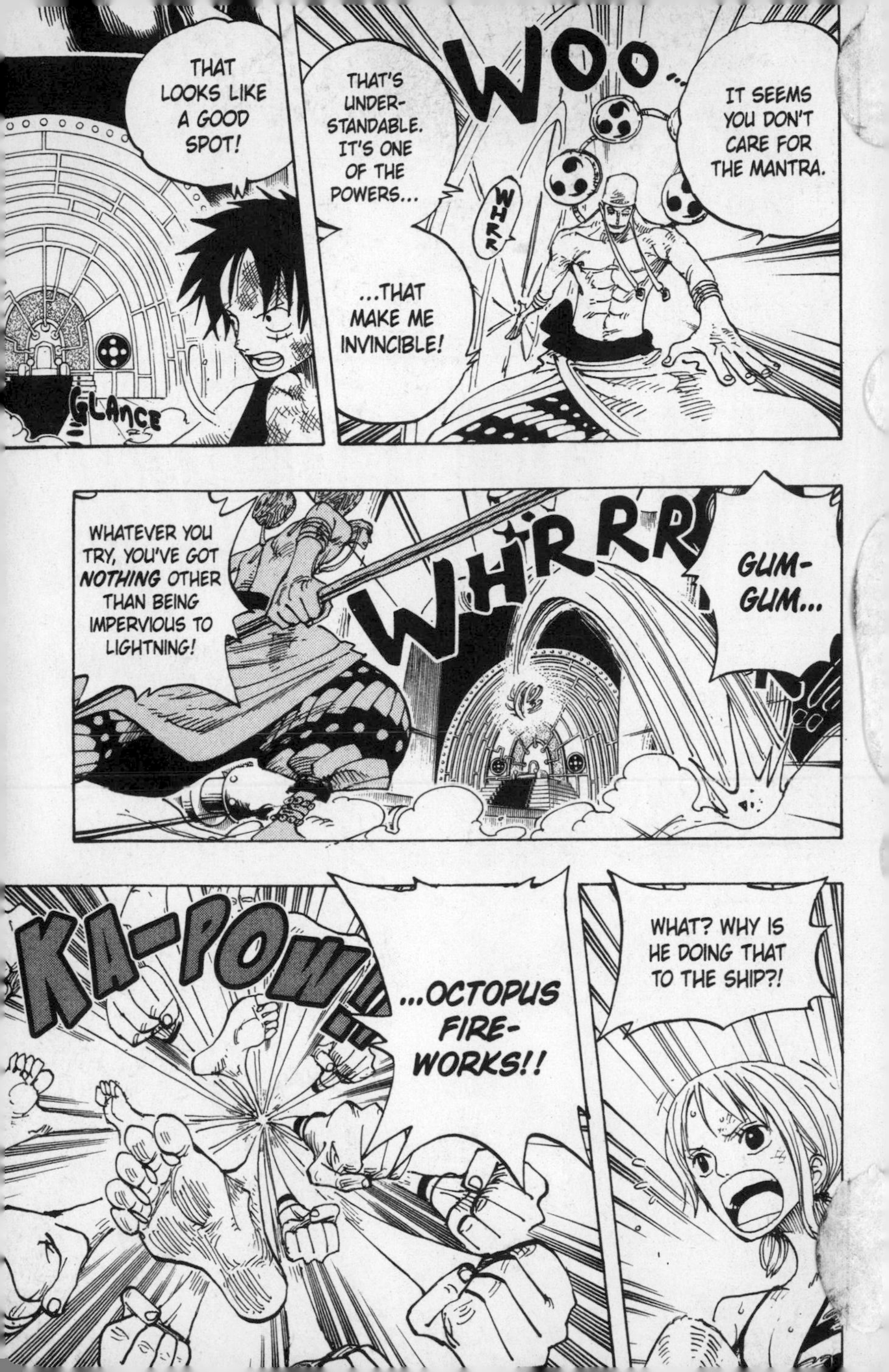
WOO...
IT SEEMS YOU DON'T CARE FOR THE MANTRA.
WHRR
THAT'S UNDER-STANDABLE. IT'S ONE OF THE POWERS...
...THAT MAKE ME INVINCIBLE!
THAT LOOKS LIKE A GOOD SPOT!
GLANCE
GUM-GUM...
WHRRR
WHATEVER YOU TRY, YOU'VE GOT *NOTHING* OTHER THAN BEING IMPERVIOUS TO LIGHTNING!
WHAT? WHY IS HE DOING THAT TO THE SHIP?!
...OCTOPUS FIRE-WORKS!!
KA-POW!!

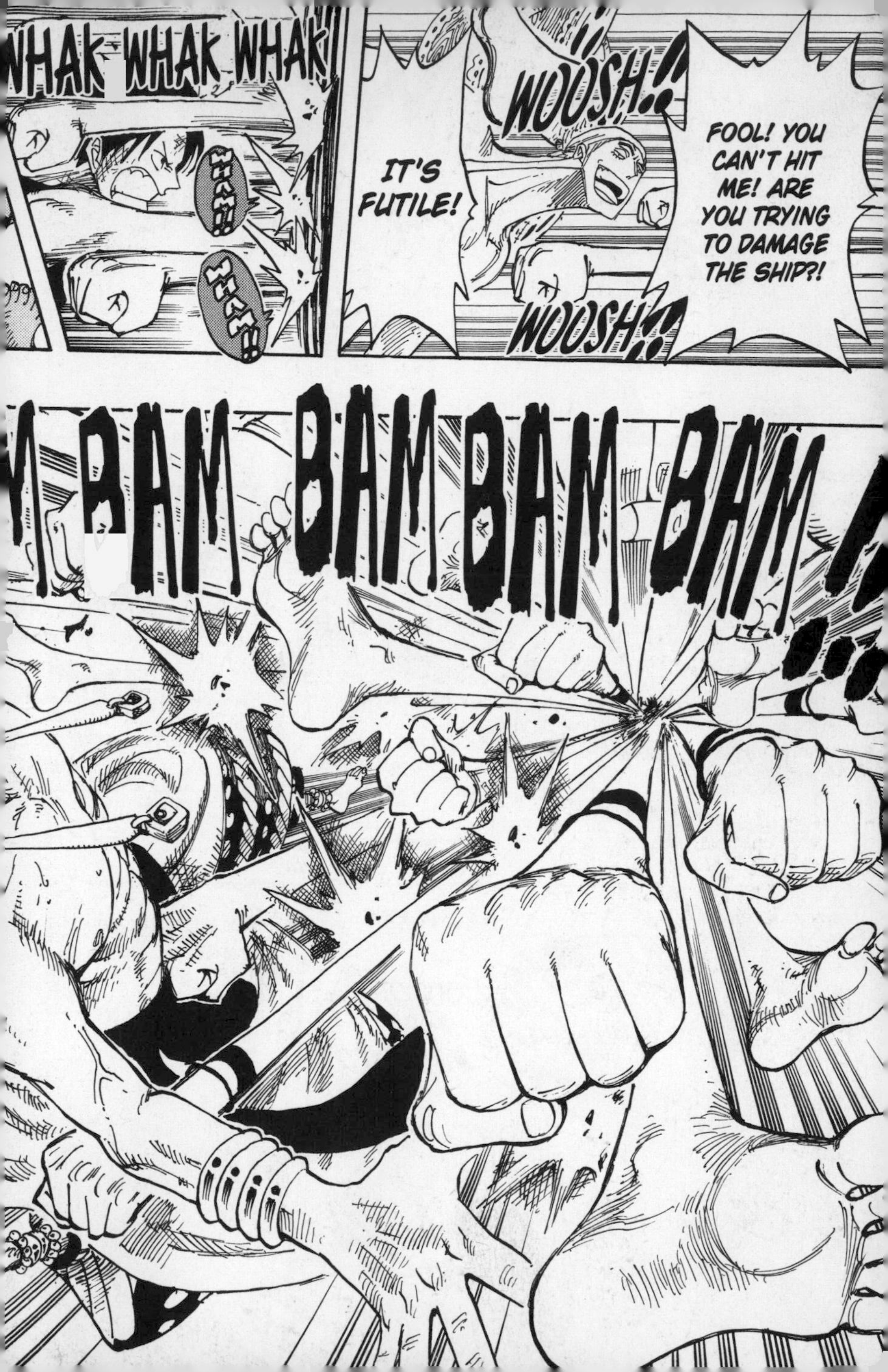
WOOSH!!
FOOL! YOU CAN'T HIT ME! ARE YOU TRYING TO DAMAGE THE SHIP?!
IT'S FUTILE!
WOOSH!!
WHAK WHAK WHAK
WHAM!!
BAM BAM BAM BAM BAM!!

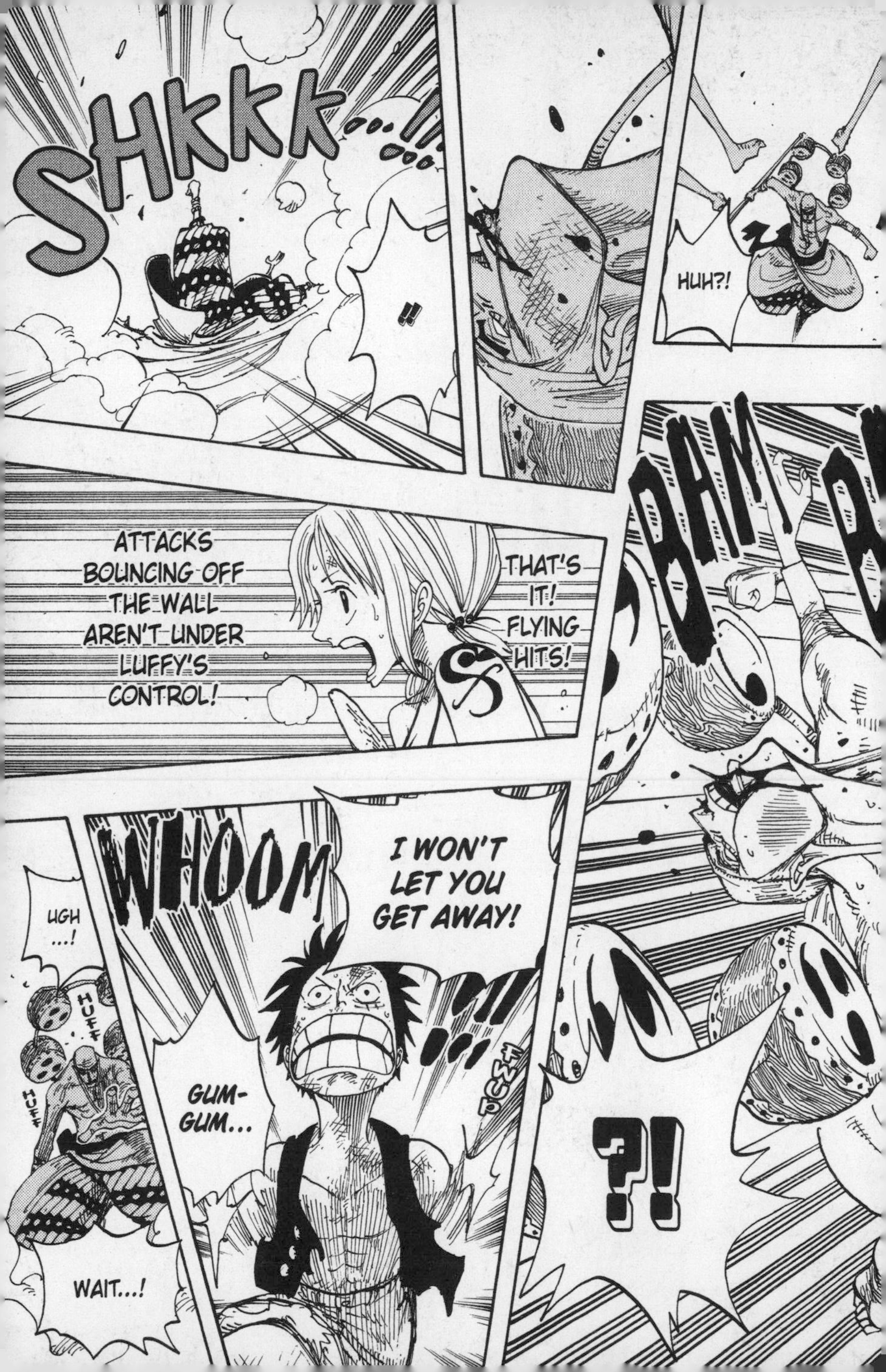
HUH?!
SHKKK...!!
!!
BAM B
?!
THAT'S IT! FLYING HITS!
ATTACKS BOUNCING OFF THE WALL AREN'T UNDER LUFFY'S CONTROL!
I WON'T LET YOU GET AWAY!
WHOOM
FWUP
GUM-GUM...
UGH ...!
HUFF
HUFF
WAIT...!

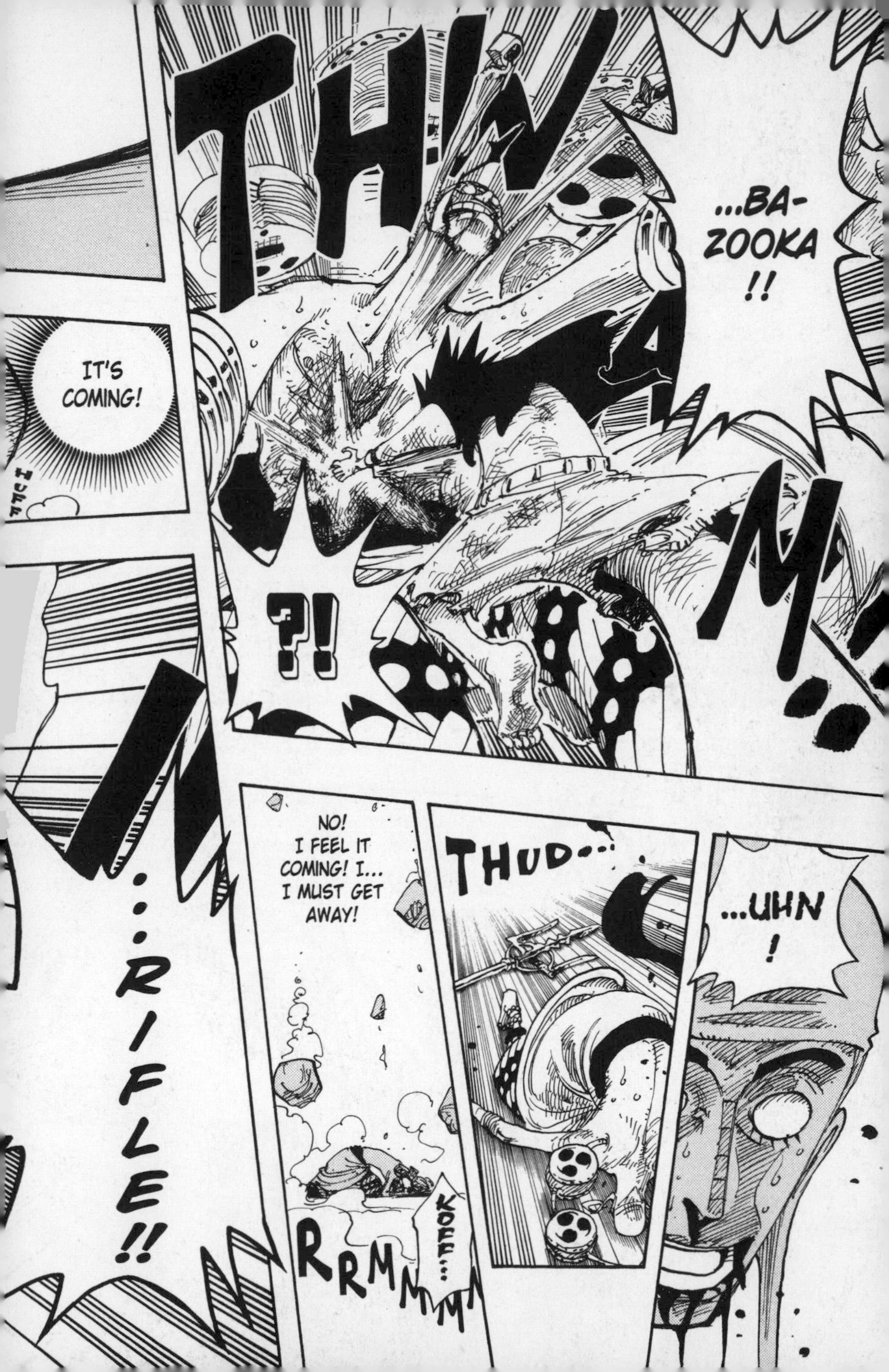

...BA-ZOOKA!!
THWAMM
?!
IT'S COMING!
HUFF
...UHN!
THUD...
NO! I FEEL IT COMING! I... I MUST GET AWAY!
KOFF...
RRMMMM
...RIFLE!!

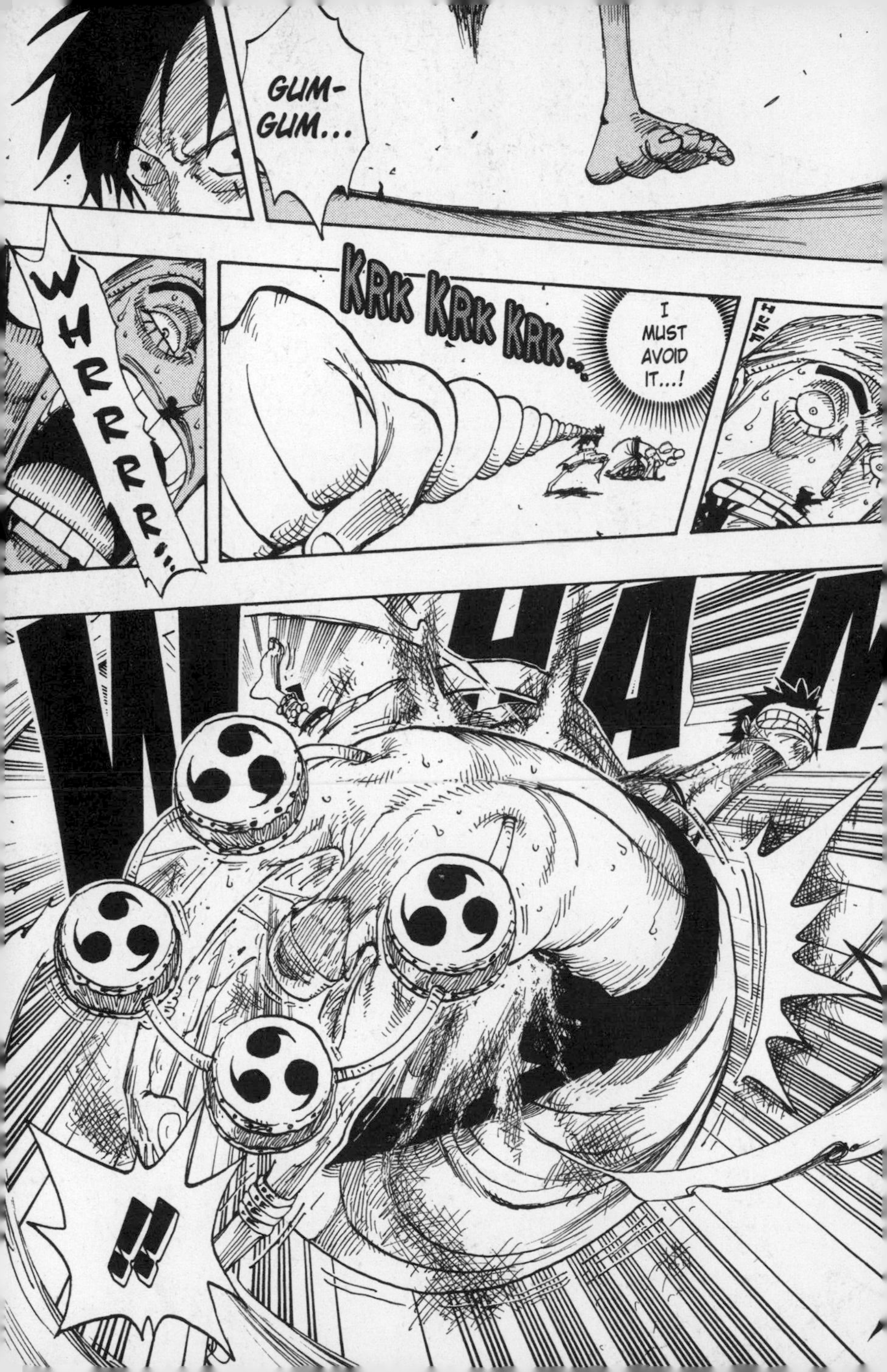
GUM-GUM...
HUFF
I MUST AVOID IT...!
KRK KRK KRK...
WHRRRR!!
!!

Chapter 282:
DESIRE

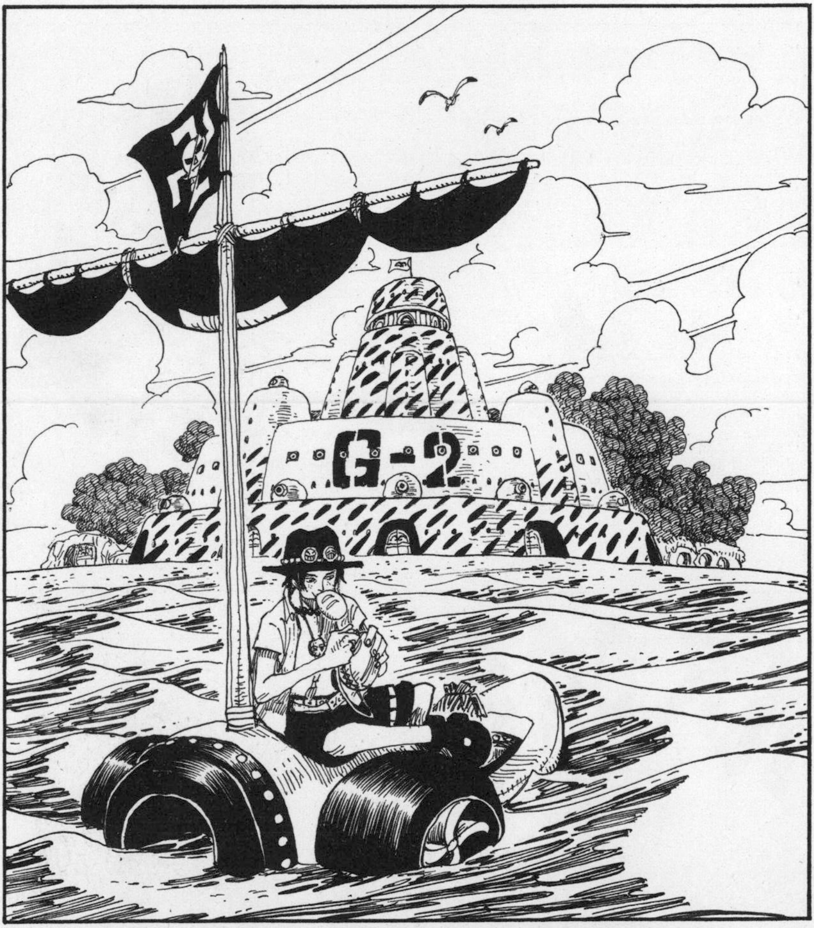
G-2

ACE'S GREAT SEARCH FOR BLACKBEARD, VOL. 10:
"GRAND LINE, NAVY BASE G-2"

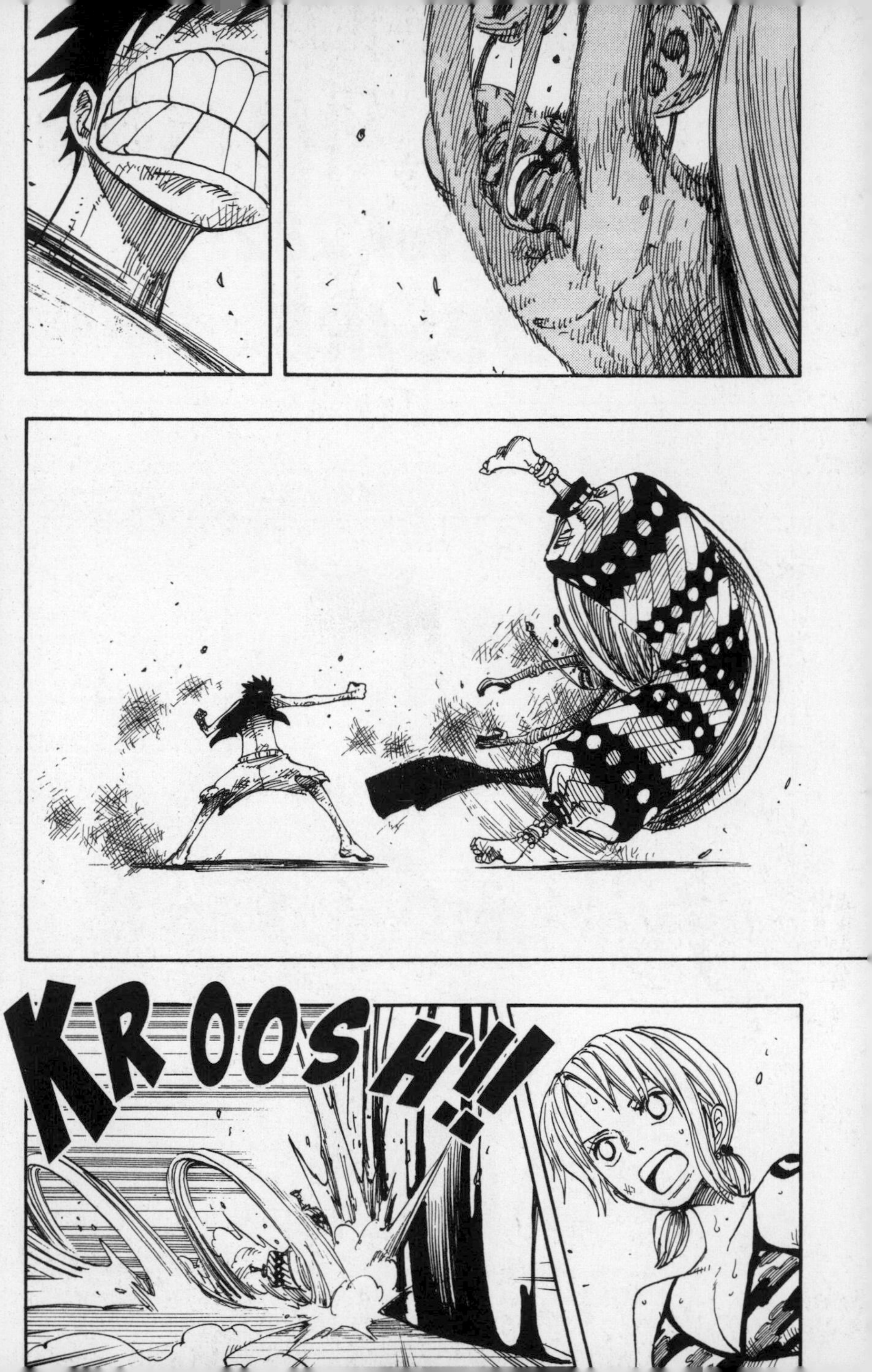
KROOSH!!

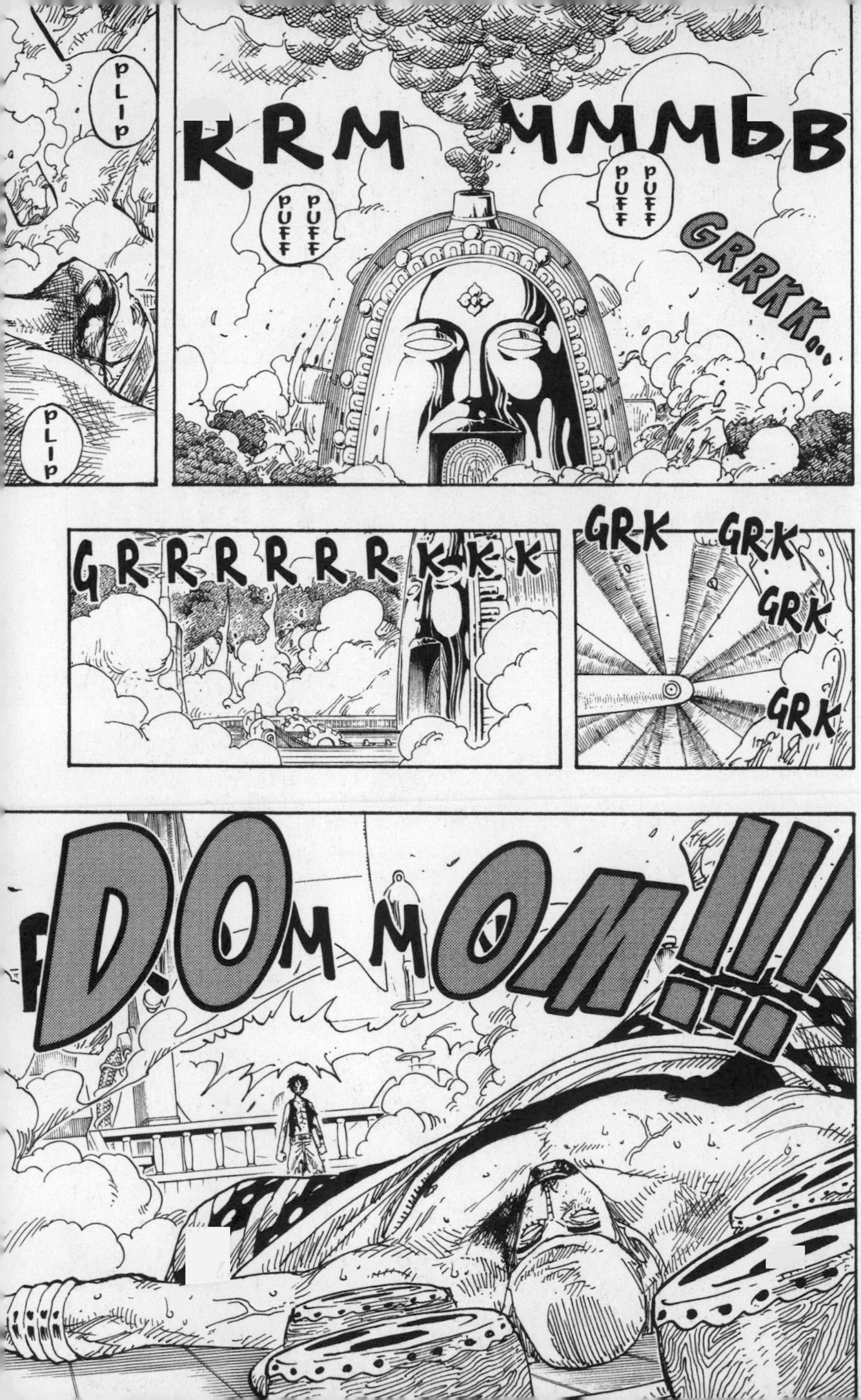

KRM MMMBB
PUFF PUFF
GRRKK...
PUFF PUFF
PLIP
PLIP
GRK GRK
GRK
GRK
GRRRRRRKKK
DOM MOM!!!

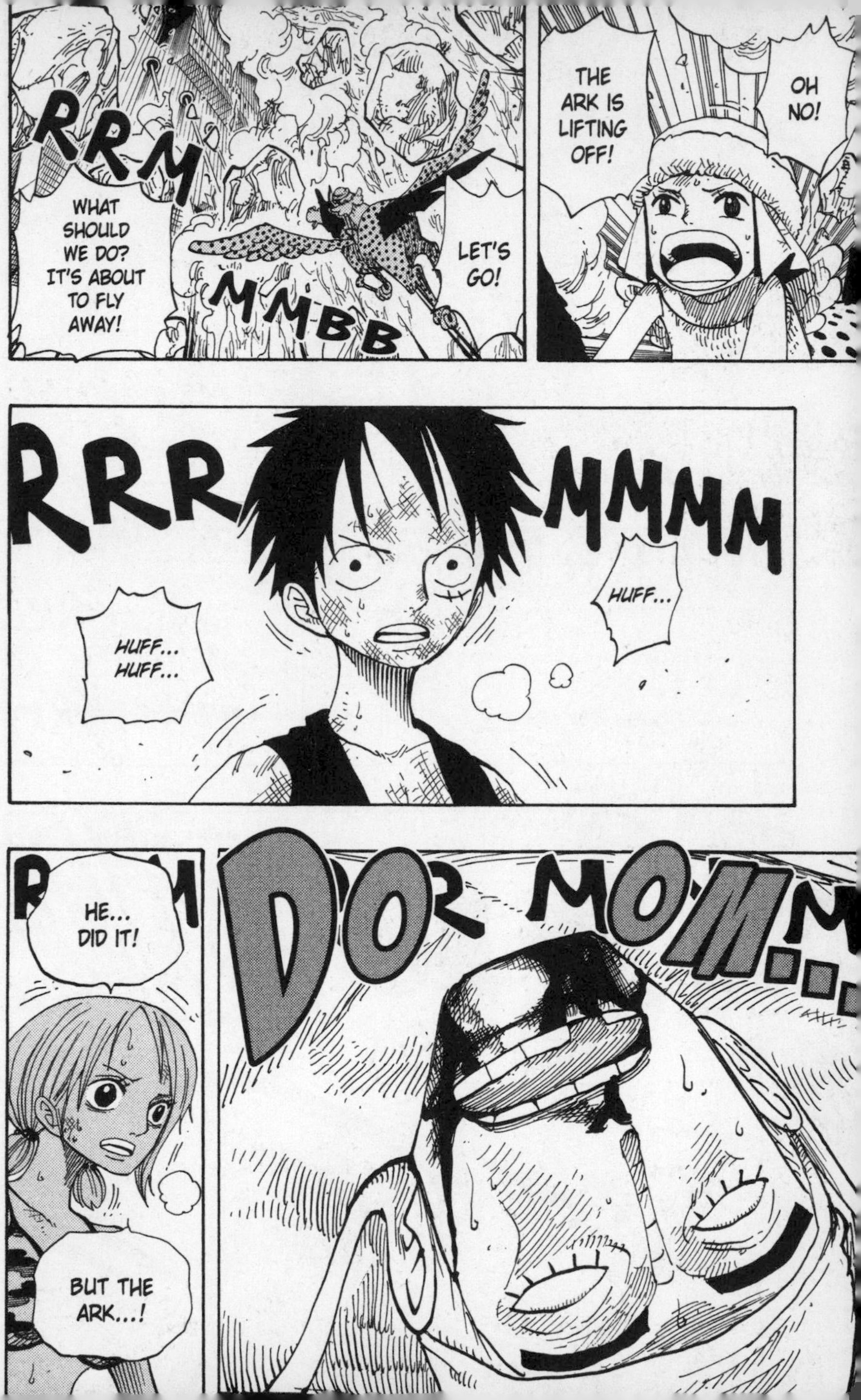
OH NO!
THE ARK IS LIFTING OFF!
RRRM
LET'S GO!
WHAT SHOULD WE DO? IT'S ABOUT TO FLY AWAY!
MMBB
RRRMMMMM
HUFF...
HUFF... HUFF...
DOR MOMM...
HE... DID IT!
BUT THE ARK...!

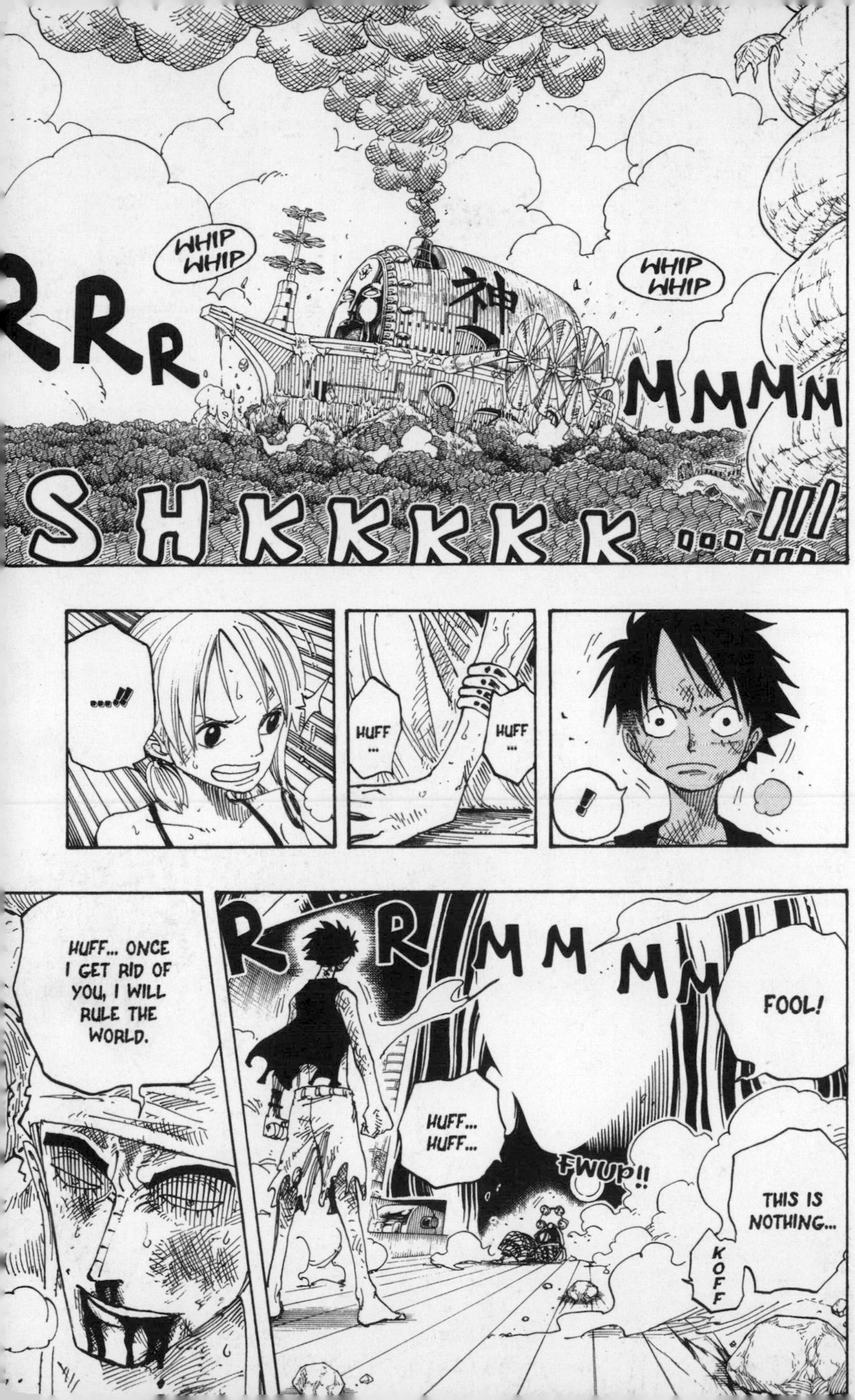
WHIP WHIP
WHIP WHIP
RRRMMMM
SHKKKKK...!!!
!
HUFF...
HUFF...
...!!
RRMMMM
FOOL!
THIS IS NOTHING...
KOFF
FWUP!!
HUFF... HUFF...
HUFF... ONCE I GET RID OF YOU, I WILL RULE THE WORLD.

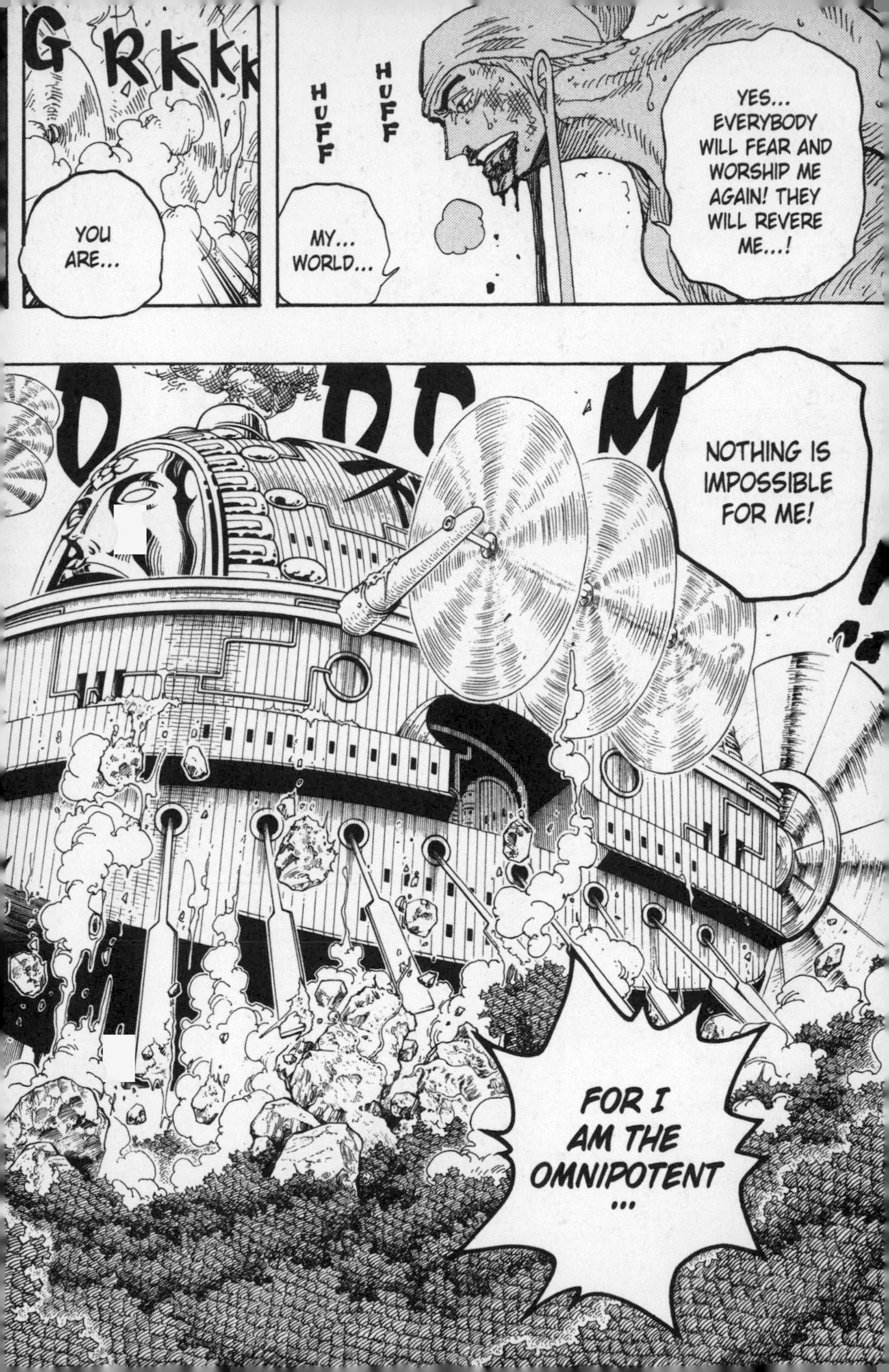
YES... EVERYBODY WILL FEAR AND WORSHIP ME AGAIN! THEY WILL REVERE ME...!
HUFF HUFF
MY... WORLD...
GRKK
YOU ARE...
NOTHING IS IMPOSSIBLE FOR ME!
FOR I AM THE OMNIPOTENT ...

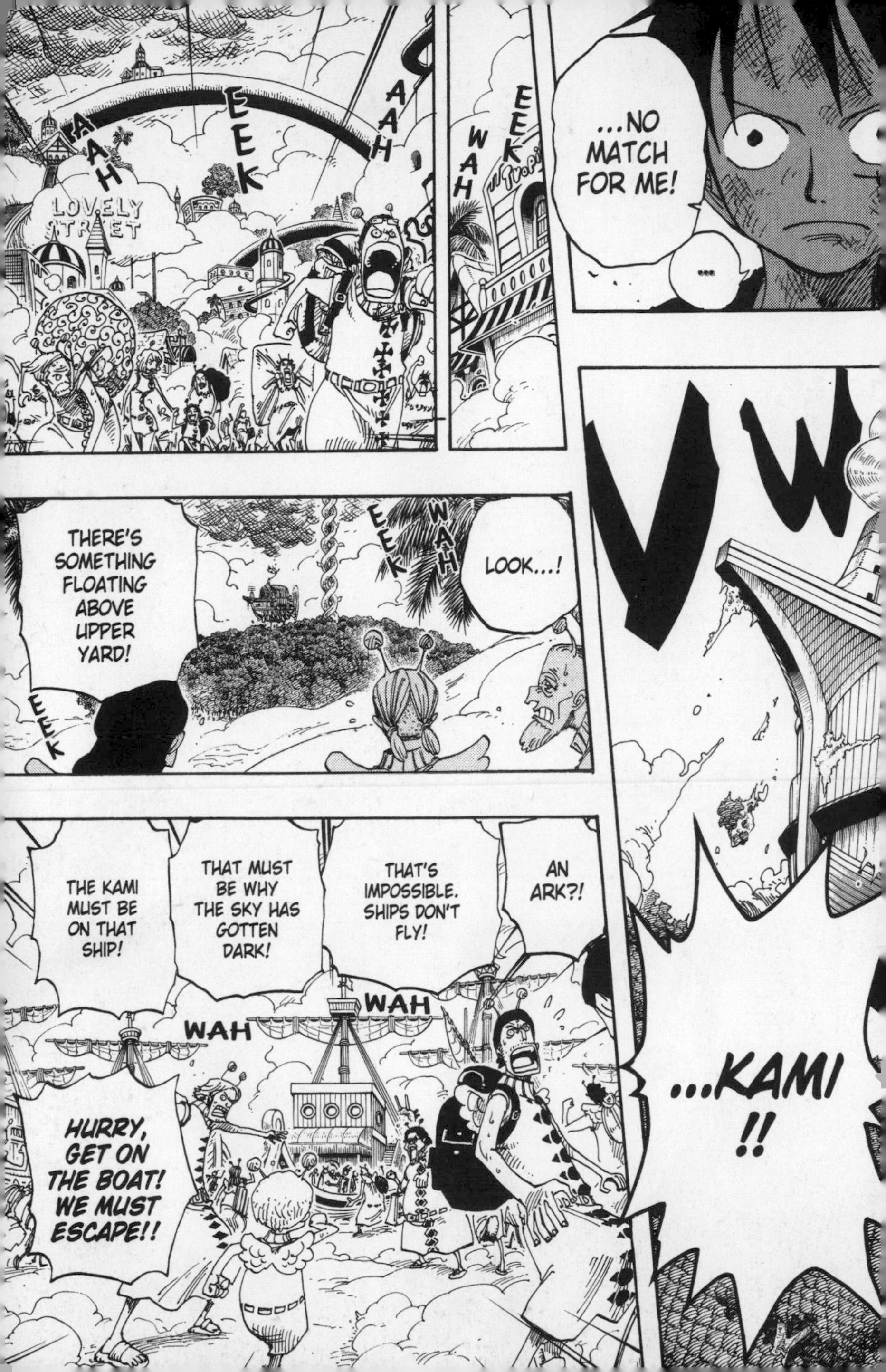
...NO MATCH FOR ME!
...
EEK
WAH
AAH
EEK
AAH
LOVELY
STR ET
VVW
...KAMI !!
WAH
EEK
LOOK...!
THERE'S SOMETHING FLOATING ABOVE UPPER YARD!
EEK
AN ARK?!
THAT'S IMPOSSIBLE. SHIPS DON'T FLY!
THAT MUST BE WHY THE SKY HAS GOTTEN DARK!
THE KAMI MUST BE ON THAT SHIP!
WAH
WAH
HURRY, GET ON THE BOAT! WE MUST ESCAPE!!

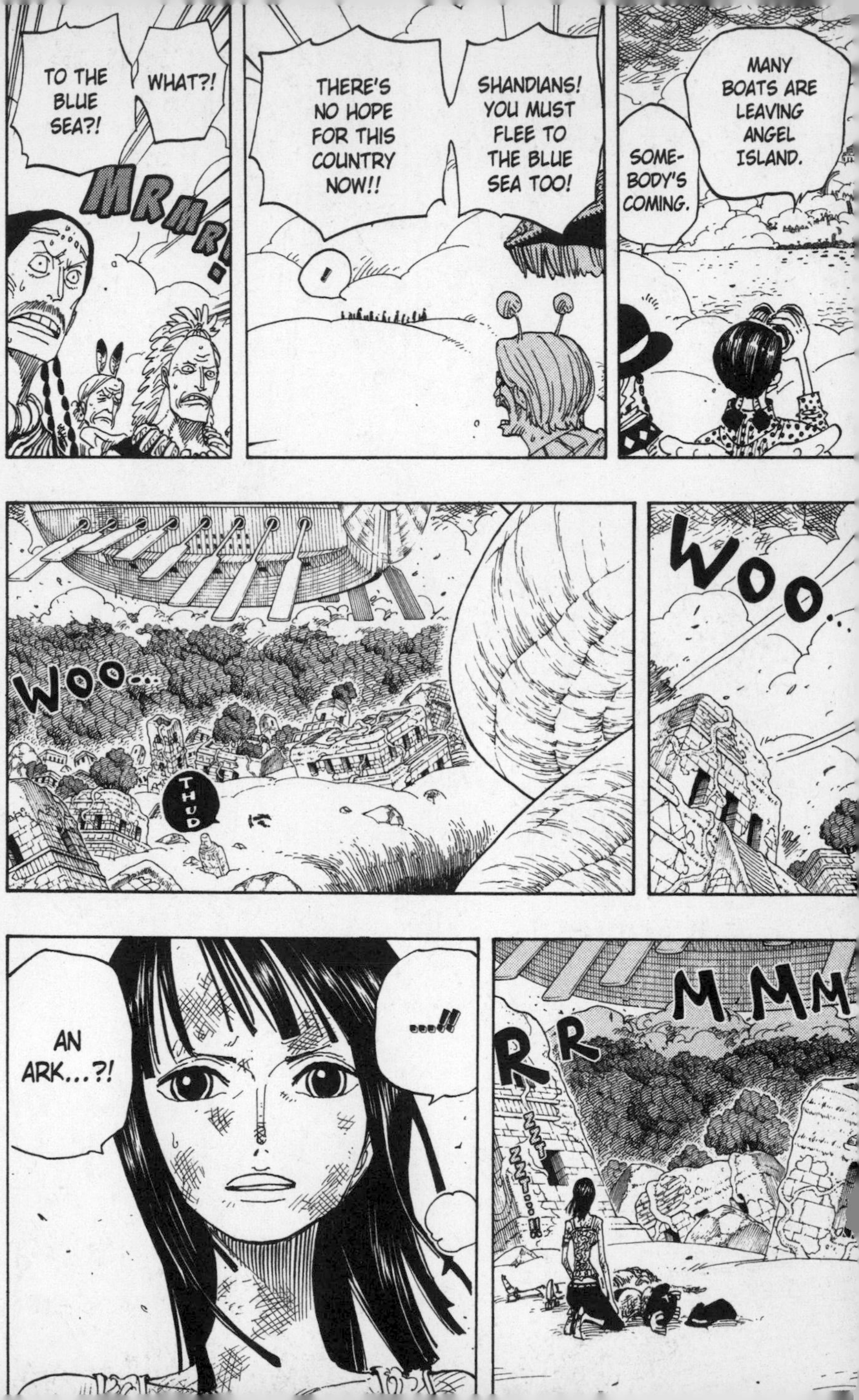
MANY BOATS ARE LEAVING ANGEL ISLAND.
SOME-BODY'S COMING.
SHANDIANS! YOU MUST FLEE TO THE BLUE SEA TOO!
THERE'S NO HOPE FOR THIS COUNTRY NOW!!
!
WHAT?!
TO THE BLUE SEA?!
MRMR
WOO...
WOO...
THUD
MMM
RR
ZZT
ZZT...!!
...!!
AN ARK...?!

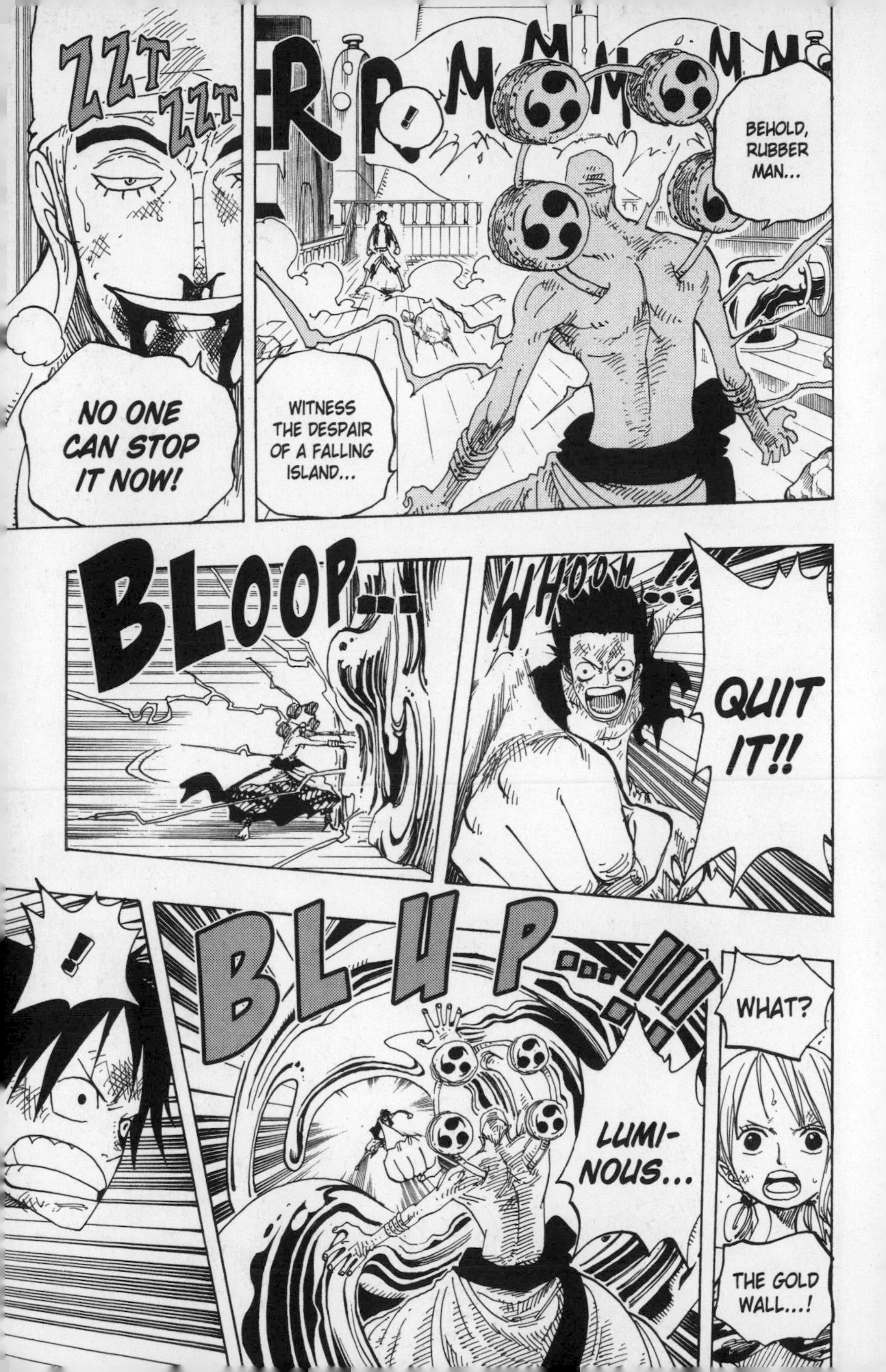
ERP! MMMMN
BEHOLD, RUBBER MAN...
WITNESS THE DESPAIR OF A FALLING ISLAND...
ZZT ZZT
NO ONE CAN STOP IT NOW!
WHOOM!!
QUIT IT!!
BLOOP...!
WHAT?
THE GOLD WALL...!
BLUP...!!!
LUMI-
NOUS...
!

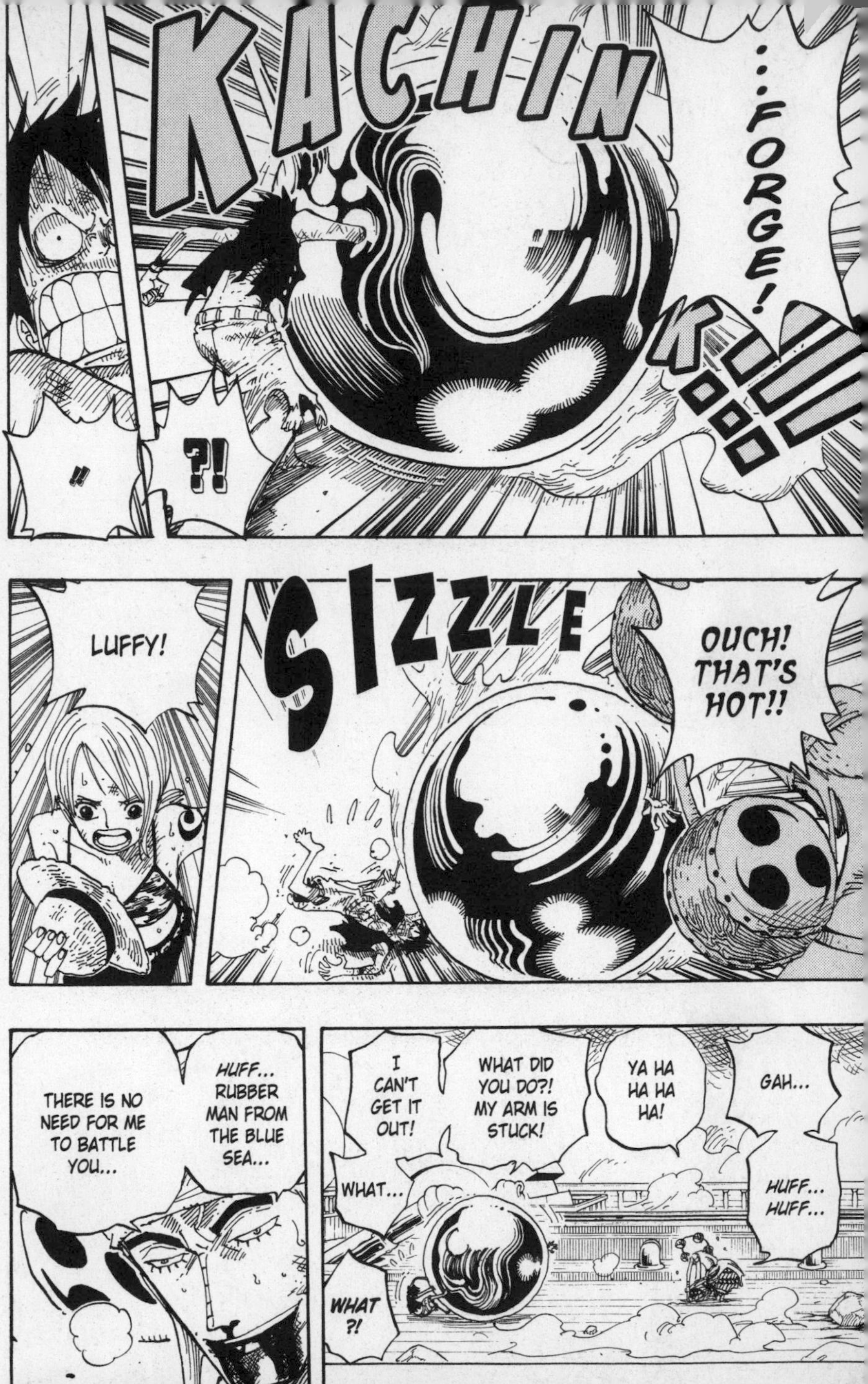
...FORGE!
KACHIN
?!
!!
OUCH! THAT'S HOT!!
SIZZLE
LUFFY!
GAH...
HUFF... HUFF...
YA HA HA HA HA!
WHAT DID YOU DO?! MY ARM IS STUCK!
I CAN'T GET IT OUT!
WHAT...
WHAT ?!
HUFF... RUBBER MAN FROM THE BLUE SEA...
THERE IS NO NEED FOR ME TO BATTLE YOU...

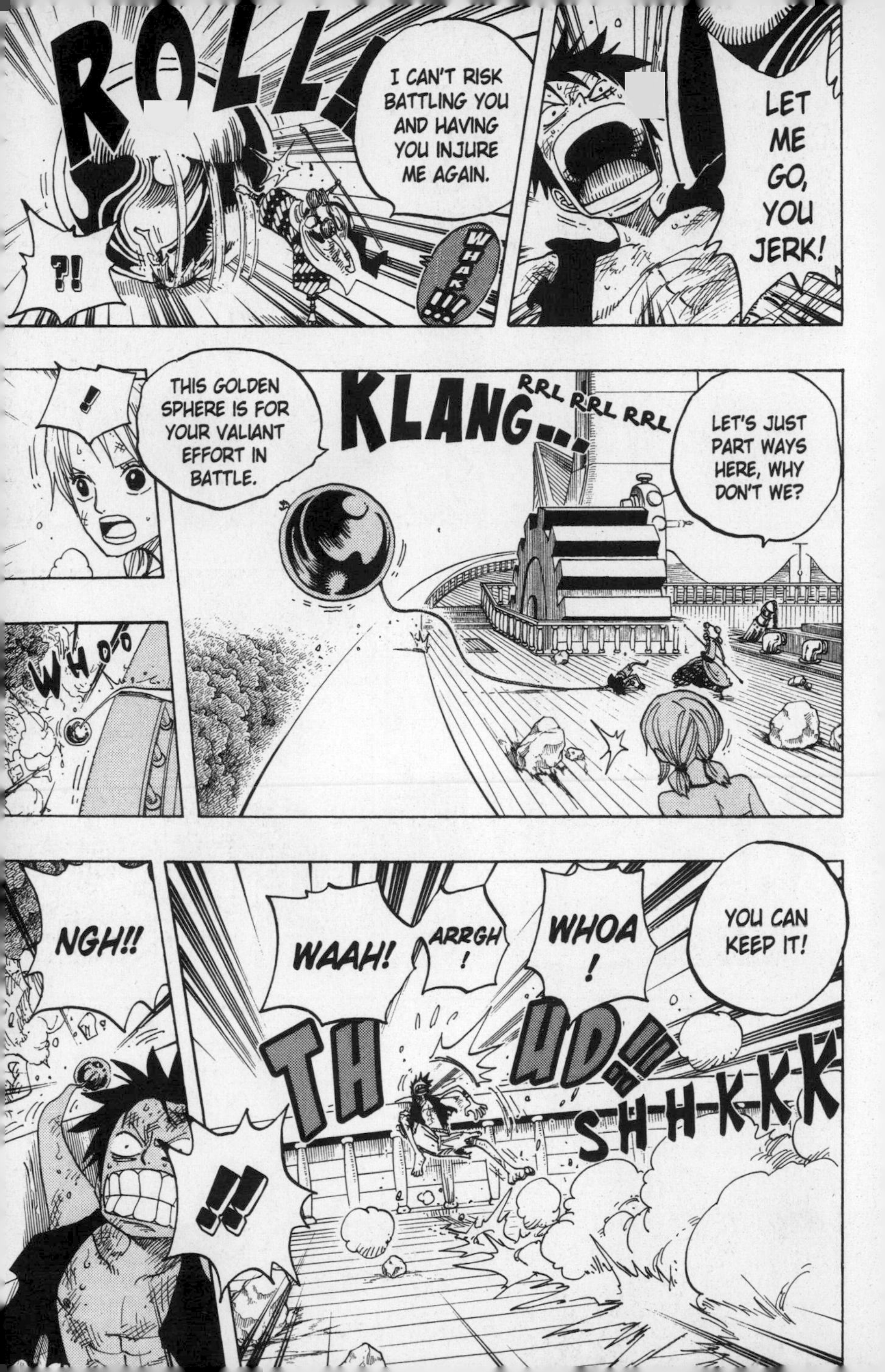
LET ME GO, YOU JERK!
I CAN'T RISK BATTLING YOU AND HAVING YOU INJURE ME AGAIN.
WHAK!!!
ROLL
?!
LET'S JUST PART WAYS HERE, WHY DON'T WE?
RRL RRL RRL
KLANG...
THIS GOLDEN SPHERE IS FOR YOUR VALIANT EFFORT IN BATTLE.
!
WHOO
YOU CAN KEEP IT!
WHOA!
ARRGH!
WAAH!
THUD!!
SHHKKK
NGH!!
!!

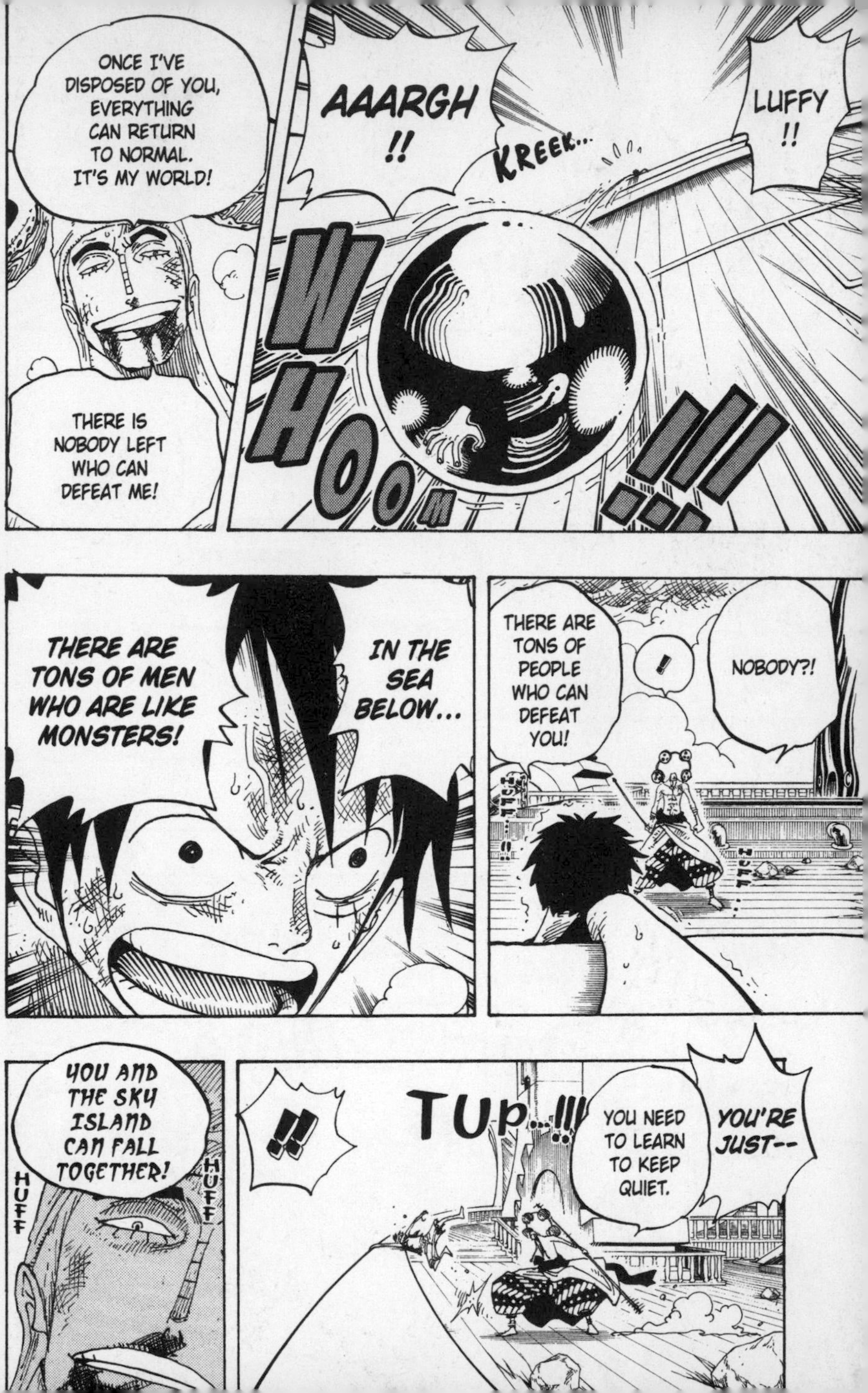
LUFFY !!
AAARGH !!
KREEK...
WHOOOM!!!
ONCE I'VE DISPOSED OF YOU, EVERYTHING CAN RETURN TO NORMAL. IT'S MY WORLD!
THERE IS NOBODY LEFT WHO CAN DEFEAT ME!
NOBODY?!
!
HUFF...
THERE ARE TONS OF PEOPLE WHO CAN DEFEAT YOU!
HUFF...!!
IN THE SEA BELOW...
THERE ARE TONS OF MEN WHO ARE LIKE MONSTERS!
YOU'RE JUST--
YOU NEED TO LEARN TO KEEP QUIET.
TUP...!!!
!!
YOU AND THE SKY ISLAND CAN FALL TOGETHER!
HUFF
HUFF

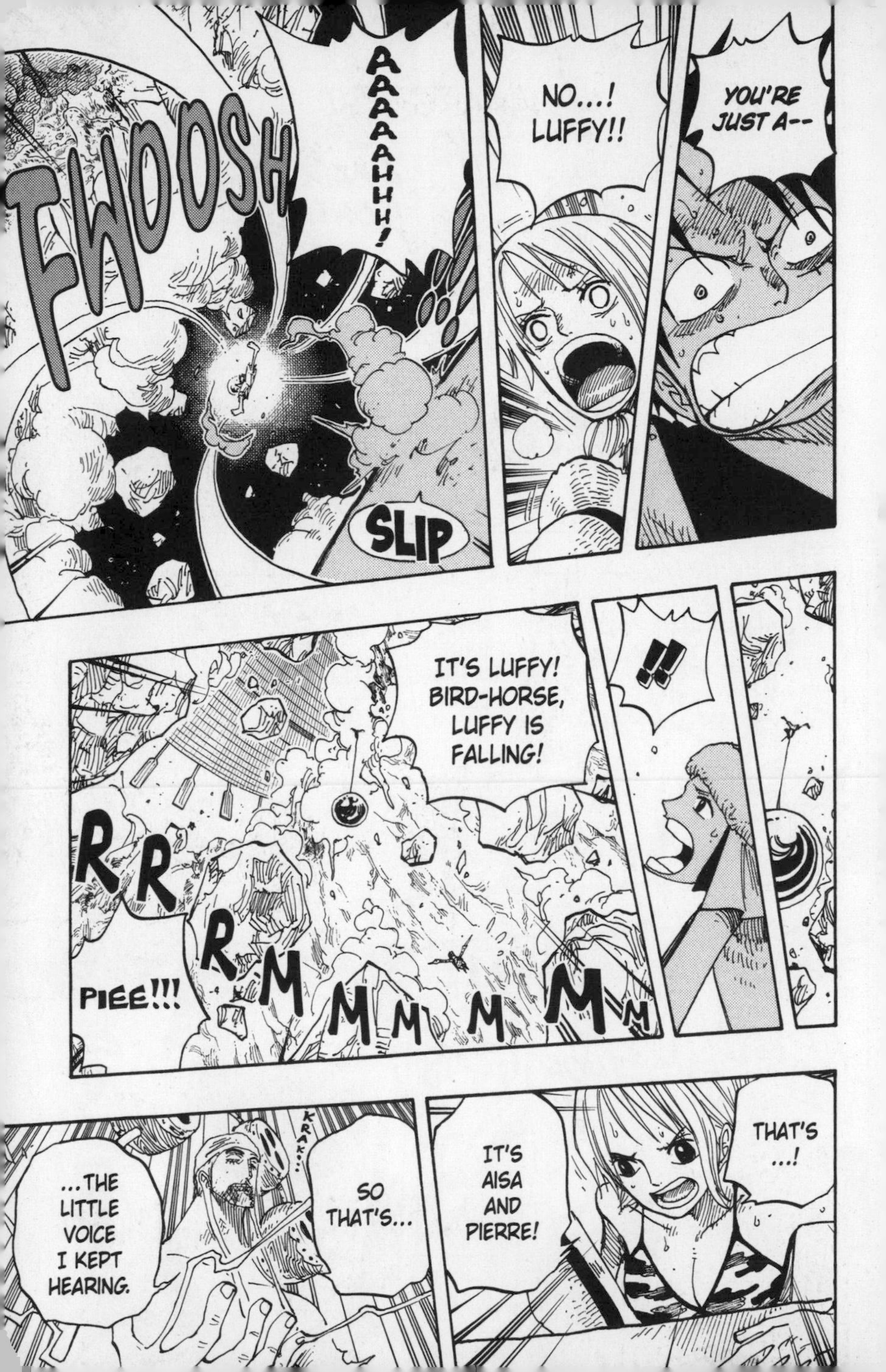
YOU'RE JUST A--
NO...! LUFFY!!
AAAAAAHHHH!
FWOOSH
SLIP
!!
IT'S LUFFY! BIRD-HORSE, LUFFY IS FALLING!
RRRMMMMMMM
PIEE!!!
THAT'S ...!
IT'S AISA AND PIERRE!
KRAK...
SO THAT'S...
...THE LITTLE VOICE I KEPT HEARING.

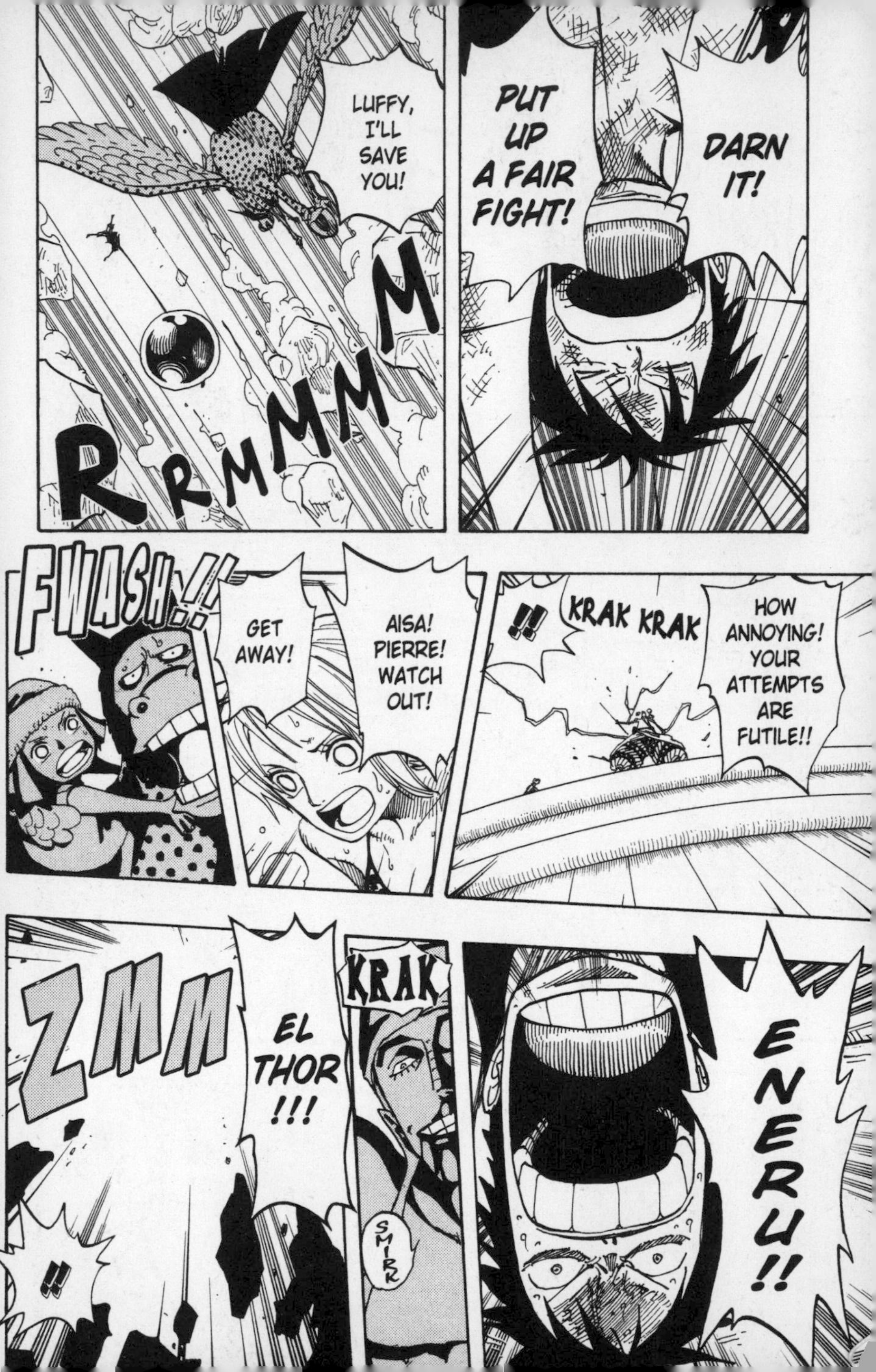
DARN IT!
PUT UP A FAIR FIGHT!
LUFFY, I'LL SAVE YOU!
RRMMMM
HOW ANNOYING! YOUR ATTEMPTS ARE FUTILE!!
KRAK KRAK
!!
AISA! PIERRE! WATCH OUT!
GET AWAY!
FWASH!!
ENERU!!
KRAK
SMIRK
EL THOR!!!
ZMM
!!

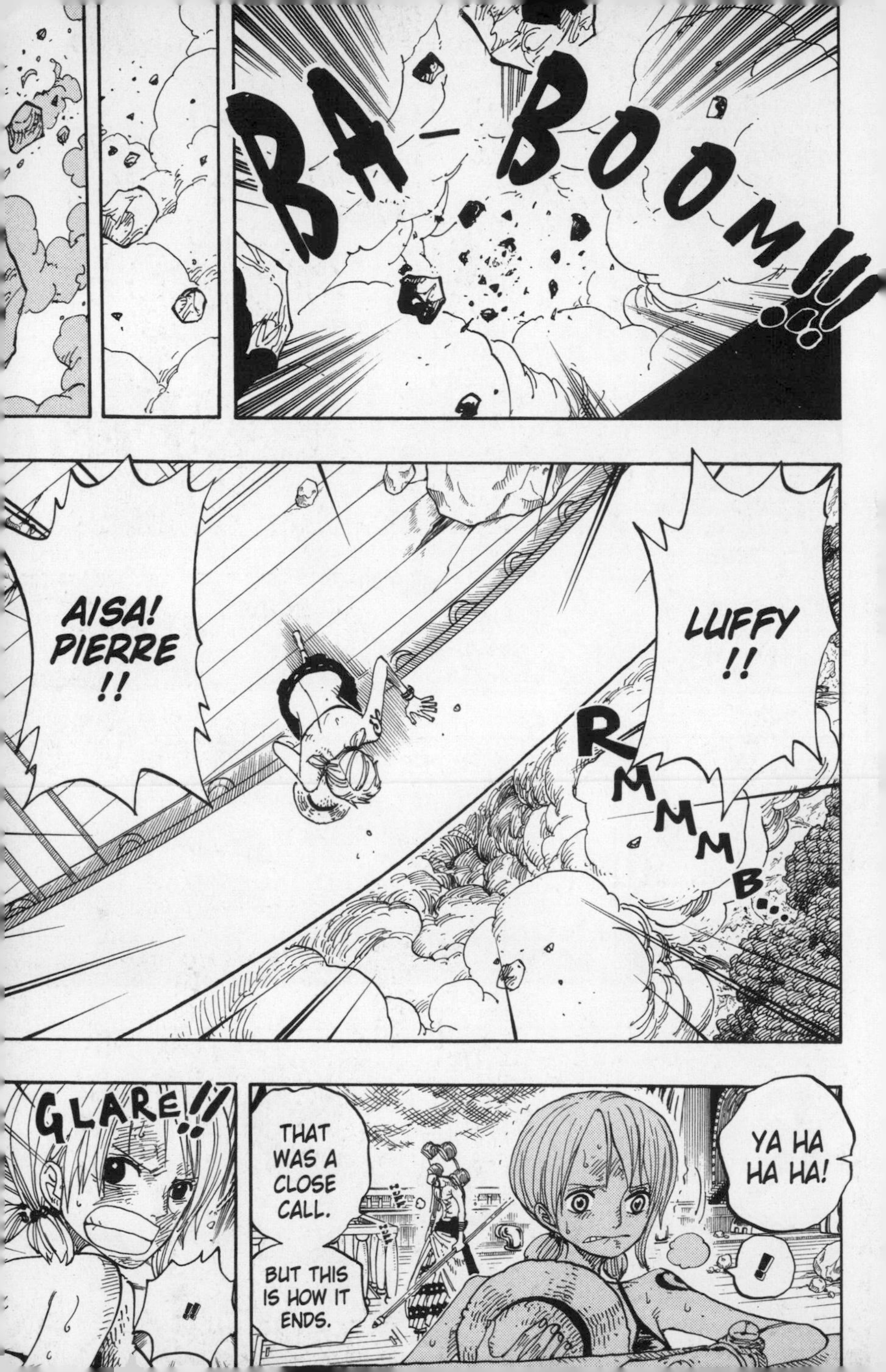

BA-BOOM!!!
LUFFY !!
RMMMB..
AISA! PIERRE !!
YA HA HA HA!
!
THAT WAS A CLOSE CALL.
BUT THIS IS HOW IT ENDS.
GLARE!!
!!

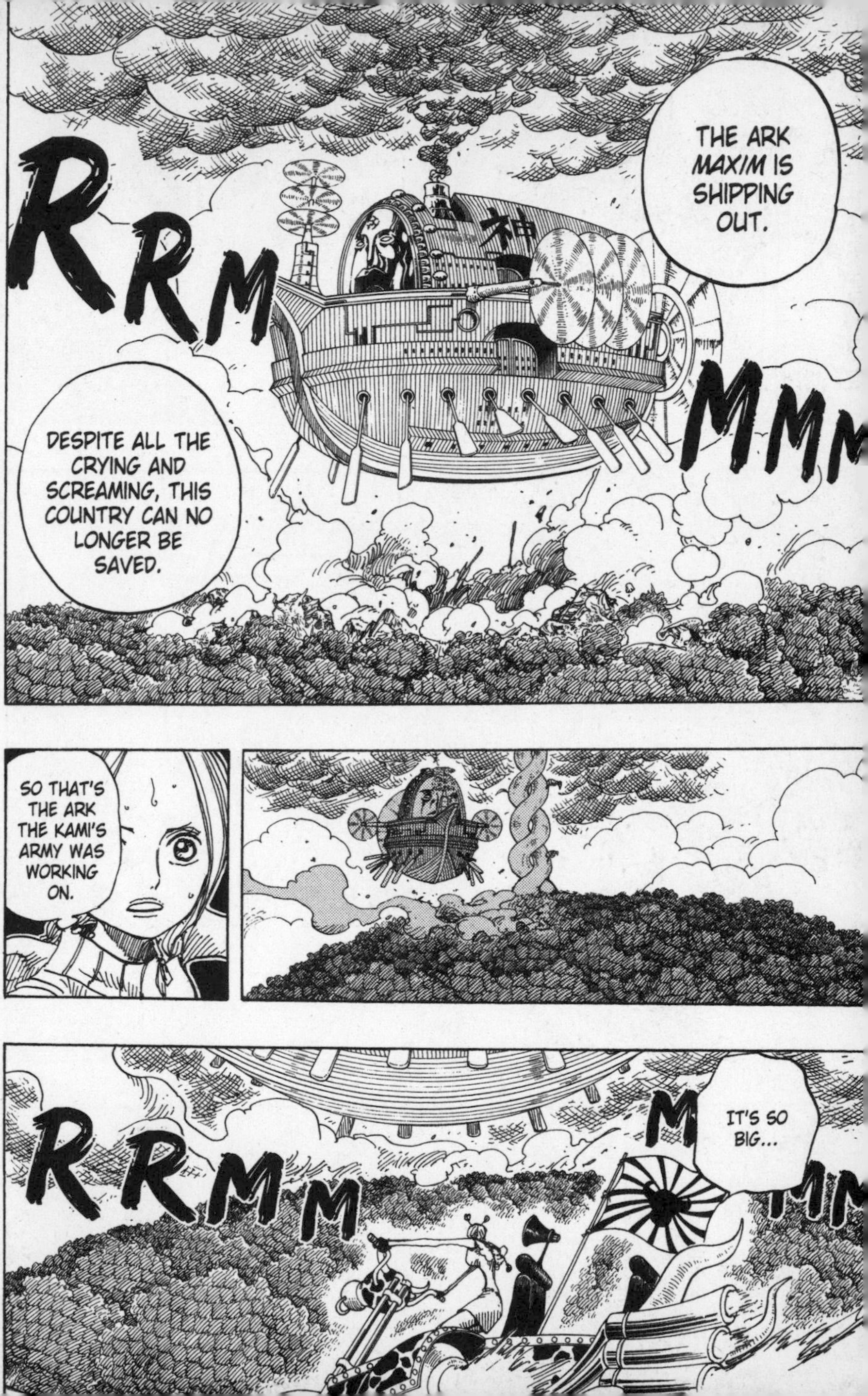
THE ARK *MAXIM* IS SHIPPING OUT.
RRMMMM
DESPITE ALL THE CRYING AND SCREAMING, THIS COUNTRY CAN NO LONGER BE SAVED.
SO THAT'S THE ARK THE KAMI'S ARMY WAS WORKING ON.
IT'S SO BIG...
RRMMM

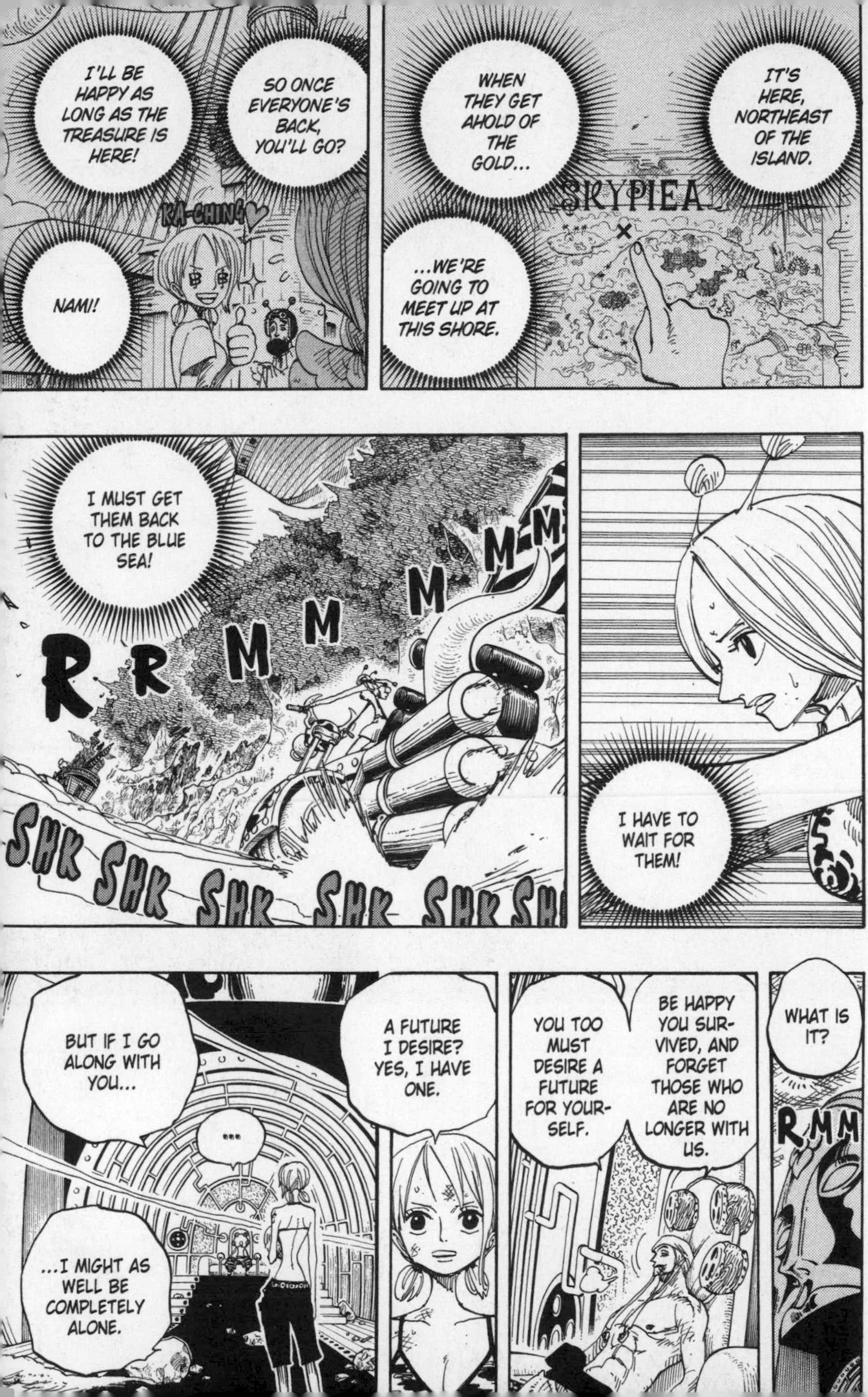
IT'S HERE, NORTHEAST OF THE ISLAND.
SKYPIEA
WHEN THEY GET AHOLD OF THE GOLD...
...WE'RE GOING TO MEET UP AT THIS SHORE.
SO ONCE EVERYONE'S BACK, YOU'LL GO?
I'LL BE HAPPY AS LONG AS THE TREASURE IS HERE!
KA-CHING
NAMI!
I HAVE TO WAIT FOR THEM!
I MUST GET THEM BACK TO THE BLUE SEA!
RRMMMMMM
SHK SHK SHK SHK SHK SH
WHAT IS IT?
RMM
BE HAPPY YOU SURVIVED, AND FORGET THOSE WHO ARE NO LONGER WITH US.
YOU TOO MUST DESIRE A FUTURE FOR YOURSELF.
A FUTURE I DESIRE? YES, I HAVE ONE.
BUT IF I GO ALONG WITH YOU...
...
...I MIGHT AS WELL BE COMPLETELY ALONE.

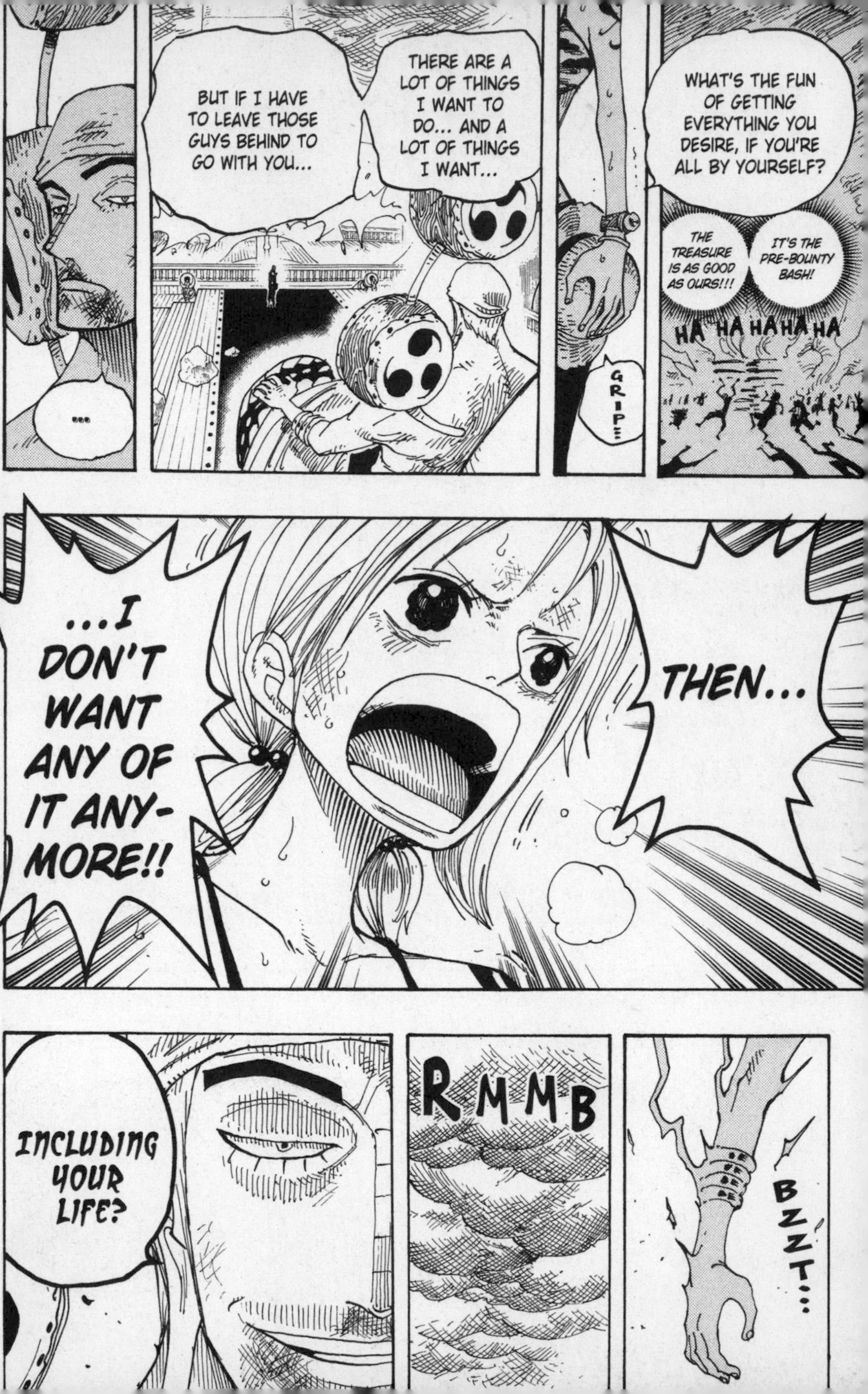
WHAT'S THE FUN OF GETTING EVERYTHING YOU DESIRE, IF YOU'RE ALL BY YOURSELF?
IT'S THE PRE-BOUNTY BASH!
THE TREASURE IS AS GOOD AS OURS!!!
HA HA HA HA HA
GRIP!!
THERE ARE A LOT OF THINGS I WANT TO DO... AND A LOT OF THINGS I WANT...
BUT IF I HAVE TO LEAVE THOSE GUYS BEHIND TO GO WITH YOU...
...
THEN...
...I DON'T WANT ANY OF IT ANY-MORE!!
BZZT...
RMMB
INCLUDING YOUR LIFE?

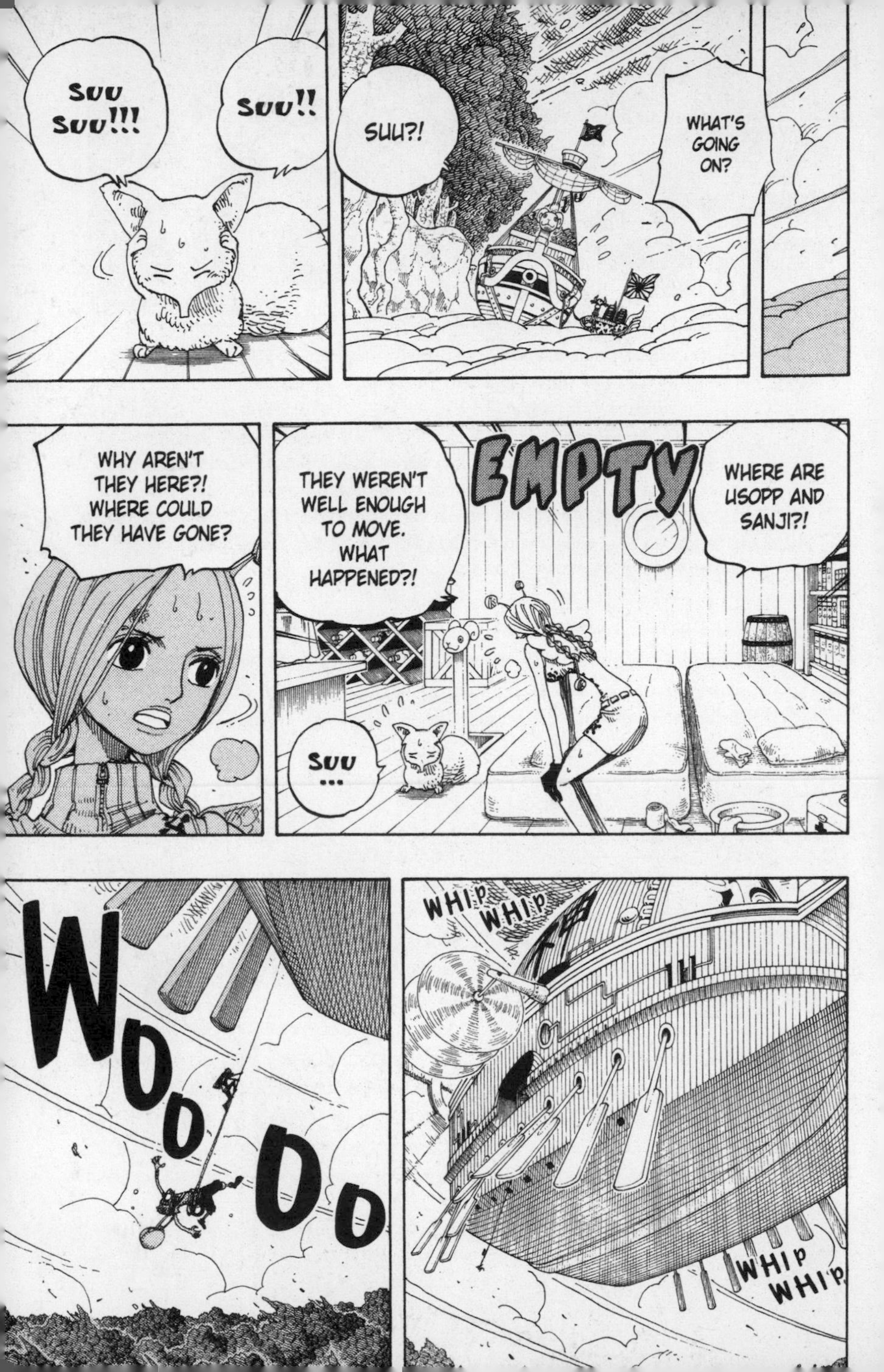
WHAT'S GOING ON?
SUU?!
SUU!!
SUU SUU!!!
WHERE ARE USOPP AND SANJI?!
EMPTY
THEY WEREN'T WELL ENOUGH TO MOVE. WHAT HAPPENED?!
SUU...
WHY AREN'T THEY HERE?! WHERE COULD THEY HAVE GONE?
WHIP WHIP
WHIP WHIP
WOOOO

Q: I think all the *One Piece* characters are so fashionable. Are you stylish too, Oda Sensei?

A: Oh, yes. As a man, I really do like to look my best every day. My hair is in a free-growing style with an emphasis on the natural look. My wardrobe consists of junk-store clothes with an eye toward the seasons. And my pants have elastic waistbands, so as not to hold me back in any way. And on my feet will be flip-flops that I'll even wear into expensive hotels.

Q: There's one thing I would like to know. In volume 27, page 130, Sanji says, "When there's enough distilled water in the bowl, pour it into the flask." Can you explain what kind of survival technique this is? I'd like to know how to do it. I'm going to go into the jungle.

--Kagawa

A: Okay, so here's how you make distilled water:

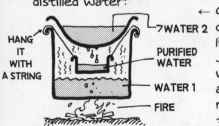

HANG IT WITH A STRING

WATER 2
PURIFIED WATER
WATER 1
FIRE

← Get three containers, like this. Just use water from a nearby river. The water in container #2 cools down the steam from the boiling water in container #1. The cooled steam will turn into water droplets and slowly drip into the pot below, creating clean drinking water. Sanji did this using Sea Clouds. Using this method, you can make drinking water in all kinds of situations!

Chapter 283:
ON THE FRONT LINE OF RESCUING LOVE

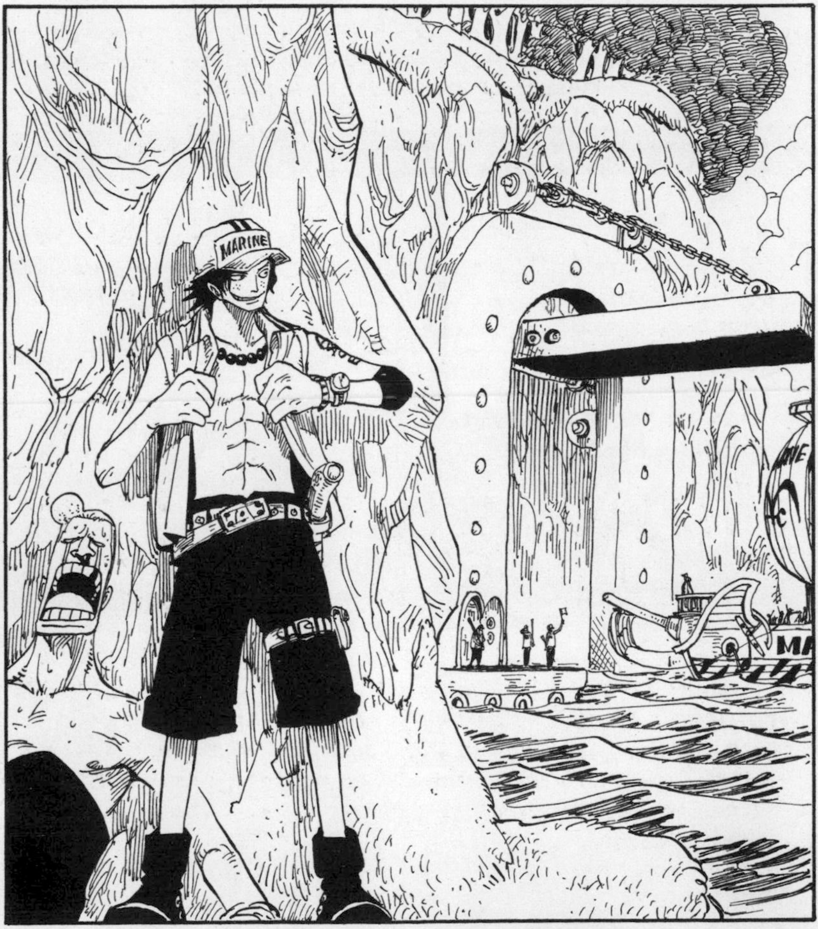
MARINE

ACE'S GREAT SEARCH FOR BLACKBEARD, VOL. 11:
"INFILTRATING THE NAVY BASE"

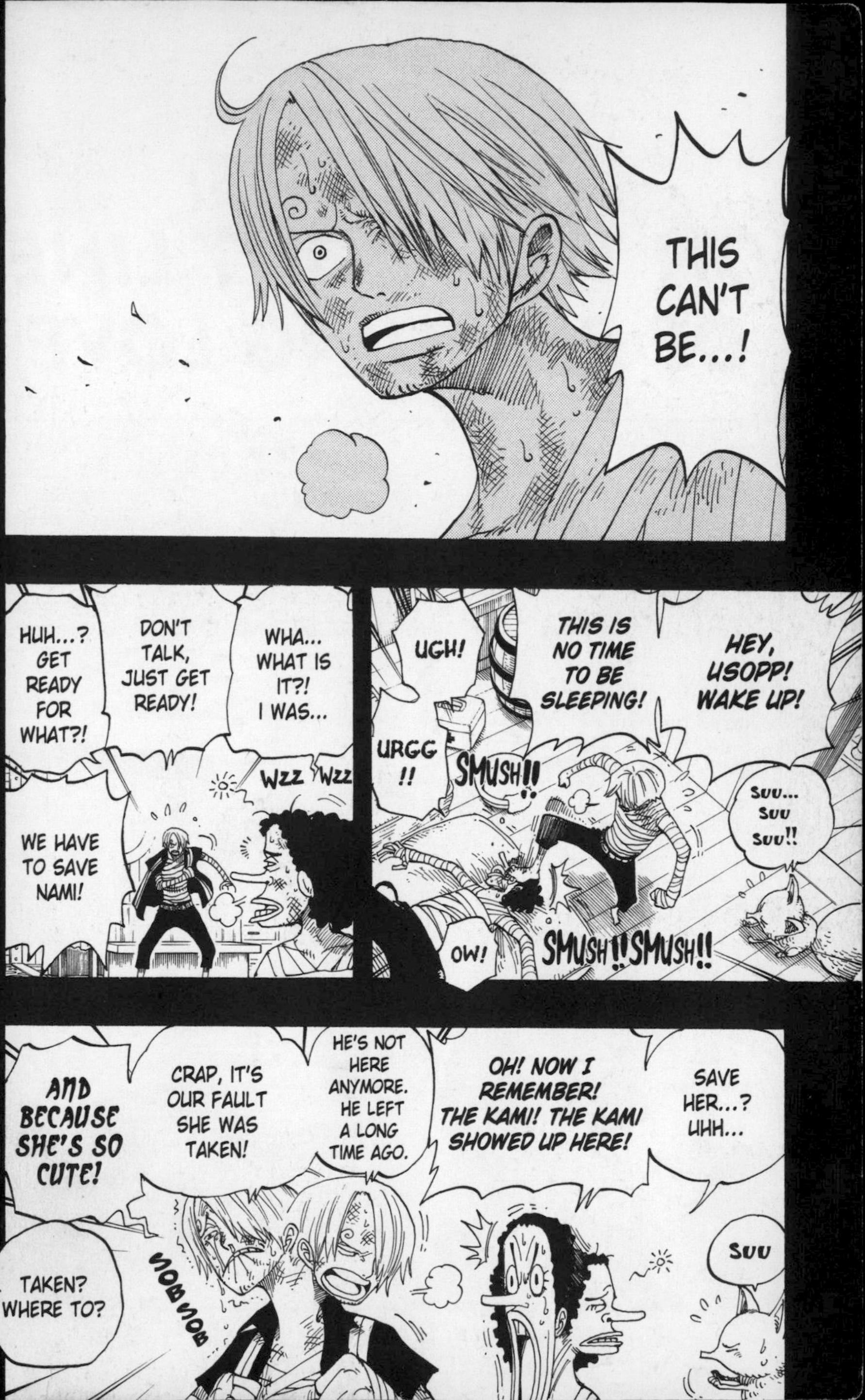
THIS CAN'T BE...!
HEY, USOPP! WAKE UP!
THIS IS NO TIME TO BE SLEEPING!
UGH!
SUU... SUU SUU!!
SMUSH!!
URGG !!
SMUSH!! SMUSH!!
OW!
WHA... WHAT IS IT?! I WAS...
DON'T TALK, JUST GET READY!
HUH...? GET READY FOR WHAT?!
WZZ WZZ
WE HAVE TO SAVE NAMI!
SAVE HER...? UHH...
OH! NOW I REMEMBER! THE KAMI! THE KAMI SHOWED UP HERE!
HE'S NOT HERE ANYMORE. HE LEFT A LONG TIME AGO.
CRAP, IT'S OUR FAULT SHE WAS TAKEN!
AND BECAUSE SHE'S SO CUTE!
SUU
SOB SOB
TAKEN? WHERE TO?

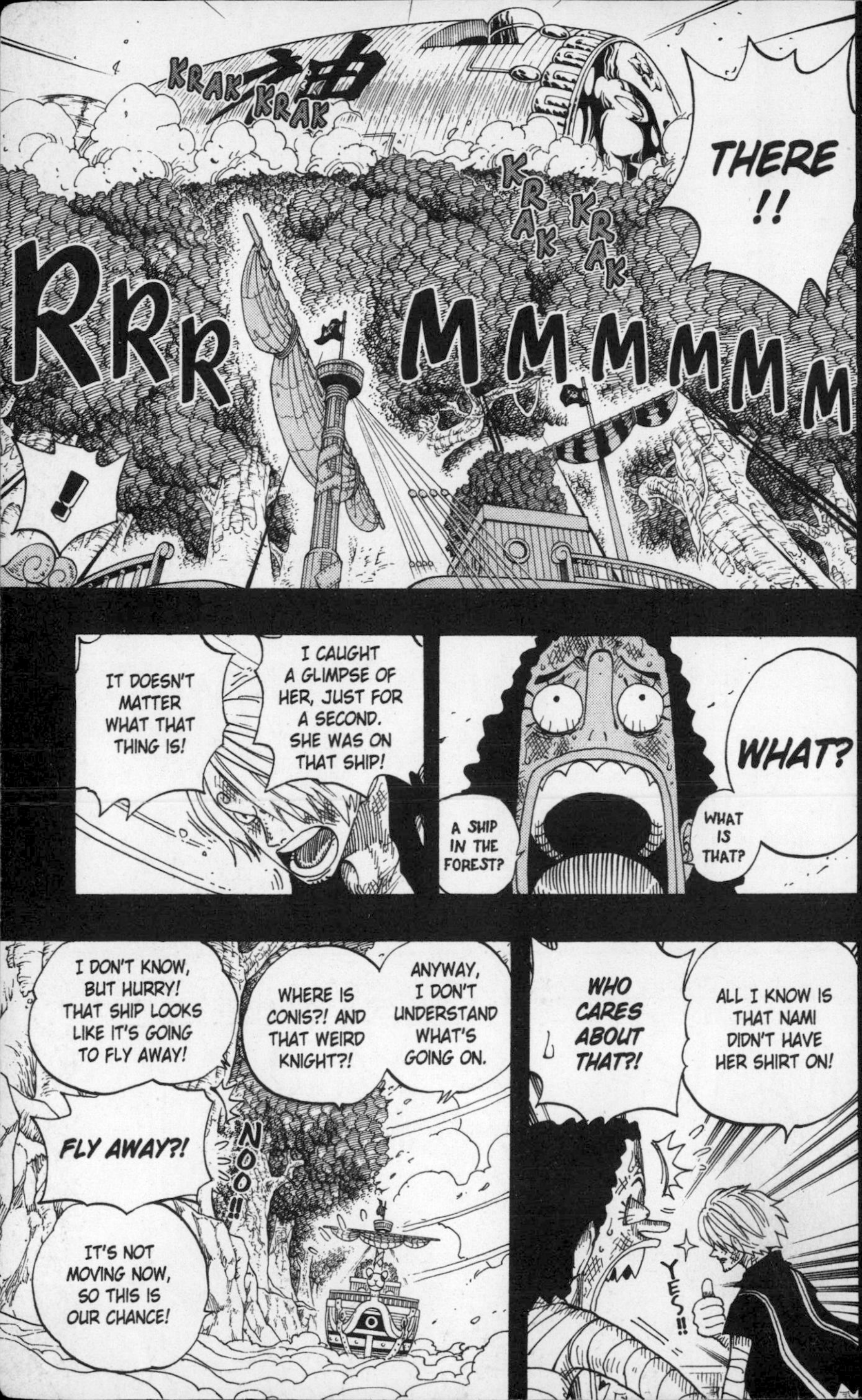
THERE !!
KRAK KRAK
KRAK KRAK
RRRMMMMMMMM
!
WHAT?
WHAT IS THAT?
A SHIP IN THE FOREST?
I CAUGHT A GLIMPSE OF HER, JUST FOR A SECOND. SHE WAS ON THAT SHIP!
IT DOESN'T MATTER WHAT THAT THING IS!
ALL I KNOW IS THAT NAMI DIDN'T HAVE HER SHIRT ON!
WHO CARES ABOUT THAT?!
YES!!
ANYWAY, I DON'T UNDERSTAND WHAT'S GOING ON.
WHERE IS CONIS?! AND THAT WEIRD KNIGHT?!
I DON'T KNOW, BUT HURRY! THAT SHIP LOOKS LIKE IT'S GOING TO FLY AWAY!
NOOO!!
FLY AWAY?!
IT'S NOT MOVING NOW, SO THIS IS OUR CHANCE!

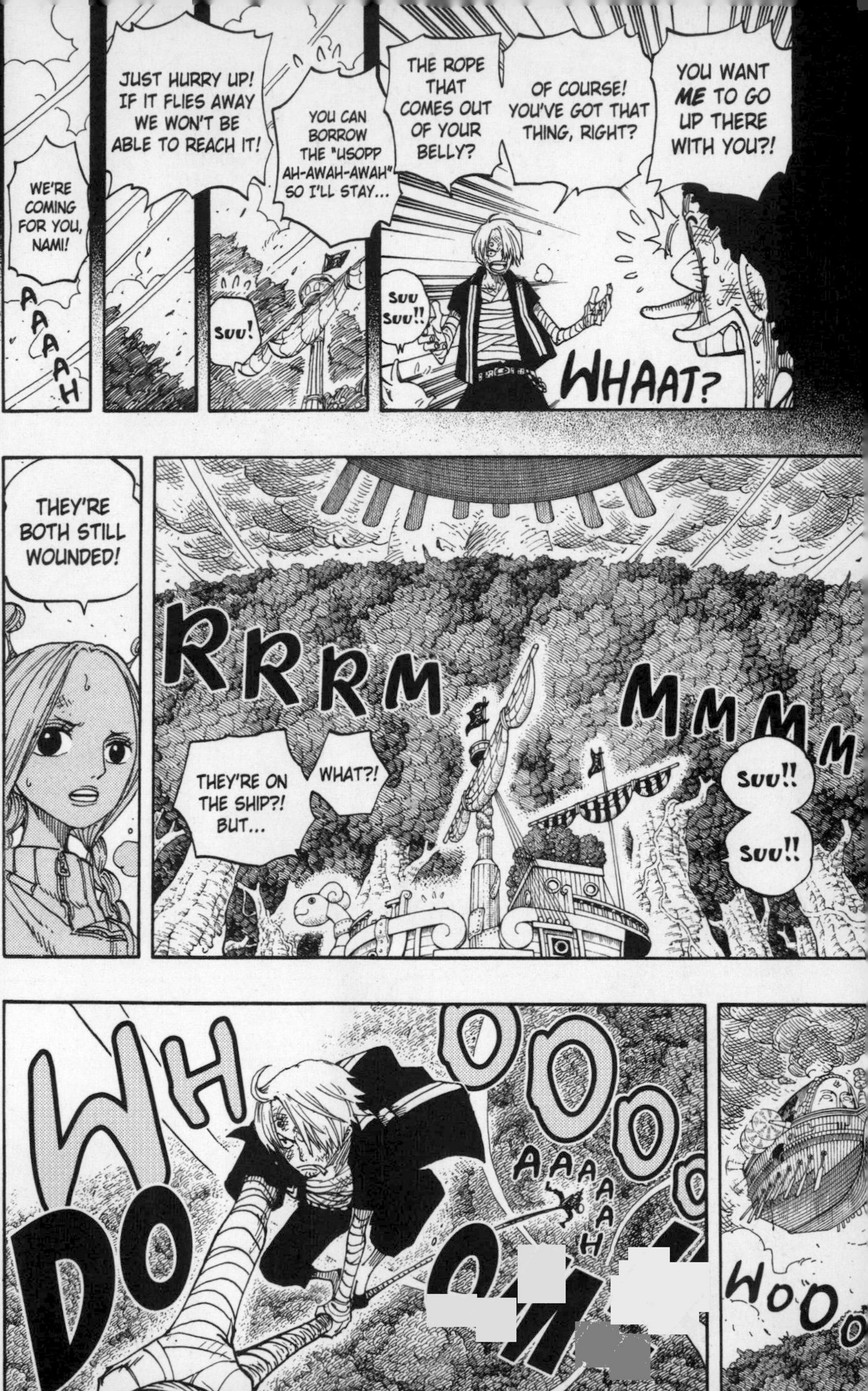

YOU WANT ME TO GO UP THERE WITH YOU?!
OF COURSE! YOU'VE GOT THAT THING, RIGHT?
THE ROPE THAT COMES OUT OF YOUR BELLY?
SUU SUU!!
WHAAT?
YOU CAN BORROW THE "USOPP AH-AWAH-AWAH" SO I'LL STAY...
JUST HURRY UP! IF IT FLIES AWAY WE WON'T BE ABLE TO REACH IT!
SUU!
WE'RE COMING FOR YOU, NAMI!
AAAAH
RRRM MMMMM
SUU!!
SUU!!
WHAT?!
THEY'RE ON THE SHIP?! BUT...
THEY'RE BOTH STILL WOUNDED!
WOOO
WHOOOOOO
AAAAAAH
DOOON

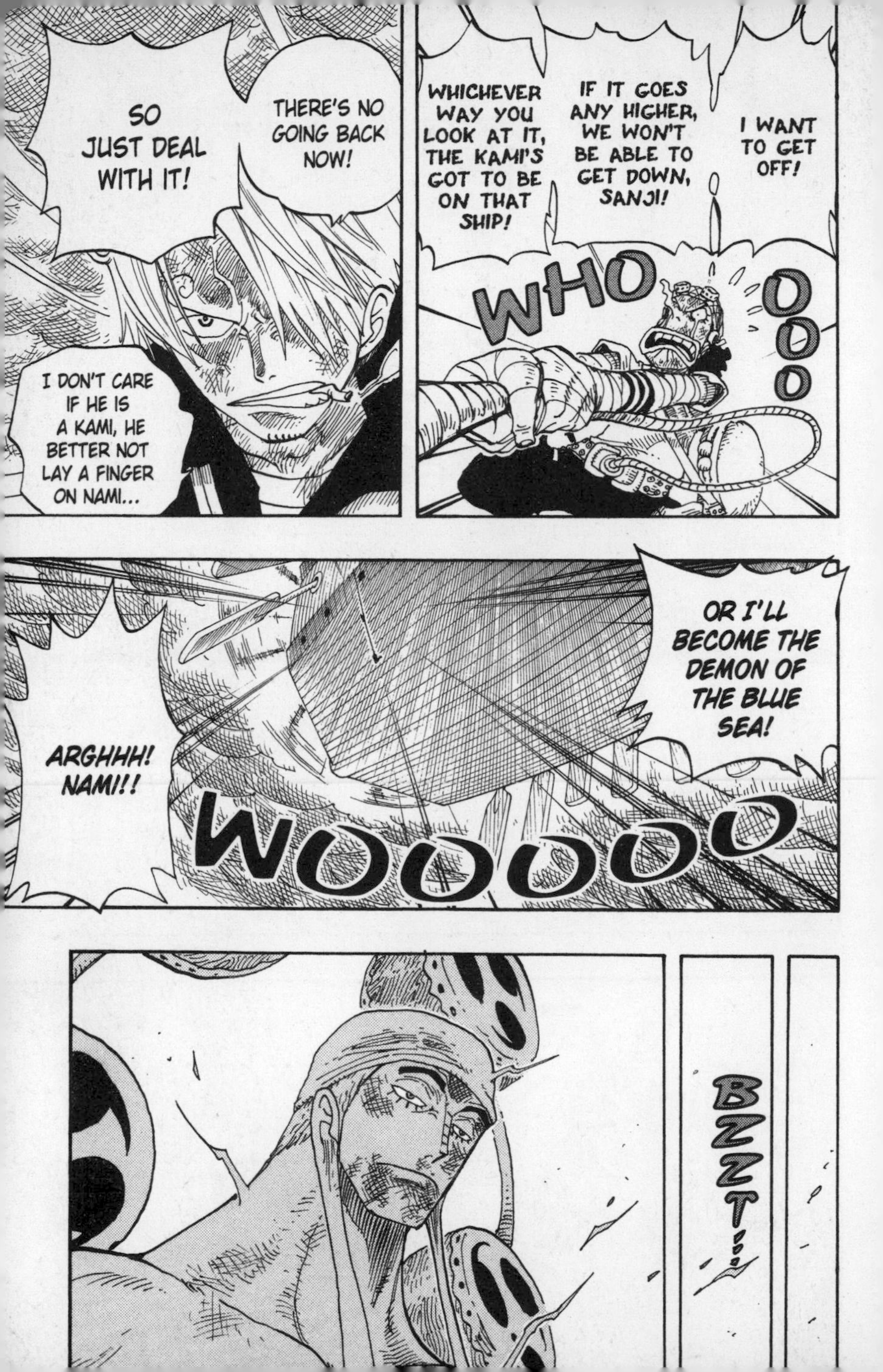
I WANT TO GET OFF!
IF IT GOES ANY HIGHER, WE WON'T BE ABLE TO GET DOWN, SANJI!
WHICHEVER WAY YOU LOOK AT IT, THE KAMI'S GOT TO BE ON THAT SHIP!
WHOOOO
THERE'S NO GOING BACK NOW!
SO JUST DEAL WITH IT!
I DON'T CARE IF HE IS A KAMI, HE BETTER NOT LAY A FINGER ON NAMI...
OR I'LL BECOME THE DEMON OF THE BLUE SEA!
ARGHHH! NAMI!!
WOOOOOO
BZZT...

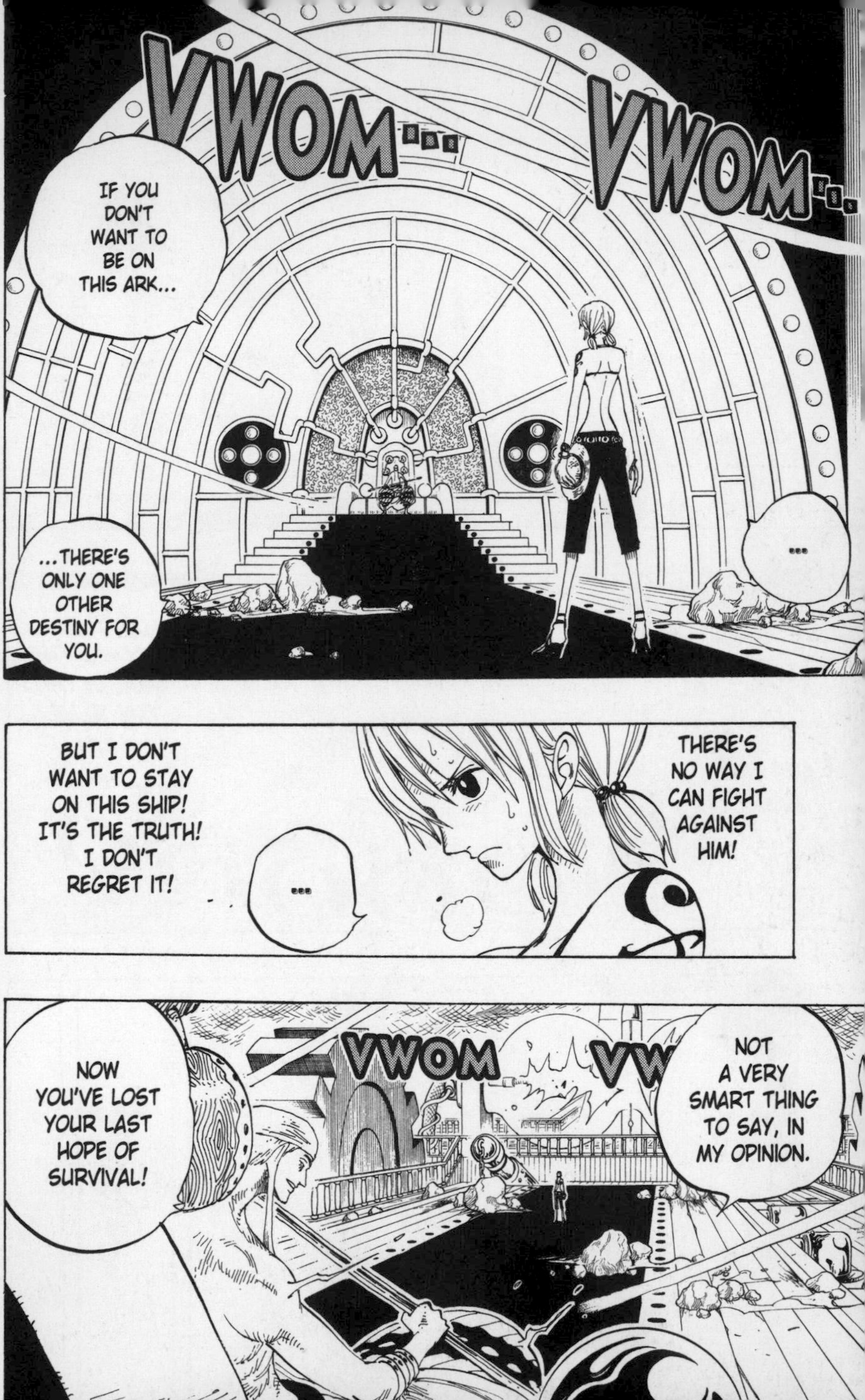
VWOM...
VWOM...
IF YOU DON'T WANT TO BE ON THIS ARK...
...THERE'S ONLY ONE OTHER DESTINY FOR YOU.
...
THERE'S NO WAY I CAN FIGHT AGAINST HIM!
...
BUT I DON'T WANT TO STAY ON THIS SHIP! IT'S THE TRUTH! I DON'T REGRET IT!
NOT A VERY SMART THING TO SAY, IN MY OPINION.
VW
VWOM
NOW YOU'VE LOST YOUR LAST HOPE OF SURVIVAL!

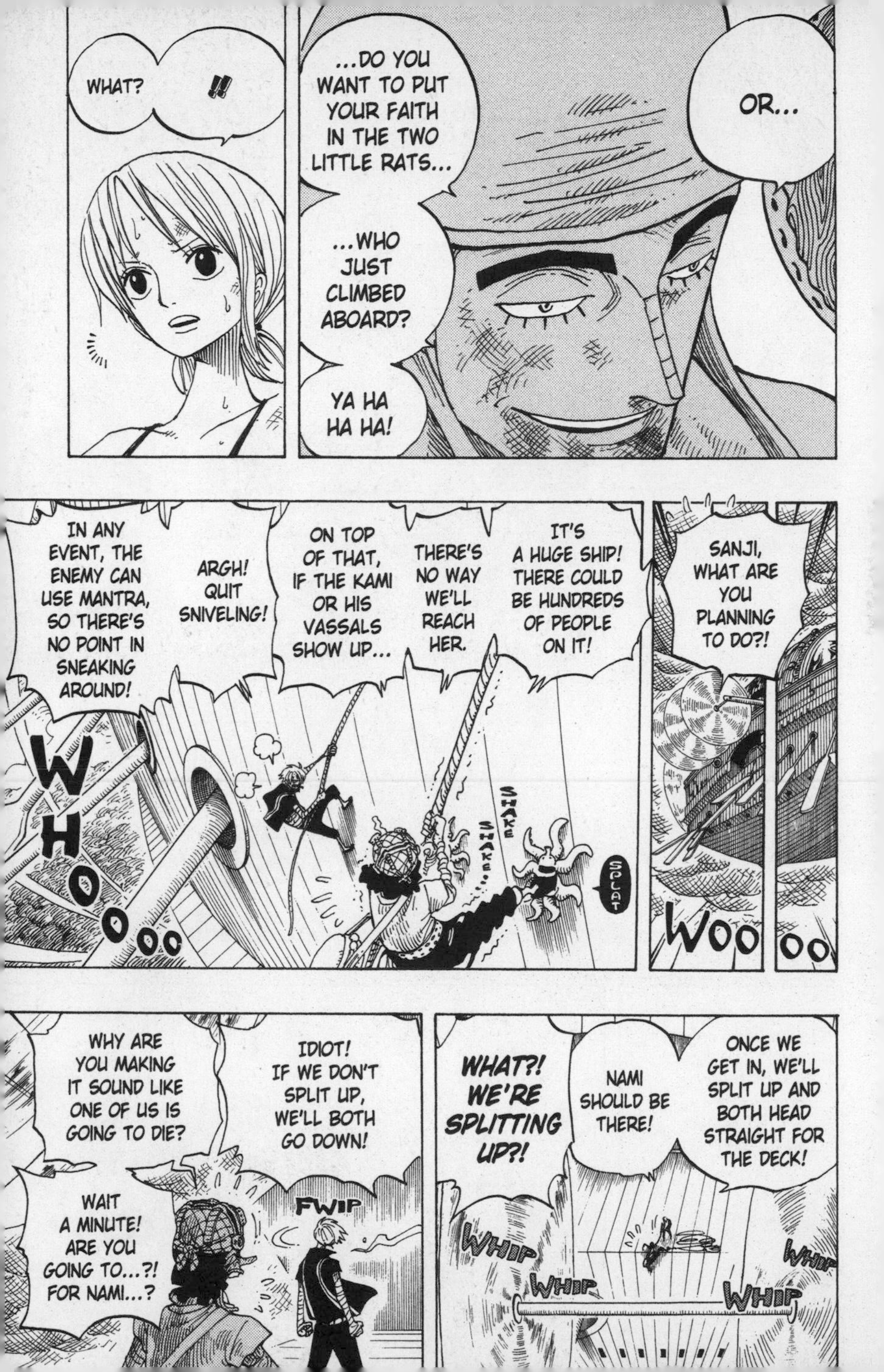
OR...
...DO YOU WANT TO PUT YOUR FAITH IN THE TWO LITTLE RATS...
...WHO JUST CLIMBED ABOARD?
YA HA HA HA!
WHAT? !!
SANJI, WHAT ARE YOU PLANNING TO DO?!
WOOOO
IT'S A HUGE SHIP! THERE COULD BE HUNDREDS OF PEOPLE ON IT!
THERE'S NO WAY WE'LL REACH HER.
ON TOP OF THAT, IF THE KAMI OR HIS VASSALS SHOW UP...
ARGH! QUIT SNIVELING!
IN ANY EVENT, THE ENEMY CAN USE MANTRA, SO THERE'S NO POINT IN SNEAKING AROUND!
SPLAT
SHAKE SHAKE...
WHOOOOO
ONCE WE GET IN, WE'LL SPLIT UP AND BOTH HEAD STRAIGHT FOR THE DECK!
NAMI SHOULD BE THERE!
WHAT?! WE'RE SPLITTING UP?!
WHIP WHIP WHIP WHIP
IDIOT! IF WE DON'T SPLIT UP, WE'LL BOTH GO DOWN!
WHY ARE YOU MAKING IT SOUND LIKE ONE OF US IS GOING TO DIE?
FWIP
WAIT A MINUTE! ARE YOU GOING TO...?! FOR NAMI...?

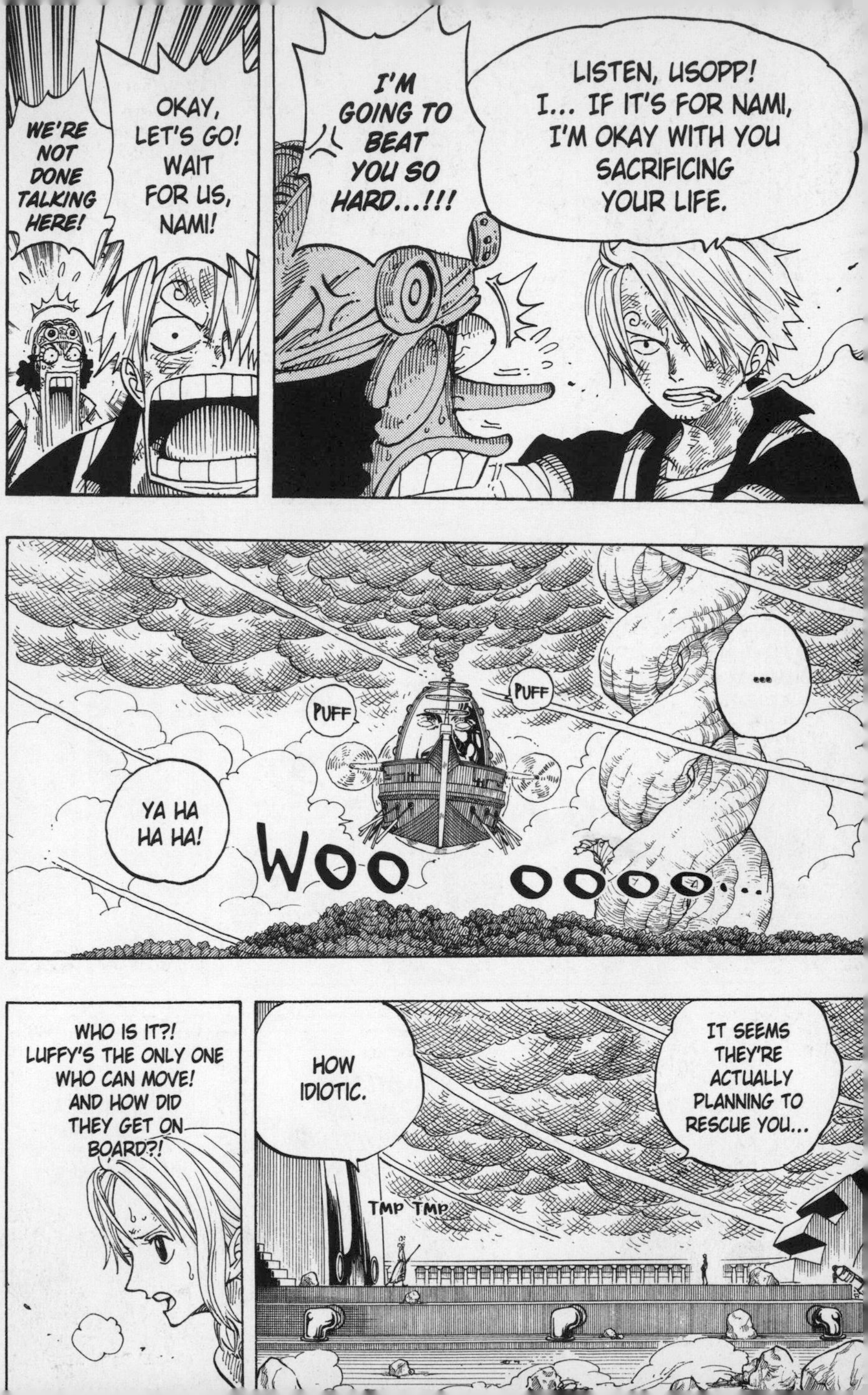
LISTEN, USOPP! I... IF IT'S FOR NAMI, I'M OKAY WITH YOU SACRIFICING YOUR LIFE.
I'M GOING TO BEAT YOU SO HARD...!!!
OKAY, LET'S GO! WAIT FOR US, NAMI!
WE'RE NOT DONE TALKING HERE!
...
PUFF
PUFF
YA HA HA HA!
WOO OOOO...
IT SEEMS THEY'RE ACTUALLY PLANNING TO RESCUE YOU...
HOW IDIOTIC.
TMP TMP
WHO IS IT?! LUFFY'S THE ONLY ONE WHO CAN MOVE! AND HOW DID THEY GET ON BOARD?!

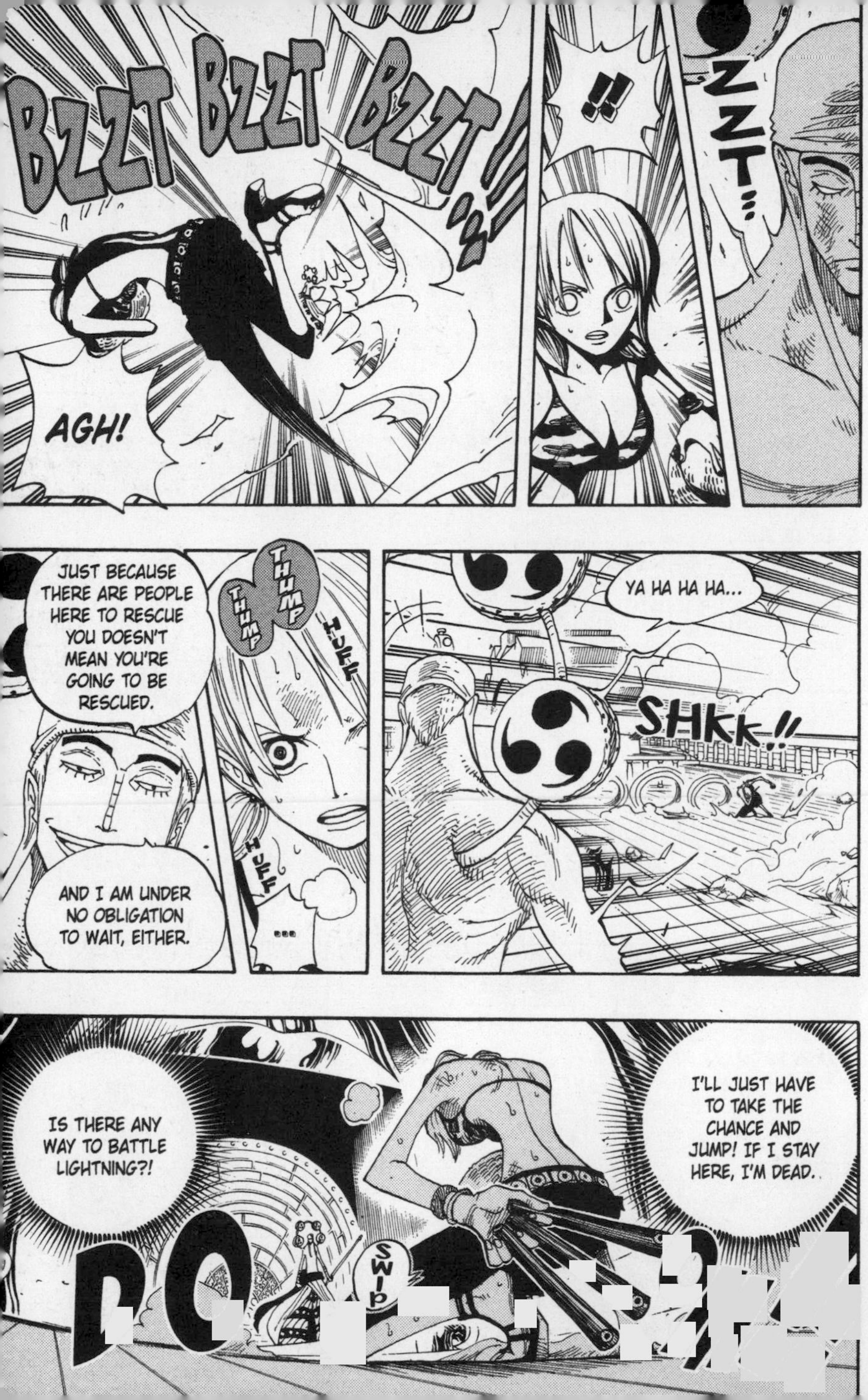
ZZZT...
!!
BZZT BZZT BZZT!!
AGH!
YA HA HA HA...
SHKK!!
THUMP THUMP
HUFF
HUFF
...
JUST BECAUSE THERE ARE PEOPLE HERE TO RESCUE YOU DOESN'T MEAN YOU'RE GOING TO BE RESCUED.
AND I AM UNDER NO OBLIGATION TO WAIT, EITHER.
I'LL JUST HAVE TO TAKE THE CHANCE AND JUMP! IF I STAY HERE, I'M DEAD.
IS THERE ANY WAY TO BATTLE LIGHTNING?!
SWIP
DO

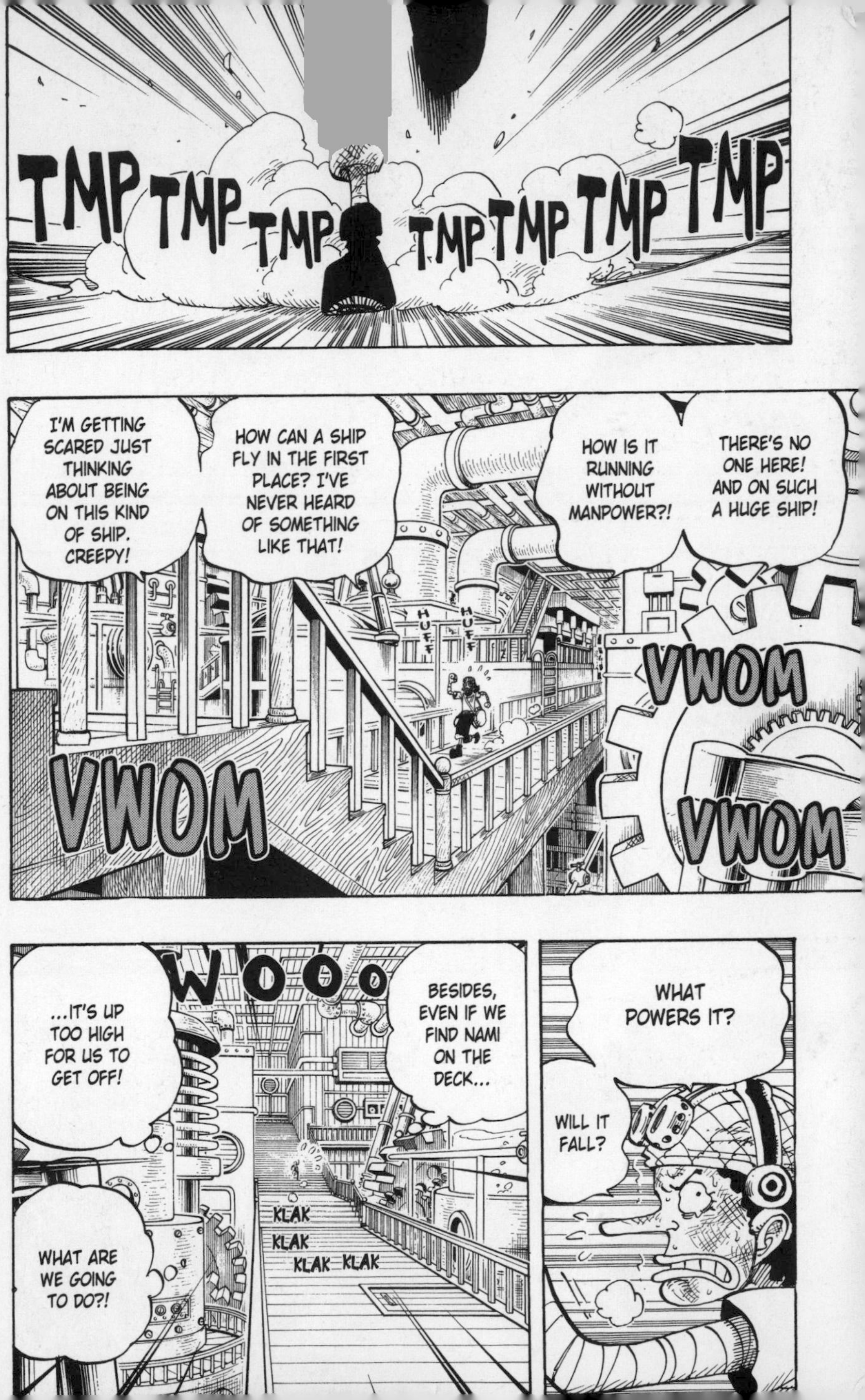
TMP TMP TMP TMP TMP TMP TMP TMP
THERE'S NO ONE HERE! AND ON SUCH A HUGE SHIP!
HOW IS IT RUNNING WITHOUT MANPOWER?!
HOW CAN A SHIP FLY IN THE FIRST PLACE? I'VE NEVER HEARD OF SOMETHING LIKE THAT!
I'M GETTING SCARED JUST THINKING ABOUT BEING ON THIS KIND OF SHIP. CREEPY!
HUFF HUFF
VWOM
VWOM
VWOM
WHAT POWERS IT?
WILL IT FALL?
WOOO
BESIDES, EVEN IF WE FIND NAMI ON THE DECK...
...IT'S UP TOO HIGH FOR US TO GET OFF!
KLAK KLAK KLAK KLAK
WHAT ARE WE GOING TO DO?!

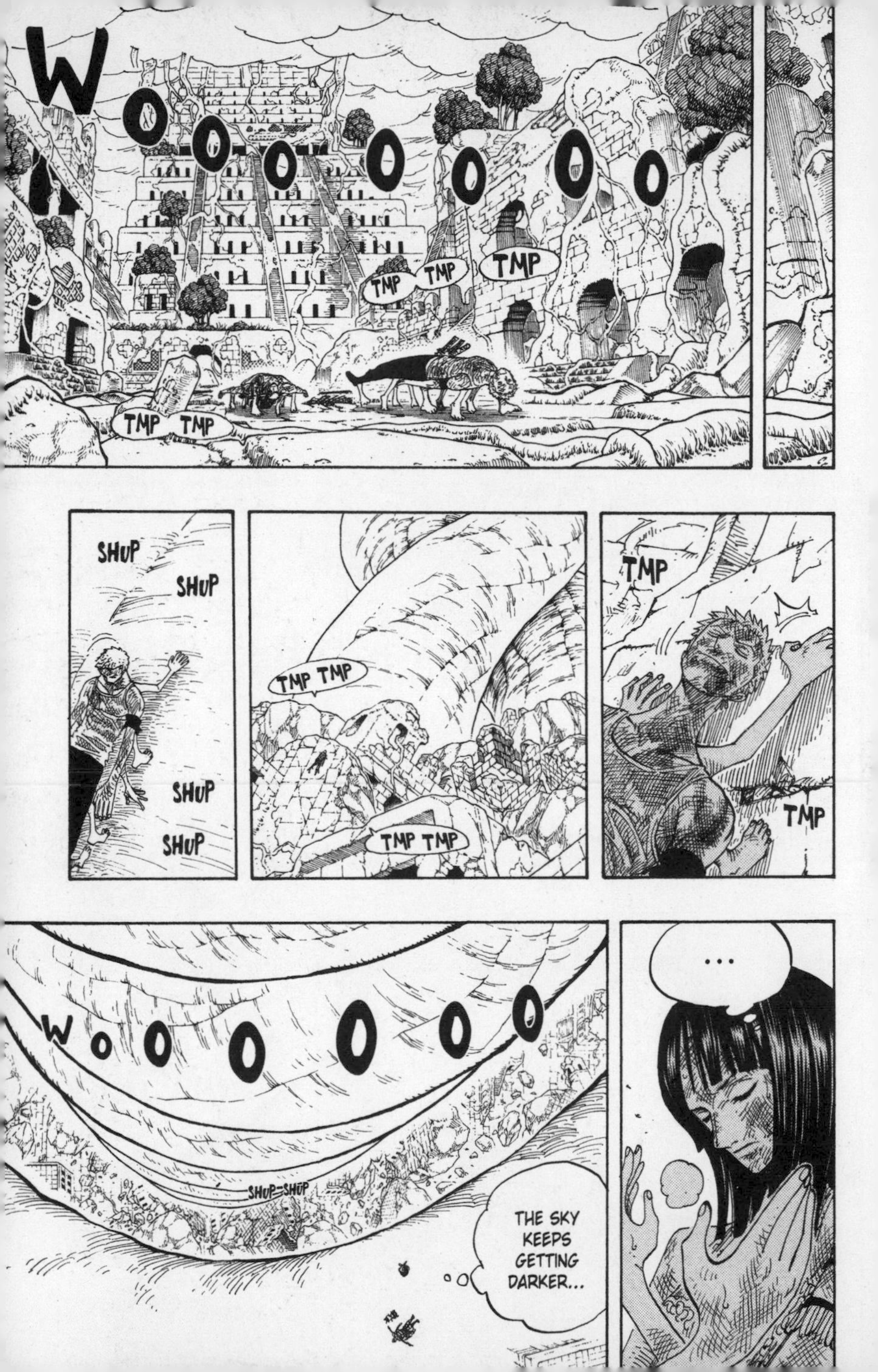
WOOOOOOOO
TMP
TMP
TMP
TMP TMP
TMP
TMP
TMP TMP
TMP TMP
SHUP
SHUP
SHUP
SHUP
...
WOOOOOO
THE SKY KEEPS GETTING DARKER...
SHUP SHUP

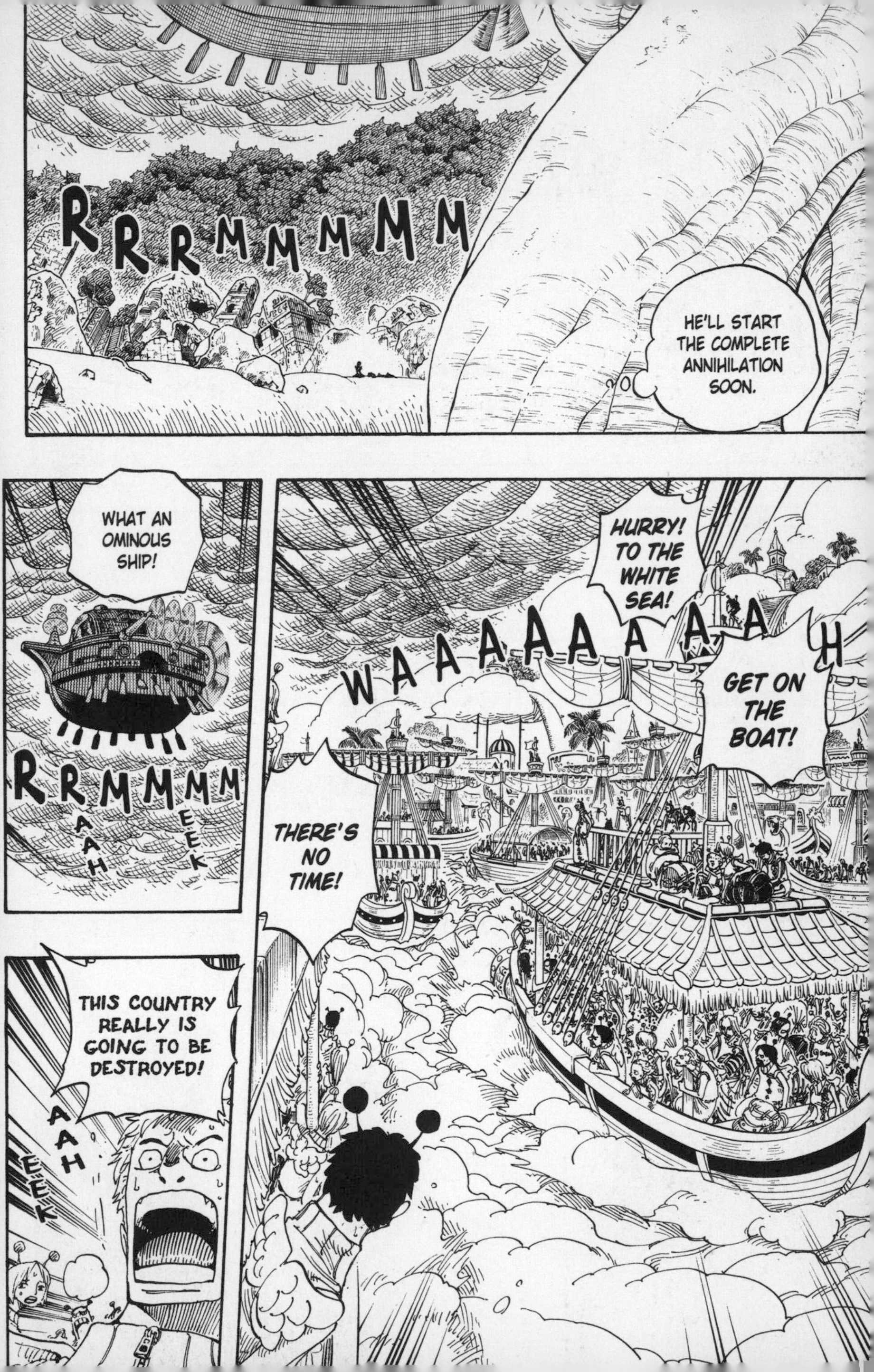
HE'LL START THE COMPLETE ANNIHILATION SOON.
RRRMMMMM
HURRY! TO THE WHITE SEA!
GET ON THE BOAT!
WAAAAAAAAH
THERE'S NO TIME!
WHAT AN OMINOUS SHIP!
RRMMMM
AAH
EEK
THIS COUNTRY REALLY IS GOING TO BE DESTROYED!
AAH
EEK

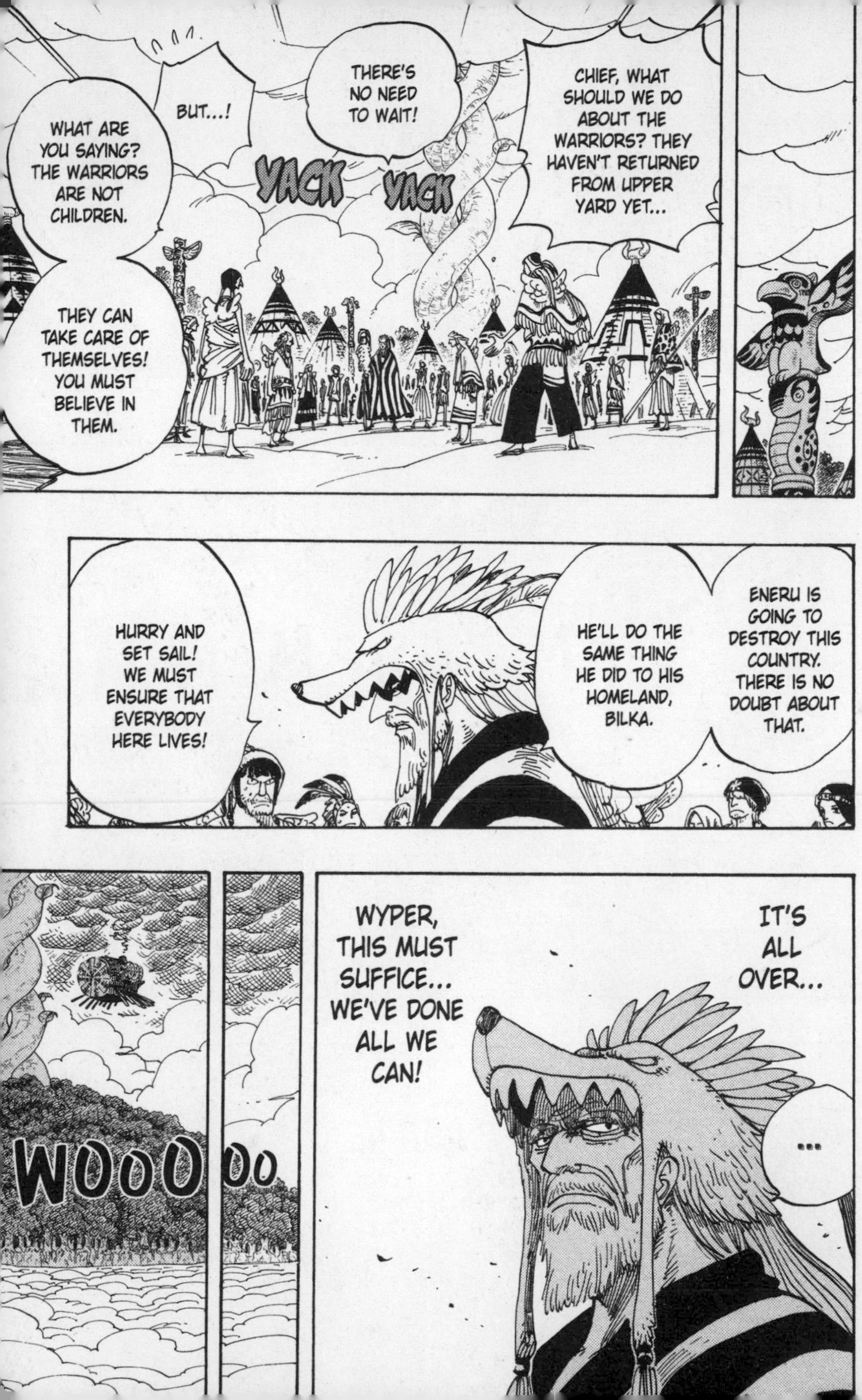

CHIEF, WHAT SHOULD WE DO ABOUT THE WARRIORS? THEY HAVEN'T RETURNED FROM UPPER YARD YET...
THERE'S NO NEED TO WAIT!
YACK YACK
BUT...!
WHAT ARE YOU SAYING? THE WARRIORS ARE NOT CHILDREN.
THEY CAN TAKE CARE OF THEMSELVES! YOU MUST BELIEVE IN THEM.
ENERU IS GOING TO DESTROY THIS COUNTRY. THERE IS NO DOUBT ABOUT THAT.
HE'LL DO THE SAME THING HE DID TO HIS HOMELAND, BILKA.
HURRY AND SET SAIL! WE MUST ENSURE THAT EVERYBODY HERE LIVES!
IT'S ALL OVER...
WYPER, THIS MUST SUFFICE... WE'VE DONE ALL WE CAN!
...
WOOOoo

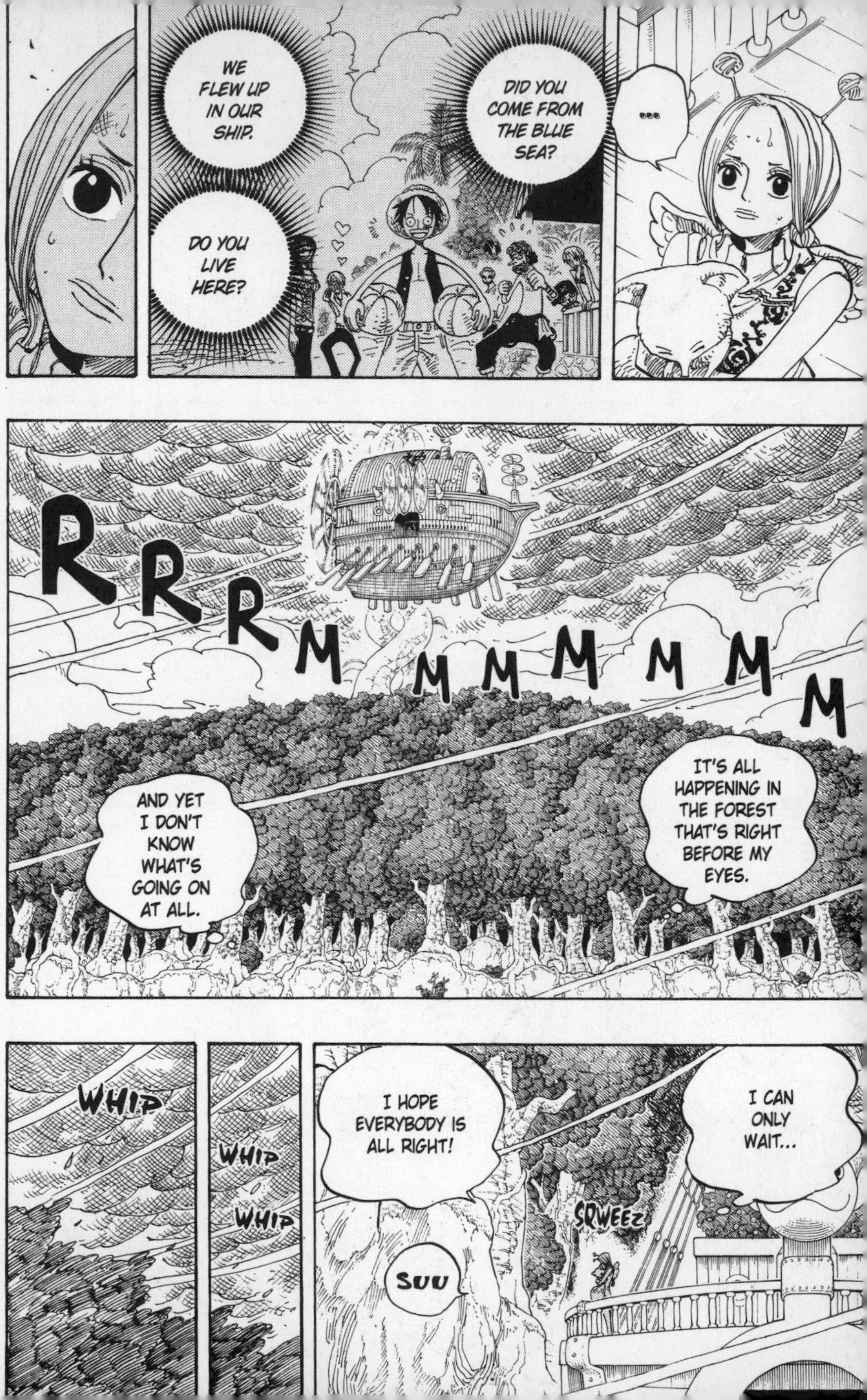
...
DID YOU COME FROM THE BLUE SEA?
WE FLEW UP IN OUR SHIP.
DO YOU LIVE HERE?
RRRMMMMMMM
IT'S ALL HAPPENING IN THE FOREST THAT'S RIGHT BEFORE MY EYES.
AND YET I DON'T KNOW WHAT'S GOING ON AT ALL.
I CAN ONLY WAIT...
SQWEEZ
I HOPE EVERYBODY IS ALL RIGHT!
SUU
WHIP
WHIP
WHIP

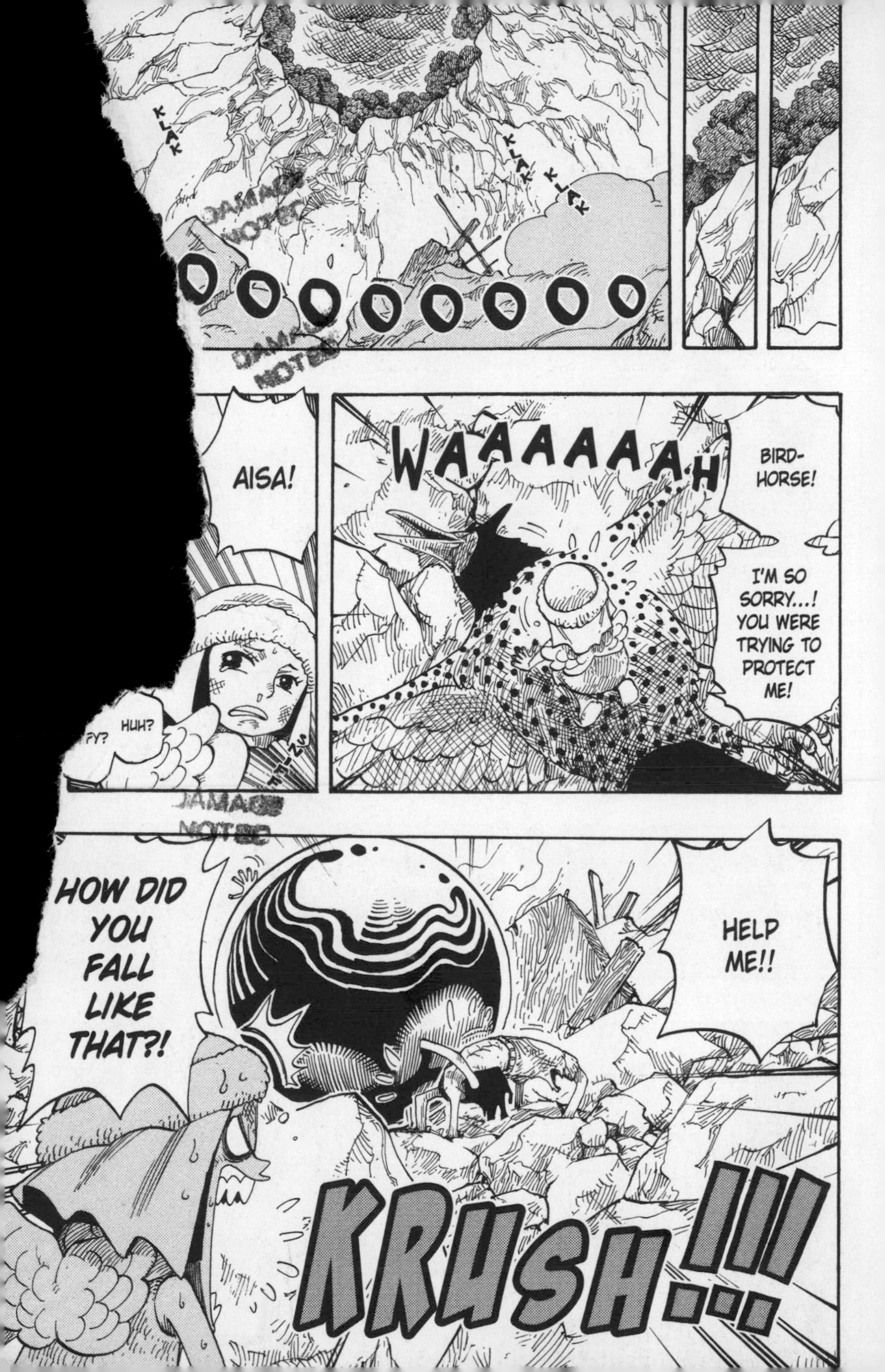
KLAK
KLAK
KLAK
OOOOOOOOO
WAAAAAAH
BIRD-HORSE!
I'M SO SORRY...! YOU WERE TRYING TO PROTECT ME!
AISA!
HUH?
HELP ME!!
HOW DID YOU FALL LIKE THAT?!
KRUSH...!!!

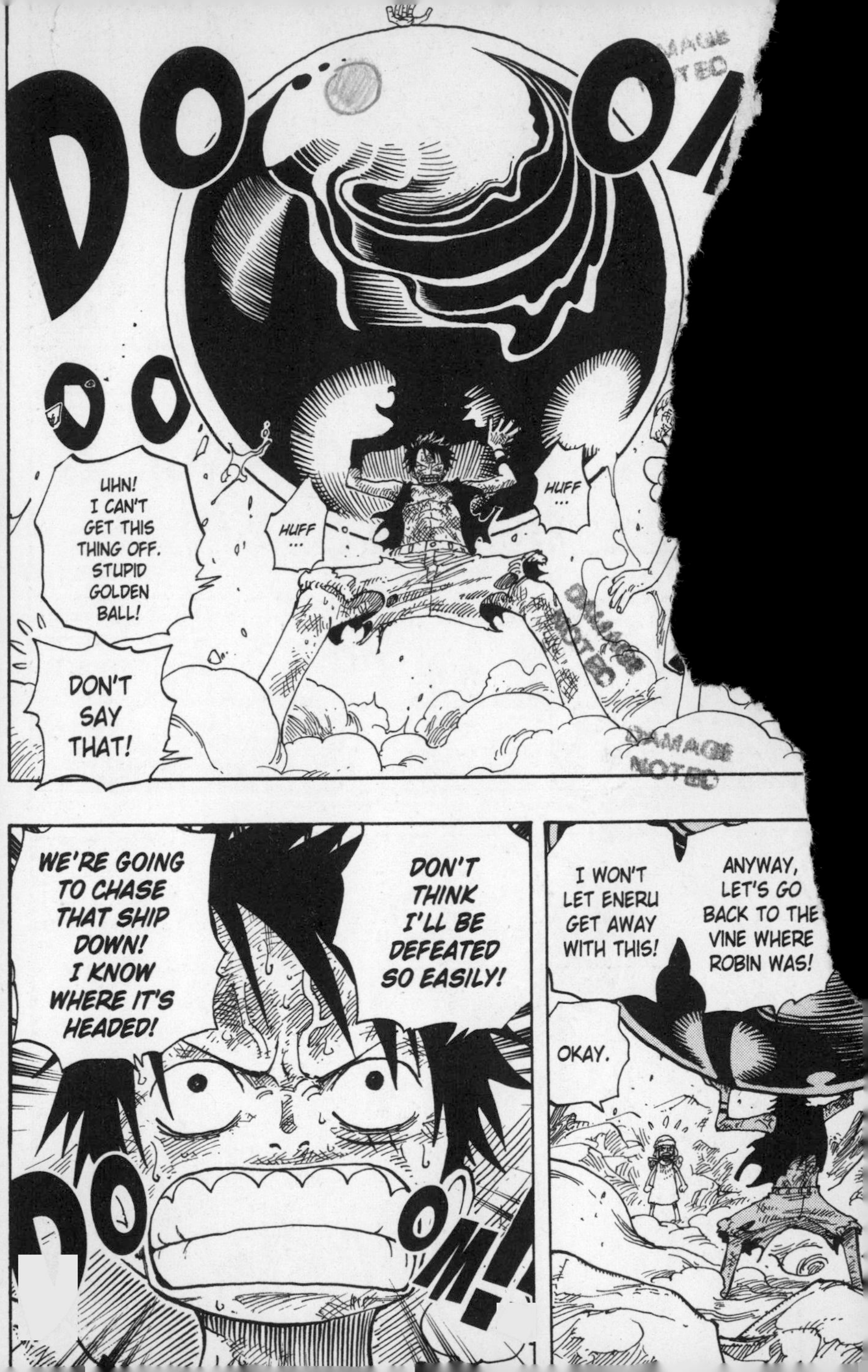
HUFF...
HUFF...
UHN! I CAN'T GET THIS THING OFF. STUPID GOLDEN BALL!
DON'T SAY THAT!
ANYWAY, LET'S GO BACK TO THE VINE WHERE ROBIN WAS!
I WON'T LET ENERU GET AWAY WITH THIS!
OKAY.
DON'T THINK I'LL BE DEFEATED SO EASILY!
WE'RE GOING TO CHASE THAT SHIP DOWN! I KNOW WHERE IT'S HEADED!

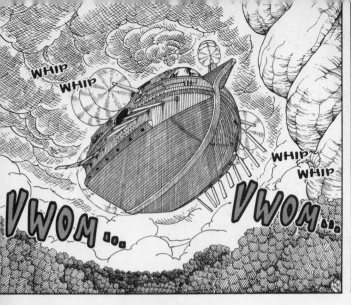

WHIP

WHIP

WHIP

WHIP

VWOM...

VWOM...

R M B L

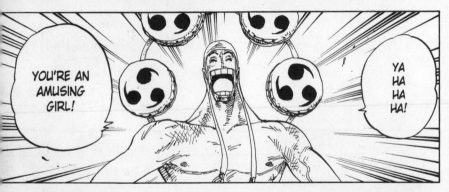

YOU'RE AN AMUSING GIRL!

YA HA HA HA!

KRAK!

SO THAT'S A BLUE SEA WEAPON, EH?

HUFF

HUFF

HUFF...

HUFF...

HUFF...

I DID IT...!

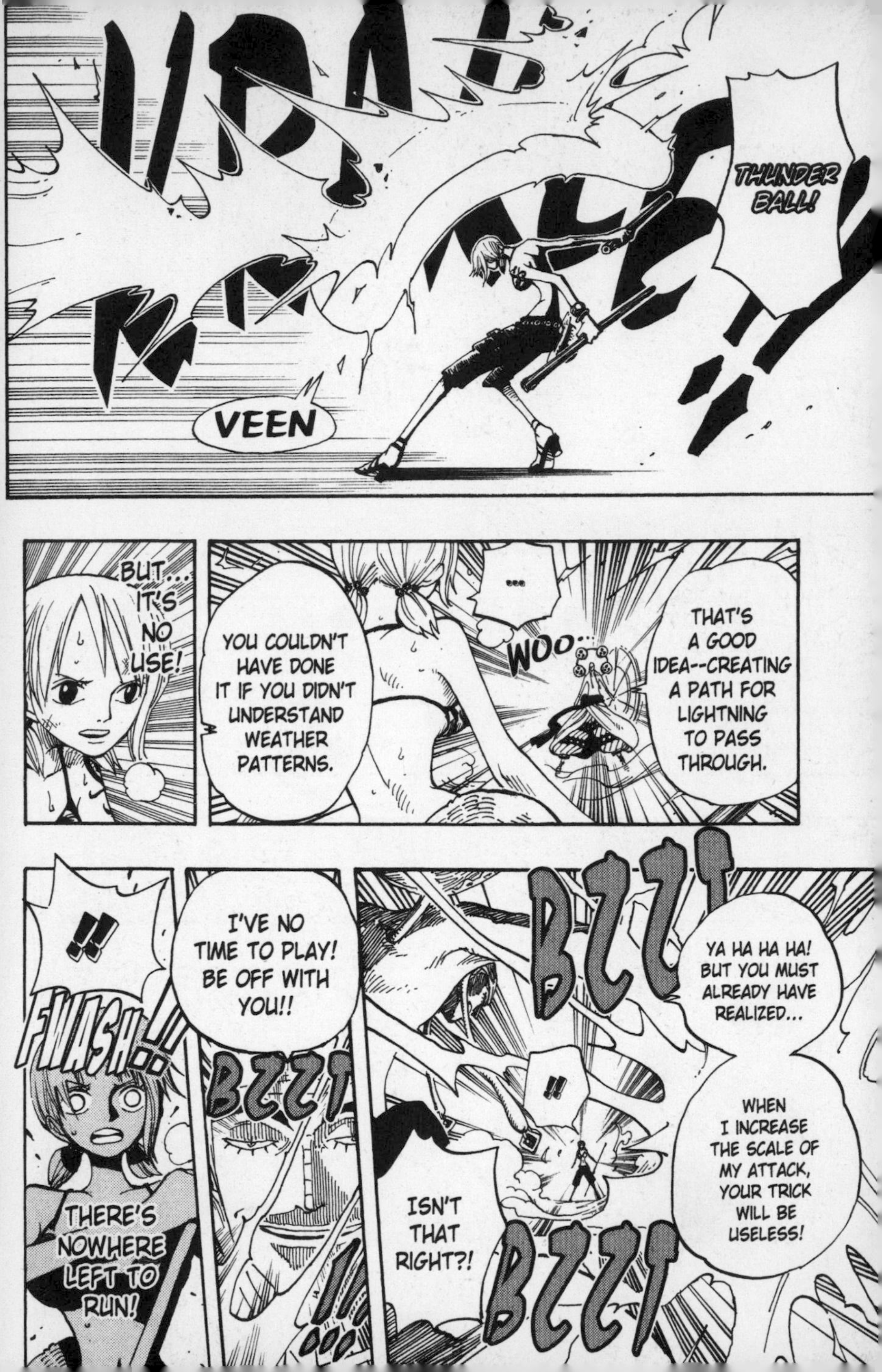
THUNDER BALL!
VEEN
THAT'S A GOOD IDEA--CREATING A PATH FOR LIGHTNING TO PASS THROUGH.
...
WOO...
YOU COULDN'T HAVE DONE IT IF YOU DIDN'T UNDERSTAND WEATHER PATTERNS.
BUT... IT'S NO USE!
BZZT
YA HA HA HA! BUT YOU MUST ALREADY HAVE REALIZED...
WHEN I INCREASE THE SCALE OF MY ATTACK, YOUR TRICK WILL BE USELESS!
!!
ISN'T THAT RIGHT?!
BZZT
I'VE NO TIME TO PLAY! BE OFF WITH YOU!!
BZZT
!!
FWASH!!
THERE'S NOWHERE LEFT TO RUN!

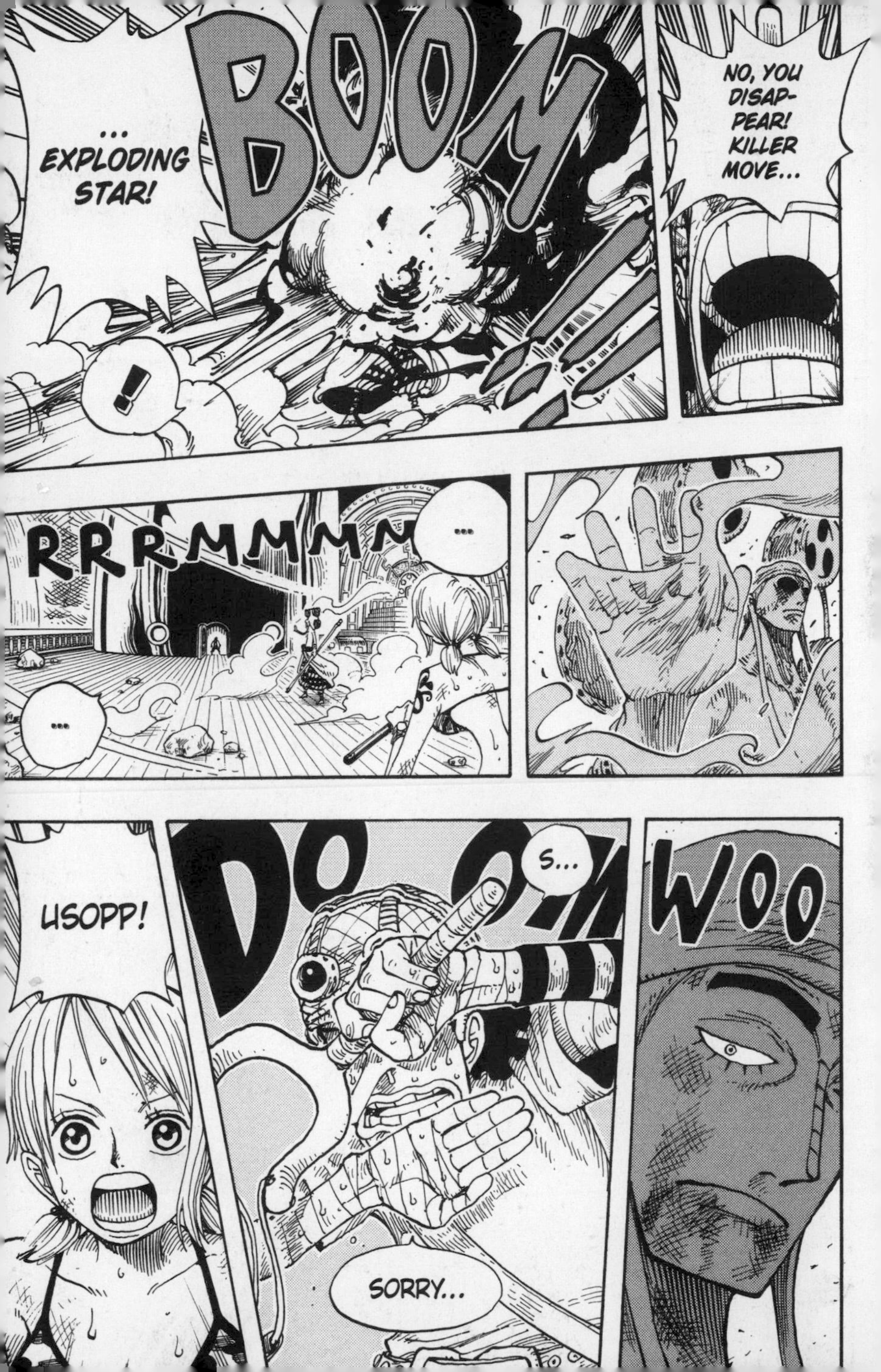
NO, YOU DISAP-PEAR! KILLER MOVE...
BOOM
... EXPLODING STAR!
!
...
RRRMMMMM
...
WOO
S...
DOOM
SORRY...
USOPP!

Chapter 284:
SORRY

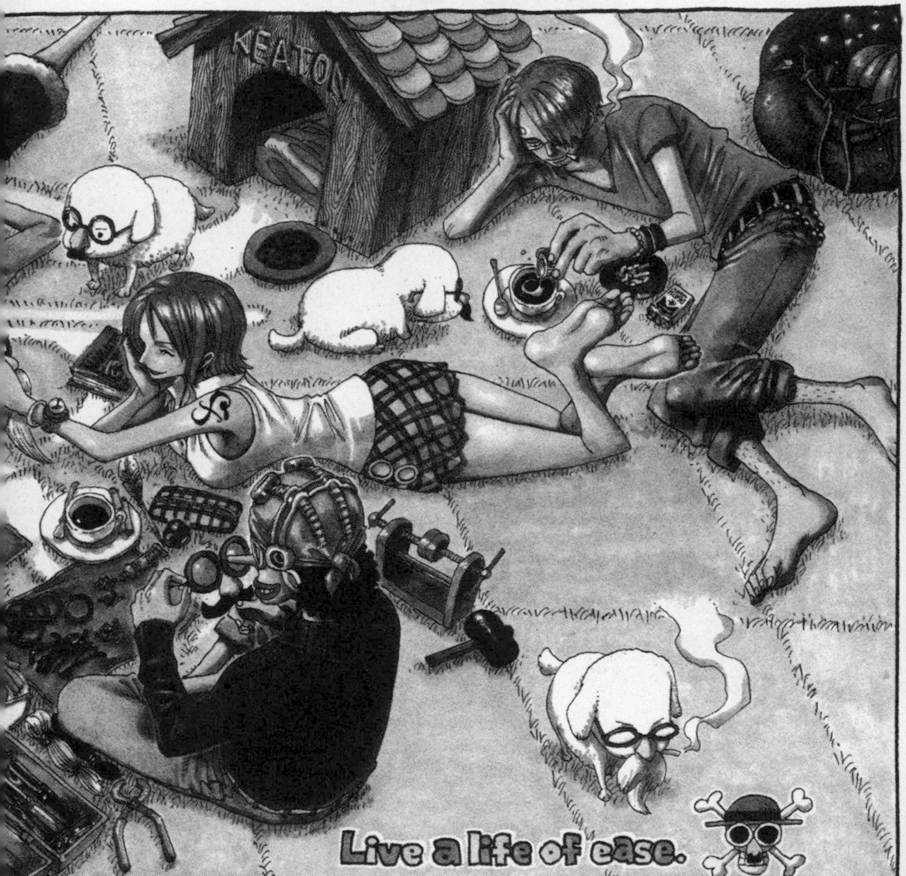

KEATON
Live a life of ease.

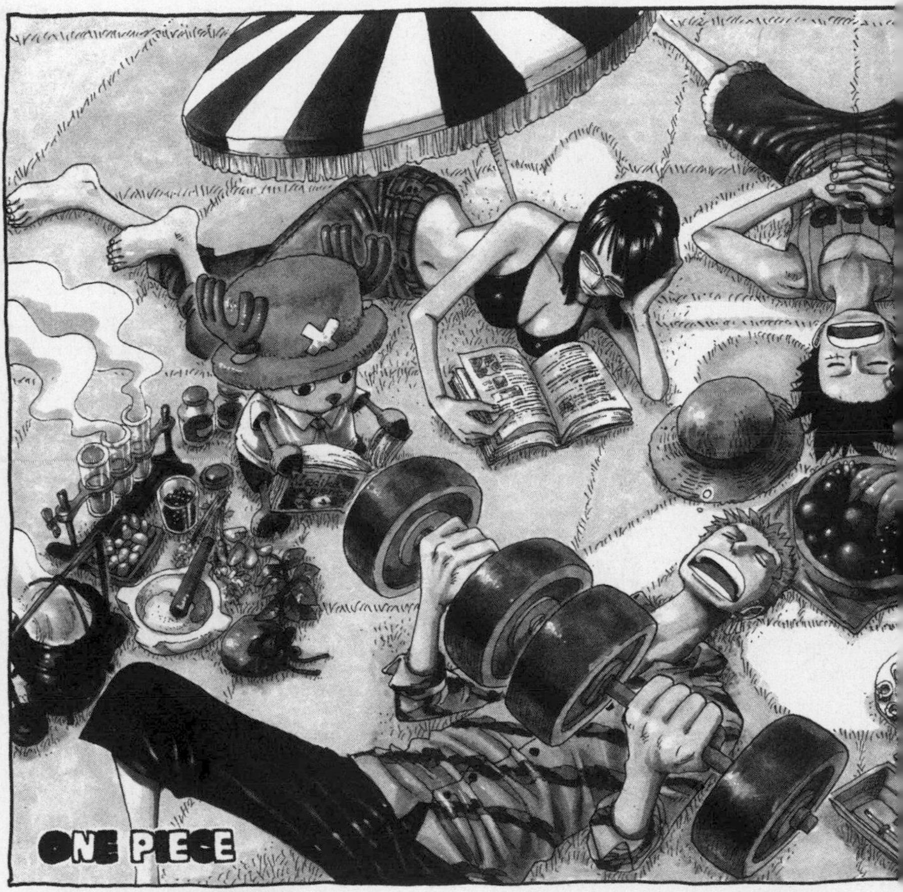
ONE PIECE

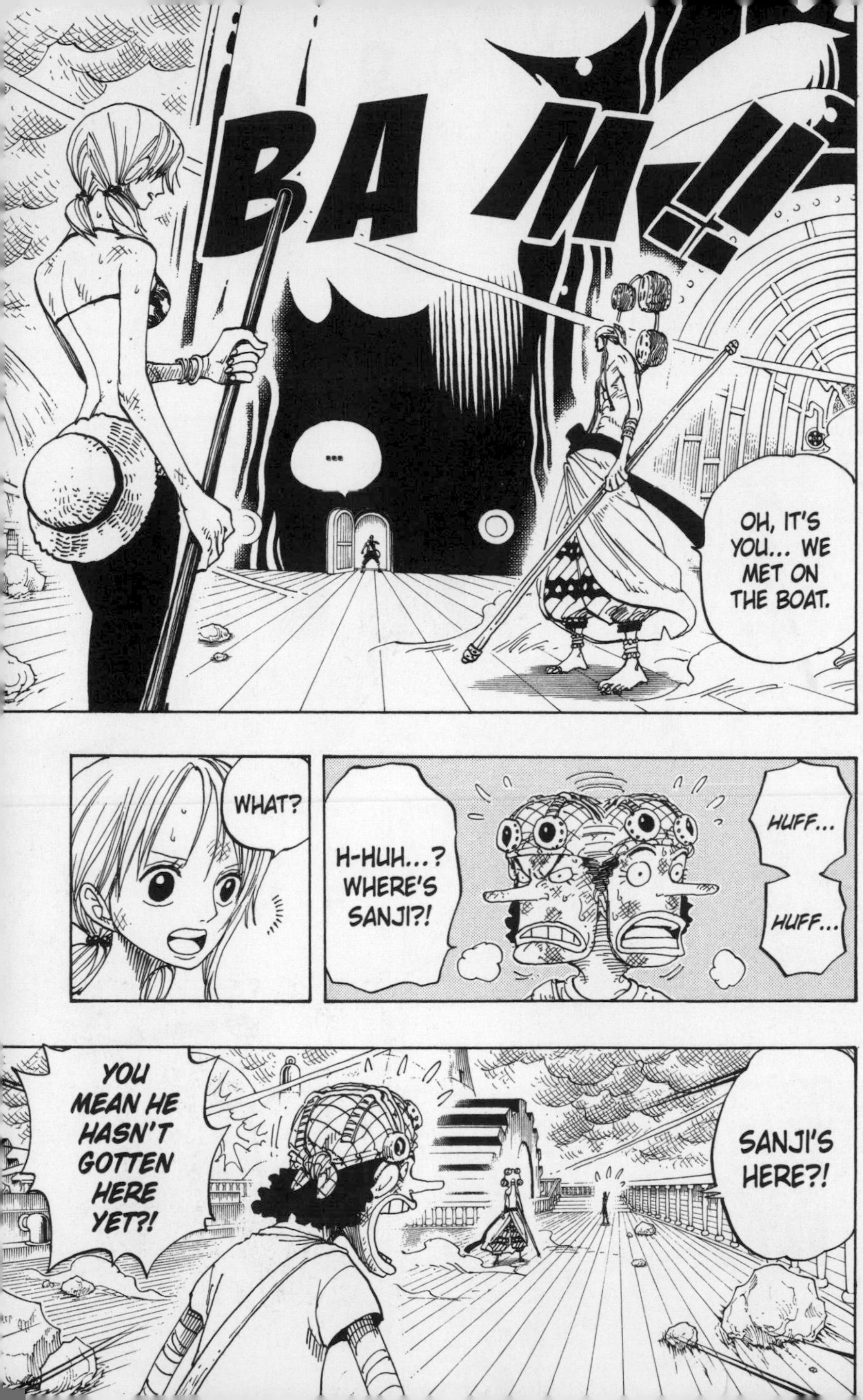
BAM!!
OH, IT'S YOU... WE MET ON THE BOAT.
...
HUFF... HUFF...
H-HUH...? WHERE'S SANJI?!
WHAT?
SANJI'S HERE?!
YOU MEAN HE HASN'T GOTTEN HERE YET?!

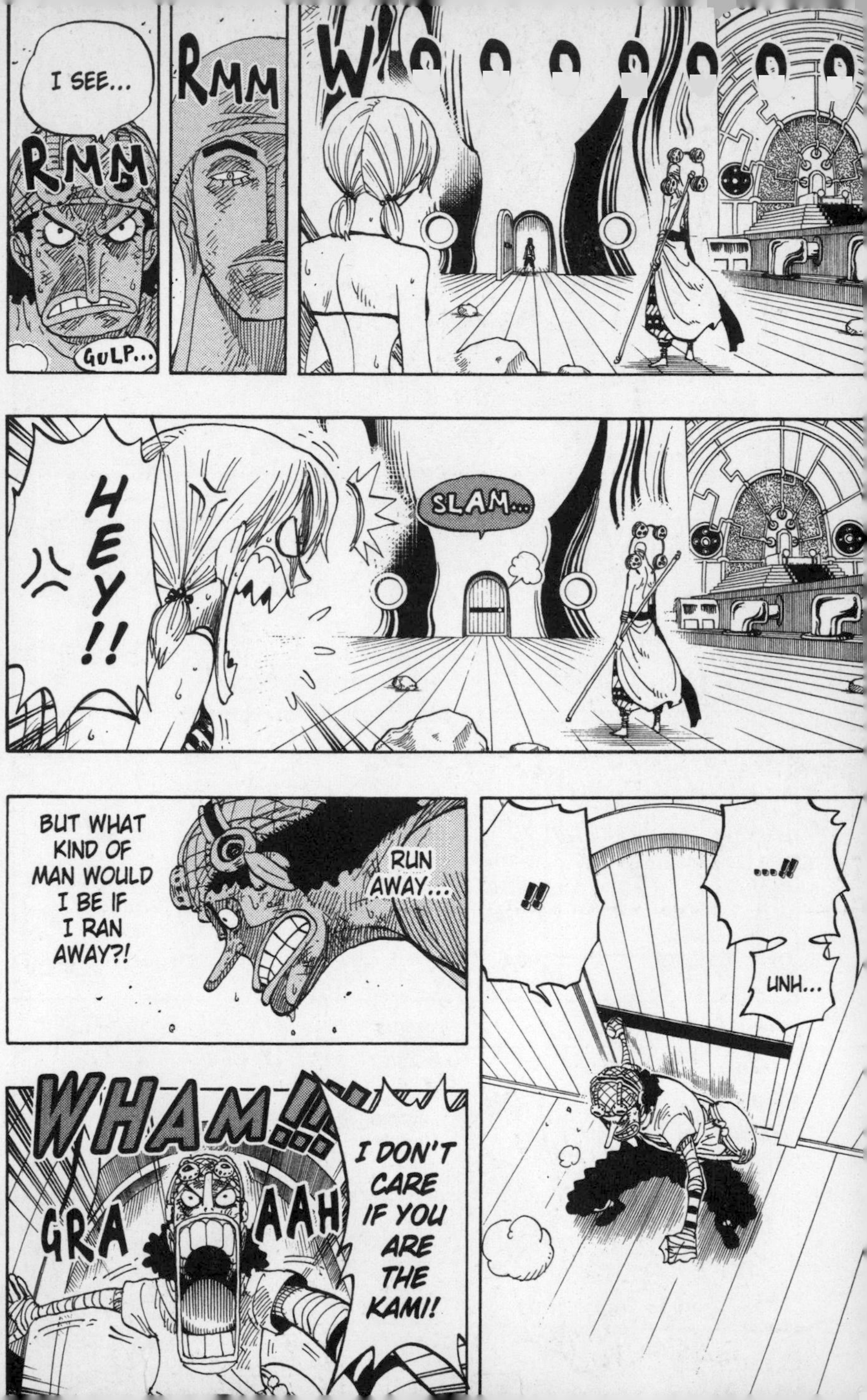
WOOOOOOO
RMM
I SEE...
RMM
GULP...
SLAM...
HEY!!
...!!
UNH...
!!
RUN AWAY...
BUT WHAT KIND OF MAN WOULD I BE IF I RAN AWAY?!
I DON'T CARE IF YOU ARE THE KAMI!
WHAM!!
GRAAAH

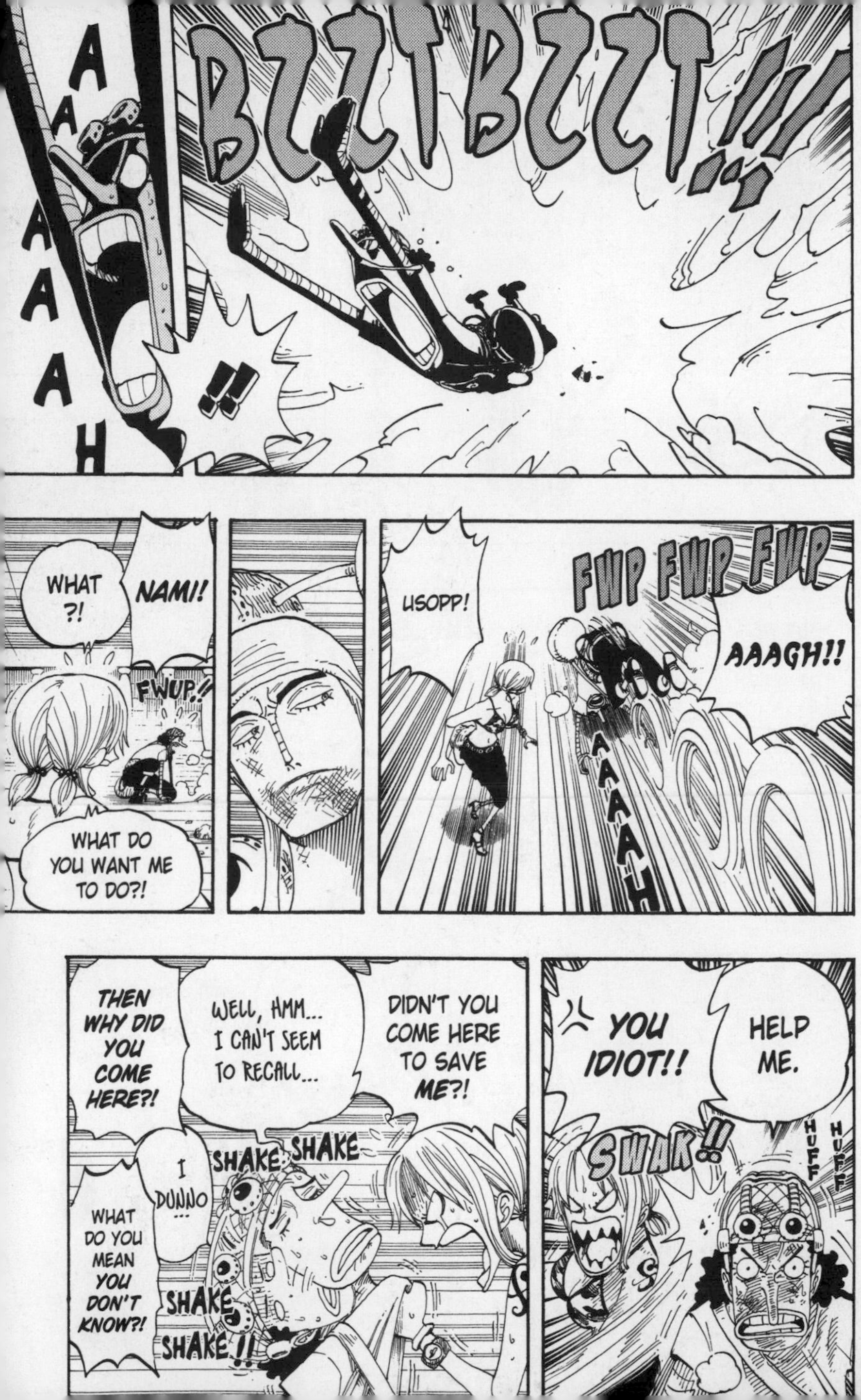
BZZT BZZT!!
AAAAAAH
!!
USOPP!
FWP FWP FWP
AAAGH!!
AAAAAH
NAMI!
WHAT ?!
FWUP!!
WHAT DO YOU WANT ME TO DO?!
HELP ME.
YOU IDIOT!!
SWAK!!
HUFF HUFF
DIDN'T YOU COME HERE TO SAVE ME?!
WELL, HMM... I CAN'T SEEM TO RECALL...
THEN WHY DID YOU COME HERE?!
SHAKE SHAKE
I DUNNO...
WHAT DO YOU MEAN YOU DON'T KNOW?!
SHAKE SHAKE!!

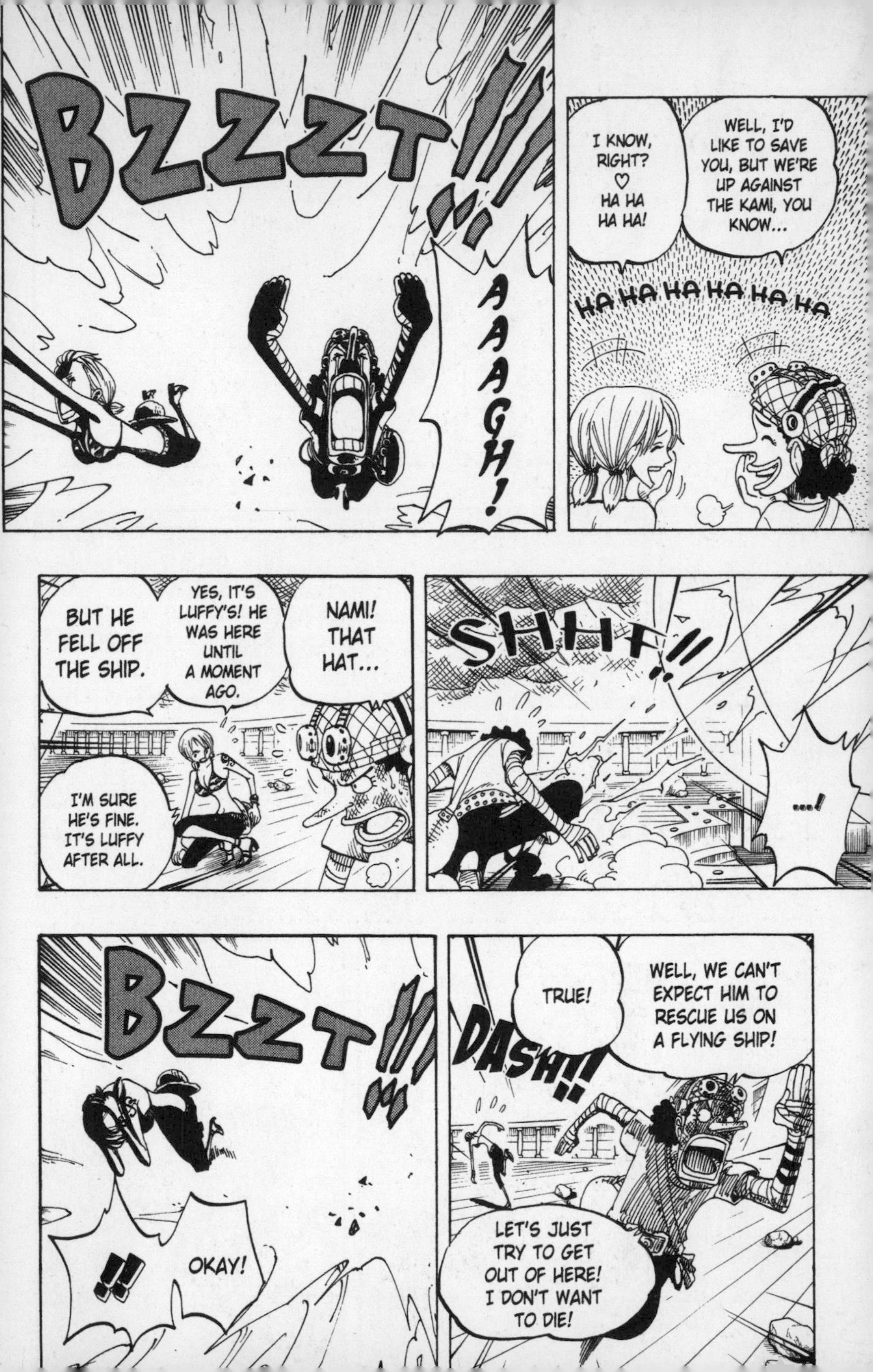
WELL, I'D LIKE TO SAVE YOU, BUT WE'RE UP AGAINST THE KAMI, YOU KNOW...
I KNOW, RIGHT? ♡ HA HA HA HA!
HA HA HA HA HA HA
BZZZT!!!
AAAAGH!
SHHF!!
...!
NAMI! THAT HAT...
YES, IT'S LUFFY'S! HE WAS HERE UNTIL A MOMENT AGO.
BUT HE FELL OFF THE SHIP.
I'M SURE HE'S FINE. IT'S LUFFY AFTER ALL.
WELL, WE CAN'T EXPECT HIM TO RESCUE US ON A FLYING SHIP!
TRUE!
DASH!!
LET'S JUST TRY TO GET OUT OF HERE! I DON'T WANT TO DIE!
BZZT!!!
!!
OKAY!

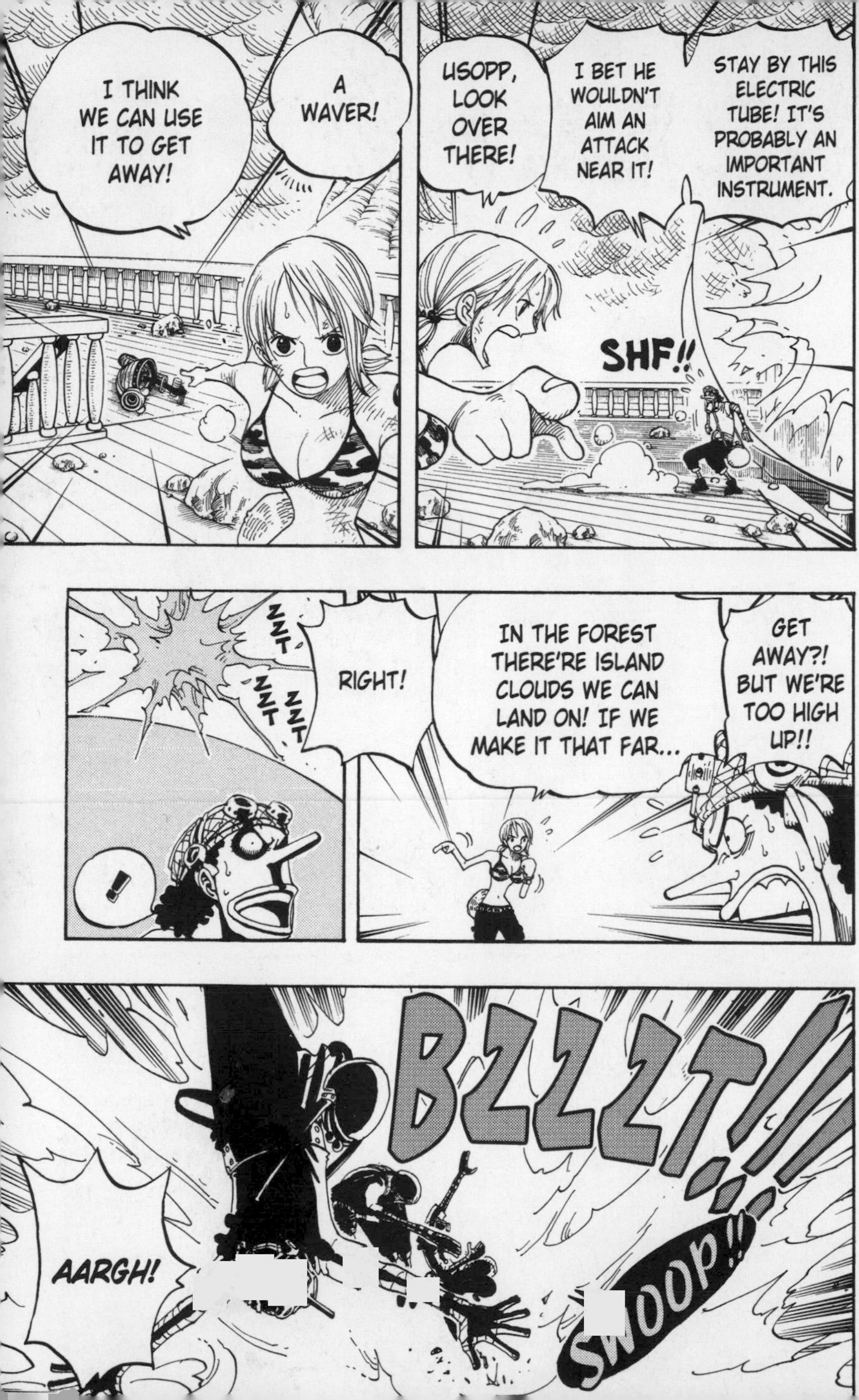
STAY BY THIS ELECTRIC TUBE! IT'S PROBABLY AN IMPORTANT INSTRUMENT.
I BET HE WOULDN'T AIM AN ATTACK NEAR IT!
USOPP, LOOK OVER THERE!
SHF!!
A WAVER!
I THINK WE CAN USE IT TO GET AWAY!
GET AWAY?! BUT WE'RE TOO HIGH UP!!
IN THE FOREST THERE'RE ISLAND CLOUDS WE CAN LAND ON! IF WE MAKE IT THAT FAR...
RIGHT!
ZZT
ZZT
ZZT
!
BZZZT!!
SWOOP!!
AARGH!

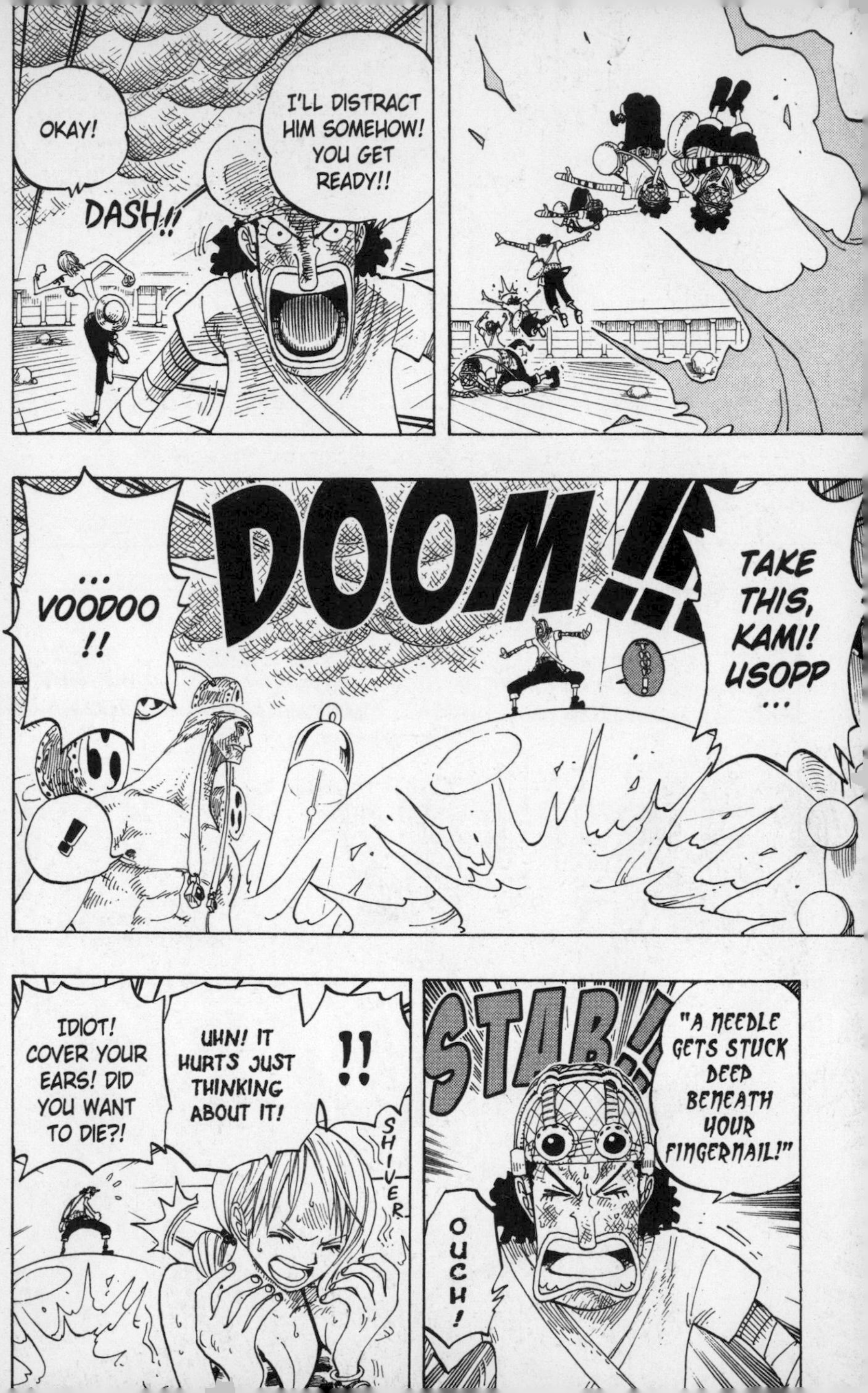
I'LL DISTRACT HIM SOMEHOW! YOU GET READY!!
OKAY!
DASH!!
TAKE THIS, KAMI! USOPP ...
DOOM!!
... VOODOO !!
!
"A NEEDLE GETS STUCK DEEP BENEATH YOUR FINGERNAIL!"
STAB!!
OUCH!
!!
UHN! IT HURTS JUST THINKING ABOUT IT!
SHIVER
IDIOT! COVER YOUR EARS! DID YOU WANT TO DIE?!

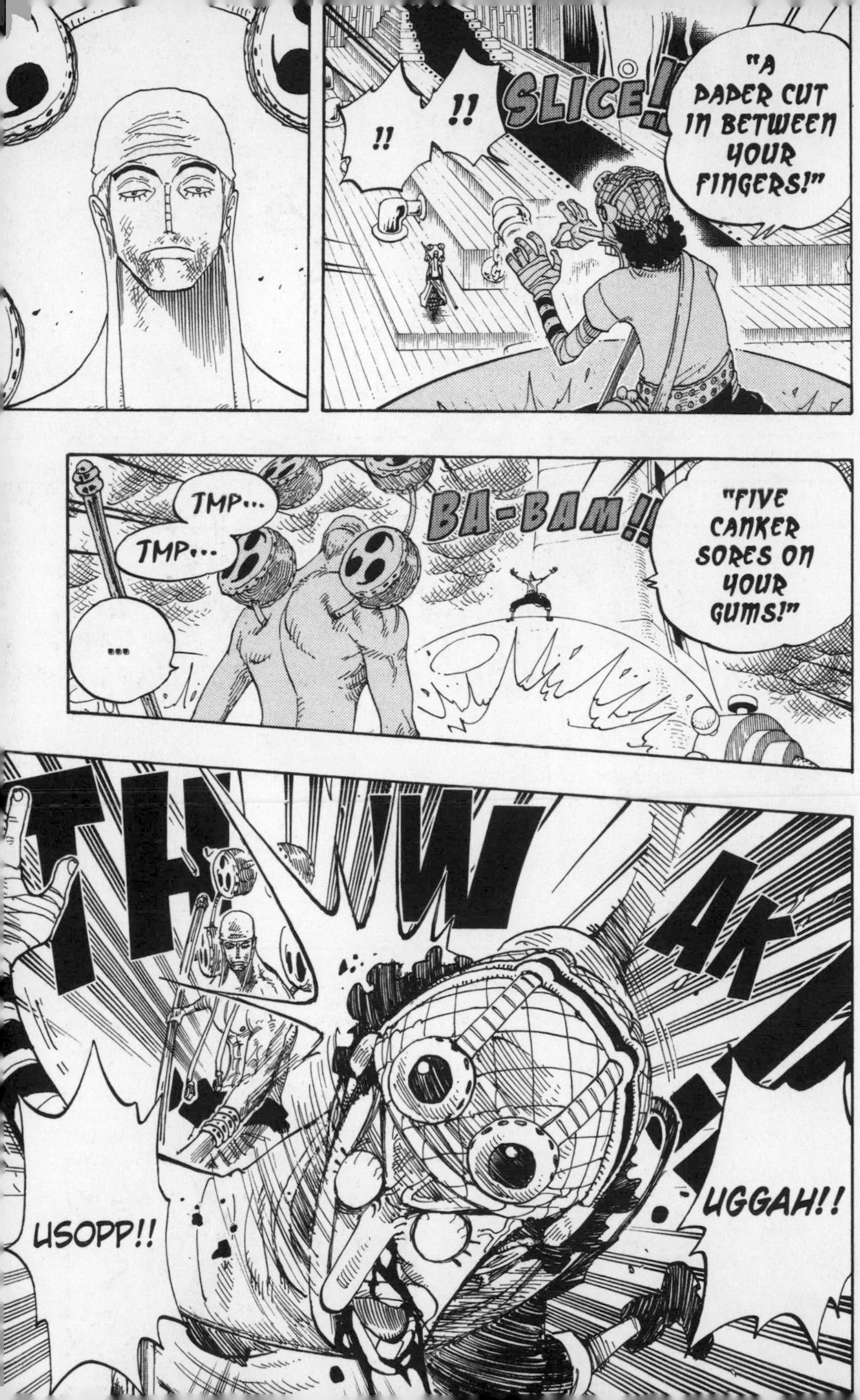
"A PAPER CUT IN BETWEEN YOUR FINGERS!"
SLICE!!
!!
!!
"FIVE CANKER SORES ON YOUR GUMS!"
BA-BAM!!
TMP...
TMP...
...
THWAK
UGGAH!!
USOPP!!

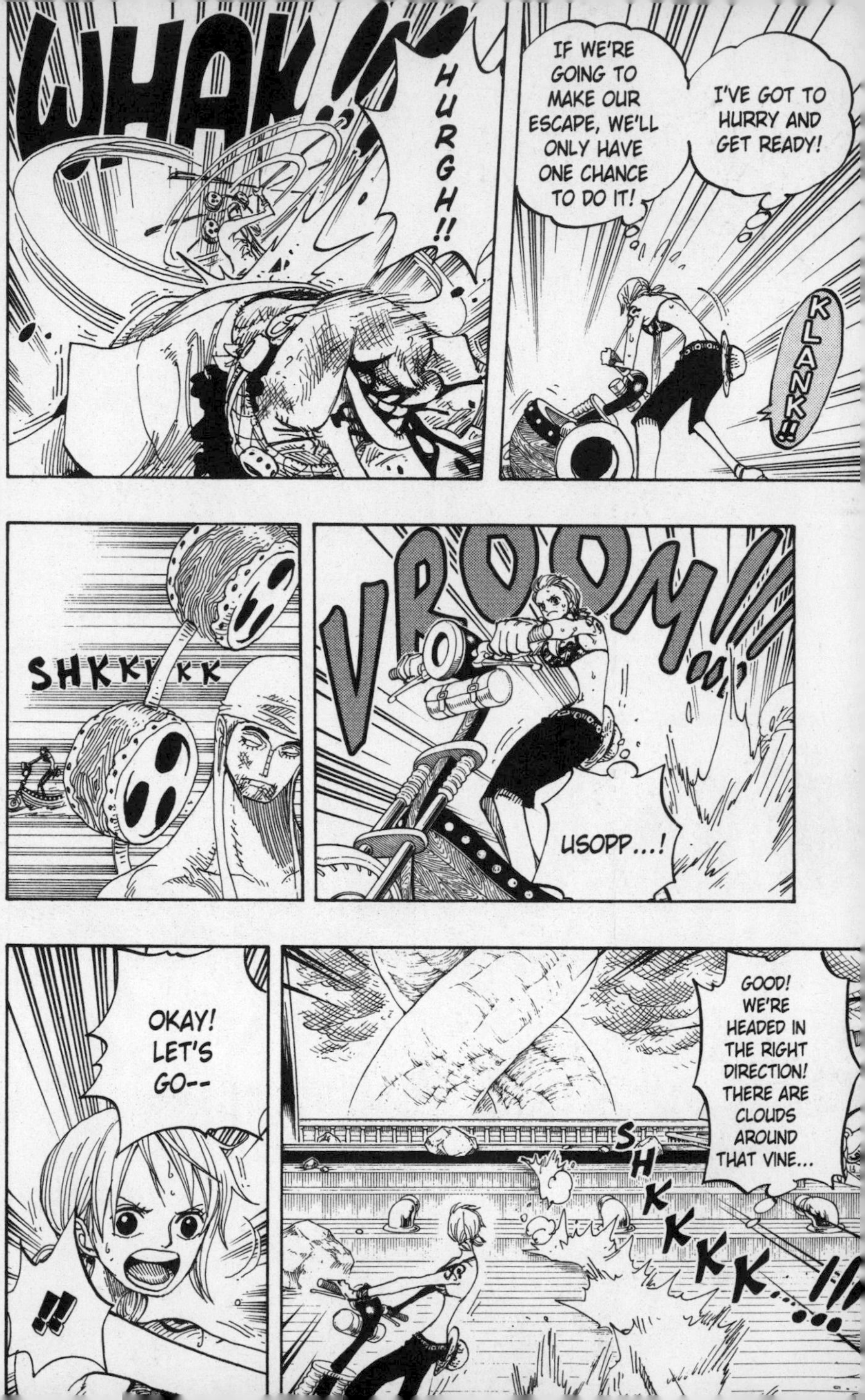
IF WE'RE GOING TO MAKE OUR ESCAPE, WE'LL ONLY HAVE ONE CHANCE TO DO IT!
I'VE GOT TO HURRY AND GET READY!
KLANK!!
WHAK!!
HURGH!!
VROOM!!
USOPP...!
SHKKKKK
GOOD! WE'RE HEADED IN THE RIGHT DIRECTION! THERE ARE CLOUDS AROUND THAT VINE...
SHKKKKK...!!
OKAY! LET'S GO--
!!

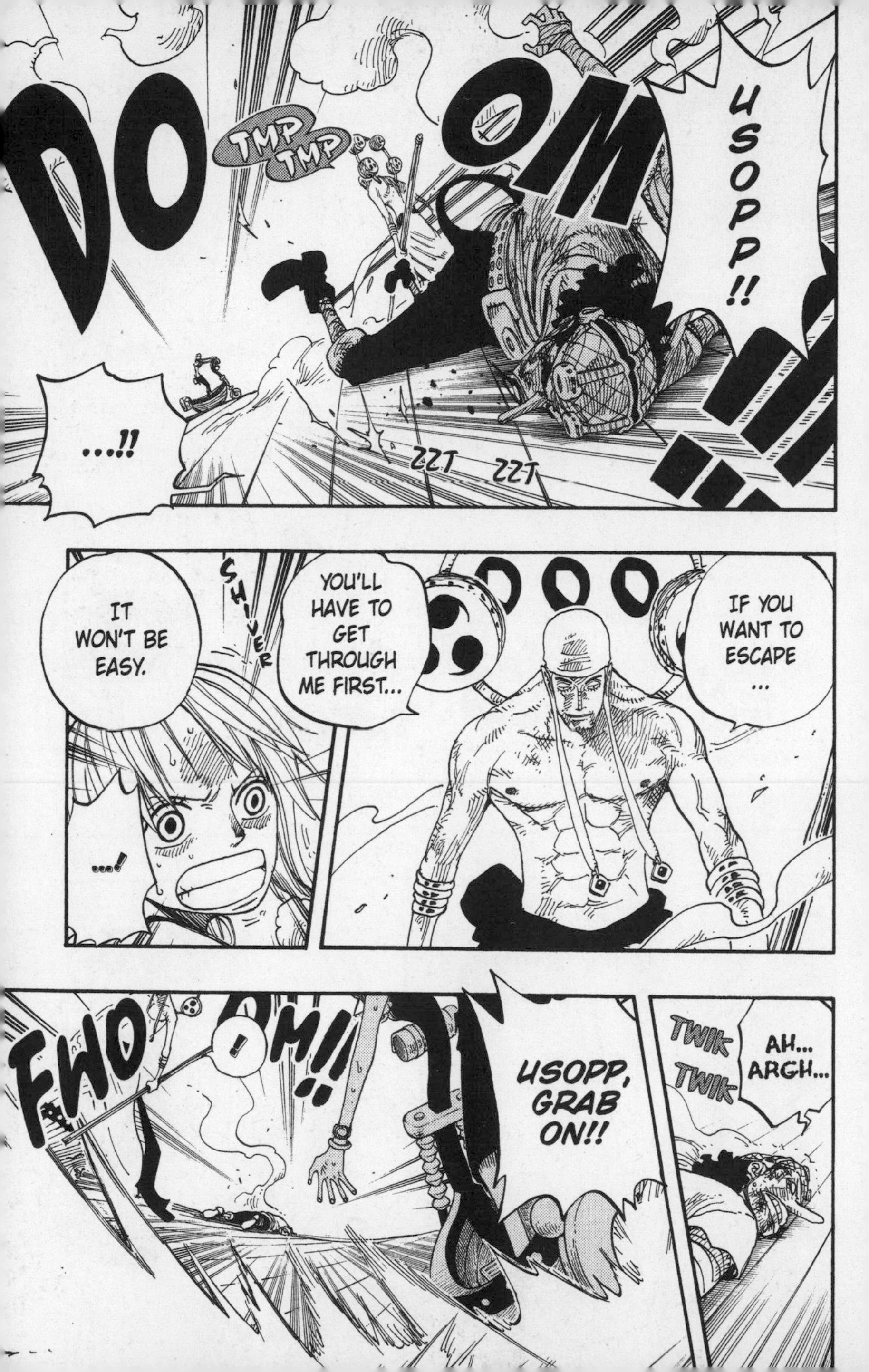
USOPP!!
DO
OM
TMP TMP
...!!
ZZT ZZT
IF YOU WANT TO ESCAPE ...
DOOO
YOU'LL HAVE TO GET THROUGH ME FIRST...
IT WON'T BE EASY.
SHIVER
...!
AH... ARGH...
TWIK TWIK
USOPP, GRAB ON!!
FWO
OM!!
!

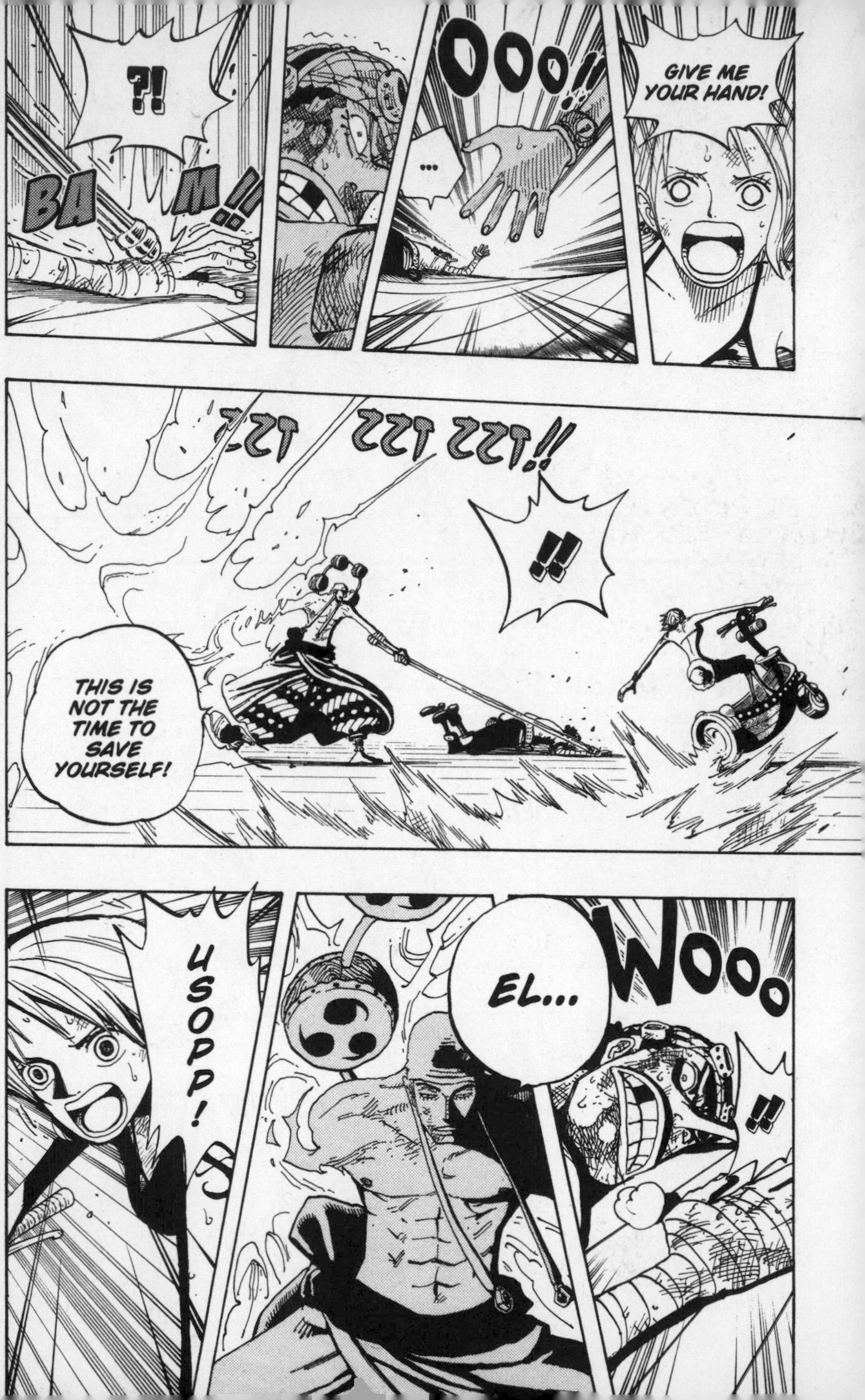
GIVE ME YOUR HAND!
OOO!!
...
?!
BAM!!
ZZT ZZT ZZT!!
!!
THIS IS NOT THE TIME TO SAVE YOURSELF!
WOOO
!!
EL...
USOPP!

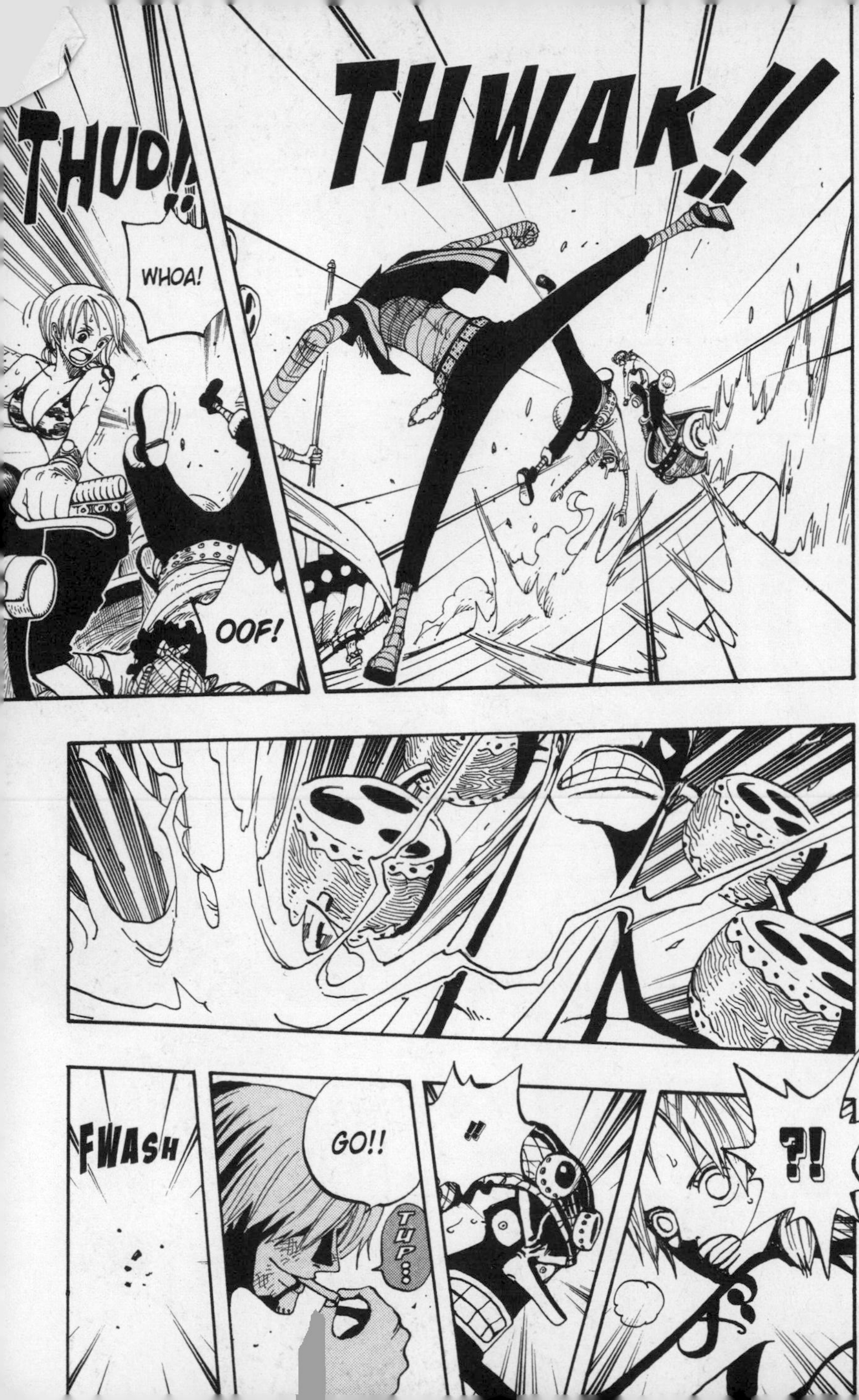
THWAK!!
THUD!!
WHOA!
OOF!
?!
!!
GO!!
TUP...
FWASH

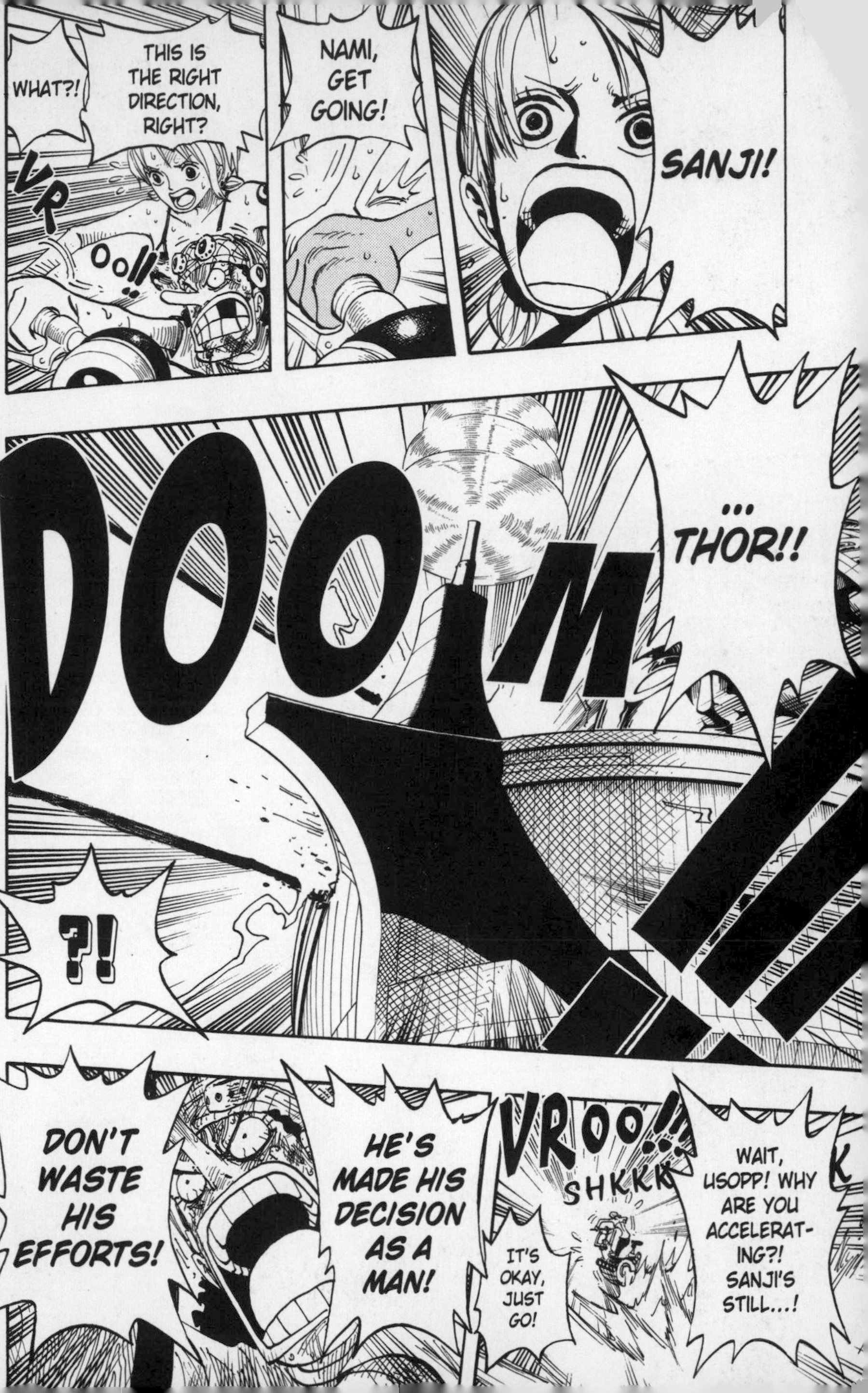
SANJI!
NAMI, GET GOING!
THIS IS THE RIGHT DIRECTION, RIGHT?
WHAT?!
VROO!!
...THOR!!
DOOM
?!
K
WAIT, USOPP! WHY ARE YOU ACCELERAT-ING?! SANJI'S STILL...!
VROO!!!
SHKKK
IT'S OKAY, JUST GO!
HE'S MADE HIS DECISION AS A MAN!
DON'T WASTE HIS EFFORTS!

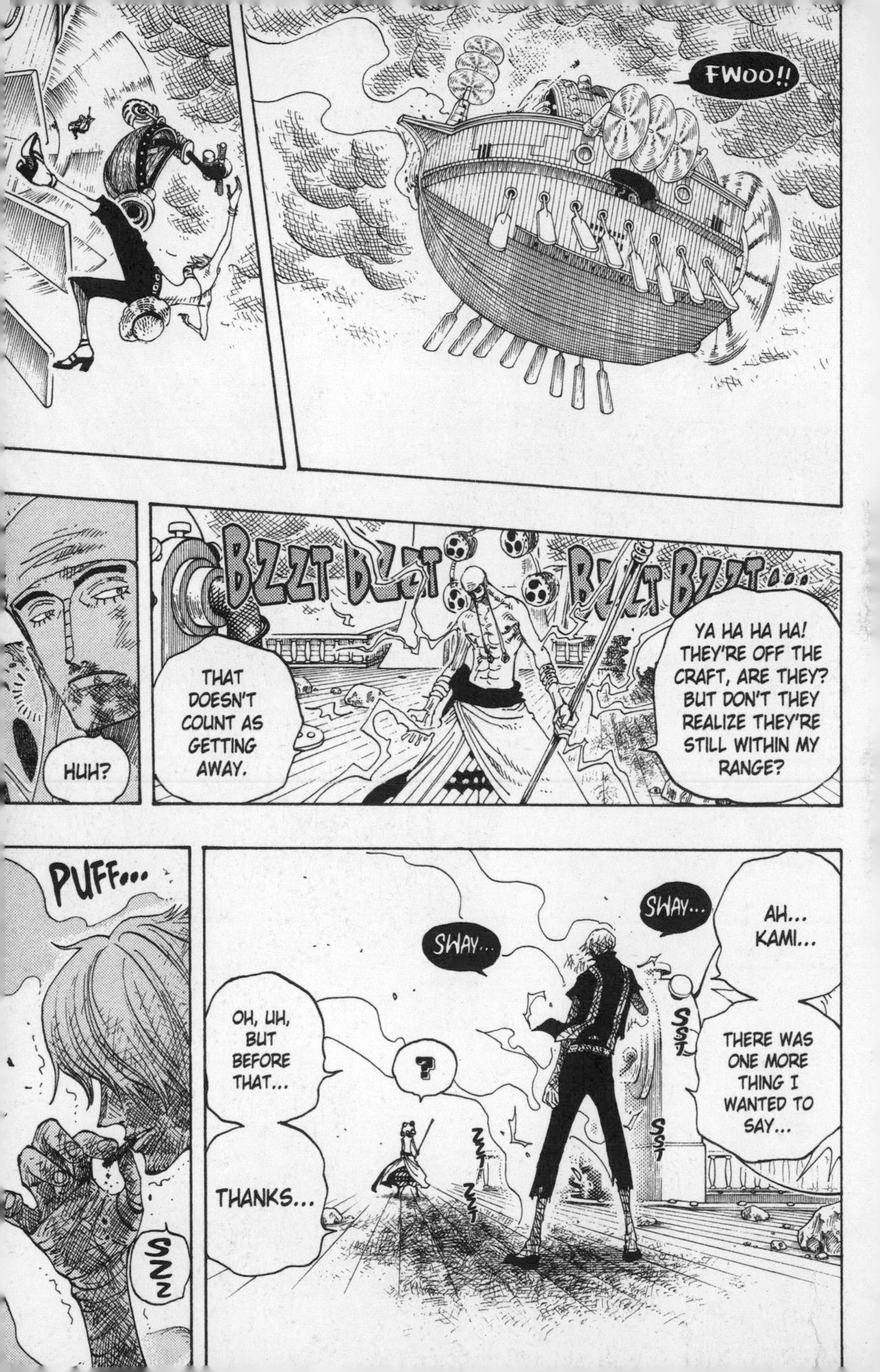
FWOO!!
BZZT BZZT...
BZZT BZZT
YA HA HA HA! THEY'RE OFF THE CRAFT, ARE THEY? BUT DON'T THEY REALIZE THEY'RE STILL WITHIN MY RANGE?
THAT DOESN'T COUNT AS GETTING AWAY.
HUH?
AH... KAMI...
SWAY...
SWAY...
SST
SST
THERE WAS ONE MORE THING I WANTED TO SAY...
?
ZZT
ZZT
OH, UH, BUT BEFORE THAT...
THANKS...
PUFF...
SZZ

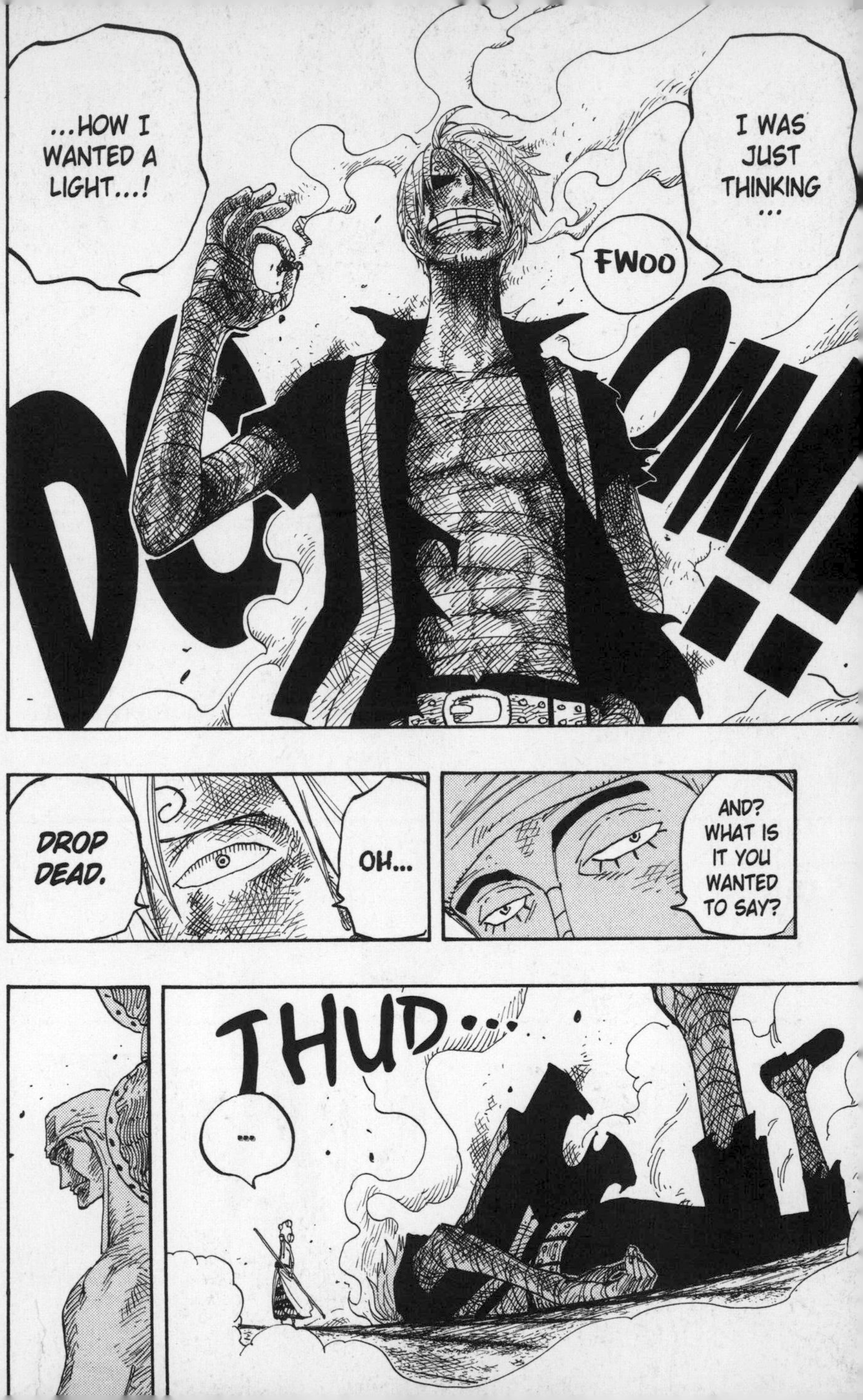
I WAS JUST THINKING ...
FWOO
...HOW I WANTED A LIGHT...!
DOOM!!
AND? WHAT IS IT YOU WANTED TO SAY?
OH...
DROP DEAD.
THUD...
...

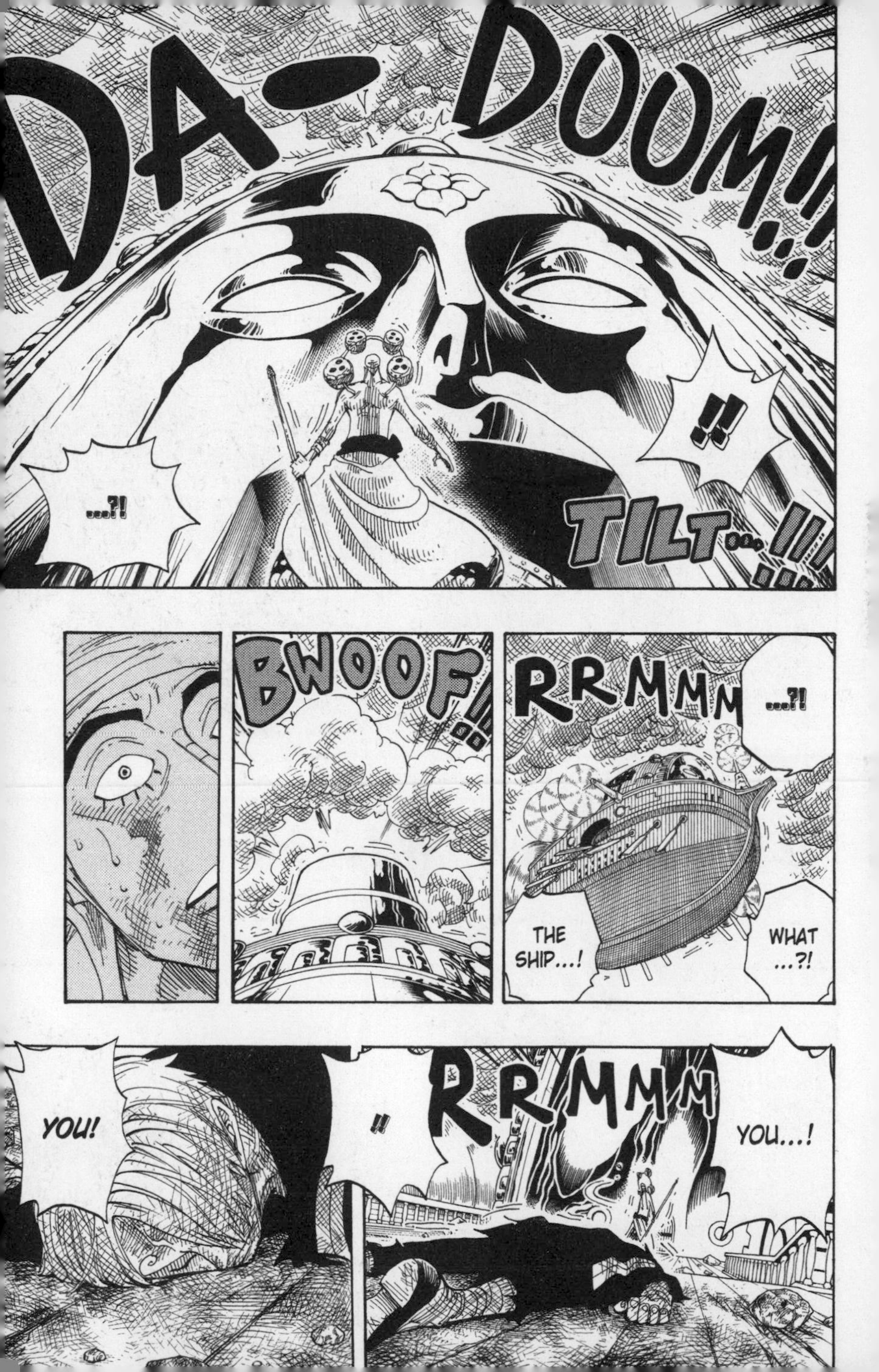
DA-DOOM!!!
!!
TILT...!!!
...?!
...?!
RRMMMM
WHAT ...?!
THE SHIP...!
BWOOF!!!
YOU...!
RRMMMM
!!
YOU!

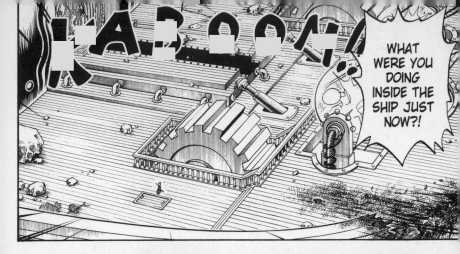

WHAT WERE YOU DOING INSIDE THE SHIP JUST NOW?!

RRMMM ...!

LOOK AT WHAT YOU'VE DONE!

GRR

HOW DARE YOU!

RRMMMM

RRRMMMMM...

THE GEARS ARE JAMMED! I HAVE TO FIX THIS!

KRAK!!

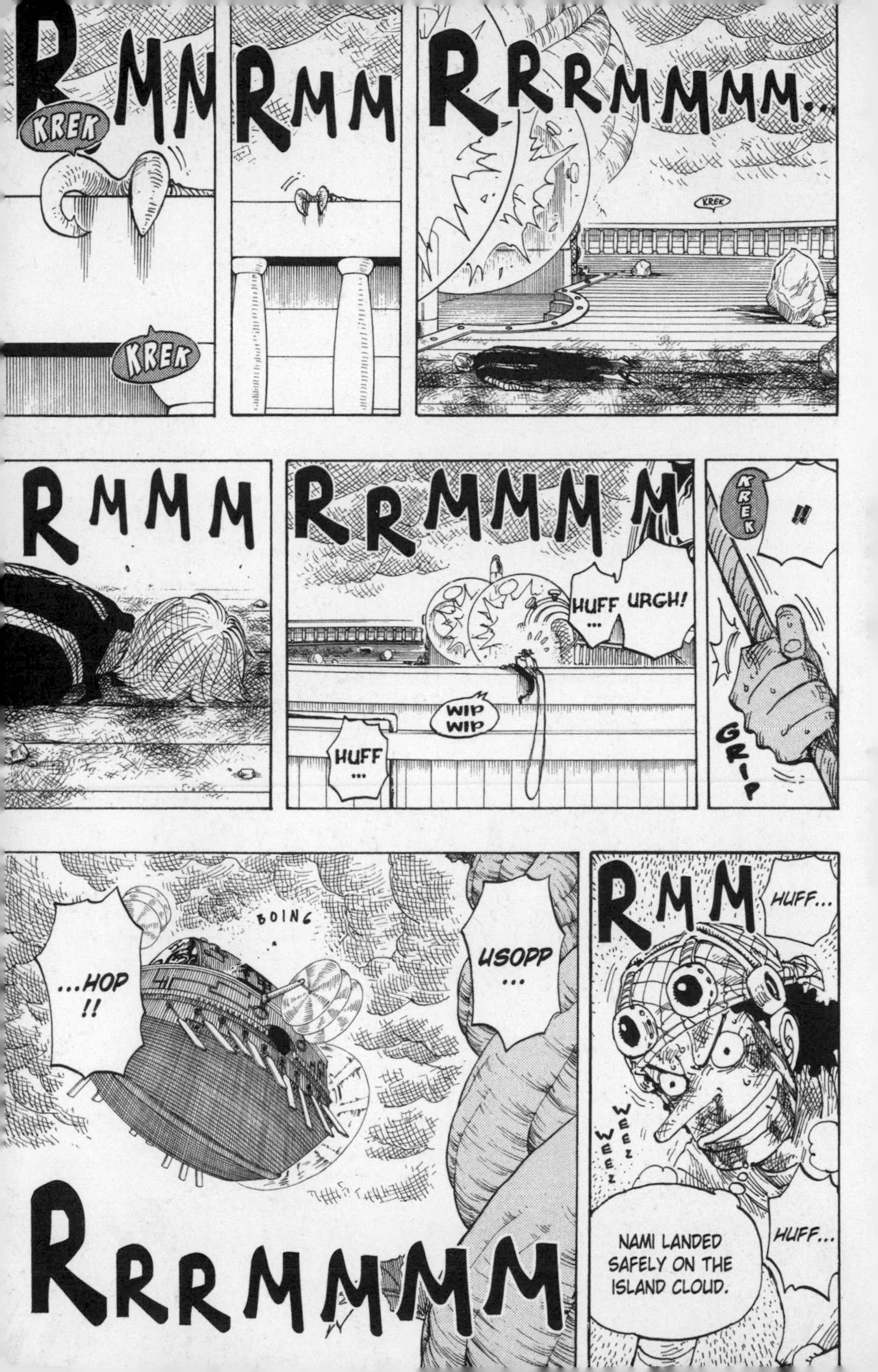
RRRRMMMM...
KREK
RMM
RMM
KREK
KREK
KREK
!!
GRIP
RRMMMM
URGH!
HUFF...
WIP WIP
HUFF...
RMMM
RMM
HUFF...
WEEZ WEEZ
NAMI LANDED SAFELY ON THE ISLAND CLOUD.
HUFF...
USOPP...
BOING
...HOP!!
RRRMMMMM

Oda: Here are the results of my experiment.
I've concluded that it's not good to draw using your mouth... So please don't ask me to do anything like this ever again. Shuuichi, my front teeth hurt! They're going to crack! We'll continue the Question Corner in the next volume!

Chapter 285: CAPRICCIO

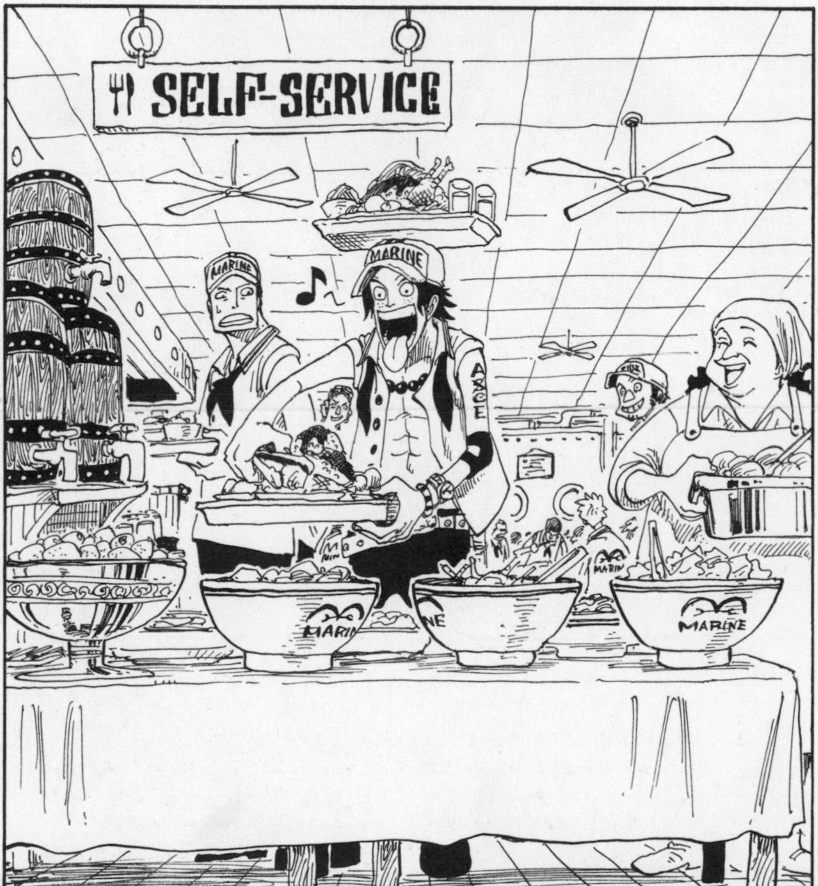
SELF-SERVICE
MARINE
MARINE
ACE
MARINE
MARINE

ACE'S GREAT SEARCH FOR BLACKBEARD, VOL. 12:
"THE NAVY'S ALL-YOU-CAN-EAT BUFFET"

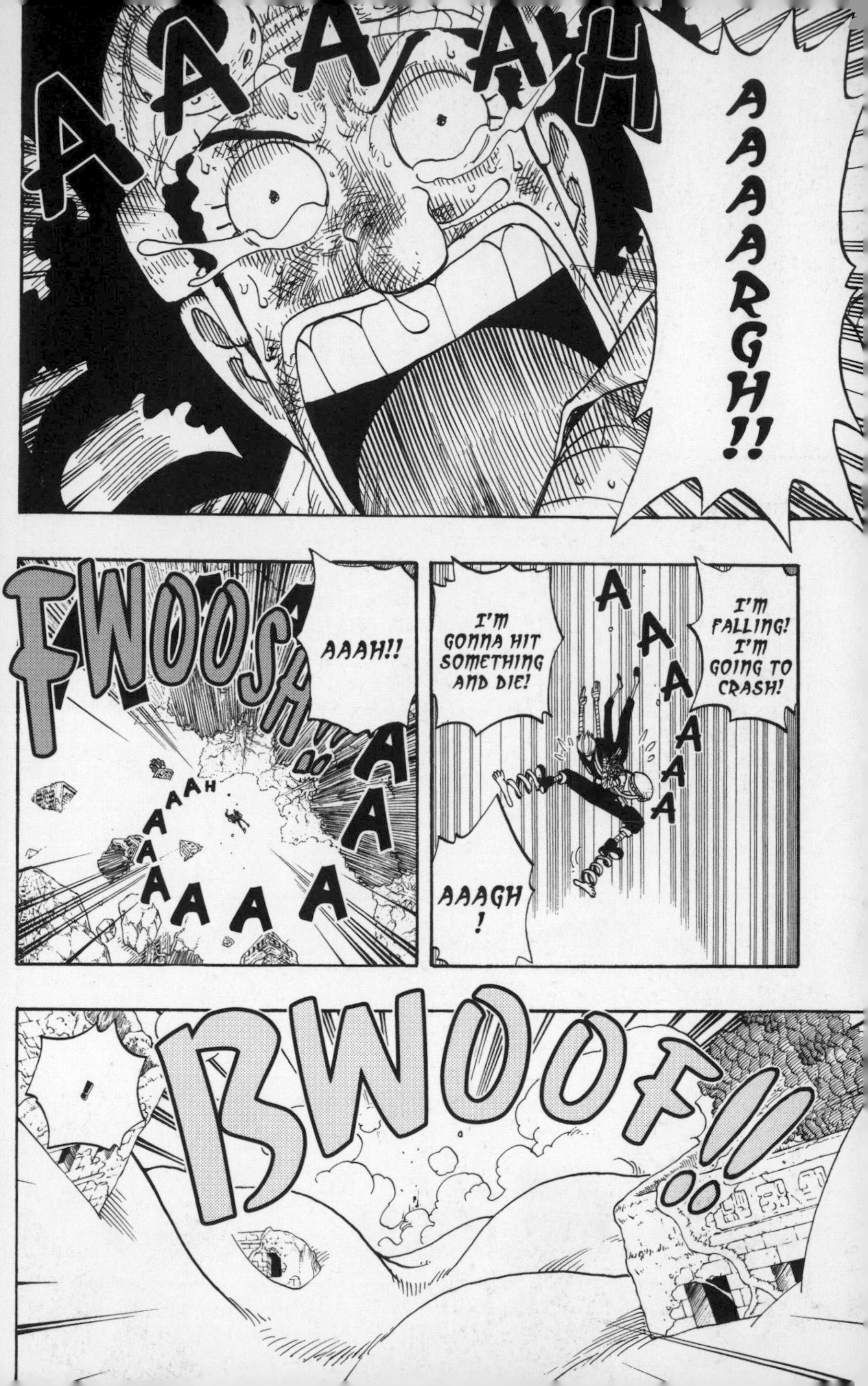
AAAAARGH!!
AAAAH
I'm falling! I'm going to crash!
AAAAAAA
I'm gonna hit something and die!
AAAGH!
AAAH!!
FWOOSH..
AAAAAAAA
AAAAAAAH
BWOOF!!
!

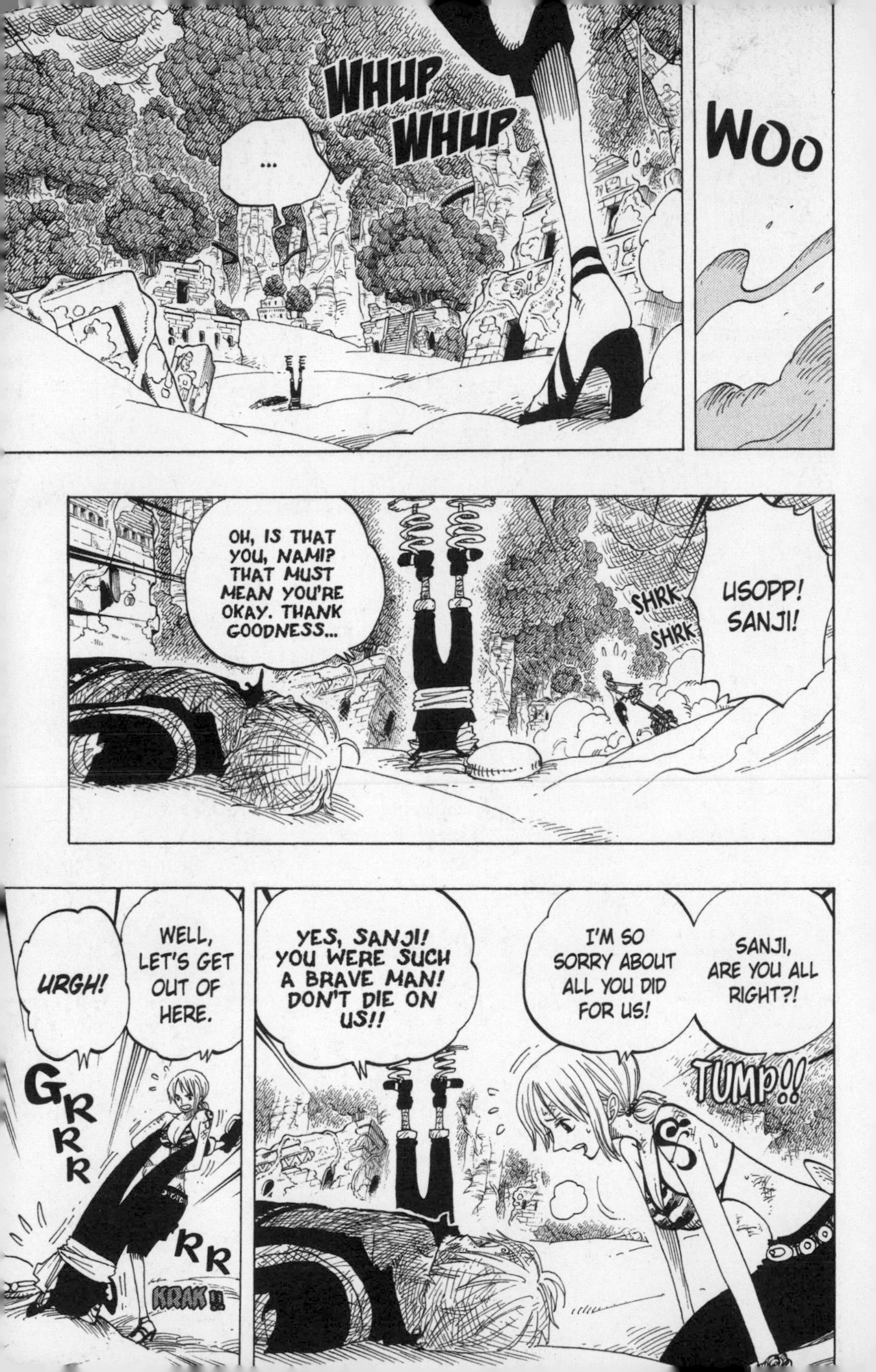
WOO
WHUP WHUP
...
USOPP! SANJI!
SHRK SHRK
OH, IS THAT YOU, NAMI? THAT MUST MEAN YOU'RE OKAY. THANK GOODNESS...
SANJI, ARE YOU ALL RIGHT?!
I'M SO SORRY ABOUT ALL YOU DID FOR US!
TUMP!!
YES, SANJI! YOU WERE SUCH A BRAVE MAN! DON'T DIE ON US!!
WELL, LET'S GET OUT OF HERE.
URGH!
GRRR
RR
KRAK!!

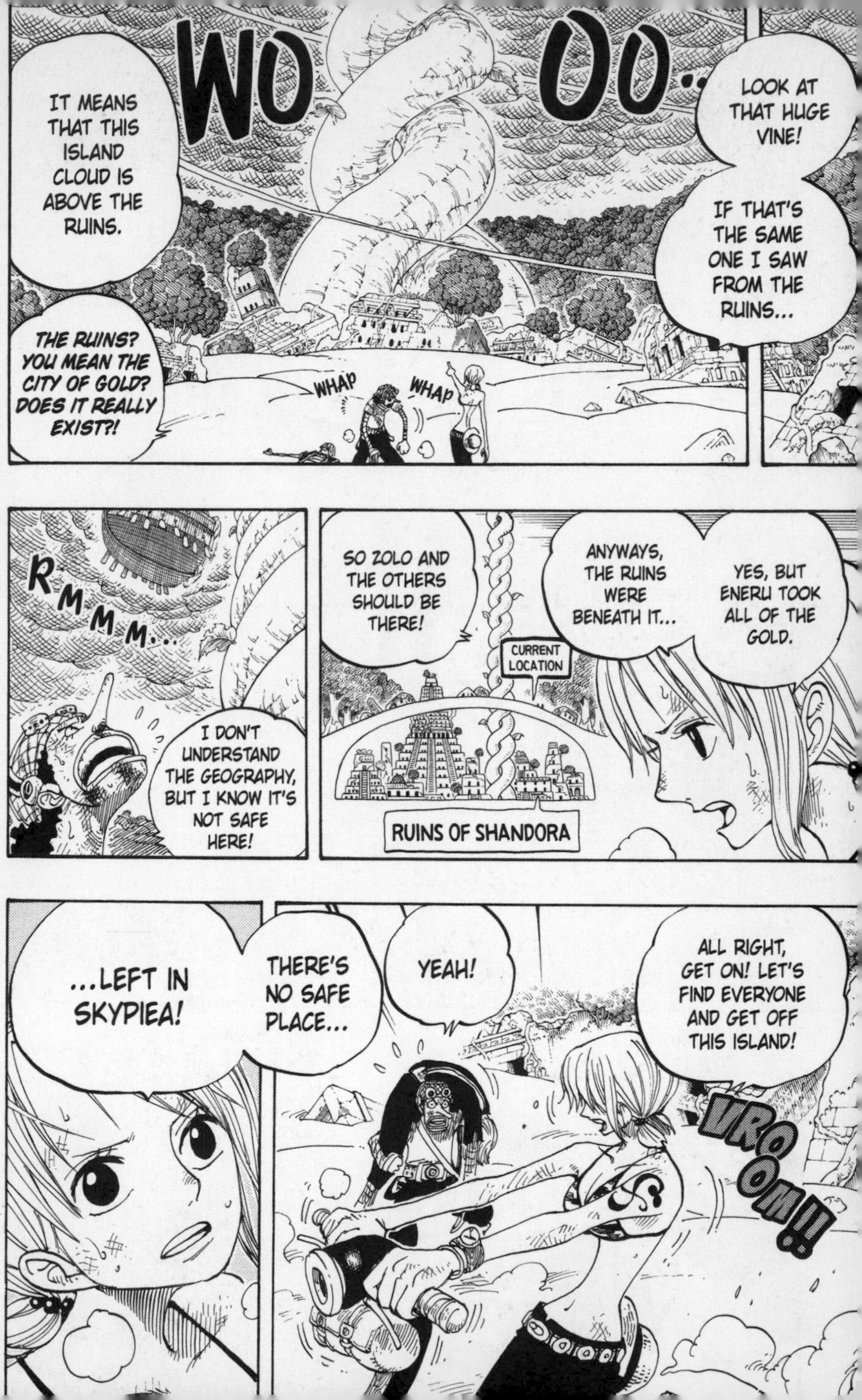
WOOO...
LOOK AT THAT HUGE VINE!
IF THAT'S THE SAME ONE I SAW FROM THE RUINS...
IT MEANS THAT THIS ISLAND CLOUD IS ABOVE THE RUINS.
THE RUINS? YOU MEAN THE CITY OF GOLD? DOES IT REALLY EXIST?!
WHAP
WHAP
YES, BUT ENERU TOOK ALL OF THE GOLD.
ANYWAYS, THE RUINS WERE BENEATH IT...
SO ZOLO AND THE OTHERS SHOULD BE THERE!
CURRENT LOCATION
RUINS OF SHANDORA
RMMM...
I DON'T UNDERSTAND THE GEOGRAPHY, BUT I KNOW IT'S NOT SAFE HERE!
ALL RIGHT, GET ON! LET'S FIND EVERYONE AND GET OFF THIS ISLAND!
YEAH!
VROOM!!
THERE'S NO SAFE PLACE...
...LEFT IN SKYPIEA!

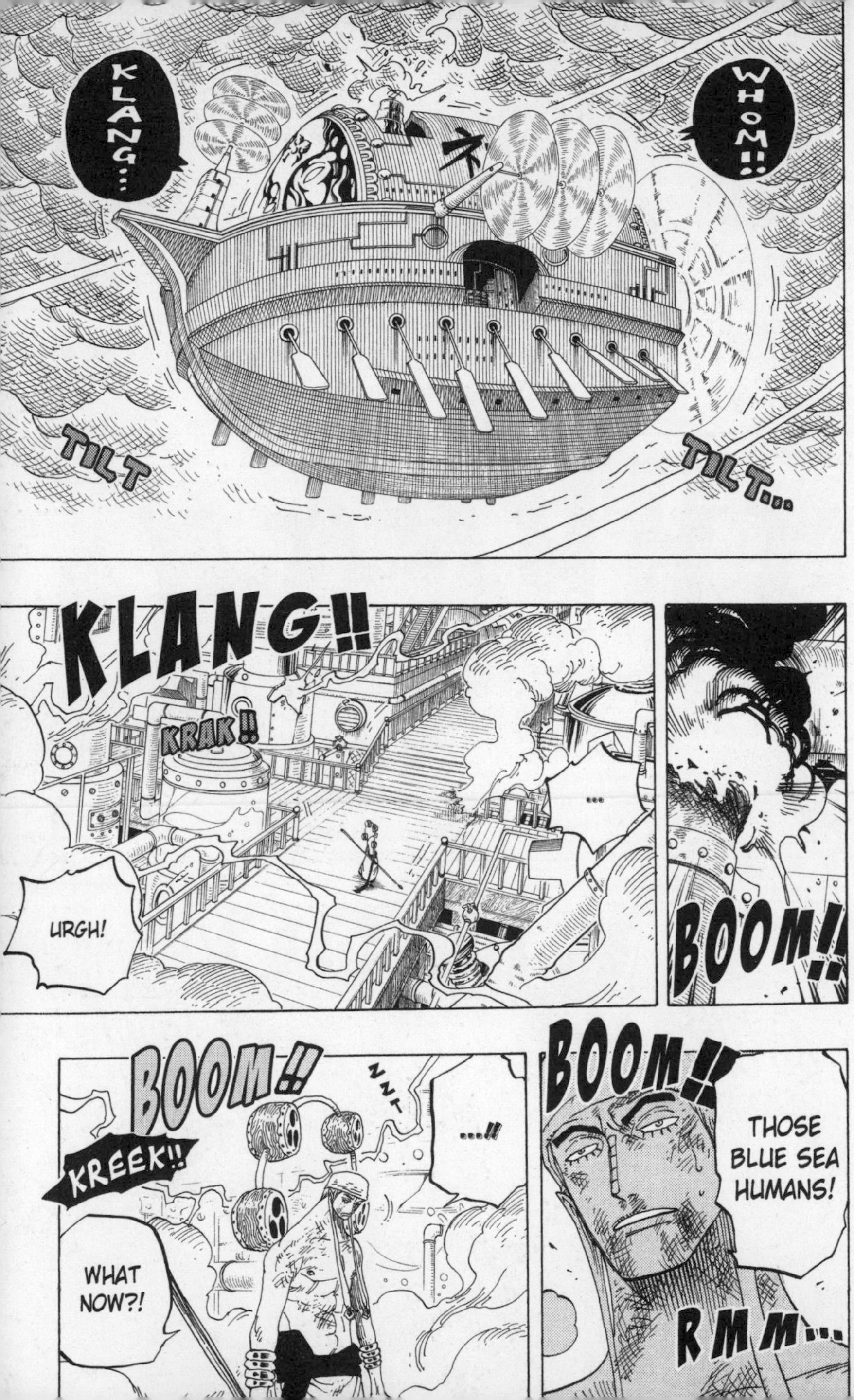
WHOM!!
KLANG...
TILT...
TILT
BOOM!!
KLANG!!
KRAK!!
...
URGH!
BOOM!!
THOSE BLUE SEA HUMANS!
RMM...
BOOM!!
ZZT
...!!
KREEK!!
WHAT NOW?!

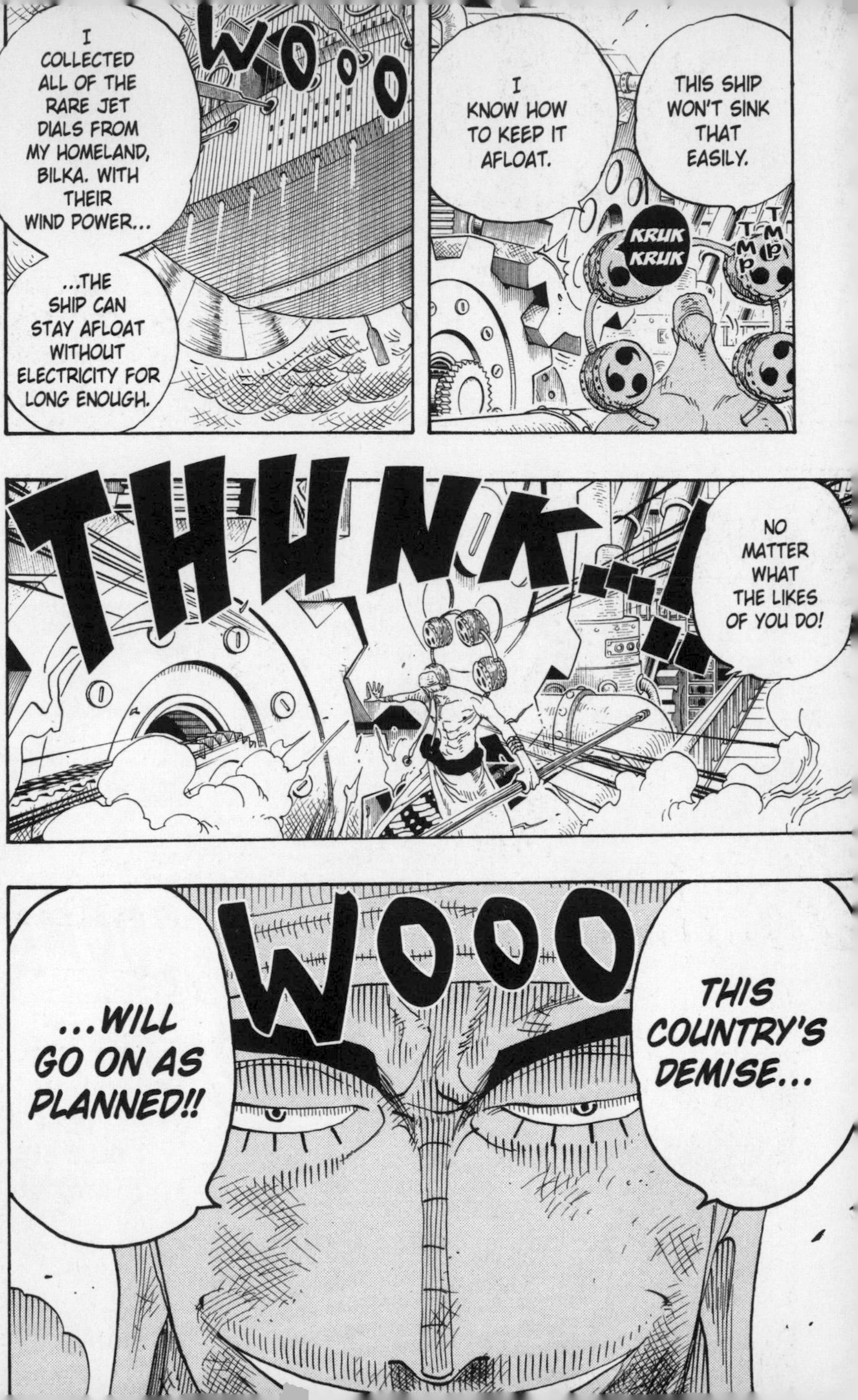
THIS SHIP WON'T SINK THAT EASILY.
I KNOW HOW TO KEEP IT AFLOAT.
KRUK KRUK
TMP TMP
WOOO
I COLLECTED ALL OF THE RARE JET DIALS FROM MY HOMELAND, BILKA. WITH THEIR WIND POWER...
...THE SHIP CAN STAY AFLOAT WITHOUT ELECTRICITY FOR LONG ENOUGH.
NO MATTER WHAT THE LIKES OF YOU DO!
THUNK..!!
THIS COUNTRY'S DEMISE...
WOOO
...WILL GO ON AS PLANNED!!

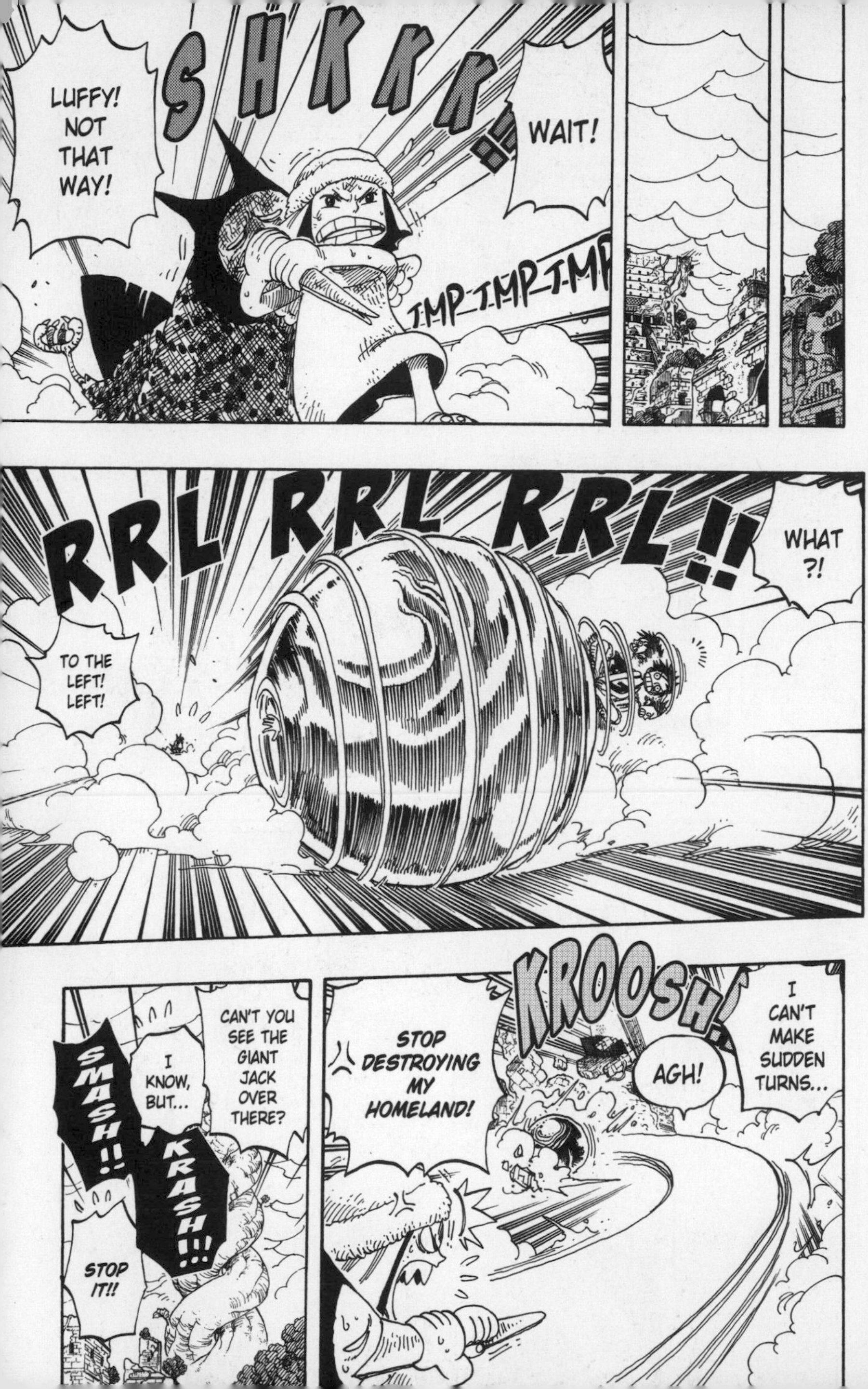
SHKKK!!
WAIT!
LUFFY! NOT THAT WAY!
TMP TMP TMP
RRL RRL RRL!!
WHAT?!
TO THE LEFT! LEFT!
KROOSH!
I CAN'T MAKE SUDDEN TURNS...
AGH!
STOP DESTROYING MY HOMELAND!
CAN'T YOU SEE THE GIANT JACK OVER THERE?
I KNOW, BUT...
SMASH!!
KRASH!!
STOP IT!!

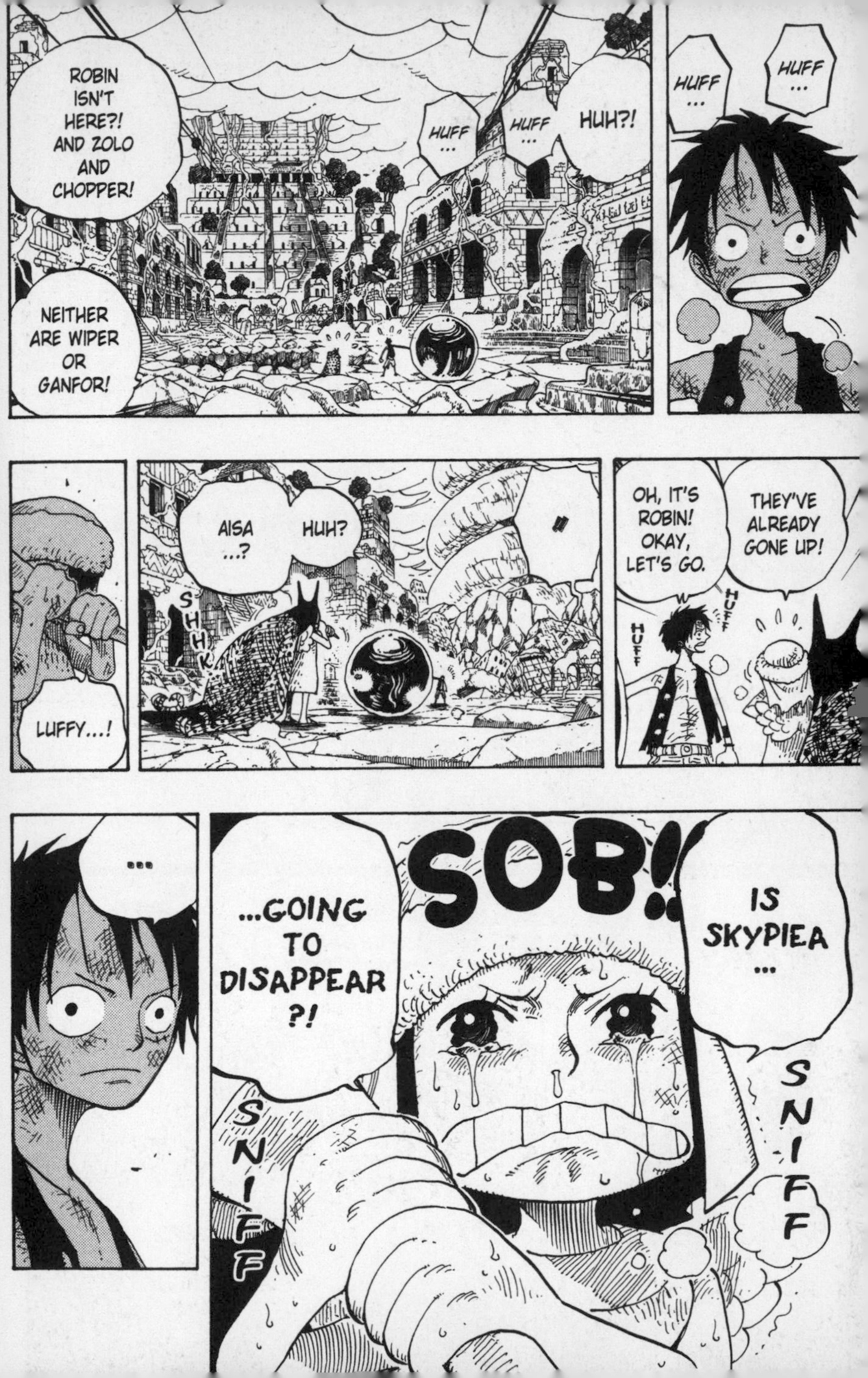
HUFF ...
HUFF ...
HUH?!
HUFF ...
HUFF ...
ROBIN ISN'T HERE?! AND ZOLO AND CHOPPER!
NEITHER ARE WIPER OR GANFOR!
THEY'VE ALREADY GONE UP!
OH, IT'S ROBIN! OKAY, LET'S GO.
HUFF
HUFF
HUH?
AISA ...?
SHHK
LUFFY...!
SOB!!
IS SKYPIEA ...
SNIFF
...GOING TO DISAPPEAR ?!
SNIFF
...

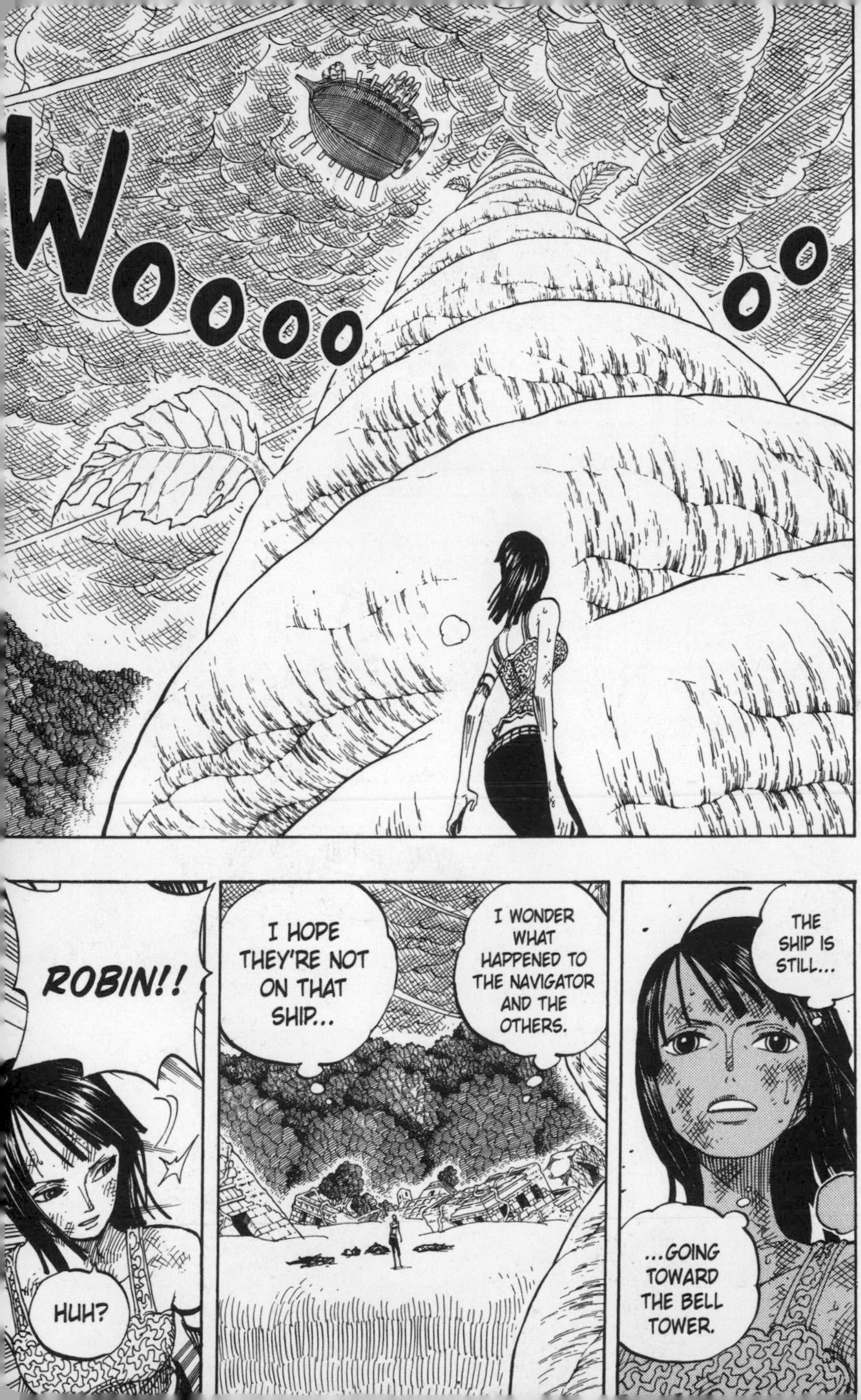
WOOOOO
OO
THE SHIP IS STILL...
...GOING TOWARD THE BELL TOWER.
I WONDER WHAT HAPPENED TO THE NAVIGATOR AND THE OTHERS.
I HOPE THEY'RE NOT ON THAT SHIP...
ROBIN!!
HUH?

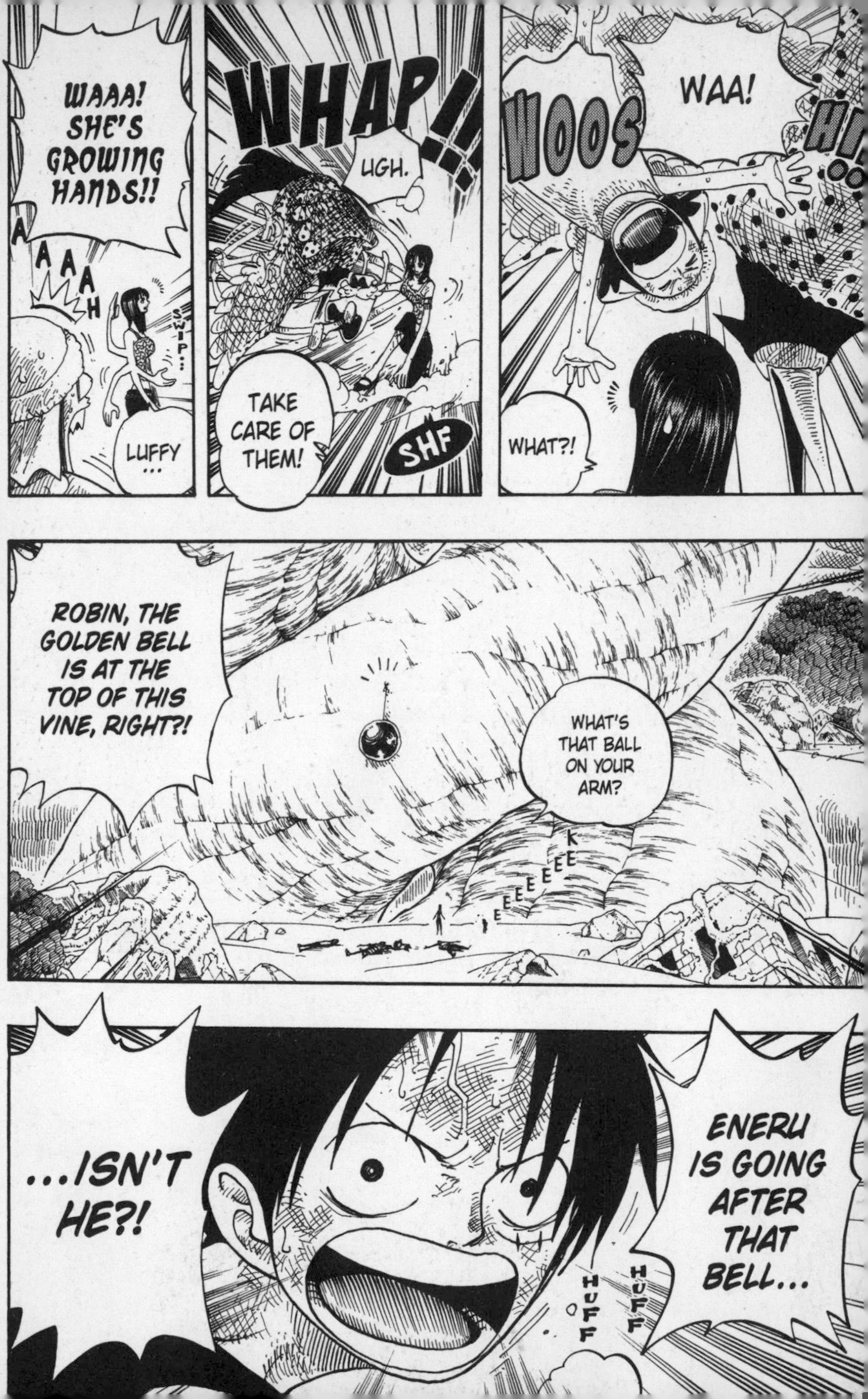
WAA!
HI!!
WOOS
WHAT?!
WHAP!!!
UGH.
TAKE CARE OF THEM!
SHF
WAAA! SHE'S GROWING HANDS!!
AAAAH
SWIP...
LUFFY...
WHAT'S THAT BALL ON YOUR ARM?
KEEEEEEE
ROBIN, THE GOLDEN BELL IS AT THE TOP OF THIS VINE, RIGHT?!
ENERU IS GOING AFTER THAT BELL...
HUFF
HUFF
...ISN'T HE?!

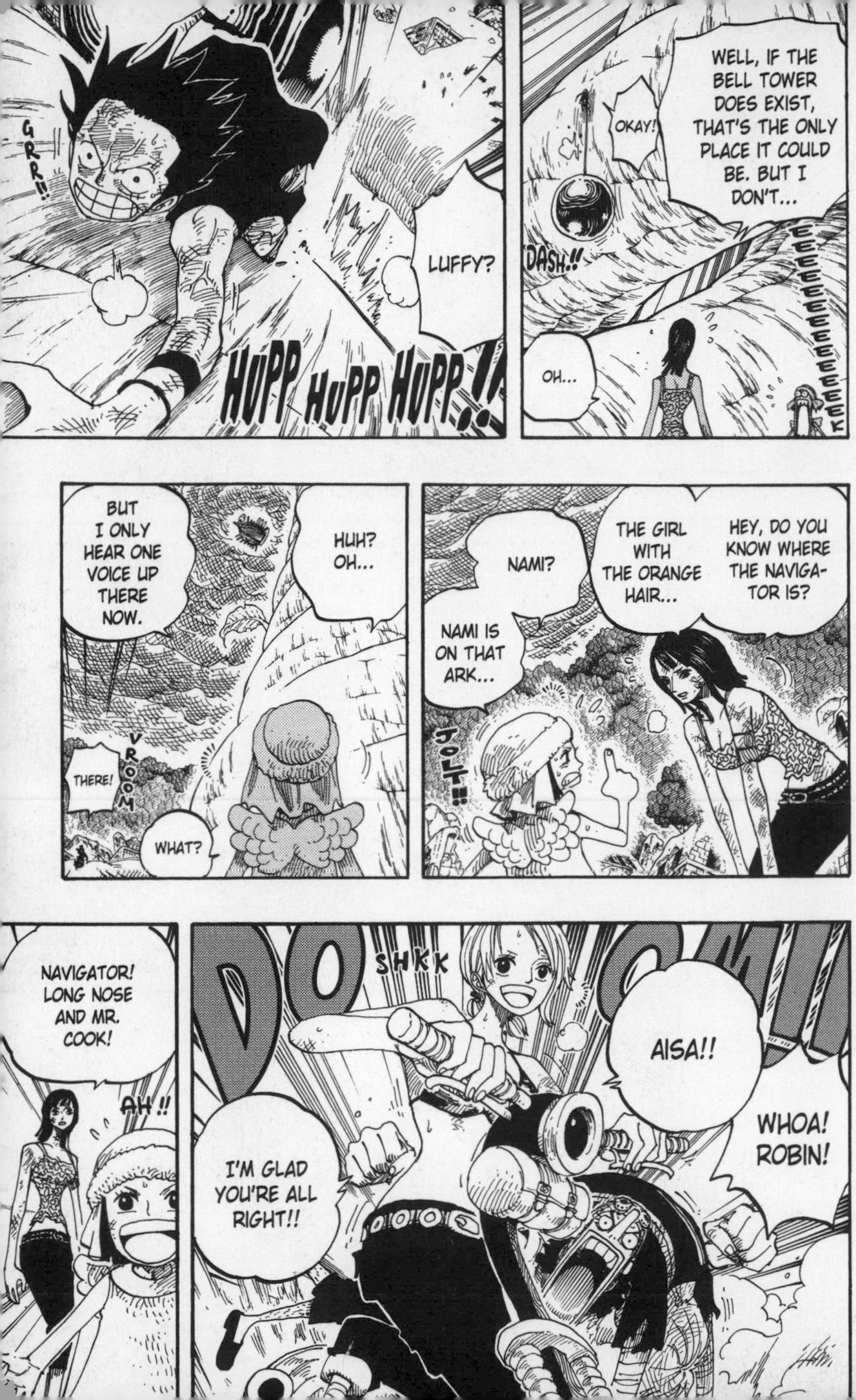

WELL, IF THE BELL TOWER DOES EXIST, THAT'S THE ONLY PLACE IT COULD BE. BUT I DON'T...
OKAY!
DASH!!
EEEEEEEEEEEEEK
OH...
LUFFY?
GRR!!
HUPP HUPP HUPP!!
HEY, DO YOU KNOW WHERE THE NAVIGATOR IS?
THE GIRL WITH THE ORANGE HAIR...
NAMI?
NAMI IS ON THAT ARK...
JOLT!!
HUH? OH...
BUT I ONLY HEAR ONE VOICE UP THERE NOW.
THERE!
VROOM
WHAT?
DOOM!!
SHKK
AISA!!
WHOA! ROBIN!
I'M GLAD YOU'RE ALL RIGHT!!
NAVIGATOR! LONG NOSE AND MR. COOK!
AH!!

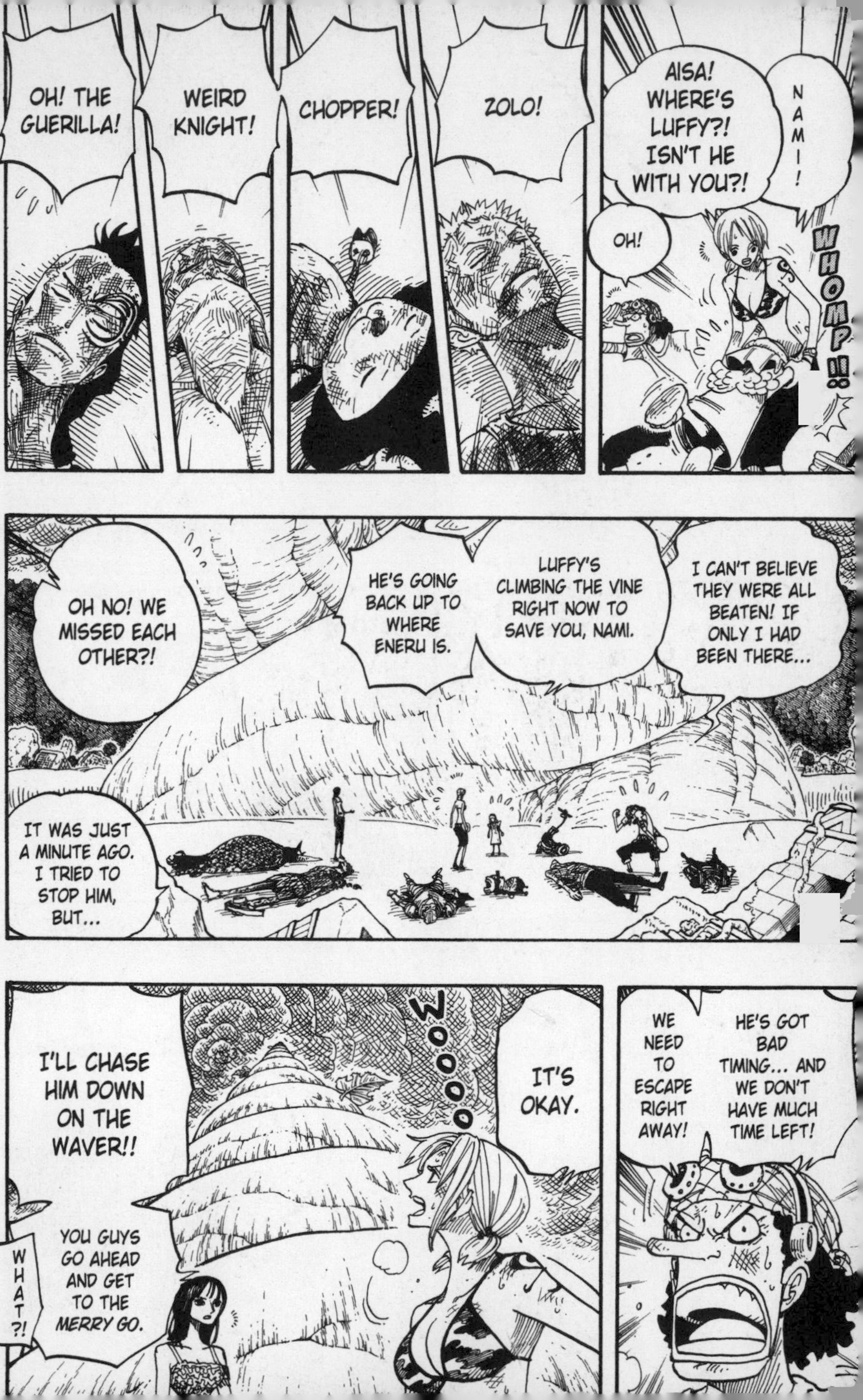
NAMI!
AISA! WHERE'S LUFFY?! ISN'T HE WITH YOU?!
OH!
WHOMP!!
ZOLO!
CHOPPER!
WEIRD KNIGHT!
OH! THE GUERILLA!
I CAN'T BELIEVE THEY WERE ALL BEATEN! IF ONLY I HAD BEEN THERE...
LUFFY'S CLIMBING THE VINE RIGHT NOW TO SAVE YOU, NAMI.
HE'S GOING BACK UP TO WHERE ENERU IS.
OH NO! WE MISSED EACH OTHER?!
IT WAS JUST A MINUTE AGO. I TRIED TO STOP HIM, BUT...
HE'S GOT BAD TIMING... AND WE DON'T HAVE MUCH TIME LEFT!
WE NEED TO ESCAPE RIGHT AWAY!
IT'S OKAY.
WOOOOO
I'LL CHASE HIM DOWN ON THE WAVER!!
YOU GUYS GO AHEAD AND GET TO THE MERRY GO.
WHAT?!

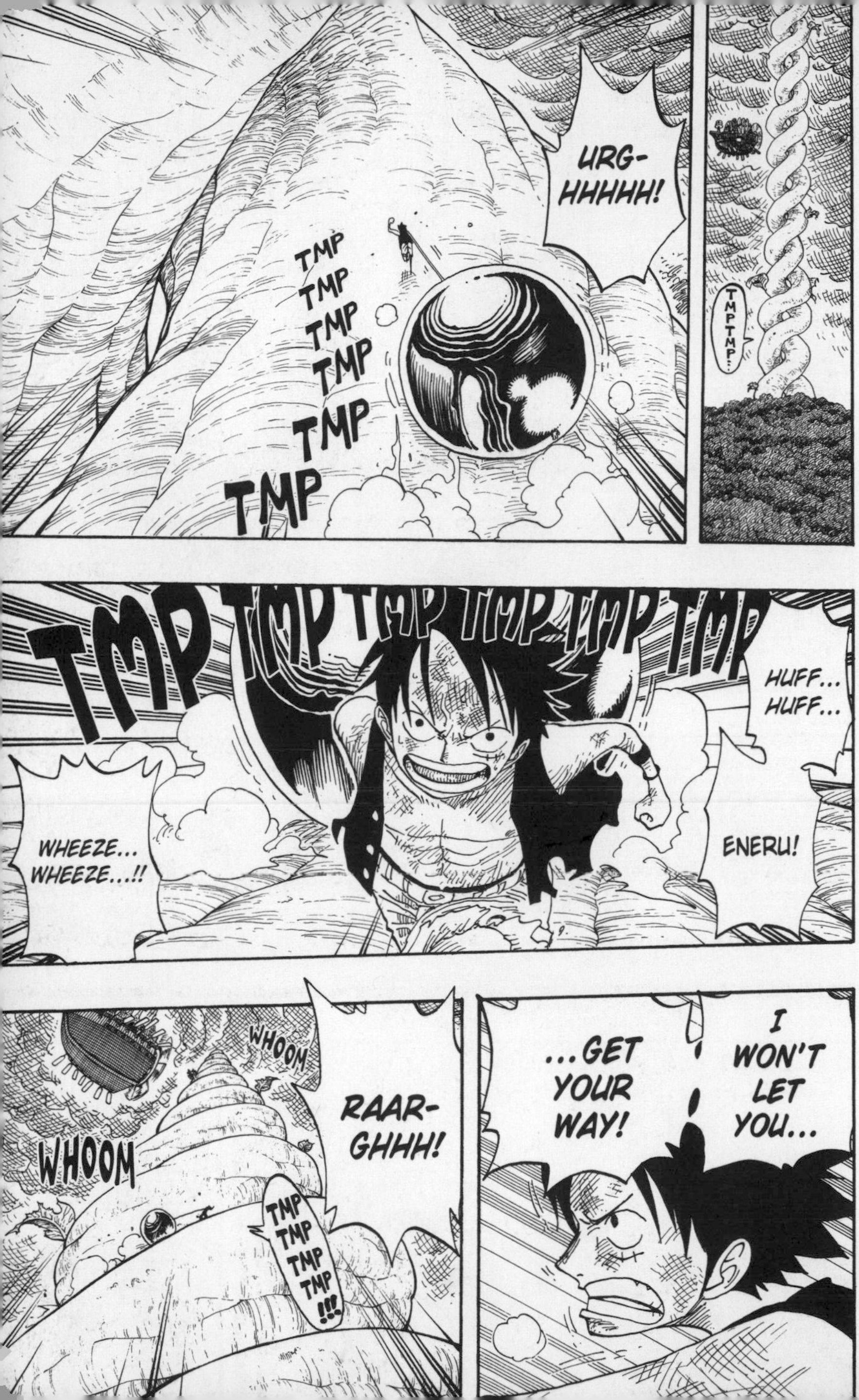
TMPTMP...
URG-HHHHH!
TMP TMP TMP TMP TMP TMP
TMP TMP TMP TMP TMP TMP
HUFF... HUFF...
ENERU!
WHEEZE... WHEEZE...!!
I WON'T LET YOU...
...GET YOUR WAY!
RAAR-GHHH!
WHOOM
WHOOM
TMP TMP TMP TMP !!!

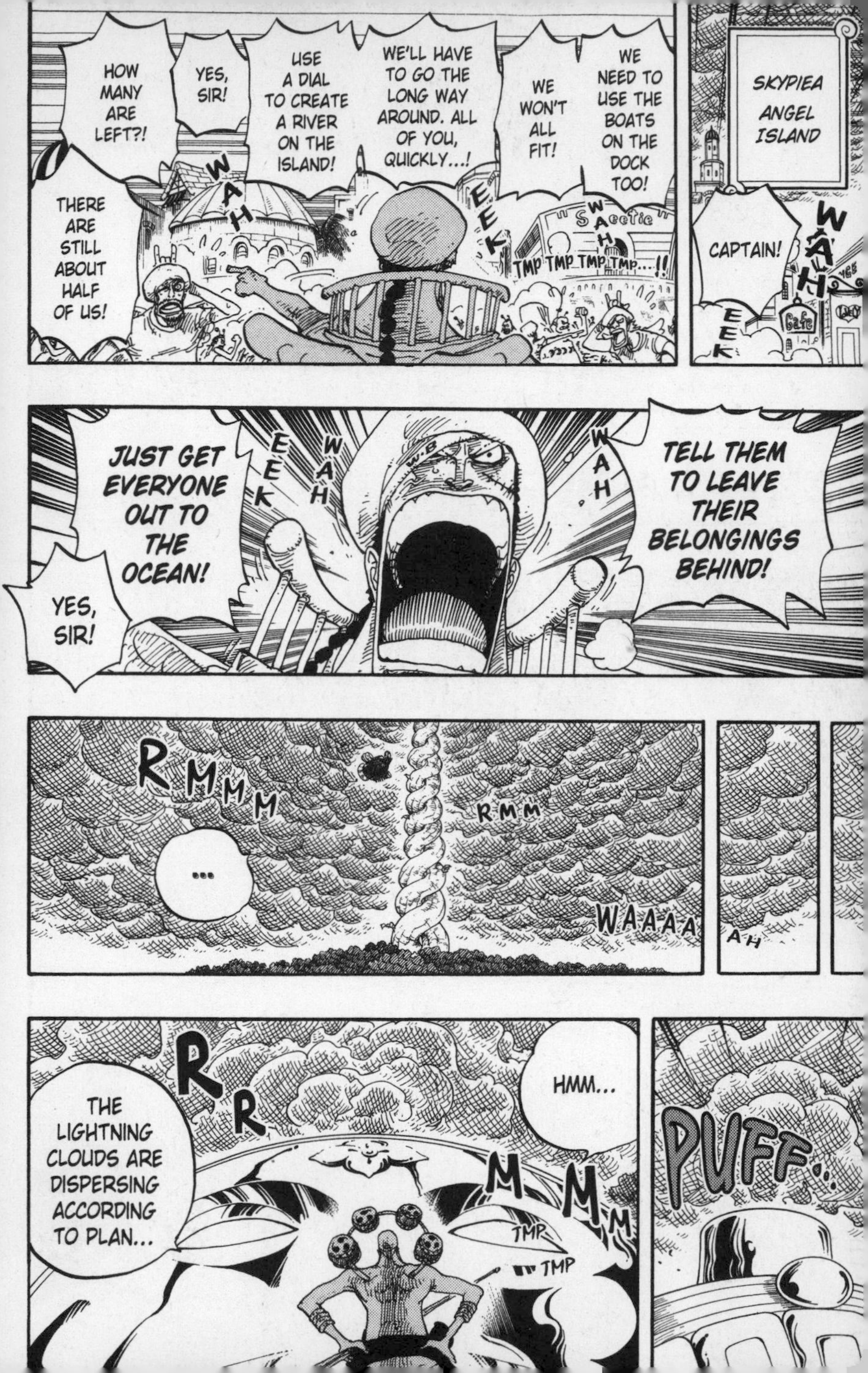
SKYPIEA ANGEL ISLAND
CAPTAIN!
WAAH
EEEK
WE NEED TO USE THE BOATS ON THE DOCK TOO!
WE WON'T ALL FIT!
WE'LL HAVE TO GO THE LONG WAY AROUND. ALL OF YOU, QUICKLY...!
USE A DIAL TO CREATE A RIVER ON THE ISLAND!
YES, SIR!
HOW MANY ARE LEFT?!
THERE ARE STILL ABOUT HALF OF US!
WAH
EEK
WAH
TMP TMP TMP TMP...!!
TELL THEM TO LEAVE THEIR BELONGINGS BEHIND!
WAH
WAH
EEEK
JUST GET EVERYONE OUT TO THE OCEAN!
YES, SIR!
AH
WAAAA
RMM
...
RMMMM
PUFF...
HMM...
RRMMMM
THE LIGHTNING CLOUDS ARE DISPERSING ACCORDING TO PLAN...
TMP
TMP

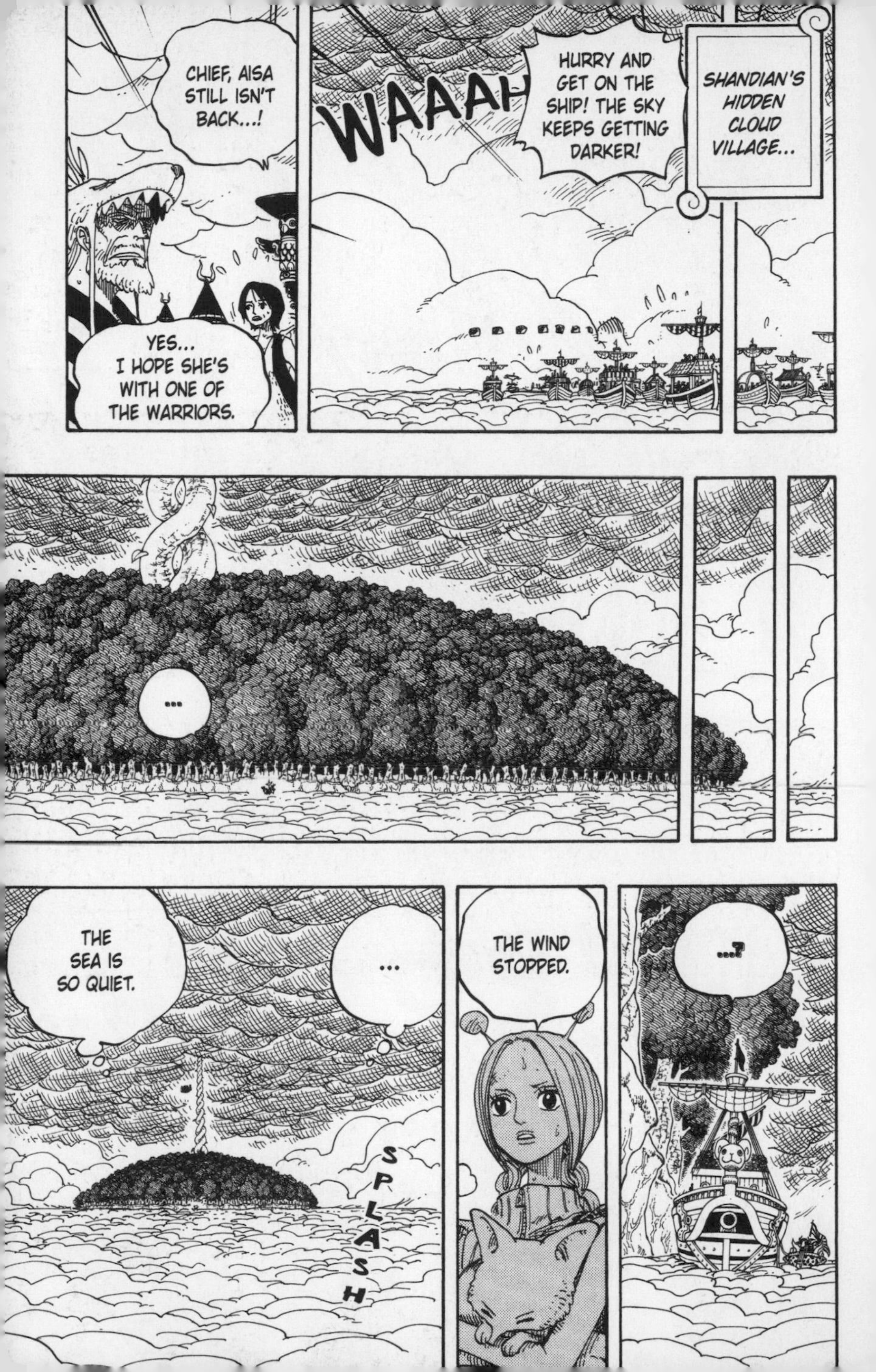
SHANDIAN'S HIDDEN CLOUD VILLAGE...
WAAAH
HURRY AND GET ON THE SHIP! THE SKY KEEPS GETTING DARKER!
CHIEF, AISA STILL ISN'T BACK...!
YES... I HOPE SHE'S WITH ONE OF THE WARRIORS.
...
...?
THE WIND STOPPED.
...
THE SEA IS SO QUIET.
SPLASH

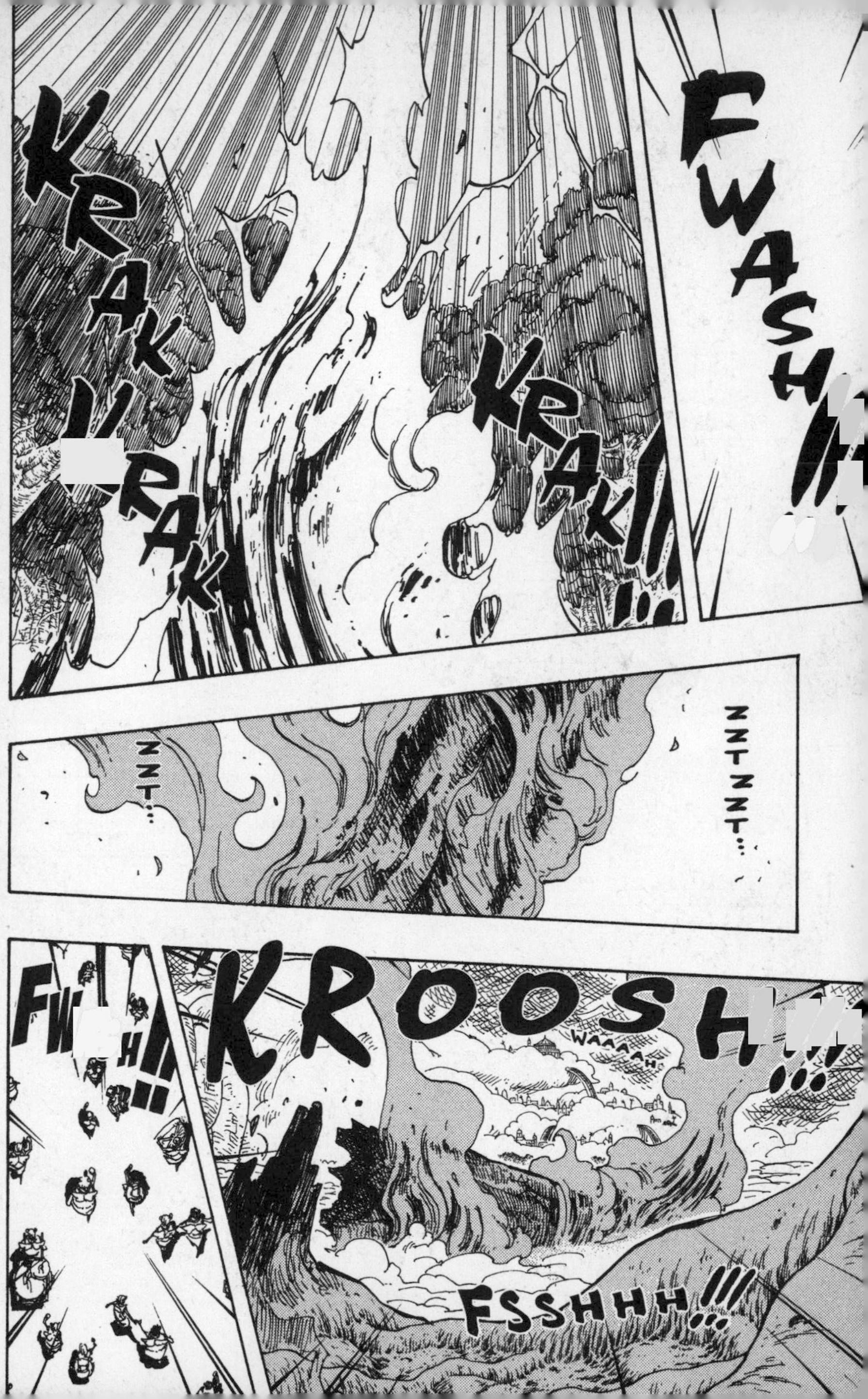

FWASH!!
KRAK KRAK!!!
KRAK KRAK
ZZT ZZT ZZT...
ZZT...
KROOSH!!!
WAAAAAH
FSSHHH!!!
FW H!!!

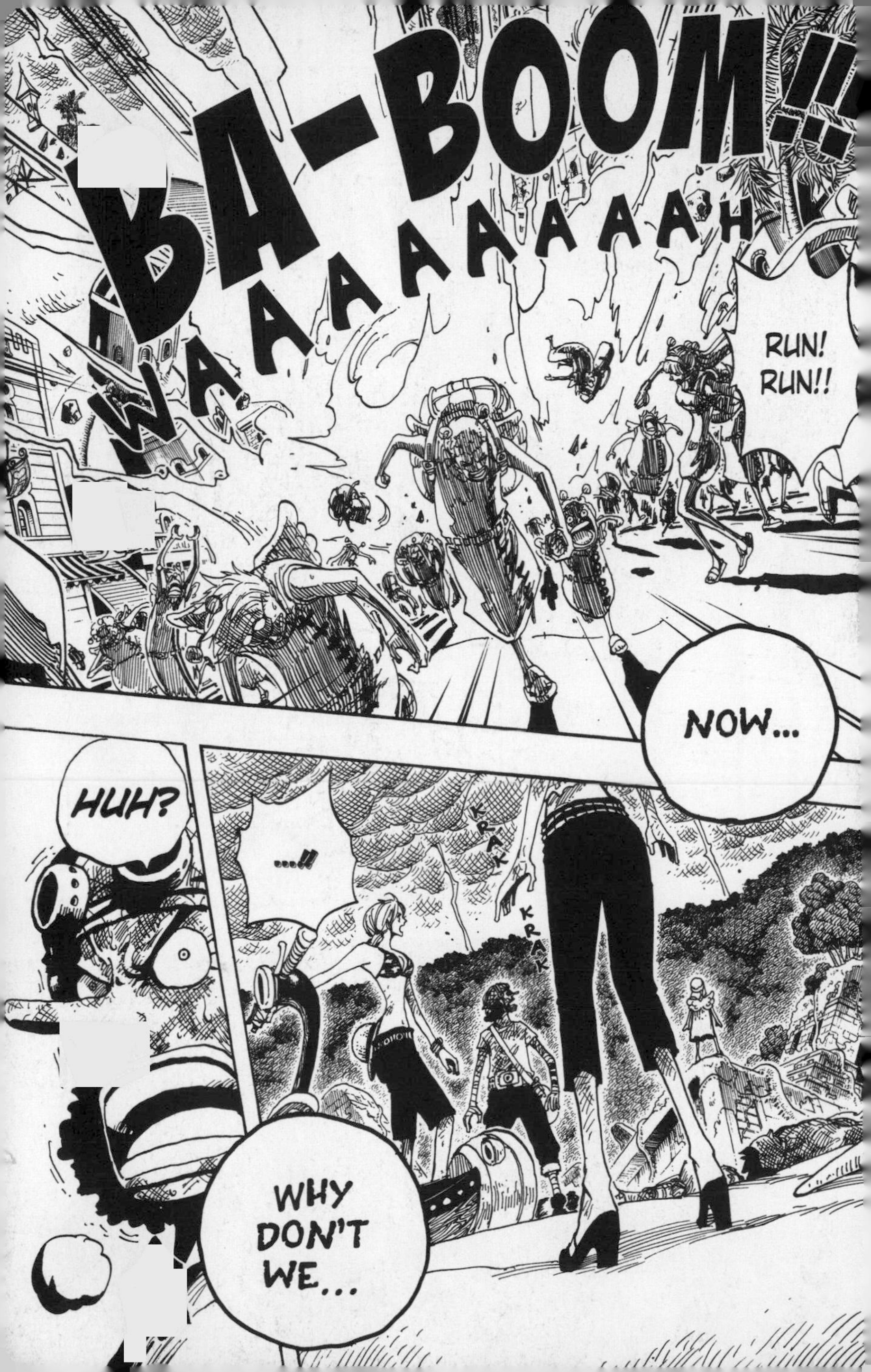
BA-BOOM!!
WAAAAAAAAH
RUN! RUN!!
NOW...
...!!
KRAK
KRAK
WHY DON'T WE...
HUH?

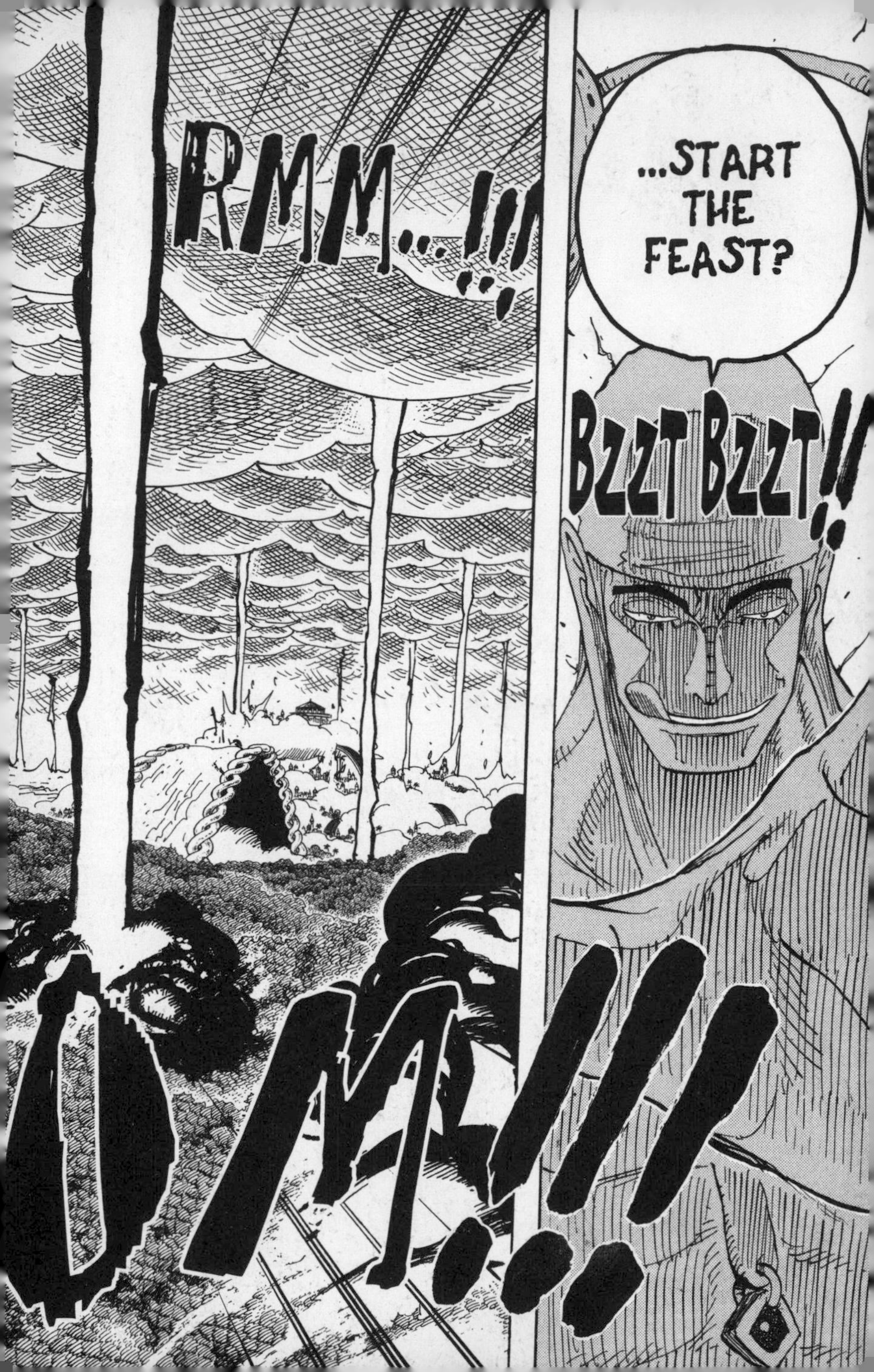
...START THE FEAST?
BZZT BZZT!!
RMM...!!!
UM...!!!

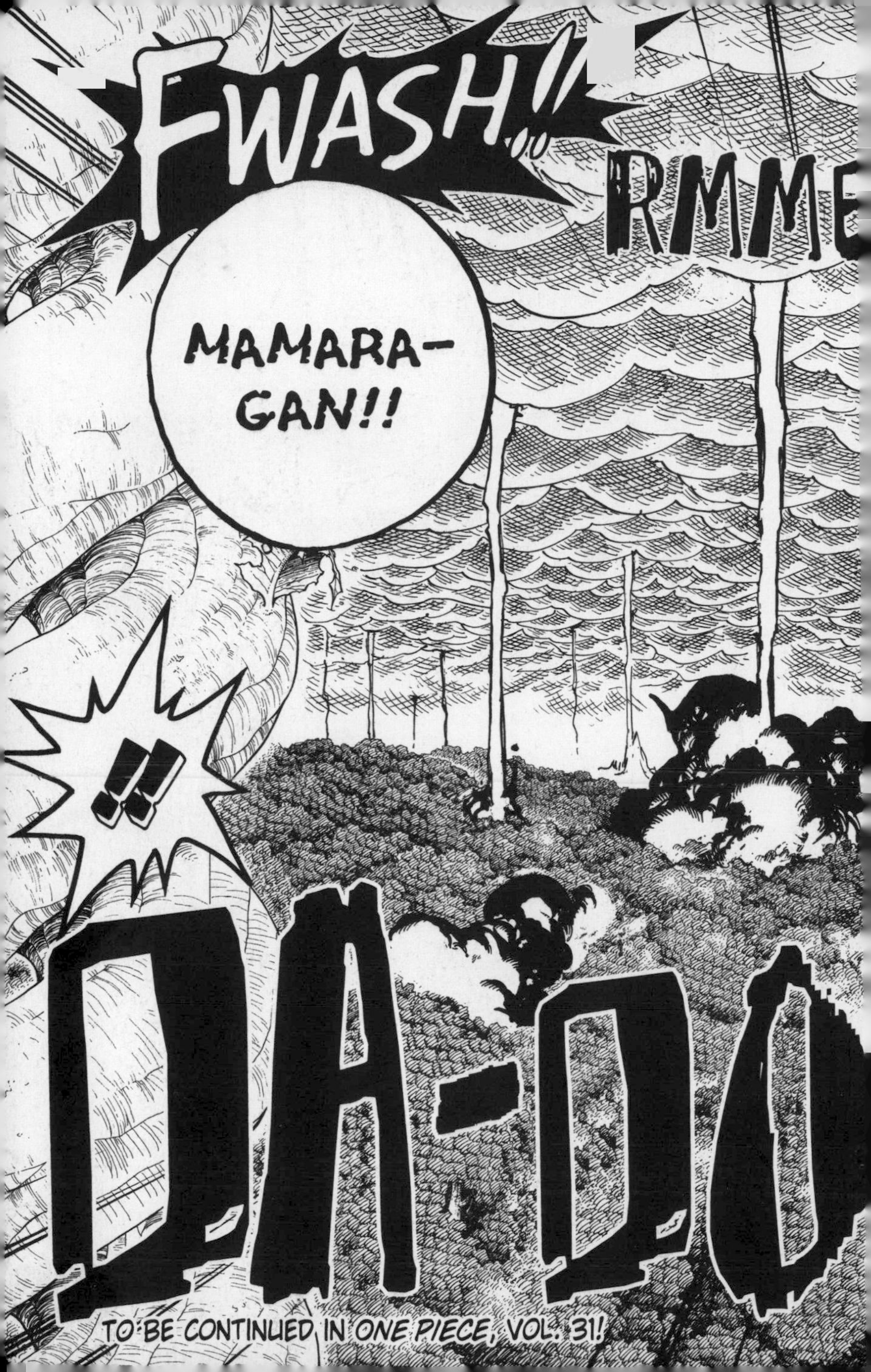
RMME
FWASH!!
MAMARA-GAN!!
!!
DA-DO
TO BE CONTINUED IN ONE PIECE, VOL. 31!

COLORING PAGE

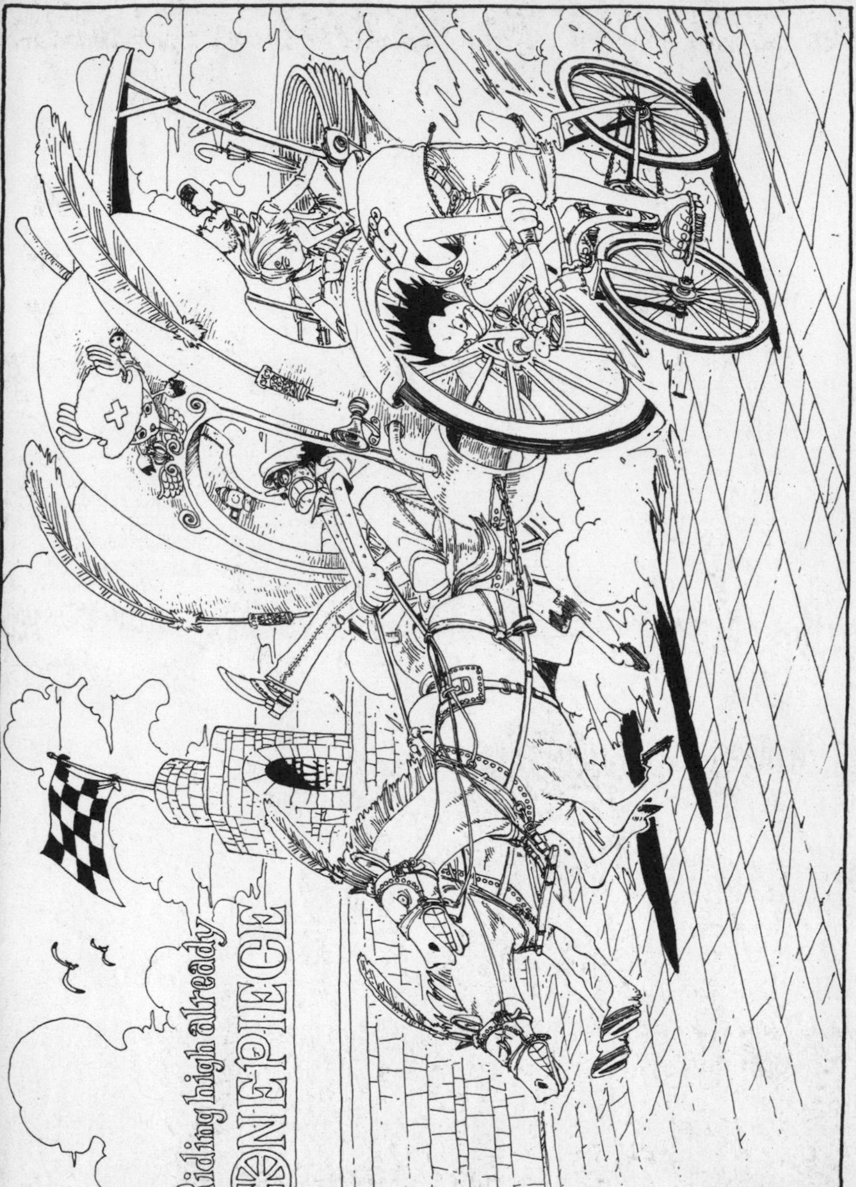
Riding high already
ONE PIECE

COMING NEXT VOLUME:

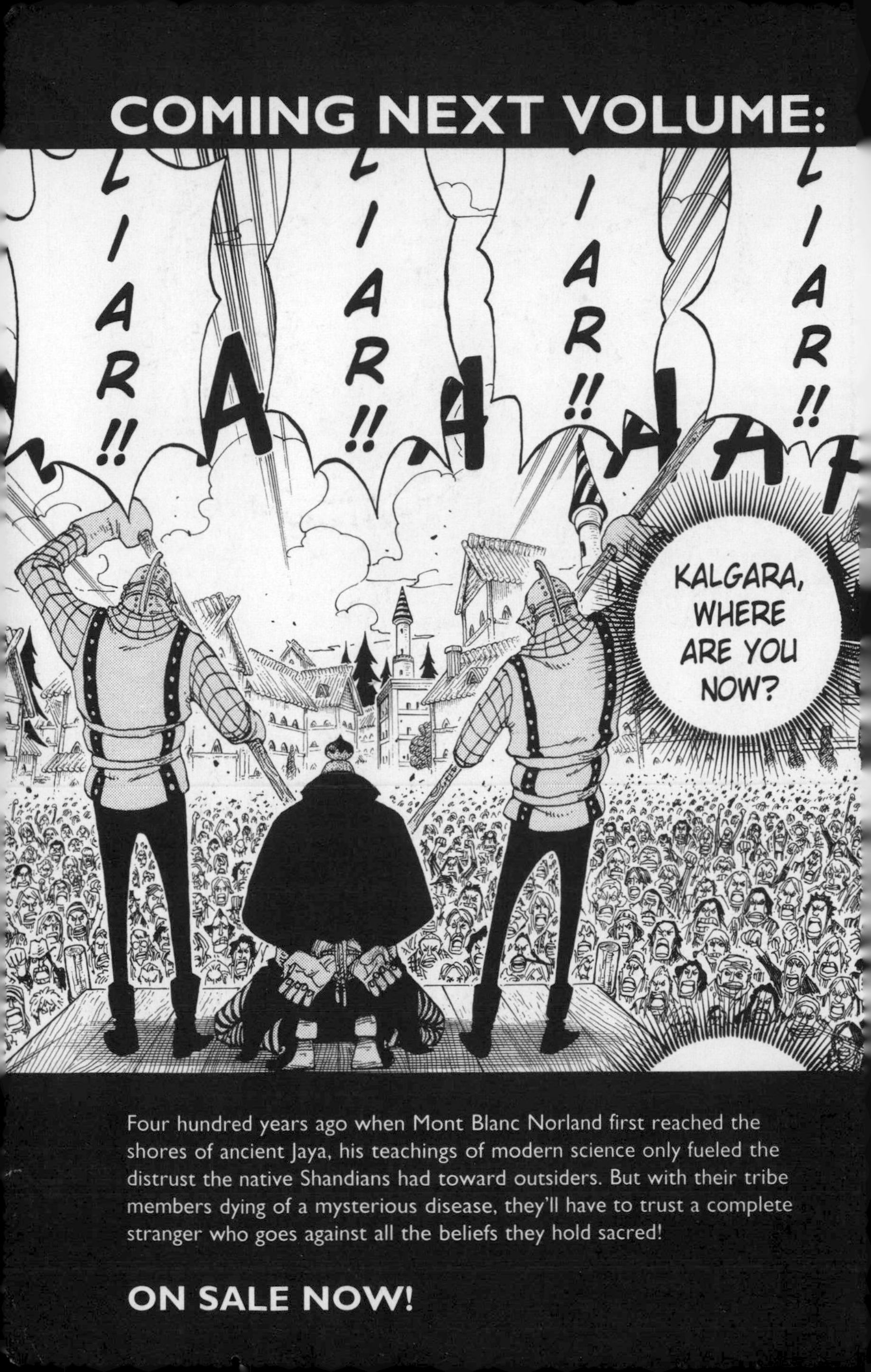
LIAR!!
LIAR!!
LIAR!!
LIAR!!
KALGARA, WHERE ARE YOU NOW?

Four hundred years ago when Mont Blanc Norland first reached the shores of ancient Jaya, his teachings of modern science only fueled the distrust the native Shandians had toward outsiders. But with their tribe members dying of a mysterious disease, they'll have to trust a complete stranger who goes against all the beliefs they hold sacred!

ON SALE NOW!

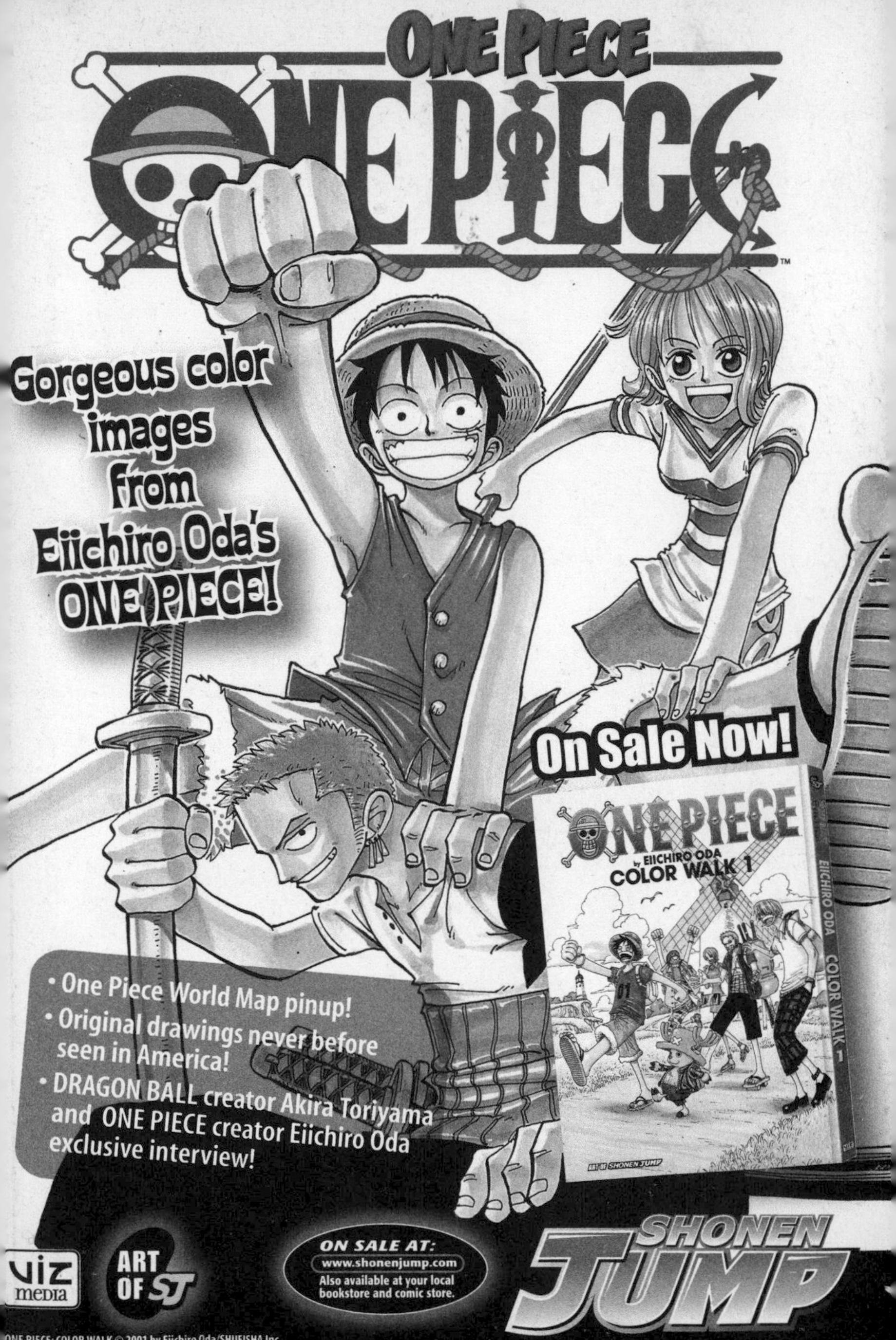
ONE PIECE
ONE PIECE
Gorgeous color images from Eiichiro Oda's ONE PIECE!
On Sale Now!
ONE PIECE
by EIICHIRO ODA
COLOR WALK 1
ART OF SHONEN JUMP
EIICHIRO ODA COLOR WALK 1
• One Piece World Map pinup!
• Original drawings never before seen in America!
• DRAGON BALL creator Akira Toriyama and ONE PIECE creator Eiichiro Oda exclusive interview!
viz media
ART OF SJ
ON SALE AT:
www.shonenjump.com
Also available at your local bookstore and comic store.
SHONEN JUMP
ONE PIECE: COLOR WALK © 2001 by Eiichiro Oda/SHUEISHA Inc.